MAP OF MEMBER COUNTRIES OF ASEAN

SOUTHEAST ASIAN AFFAIRS 2001

SOUTHEAST ASIAN AFFAIRS 2001
EDITORIAL COMMITTEE

Chairperson	*Chia Siow Yue*
Editors	*Daljit Singh*
	Anthony Smith
Production Editor	*Roselie Ang*

SOUTHEAST ASIAN AFFAIRS 2001

 INSTITUTE OF SOUTHEAST ASIAN STUDIES

ISEAS Library Cataloguing-in-Publication Data

Southeast Asian affairs.
1974–
Annual
1. Asia, Southeastern.
I. Institute of Southeast Asian Studies.
DS501 S72A

ISSN 0377-5437
ISBN 981-230-128-3 (softcover)
ISBN 981-230-129-1 (hardcover)

Published by
Institute of Southeast Asian Studies
30 Heng Mui Keng Terrace
Pasir Panjang
Singapore 119614

Internet e-mail: publish@iseas.edu.sg
Website: http://www.iseas.edu.sg/pub.html

Typeset by International Typesetters Pte Ltd.
Printed in Singapore by Seng Lee Press Pte Ltd

FOREWORD

We are pleased to present the twenty-eighth issue of *Southeast Asian Affairs*, a comprehensive annual review of the political and economic trends and developments in Southeast Asia.

Designed to be easily readable yet in-depth, informative and analytical, the annual has come to be a standard reference for scholars, policy-makers, private sector executives, and journalists, who seek to understand and keep up to date on the dynamics of Southeast Asian developments.

The year 2000 saw the economies of Southeast Asia recovering further from the regional economic crisis against the background of strong growth of the American economy, but the much needed banking and corporate sector reforms were not being implemented fast enough. Political stability remained a problem in certain key countries. Indonesia continued to face severe challenges.

I take this opportunity to thank the authors who have contributed to this publication. While the Institute encourages the statement of all points of view in the publication, the authors alone are responsible for the facts and opinions expressed in their articles. Their contributions and interpretations do not necessarily reflect the views of the Institute.

Chia Siow Yue
Director
Institute of Southeast Asian Studies

April 2001

CONTENTS

INDONESIA

LAOS

MALAYSIA

MYANMAR

THE PHILIPPINES

SINGAPORE

THAILAND

VIETNAM

INTRODUCTION

For the Southeast Asian economies, 2000 was the best year since 1997 as countries recovered further from the regional crisis which began that year. The strong performance of the U.S. economy contributed to this relatively robust outcome. Singapore grew 9.9 per cent, Malaysia 8.5 per cent, and Vietnam 6.1 per cent. Even Indonesia, with its many problems, managed 4.8 per cent growth, while Thailand and the Philippines registered 4.2 and 3.9 per cent respectively.

However, there was still much unfinished business — in Indonesia, Thailand, and Malaysia — in the way of banking and corporate restructuring. This work will need to continue under the more difficult conditions of sluggish growth in 2001 because of the slowdown in the United States.

Moreover, the broader economic trends did not favour Southeast Asia. The flows of foreign direct investment (FDI) were still significantly below pre-crisis levels because of negative perceptions of the region among international investors, on account of its political problems and the slow pace of reforms. The greater attraction of China as an FDI destination also cast a shadow on the region's prospects.

The Association of Southeast Asian Nations (ASEAN) remained enfeebled by political uncertainty, economic problems, and weak or besieged leaderships in some of the key member countries. It was also not moving fast enough to bring about economic integration of the region. ASEAN's push for East Asian regionalism through its ASEAN Plus Three process was not making up for its credibility deficit, at least not in the short term.

Indonesia, which looms large in Southeast Asia, experienced serious trials and tribulations throughout the year 2000. The failure to address underlying structural problems was compounded by the lack of effective political leadership to deal with a myriad of political, economic, and social difficulties. President Abdurrahman Wahid, by the end of 2000, was facing growing opposition from Parliament and society, including from many who had initially supported his bid for the presidency. The ongoing conflicts within the provinces of Aceh, Irian Jaya, Maluku, and North Maluku, were marked by brutality and apparent intractability.

Some other parts of Southeast Asia also witnessed political unrest or change. The Philippines narrowly averted civil disorder during a bid (successful) to change the executive through the use of "people's power". Malaysia was still grappling with the political fallout from the detention, trial, and conviction of former Deputy Prime Minister Anwar Ibrahim. The political deadlock in Myanmar continued, and its longstanding ethnic minority problem was only contained, not solved. Thailand's young democracy experienced a peaceful change of government.

The broader regional security environment remained relatively salubrious in 2000. U.S-China relations showed progress, although the Taiwan issue ensured continued underlying frailty. The historic summit between South and North Korean leaders suggested that a thaw on the last Cold War frontier in East Asia might at last be coming. There were no significant developments in relation to the South China Sea disputes.

Southeast Asian Affairs 2001 addresses some of these issues from a regional perspective in the first six chapters. The rest of the volume consists of ten country surveys and seven special theme articles.

Daljit Singh
Anthony Smith
Editors
Southeast Asian Affairs 2001

THE REGION

SOUTHEAST ASIA IN 2000
Many Roads, No Destination?

Daljit Singh

Introduction

The Association of Southeast Asian Nations (ASEAN) continued to weaken in 2000 and key member countries experienced political difficulties while making slow progress on economic reform. In particular, ASEAN's largest member, Indonesia, remained mired in serious domestic problems, providing hospitable conditions for the growth of extremist groups. ASEAN was pushing ahead with East Asian regionalism through the ASEAN Plus Three (APT) process, although this could further impair its own identity and cohesiveness. The year was also marked by the quest for bilateral free trade deals by Singapore (and others), a quest born out of a certain disappointment with Southeast Asian regionalism, in particular its economic liberalization agenda. Advocates of such bilateral agreements expressed the hope that they would serve as catalysts for accelerated regional and global trade liberalization. Asia–Pacific regionalism, manifested in the Asia–Pacific Economic Co-operation (APEC) forum, had lost momentum, although APEC continued to matter for its leaders' summit and for its geopolitical significance as a link between the two sides of the Pacific.

Meanwhile, in East Asia, two events that occurred in 2000 may change the security environment permanently. The first was the election in March of opposition leader Chen Shui-bian as the new President of Taiwan. The significance of this event lay not only in the fact that Chen is leader of the Democractic Progressive Party that has been identified with independence for Taiwan but also that he was the choice of the Taiwanese electorate in a competitive democratic election. The development seemed to ensure that Taiwan would continue on the path of *de facto* independence that former President Lee Ting Hui had embarked upon. Whatever tactical flexibility Chen Shui-bian might show to mollify China's wrath, the perceptions of Taiwan in China, in the United States, and among Taiwanese seemed set to change, with consequent implications for U.S.-China relations.

The second event was the historic North–South summit in Korea in June, even though by the end of 2000, the summit had only raised expectations without a reduction of military tensions or any tangible progress on issues

Daljit Singh is Senior Research Fellow at the Institute of Southeast Asian Studies.

dividing the peninsula. Yet it seemed to signal an impending end to the confrontation on the peninsula, and this by itself suggested unpredictable alterations to the great power postures in Northeast Asia in the medium and longer terms, including the deployments of U.S. forces in East Asia.

Still, there was confidence in the region that the United States would remain militarily engaged in Asia, even if the configuration of forces forward deployed might change. The U.S. presence in East Asia is required to provide a framework of security and stability in which the economic and political development of East Asia can continue. For this, America and its allies will need to have military preponderance for a long time, backed by skilful diplomacy, to ensure that while the rising or revived powers — China, India or Russia — can have their legitimate influence in Asia, none would misuse their new-found strength.

In 2000, the three great powers that matter most to Southeast Asia — the United States, China and Japan — remained focused more on Northeast than Southeast Asia. Yet Southeast Asia will remain an arena in their competition for influence. The most important great power relationship in East Asia, the U.S.–China one, showed a continuing underlying fragility. Japan remained mired in economic stagnation and political weakness. Russia was showing a greater diplomatic interest in Asia, while India, encouraged by better recognition of it as an emerging power, was paying more attention to Southeast Asia.

The chapter will first deal with developments relating to ASEAN, the APT, and APEC. It will then examine the postures of the major powers in East and Southeast Asia from the vantage point of 2000.

REGIONALISM: SOUTHEAST ASIA, EAST ASIA, AND ASIA–PACIFIC

The Association of Southeast Asian Nations (ASEAN)

During 2000, ASEAN continued the struggle to overcome perceptions of ineffectiveness by its main trading partners and sources of investment. Such perceptions were affecting the region's economic recovery. Foreign direct investment (FDI) flows to Southeast Asia were still significantly lower than the levels attained before the 1997 Asian financial crisis and analysts attributed this to incomplete banking and corporate restructuring, continued political instability in key regional countries, as well as the greater attractions of Northeast Asia as an investment destination, specifically in view of Beijing's impending membership of the World Trade Organization (WTO).

"We must have less talk, more action", Singapore Prime Minister Goh Chok Tong declared after the fourth informal ASEAN Summit in Singapore in November 2000. The remark summed up the problem at this juncture of the regional organization's history.

There was no shortage of ideas, many of them good. The problem related to timely and meaningful implementation. The Singapore informal summit agreed to launch an Initiative for ASEAN Integration (IAI) which would focus on education, worker training, and skills development, in order to narrow the economic divide within ASEAN and to enhance the competitiveness of the region. Although it is an essential scheme, it will have no immediate impact on ASEAN's standing in the world. The heads of government also signed an e-ASEAN Framework Agreement to move ASEAN into the New Economy. Among other things, it would help to develop a free trade area for goods, services, and investments for the info-communications and telecommunications industries within ASEAN. The ASEAN Eminent Persons Group — Vision 2020, convened in June 1999, came out with its report containing a list of recommendations. They included the need to create "a dynamic and competitive" ASEAN region able to meet the challenges of globalization; as well as a "caring and responsive" ASEAN in which the development of civil society is to be encouraged.[1] Implementation was to be over a safe span of twenty years.

The ASEAN Ministerial Meeting (AMM), assembled earlier in July in Bangkok, encouraged non-Southeast Asian states, particularly the dialogue partners, to accede to the Treaty of Amity and Co-operation (TAC) as an expression of their commitment to the Treaty's purposes and principles. The AMM also reiterated its call to all nuclear weapons states to accede to the protocol to the treaty for a Southeast Asian Nuclear Weapons Free Zone (SEANWFZ). Given the realities of international power politics, in neither case were the responses, or non-responses, likely to be of more than symbolic import. The Draft Rules of Procedure for the High Council under the TAC were apparently still being worked out, but it is difficult to envisage members utilizing the High Council to settle disputes among themselves. The foreign ministers also approved a paper setting out the principles and purposes of an ASEAN Troika at ministerial level, and the procedures for its constitution. It is unlikely that the Troika will be able to function meaningfully, given the conditionalities likely to be demanded by members, in particular the newer ones, because of sensitivities about sovereignty and "interference" in domestic affairs. A code of conduct between ASEAN and China in relation to the South China Sea claims, which avoids the sovereignty issue, had still not been agreed upon. China may not want to sign a document unless it is watered down close to effeteness.

The foreign ministers reiterated their support for the territorial integrity of Indonesia, "which includes the Provinces of Aceh and Irian Jaya (Papua)".[2] On the Taiwan issue, they reaffirmed their "One China" policy, but without any call for the exercise of restraint on the part of both parties. Instead, on a matter of such importance to regional security as the cross-straits relationship, the ministers anaemically "expressed the hope to see positive developments".[3]

The ministers also endorsed the work done by the ASEAN Regional Forum (ARF) in confidence-building, even as they gingerly noted that while confidence-building measures (CBMs) remained the "primary focus" of the ARF process, "the ARF could advance in the development of the overlap between CBMs and preventive diplomacy (PD) as well as the concepts and principles of PD."[4] However, in 2000 the ARF was still unable to move in that direction. The ARF remained a useful forum for dialogue and for undertaking limited confidence-building measures. There is merit in the claim that the process is more important than concrete results — so long as there are no exaggerated expectations of it in the context of Asian security realities.

A minor consolation was the resumption in 2000 of the ASEAN-EU foreign ministers' meetings, which had been suspended since 1997. The 13th ASEAN-EU Ministerial Meeting, held in Vientiane, Laos, in December was attended on the European side by mostly junior ministers. The meeting was the product of a painfully worked out compromise, which included prior agreement to allow the discussion of the human rights situation in Myanmar, and a EU delegation to visit Myanmar in January 2001 to look at the human rights situation and meet the opposition.

If security and politics were difficult areas to register solid achievements to bolster credibility, unfortunately ASEAN failed to achieve such breakthrough in the crucial area of economic integration. It is true that by 2000, tariff rates for 85 per cent of ASEAN manufactured goods among the original six members had been brought down to the 0–5 per cent range. However, the removal of non-tariff barriers and the liberalization of services and harmonization of investment regimes still had a long way to go. Thus, while ASEAN was indeed making progress in economic integration, it was not fast enough when viewed against the backdrop of changes in the global and Asia–Pacific landscapes, and the expectations of investors. Well publicized moves by Malaysia in 2000 to extend protection of its automobile industry until 2005 did not help perceptions of ASEAN in the outside world, or add to ASEAN's credibility.

Nor for that matter did the opposition of Malaysia and Indonesia, on political grounds, to the formation of a free trade area between ASEAN and the Closer Economic Relations (CER) countries, namely, Australia and New Zealand. The establishment of this free trade area (FTA) was strongly recommended by a High Level Task Force on the subject, which had been set up in 1999. An ASEAN-CER FTA would send a strong signal to investors: it would have a gross domestic product (GDP) of over US$1 trillion, nearly twice that of AFTA, contain developed institutions of government and governance in the two CER countries, and possess an enhanced ability for capacity-building among the newer ASEAN members. The two CER countries traditionally also have strong security ties with Southeast Asia (for instance, both are members of the Five Power Defence Arrangements — FPDA). The ASEAN Economic Ministers' meeting in Chiang Mai in October 2000, which considered the subject of FTA with the CER countries, settled instead for a compromise Closer Economic Partnership (CEP) with Australia and New Zealand. Starting in 2002, senior officials from the two groupings will flesh out details for the CEP.

Political Stability and Bilateral Relations
Domestic political instability, failures in leadership and governance, and difficulties in bilateral relations also contributed to adverse perceptions of

ASEAN. Political leaders in some ASEAN countries failed to appreciate that as a consequence of globalization and the information revolution, reactions of markets had become very important. The assessments of the investment climate by fund managers and investment bankers, seen and heard daily on CNN, CNBC and other media outlets, were arguably no less important than what the ASEAN political leaders themselves said about economic or political prospects in their countries. Furthermore, the headquarters of investment firms and security houses in London, New York, or Frankfurt tended to see Southeast Asia as virtually one undifferentiated region for investment purposes, with the result that in terms of investor confidence, the sins of one country were visited upon the others in the region.

In 2000, Indonesia was clearly the biggest concern. In many ways, Jakarta faced a dismal no-win situation: without the necessary corporate reforms and restructuring, the economy could not grow nor stability improve; yet without stability it was difficult to generate confidence so that a flow of investments would be forthcoming. With a weak and erratic leadership by a physically handicapped President who by year's end was losing support from most sectors of the political spectrum, the country seemed to be in a state of political paralysis. Feeble state institutions — a legacy of the Soeharto years — corruption, and a military often beyond the control of the President, ensured that even sensible and well intentioned writs of the government could be ignored or somehow by-passed. There was no immediate prospect of national fragmentation, despite separatist activity in Aceh and West Papua (Irian Jaya). However, there was the danger of a slide into increasing anarchy, producing a situation in which Indonesia's geographical territory becomes a fertile breeding ground for various extremist (Islamic) and criminal groups, domestic as well as international, and a source of migration of distressed people to neighbouring countries.

In Malaysia, the 1999 general election had shown a significant loss of Malay support for the United Malays National Organization (UMNO). In 2000, this apparent lack of confidence in UMNO continued, given the weak by-election results and growing disaffection within the party rank and file about leadership and party policies.[5] The Anwar Ibrahim factor remained a central issue in both internal Malay and national politics. The progressive weakening of UMNO and of the Prime Minister's position generated uncertainty about the future. Adverse international publicity on Malaysia focused on the country's judiciary and its role in the Anwar trial, and reports of political intervention (and lack of transparency) in corporate affairs. Dr Mahathir's tirades against the West and criticisms of the International Monetary Fund (IMF) did not help.

Political troubles mounted in the Philippines too. The bad news appeared early in the year under the whimsical and feeble leadership of President Joseph Estrada, marked by cronyism and stalled economic reforms. The kidnapping by the radical Islamic guerrilla group Abu Sayyaf of Western and Asian hostages from the Malaysian resort island of Sipadan, and the protracted and murky handling of the situation, ensured adverse international attention. However, the worst was yet to come: the explosive revelations in October by Luis "Chavit" Singson, governor of the northern Luzon province of Ilocos Sur, who claimed that Estrada had received large sums of money from illegal gambling rackets. The subsequent impeachment of the President by the House of Representatives and his trial by the Senate were dramatic developments quickly seized upon by the international media. The long shadow of the Marcos era was again suddenly cast across the nation, a reminder of how easily good government can be subverted by careless and inadequate leadership.

Elsewhere, the politics of the newer members of ASEAN were marked by regime insecurity. In Myanmar, a decade after its genesis, the deadlock between the military regime and the National League for Democracy seemed no nearer resolution at the end of 2000.[6] Furthermore, the country's economic and social conditions, and key relationships with neighbouring Thailand, sank to new lows. In Vietnam, though hopes for a *Doi Moi II* were revived after the signing of a landmark trade agreement with the United States, the Communist Party leadership remained apprehensive about change, waiting to see whether the Chinese experiment of joining the WTO would work to Beijing's advantage. In Laos, economic distress and a Hmong insurgency forced a basically insecure regime to seek succour from Vietnam and China for its survival.

The quality of interstate relations between ASEAN member states, another indicator of the state of health of the Association, had deteriorated under the stresses of the 1997 economic crisis and its political fallout. There seemed to be some improvement in 2000 compared to 1999, but not significantly.

In the case of Malaysia–Singapore relations, a number of developments suggested progress. These included Singapore Senior Minister Lee Kuan Yew's visit to Kuala Lumpur in August 2000, the first since he stepped down as Prime Minister. There was also a surprisingly low-key Malaysian response to the publication of the second volume of Lee's memoirs (in contrast to the voluble reaction to the first). Malaysian Deputy Prime Minister Abdullah Badawi's visit to Singapore in January 2001 seemed upbeat enough. However, in reality there was little concrete progress in resolving outstanding bilateral issues. Furthermore, new issues and incidents emerged later in 2000 as irritants in the relationship.[7]

Relations between Jakarta and Singapore had improved significantly after Abdurrahman Wahid (Gus Dur) became President of Indonesia in 1999, but turned testy again following Wahid's imprudent remarks about Singapore in November 2000.[8] Though the damage caused by these remarks was subsequently contained, the underlying relationship remained uneasy at the end of the year. Malaysia–Indonesia relations were, if anything, marked by even more underlying tension beneath the external veneer of normalcy. To its domestic constituencies, Kuala Lumpur kept contrasting the stability in Malaysia to the chaos that change of regime and democracy had brought to Indonesia. Meanwhile, parliamentary and civil society leaders in Indonesia continued to receive opposition figures from Malaysia.

Philippines–Malaysia relations, while placid on the surface by the end of 2000, had been affected earlier in the year by the way the crisis over the kidnapping of tourists from the Malaysian resort of Sipadan was handled. Further back, in 1999, relations had been soured when Malaysia was found to have erected a structure, with a helipad, on Investigator Shoal in the Spratly Islands — since the Shoal was also claimed by the Philippines. Manila had then lodged a formal protest with Kuala Lumpur, which the latter ignored, merely reiterating that the reef was Malaysian territory.

However, potentially the most difficult bilateral relationship was that between Thailand and Myanmar. Border issues between the two countries involving refugees and illegal immigrants, both Burman and ethnic minorities, have for many years been irritants in relations. More recently, Thailand has been afflicted by a serious drug problem caused by a flood of methamphetamines produced in factories located in the eastern Shan state of Myanmar controlled by the Wa ethnic minority. Unless the Myanmar regime can lean on the United Wa State Army to control or eradicate the problem, it could test ASEAN's principle of non-use of force in dealings between members. Thailand's "flexible engagement" initiative in ASEAN was designed to help deal with just such transnational issues. There are indications that Thailand may be writing off ASEAN in search of a solution to this problem, hoping to rely more on China and on bilateral efforts with the Myanmar regime.

Prospects for ASEAN

Yet, with all its perceived shortcomings, Southeast Asia still needs an organization like ASEAN. It provides this subregion of Asia with a unifying framework, without which it would once again be fragmented. The ASEAN countries are well aware that together they have a better chance of managing relations with the major powers than individually. ASEAN cohesiveness is also necessary for the evolution of the ASEAN Plus Three process, and for ASEAN's role in the ARF.

However, can ASEAN recover its former credibility? It can reclaim some of it if, over the next 3–5 years, its member countries can marshal better economic performance, accelerate economic integration, and avoid bilateral conflict. An improvement of the economic and political situation in Indonesia, the largest member country, would also be necessary. At the close of 2000, the prospects for such amelioration could at best be described as uncertain.

Yet, amidst the gloom, it is easy to forget the region's positive features. Shortcomings in banking and corporate governance in Southeast Asia will continue to be addressed, even if not fast enough. The Southeast Asian political landscape is not uniformly bleak. There is, for instance, a reasonably good basis for political stability in Thailand, even with the problems facing the new Prime Minister. In Malaysia, it is virtually impossible for the Islamic Parti Islam SeMalaysia (PAS) to capture power without being part of a multiracial coalition to which it also has to adjust its policies.

International investors and fund managers shift their attention from region to region, and a conjunction of developments in the next 3–5 years could again alter their perceptions of Southeast Asia. These developments could include economic recoveries in America and Japan and possible investor disenchantment with China, even if temporary. The latter could arise from perceived difficulties in complying with WTO conditionalities, economic slowdown, or political uncertainty. A Japanese recovery will undoubtedly have a significant positive impact on Southeast Asia.

However, higher growth rates, if achieved, will not be sustainable for long if ASEAN countries do not rapidly dismantle barriers to trade and investments and address other structural impediments to growth (like deficient educational systems). The competition from countries like China and India will be a protracted long-term challenge.

Moreover, with greater diversity of interests in the ten-member Association and the fact that the newer members are only partially in the market economy, ASEAN will continue to lack cohesion, making it difficult for the Association to act as a diplomatic community, as it was able to do in the 1980s, to secure its common interests in relation to outside forces, however defined, and especially the major external political and economic powers. For the same reasons, ASEAN will continue to be handicapped in addressing issues like human rights and democracy. In this context, the 26th AMM in Singapore in 1993 had decided to consider the establishment of "an appropriate regional mechanism on human rights". Yet at the 33rd AMM in Bangkok in 2000, the foreign ministers were only able to note with appreciation the consultations between the ASEAN Senior Officials and the Working Group for an ASEAN Human Rights Mechanism.

Asean Plus Three
The ASEAN Plus Three process continued to see a spate of activities. The APT finance ministers met in Chiang Mai in May 2000, and the economic ministers in October in the same city, following the annual meetings of the ASEAN finance and economic ministers respectively. The foreign ministers met for the first time in July in Bangkok after the ASEAN Annual Ministerial Meeting there, and will continue to do so after each AMM. The heads of government met in Singapore in November after the informal ASEAN summit.

In terms of substance, perhaps the Chiang Mai meeting was the more significant because the ministers agreed to a "currency swap" mechanism. Also known as the Chiang Mai Initiative, it involves an expanded ASEAN Swap Arrangement (ASA) that would include all ASEAN countries, and a network of bilateral swap arrangements (BSA) among the ASEAN countries, China, Japan, and South Korea. The scheme is intended to provide support for member countries facing short-term foreign exchange difficulties. It would hopefully discourage a repeat of the 1997 crisis, given the formidable pool of foreign exchange reserves of nearly US$1 trillion in the region. This agreement could also one day form the basis of an Asian Monetary Fund.

At the Singapore summit itself, the host, Singapore Prime Minister Goh Chok Tong, said that "the two big ideas" evolving from discussions were the proposal for an East Asian summit and an East Asian free trade zone. An East Asian summit, as distinct from an ASEAN Plus Three summit, would take the APT process towards an East Asian grouping. Goh made two key observations about this prospect. Firstly, there was no harm in East Asian countries coming together as others were also forming their own groupings — a reference obviously to the European Union (EU) and the North American Free Trade Agreement (NAFTA). The essential thing was open regionalism, that is, not seeking to keep others out of the club. Secondly, the circumstances were different from those in the early 1990s when the United States had opposed the formation of the East Asian Economic Grouping (EAEG), because now APEC was much better established. There was therefore less danger of the two sides of the Pacific being divided, he maintained. It was left to be seen whether the new Bush Administration would be assured by these arguments. The importance of trans-Pacific geopolitical links was also emphasized in the Singapore premier's rationale for wanting to negotiate a U.S.–Singapore Free Trade Agreement.

There was an apparent attempt to play down East Asian regionalism. Goh claimed: "Speaking for Singapore, I would prefer a gradual approach. I would emphasize ASEAN solidarity."[9] Likewise, Malaysia's Dr Mahathir Mohamad noted that although the idea of closer co-operation between ASEAN and the three northeast Asian countries was very good, "it is not going to happen anytime soon" and that such an arrangement should not put developing ASEAN countries at risk.[10]

Yet it has also been clear that East Asian regionalism will be pursued even if doubts persist among some members about its ultimate aims, given the fact that the vast area is too diverse and the interests of China and Japan too different. In private conversations, Japanese officials have indicated that the scheme would not likely emerge as a free trade area, though they supported the idea of more East Asian co-operation in order to engage China, and to improve intra-East Asian relations in general.[11] To the Japanese and Koreans, the impact of the scheme on the American presence in Asia, and in particular their own relations with the United States, their security guarantor and vital economic market, was also crucial in their approach to the APT.

The main original impulse behind the new East Asian regionalism was a sense of ASEAN weakness and helplessness in the face of international financial factors that precipitated the Asian crisis in July 1997. Such regionalism might also allow East Asia in general to deal from a position of strength with powerful countries or groupings on other issues. These include issues of protectionism[12] and perceived U.S. arrogance and unilateralism. The 1997 Asian crisis will be remembered by some in Asia not only for the speculative attacks on regional currencies, but also for the manner in which the Soeharto regime was brought down by stringent IMF conditionalities. Singapore seems to be a leading force behind this East Asian thrust. Part of the motivation for this position is the desire for a more "multipolar" world. This is one in which the United States, the EU, and "a more united East Asia" constitute three poles, a world that "would be more balanced, comfortable and safe" than a unipolar one under U.S. dominance.[13] Singapore realizes that a successful East Asian regionalism would depend on a historic reconciliation between China and Japan, but acknowledges also the Herculean character of the task of trying to bring about such an accommodation. At the same time, Singapore also continues to recognize the importance of the U.S. presence in East Asia as a balance to China "if we are to have elbow room for ourselves",[14] for the East Asian club is unlikely to have an internal balance.

While nobody was prepared to forecast where the APT process will lead to, the outside world was starting to take notice of its potential. Fred Bergsten, the Director of the Institute of International Economics in Washington D.C., writing in the *The Economist,* opined that, in the medium term, "the most important changes to the world's financial architecture" were likely to come from the arrangements being fashioned by the APT countries. "For the first time in history," he went on to observe, "the world is becoming a three block configuration. Not only global economic relationships, but political ones too, will turn on the direction the new agreements will take — and how the United States and others outside the region decide to respond to them."[15]

The Asia–Pacific Economic Co-operation (APEC) Forum
Meanwhile, Asia–Pacific regionalism as represented by the APEC forum was alive, if somewhat sickly. With the failure of the second WTO summit in Seattle in 1998 to produce a new round of multilateral trade talks, and with greater caution about globalization felt in East Asia following the economic crisis of 1997–98, APEC was no longer functioning as an engine to push the WTO to start a new round of global trade talks. (In the early 1990s, it had contributed to a successful conclusion of the Uruguay Round and the establishment of the WTO).

The joint statement by the foreign and trade ministers of the twenty-one member countries that met in Brunei in November urged negotiators at the WTO in Geneva to agree to an agenda in 2001 "that [is] balanced and sufficiently broad-based to respond to the interests and concerns of all members". This went to the heart of the divide between those who wanted a new round of global trade talks in 2001, and those, principally the developing countries, who refused to meet until an agenda could be agreed upon first. This hiatus was not entirely closed by the willingness of the leaders at their summit to go further by calling for the actual start of multilateral trade negotiations in 2001.

APEC 2000 was highlighted by the announcement of moves for a series of bilateral free trade agreements (FTAs). Singapore formally signed such an agreement with New Zealand on the sidelines of the APEC meeting and announced it was going to begin negotiating a FTA with the United States.

Singapore was also planning to negotiate FTAs with Japan, Mexico, Australia, and Canada. All these FTAs were to go well beyond liberalization of trade and involve significant liberalization in services.[16]

The APEC leaders in Brunei endorsed the bilateral FTAs as potential building blocks for multilateral freeing of markets so long as they remained consistent with WTO rules. Singapore's Senior Minister Lee Kuan Yew was later to depict Singapore's strategy as one of leapfrogging the region and reaching out to developed countries in order to diversify its markets and links.[17] Singapore also justified its proposed FTA with the United States in strategic terms, that is, to strengthen the links between the two sides of the Pacific. In this regard, Prime Minister Goh Chok Tong also noted: "Singapore is a building block for the U.S.' wider interest in ASEAN".[18] According to media reports, various other countries were also actively pursuing the bilateral route.[19]

Despite the loss of momentum in APEC during the past few years over trade liberalization, the organization remains vital for Southeast Asia. Firstly, the leaders' meetings have an import well beyond economics. Such gatherings are particularly useful in times of tension by providing opportunity to meet on the sidelines. Secondly, APEC is one of the vehicles which helps to keep the two sides of the Pacific connected, given the crucial importance of continued U.S. engagement in East Asia. Taking a longer view, there need not be too much dismay if in the past few years APEC has not moved forward fast enough on regional trade liberalization. It is not surprising for regional co-operation to be marked by periods of good progress punctuated by periods of apparent stagnation, as the history of regional co-operation in Western Europe since the 1950s shows.

THE GREAT POWERS AND SOUTHEAST ASIA

The broader Asian region which stretches in an arc from the Russian Far East in the east, through Southeast Asia, to Pakistan in the west, is home to four big powers — China, Japan, Russia, and India — while a fifth, the United States, is also deeply involved in its affairs. Four of these five powers have nuclear arms. The largest standing armies in the world are distributed among them and the two Koreas. The security situation in the whole region is dangerous and fluid, marked by historical animosities, contemporary rivalries, and deep distrust between some of the leading players. The area is also one of potential "hegemonic transition" that in past history has often been associated with major conflict. East Asia is the only place in the world today where a war between the major powers, most likely the United States and China over Taiwan, could break out with little advance warning, even if on rational calculation, it may not be in the interest of either country to have such a conflict. South Asia, described by former U.S. President Bill Clinton as the most dangerous place in the world, is witnessing a perilous nuclear arms race and faces a growing menace of international terrorism.

The U.S.–China Relationship
No great power relationship is more important to Southeast Asia than the
Washington–Beijing one. There was good progress during the last year of the
Clinton Administration in bilateral issues between the United States and China:
contacts between defence officials at the highest levels were resumed and the
U.S. Congress passed China's entry into the WTO, ending America's
twenty-year annual review of China's preferred-nation trade status. China on
its part pledged not to help any country to develop ballistic missiles that can
be used to deliver nuclear weapons, paving the way for satellite and other high
technology deals between the United States and China, and waiver of U.S.
sanctions against Chinese firms previously involved in such proliferation.[20]

However, the underlying relationship was fragile and unstable because of
the Taiwan problem and different perceptions of each other's role and
intentions in Asia. The United States increasingly feels that China does not
accept the notion that East Asia is large enough for both of them, and that it
wants the United States to be evicted from Asia. On the other hand, there is
a growing feeling in China, especially in the Chinese military, that the United
States wants to curb the rise of China and has embarked on a policy of
containment.

The election, in March, of Chen Shui-bian as President of Taiwan raised
tensions. His Democratic Progressive Party (DPP) has been identified with an
independent Taiwan. However, Chen showed the flexibility to avoid a crisis.
Nevertheless, the China–Taiwan relationship will remain charged with danger,
with the ever-present risk of miscalculation by either side, especially by China.
China is steadily building an assault capacity of short-range M-9 and M-11
ballistic missiles on the Fujian coast opposite Taiwan, reportedly about 250 in
mid-2000, and increasing by about 50 a year[21] — a development that is likely
to feature importantly in the new Bush Administration's choice of weapons
systems to update Taiwan's defences.

At the end of the year, it was clear that 2001 could subject the U.S.–China
relationship to new tests. The Bush team will have a whole range of issues to
attend to, including new arms for Taiwan, National Missile Defence (NMD),
Theatre Missile Defence (TMD), China's implementation of the non-
proliferation pledge of November 2000, and the State Department's review of
human rights in China. Anyone of these issues, depending upon how it is
handled, could derail the progress made in relations during 2000. Further
down the road, China may find it politically impossible to abide fully by all the
conditions for entry into the WTO and thereby provide further ammunition
to anti-China hawks in Washington.

There are two other factors that have to borne in mind. Firstly, there is
growing nationalism in China. While it has been manipulated by the regime
in the past, it is clearly a double-edged sword and not always easy to manage,
given the country's greater openness. Perceived slights to Chinese dignity
and pride on issues like Taiwan could give this nationalism a dangerous

anti-American bent. The Internet in China has been used to pressure the PRC (People's Republic of China) government to take a more aggressive attitude towards other countries — for instance, in relation to atrocities against ethnic Chinese in Indonesia in May 1998.[22] It could be used again in relation to Taiwan, perceived bullying of China, or perceived persecution of ethnic Chinese in Southeast Asia, potentially bringing about a tougher official reaction to such issues.

Secondly, China is facing leadership transition in 2002. It is not clear how much influence Jiang Zemin will wield after he steps down as party leader and President in 2002 and whether his successors will be strong enough and committed enough to maintain priority for economic development and remain level-headed in a crisis. Just as there are anti-China hawks in the United States, there will continue to be anti-U.S. hawks in China. It has to be a consideration in the policy of any U.S. Administration not to strengthen their hand.

Internationally, China continued to seek to curb U.S. power by promoting global multipolarization, arguing that the current situation in which one country is too powerful is unhealthy and prone to instability. It has sought to forge a united front with like-minded powers, principally Russia, to achieve this. It has tried to mend fences with others in Asia, particularly India and ASEAN, which might be tempted to ally themselves more closely with the United States, so that it can concentrate its energies on dealing with the United States over the Taiwan issue. The United States is portrayed by the Chinese state media as a possible adversary, and in military science publications strategists openly discuss war with the United States over Taiwan. China's third Defence White Paper, issued in November 2000, says "Certain big powers are pursuing neo-interventionism, neo-gunboat diplomacy and new economic colonialism which are ... threatening world peace and security." Chinese nationalism includes the desire for a powerful, well equipped military. China is devoting considerable resources and energy to developing a new class of land-based (DF-41 and DF-31) and submarine-based (JL-2) intercontinental ballistic missiles (ICBMs), on the chilling assumption that it would be necessary to neutralize America's strategic advantage in any war with the United States over Taiwan.[23]

The United States in Asia

In the year 2000, reviews were under way of the approximately 100,000 forward deployed U.S. troops in East Asia/Western Pacific, and the findings will be used in the Quadrennial Defence Review (QDR) which is due to be out in 2001. The advent of a new Administration in January 2001 led to a further internal Pentagon review of U.S. military strategy (under the direction of Andrew Marshall, Director of the Pentagon's Office of Net Assessment), the results of which will also be used in the QDR.

While the United States is likely to remain committed to the security of the region because of its geopolitical and economic importance to American interests, the means of fulfilling this commitment could well change, depending on the political and security environment of Asia. American security specialists have argued for some time that there should be nothing magical about the figure of 100,000 troops in East Asia. Technological developments by themselves could provide the required deterrent and the desired "presence" with less than 100,000 forces. All new administrations in the United States take time to settle down and adjust their early policy instincts to international realities and domestic budgetary constraints. Still, there was some sense of uncertainty ahead because of the new Bush team's apparent determination to proceed with a national missile defence (with its connotations of a "Fortress America"), media speculation that its instincts might be to develop power projection capabilities based in U.S. territory, and reports that the Marshall review could lead to reductions of forward deployed forces over the longer term.

The most dramatic image of impending change in Asia was the historic North–South Korea summit, which gave rise to uncertainties about the future deployments of U.S. forces in East Asia.[24] Although President Kim Dae-Jung has said that his northern counterpart had agreed with him that U.S. troops contributed to the stability of the region, U.S. military planners were not taking this comment at face value. Korean nationalism may make it difficult to keep U.S. ground troops if there is substantial improvement of relations between the two Koreas and de-escalation of military tensions. Meanwhile, the strength of the anti-U.S. forces sentiment in Okinawa, combined with stirrings of nationalism in Japan as a whole, may require adjustments to the Marine Corps in Okinawa, even though the U.S.-Japan Mutual Security Treaty has been strengthened in recent years by the adoption of new operational guidelines. Indeed, the Korean summit and protests against U.S. forces in South Korea and Japan were provoking an intense scrutiny of options for forward troop deployment.

There are other considerations too. The increasing accuracy of conventional ballistic missiles in the hands of Asian countries has made U.S. bases in Northeast Asia more vulnerable. The progressive modernization of China's armed forces will also raise the costs, in human and material terms, of potential conflict arising from America's commitments to Taiwan.

Yet, whatever the exact numbers or configuration of forces considered necessary, it is clear that U.S. strategic attention has gradually been shifting from Europe towards Asia. This is suggested by efforts made since the mid-1990s to strengthen bilateral alliances with Japan and Australia, and intensify training and interactions with Thailand, the Philippines, and Singapore. There is a growing sense in the U.S. armed forces that Asia is the most likely place that the United States will be involved in conflict and that the stakes here are perhaps bigger than anywhere else.[25] This shift towards Asia is likely to become more pronounced under the Bush Administration.

The alliance with Japan is crucial for U.S. security strategy in East Asia. The Bush Administration has pledged to revitalize the relationship with Japan and to give it more importance than President Clinton did. Japan had felt slighted by the Clinton Administration's apparent neglect of it in favour of a "strategic partnership" with China. It has long been noted by American analysts that while the U.S.–Japan alliance provides invaluable facilities for forward deployment, it also has serious limitations, from the military perspective. If America has to fight a war in Korea or in the Taiwan Straits, Japan would provide, at most, some rear end logistic support — out of harm's way.

The new U.S. Administration is likely to push Japan towards burden-sharing in the sense of more direct involvement of Japanese forces in conflict, if one were to break out in the vicinity of Japan and involve U.S. troops. In other words, Washington may want to alter the character of the alliance to one of collective defence. A bipartisan study group that included Richard Armitage (who has now assumed a senior position in the State Department in the new Administration) and Professor Joseph Nye concluded in autumn 2000 that Japan's restrictions on the use of militay power are "a constraint" on the U.S.–Japan alliance and that it is time for "burden-sharing to evolve into power-sharing".[26] This will not be easy and will take time to achieve, even if, in the first instance, it is negotiable at all. It may require the amendment of Japan's "peace" constitution, which will be a major undertaking, though there has been some change in sentiment in Japan on this issue. (See section on Japan below.) However, Japan at present is too weak psychologically and politically, too diffident, to embark on a course which is likely to invite strong reaction from China. Although its relations with China are difficult, Japan would not want to turn it into an enemy.

In Southeast Asia, attitudes towards the United States remain ambivalent. At the strategic level, almost all countries favour a U.S. military presence to balance China. At the political level, there is the old unhappiness among some over the perceived tendency for the United States to be unilateralist and interventionist on issues of human rights and democracy; to it has been added resentment over some of America's actions or omissions in relation to the Asian economic crisis.[27] Such a situation calls for a more sophisticated and skilful diplomacy on the part of the United States, including more attention to those regional institutions and forums that Asians consider important, even though they may seem to be no more than "talk shops", while at the same time, a strong military presence is maintained and the key alliances are sustained and nurtured. Asia is traditionally a place where appearances, "face" and pride matter a great deal, and insensitivity to them can have potentially serious consequences.

Southeast Asians will resent too intrusive a U.S. policy on human rights and democratization, even though they know that this issue serves the important domestic purpose of sustaining U.S. engagement abroad. In comparing American military power with that of regional states, there is sometimes insufficient appreciation among Southeast Asians that the United States needs more than a military "balance" with a potential adversary. From the American perspective, a U.S. military preponderance in East Asia of a kind which allows it to prevail without too much human and material cost is essential to sustain domestic U.S. support for its security commitments and forward deployments, making any notion of a military equality, in particular for air and naval warfare, unacceptable. If among East and Southeast Asia's biggest anxieties is possible conflict between the United States and China over Taiwan, many in the region are also fearful of the United States backing down in the face of an unprovoked Chinese attack on the island — because of the deleterious consequences this could have on the U.S. position in Asia.

The only country in Southeast Asia which received a state visit from the President of the United States in 2000 was Vietnam, a former enemy of Washington. Vietnam borders China, has been its historical foe, and possesses a strategically located naval base at Cam Ranh Bay. President Bill Clinton's visit in November was preceded by that of then Defence Secretary William Cohen. Cohen encouraged the Vietnamese to work closely with ASEAN to deal with China's claims in the South China Sea. He held out the offer of military ties and raised the possibility of American warships visiting Cam Ranh Bay. In July, the two countries signed a landmark trade deal, which, if honoured, would lead to wide-ranging cuts in U.S. tariffs on Vietnam's exports to the United States and removal of bureaucratic impediments in Vietnam to U.S. investors. President Clinton's visit was the first by an American President since Richard Nixon's journey to South Vietnam in 1969 at the height of the Vietnam War. The Vietnamese public, more than half of which belongs to the post-Vietnam war generation, responded enthusiastically to Clinton, but the old guard conservatives in the government and the Communist Party, who see America as wanting to change the Vietnamese political system, were wary. Their ideological solidarity with the Chinese on this score, and the improvement in Sino-Vietnamese relations in recent years, ensured that Hanoi would turn down the offer of military co-operation from the Americans. Still, seeking both an economic opening up and strategic co-operation, and not unaware that the younger generation in Vietnam is more amenable to seeing the United States as a counterweight to China, the United States left the offer on the table in the hope that in different times and circumstances it could elicit a favourable response. Judging by the flurry of Vietnamese statements and meetings with Chinese officials to assure them about the visit, Clinton could only have strengthened Vietnam's hand *vis-à-vis* China.

It was interesting that while Vietnam received strategic attention, Indonesia, the largest country in Southeast Asia, and arguably the strategically most important, received little U.S. interest besides the focus on democratization and human rights. Yet a fragmentation of Indonesia or a descent into chaos could have significant implications for U.S. interests, especially given the fact that Indonesia straddles strategic waterways linking the Pacific and Indian Oceans.

On the broader Asian canvas, the year 2000 saw a discernible tilt towards India in U.S. relations with South Asian countries. The factors behind this shift were the growing importance of India in Asian geopolitics and to the U.S. high-tech economy, a shared concern about terrorism originating from the Afghanistan-Pakistan region, and a growing influential Indian lobby in America. Self-evidently, India, with its huge population base and modernizing economy, has the potential to be a balance to a prosperous and powerful China. At the same time, neither India nor the United States want to present their developing relationship as some kind of anti-China axis, since both are simultaneously seeking to engage China.[28] American outreach to India was dramatically illustrated by President Clinton's week-long visit in March (by contrast, he spent only a few token hours in Pakistan), the first by a U.S. President since 1978. The upshot is that dialogue between the two countries will be institutionalized, with annual foreign ministers' meetings, and special regular dialogues on a whole host of issues, including Asian security, terrorism, technology, and trade. The indications were that the Bush Administration would seek to continue and deepen U.S.–India links.

China and Southeast Asia

It was a good year for China's bilateral relations with Southeast Asia. Leaders of many Southeast Asian countries visited China and signed agreements on matters ranging from economic co-operation to border demarcation. Geostrategic and economic realities lay behind these developments. Southeast Asian nations, and especially those sharing borders with China, want to have friendly relations with the neighbourhood giant whose long-term intentions are a cause of some unease in many capitals. On China's part, there is the desire to build goodwill and avoid contentious issues as part of an united front strategy directed against America. China has been adept at contrasting its own behaviour with U.S. demands on Southeast Asian nations for political and economic reforms, and its criticisms of human rights violations. Chinese Vice-President Hu Jintao, in a visit to Jakarta in July, denounced "Cold War mentality, hegemony, and power politics", promising that China on its part would ensure "genuine mutual respect, mutual co-operation, consensus through consultation ... rather than bullying, confrontation and imposition of one's will upon others."[29] The visit came after Robert Gelbard, the U.S. Ambassador in Jakarta, had been accused by the Indonesians of interfering in domestic Indonesian politics, resulting in anti-American demonstrations.

Among individual Southeast Asian countries, relations were closest with Myanmar, where the military junta, facing boycotts and sanctions from Western powers, has come to depend heavily on arms and other assistance from China. Since 1991, Chinese experts have been helping to upgrade Myanmar's infrastructure, especially badly maintained roads and railways, and Chinese military advisers arrived that year, the first foreign military personnel to be stationed in Myanmar since the 1950s. The total value of Chinese arms delivered to Myanmar in the 1990s is estimated at US$1–2 billion, with most acquired at a discount, through barter deals or interest-free loans.[30] China has also been assisting Myanmar to upgrade its naval facilities, including four electronic listening posts on the Bay of Bengal, and in the Andaman Sea. There is also a China-built radar station near Mergui in southeastern Myanmar, operated at least in part by Chinese technicians.[31]

China's influence has been increasing in the three Indochina countries, in part because of their concerns about U.S. policies or about dissidents linked to the United States. President Jiang visited both Laos and Cambodia in 2000. In Laos, economic distress, growing disquiet about the Hmong insurgency, and calls by Lao and Hmong Americans for political liberalization has driven a nervous Vientiane to seek closer co-operation with both Vietnam and China. President Jiang visited Laos for the first time in November 2000 and promised more economic aid.[32] In Cambodia, Prime Minister Hun Sen's 1997 violent coup against the coalition government to seize full control of the country resulted in the cut-off of U.S. aid, but by 2000 China was giving US$200 million in aid, including US$2.7 million in military training.[33] China capitalized upon Hun Sen's displeasure over American demands that the Khmer Rouge leaders be tried by an international tribunal, stating that foreign countries should not dictate to Cambodia on the issue. Vietnam's communist leadership has placed emphasis on improved relations with China, with the year 2000 seeing several visits by leaders, especially from Hanoi to Beijing. In December, the two countries issued a joint statement demarcating their Gulf of Tonkin sea border after years of bitter dispute. However, the disputes about sovereignty over the Paracels and the Spratly Islands remain unresolved. China has also been building a network of roads from Yunnan province into Myanmar and Laos, at certain points almost reaching the Thai border. There are good economic and commercial reasons for these constructions: the development of cross-border trade is benefiting both China and the Southeast Asian countries bordering it. However, these highways also have a strategic dimension that cannot be ignored.

Thailand, a pivotal Southeast Asian state, enjoys cordial relations with China.[34] So do Singapore, Malaysia, and Indonesia. Yet China's rise as a great power also arouses anxieties in Southeast Asia. This is not surprising, given China's size, its growing wealth and power, and its geographical location adjacent to Southeast Asia. Will a powerful China also be a benign China which respects international norms of behaviour? The answer to this key question is not clear, and may not be for a long time, given the domestic economic, political, and leadership changes China is likely to go through in the coming decades. The answer will also depend on how others, principally the United States, manage their relations with China. The signs so far are not entirely reassuring, given China's growing nationalism, great power ambitions, strident rhetoric, and its troubling claims to the South China Sea.[35]

Most Southeast Asian governments are realistic and would seek to balance relations with China with those with other powers. This would be particularly true of the six older members of ASEAN. Even with regard to countries sharing borders with China, Beijing cannot take close relations for granted. For instance, Vietnam has a strong tradition of independence and a past history of animosity against China. Myanmar too has a rugged sense of independence, even xenophobia, and would probably try not to be too dependent on China once other options become available.

Thus, while geographical proximity, combined with growing wealth and power, would seem to confer upon China an unassailable position in Southeast Asia in the future, the realities may not be so simple. Southeast Asian nationalisms and the very paradox of power, which generates resentment (as the United States has often found), may complicate the picture. China will have to tread carefully in the Southeast Asian minefield, which, paradoxically again, also includes the presence of ethnic Chinese communities — any Chinese zeal on their behalf could trigger fierce anti-Chinese reactions from the indigenous populations. There will be no dearth of issues to test relations, be they illegal Chinese immigrants or cheap Chinese goods smuggled across borders to the detriment of local industries. Furthermore, one cannot assume that twenty years down the road the strategic latitude that China has enjoyed in East Asia since the end of the Cold War, given a weak Japan and Russia, will continue in the same way.

Japan and Sino-Japanese Relations[36]

With its economy in stagnation for more than a decade, it is easy to underestimate Japan's power and influence in Asia and its crucial role in the past in the economic development of Southeast Asia. Japan remains the world's second biggest economy, the biggest in Asia, and several times larger than the Chinese economy.

Nonetheless, the prolonged economic malaise, the blow to its self-perception as an economic leader and pace-setter for Asia in the "flying geese model", and a sense of loss of its privileged position with the United States on matters dealing with Asia (in view of the importance attached to China by the Clinton Administration) have contributed to a collective self-doubt and increased questioning, especially among the younger generation, of the economic and political assumptions of the previous half century.[37] Developments on the Korean peninsula, the rise of China and its attitude to Japan, and the dynamics of American policy will interact with the profound changes under way in the Japanese economy and society to eventually forge a new consensus on Japan's role.

The younger generation of Japanese scholars, politicians, and officials are inclined to favour Japan becoming a more "normal" country, willing to assume a role in security affairs, such as United Nations peacekeeping, and participation in regional activities like anti-piracy operations. Constitutional issues, including the possible revision of Article 9 (which forbids the country from waging war), are openly discussed, as is the long-term viability of the U.S.–Japan security partnership. There is a stronger sentiment in favour of greater equality in the alliance with the United States. Though support for the alliance remains strong, there seems to be an accelerated questioning among the younger generation about the desirability and necessity of having foreign soldiers based on Japanese soil. Japanese nationalism, sublimated until the 1990s by the country's spectacular economic achievements, is coming more to the fore in response to the prolonged economic distress and troubling perceptions of Japan's place in the world.

Likewise, in this context, the year 2000 saw a hardening of the official Japanese policy towards China in response to the views of a new generation of politicians, academics, and journalists. They resent continuous Chinese hectoring about Tokyo's World War II misdeeds, which they see as an attempt to keep contemporary Japan down, and China's unwillingness to accept that Japan too has legitimate security concerns and can play a positive regional role. China's resistance to the convening of trilateral U.S.–China–Japan security talks, its opposition to Japan's quest for a permanent membership of the United Nations Security Council, and its criticisms of the U.S.–Japan security alliance, are also evaluated in this light. These factors, together with China's military modernization, have eroded public support for Japanese official development assistance (ODA) to China, which since 1979 has amounted to more than 2 trillion yen (close to US$20 billion). The possible reunification of Korea is viewed with unease as it foreshadows Sino-Japanese jockeying for influence on the peninsula. Public attitudes towards China have also been affected by illegal Chinese migrants in Japan, blamed for a surge of petty crime.

In various vital ways, economic links have been growing, though economics do not necessarily determine politics. Trade between the two countries, heavily in favour of China, was expected to surpass US$80 billion in 2000, with Japan ranked as China's biggest trading partner and China constituting Japan's second biggest trading partner after the United States. Japanese companies were also planning to invest more in China in view of its coming WTO membership.

During 2000, publicity given to ill-considered sailings of Chinese naval intelligence vessels within Japan's 200-mile exclusive economic zone, or EEZ (there were fourteen such sightings in the first five months of 2000 alone) did not improve Japanese attitudes to China, though the matter was apparently resolved, after being taken up at the highest levels of government.

There can be little doubt that Southeast Asia will be an arena of Sino–Japanese competition for influence. One development which illustrated the distrust between the two countries was China's attitude to Japan's proposal to combat the growing incidence of piracy in Southeast Asian waters through which a large part of Japan's trade passes. The proposal for regional joint exercises and patrols involving Japanese coastguard vessels was opposed strongly by China.

Russia and India

Despite many domestic problems, President Vladimir Putin has made it clear that Russia has a diplomatic role to play in Asia, especially in Northeast Asia.

His visits to Pyongyang and Seoul also serve notice that Moscow is not about to abandon its traditional interest in the fortunes of the Korean peninsula, a position that seems to be endorsed by both Korean capitals. It may also revive its diplomacy with Japan on critical unsettled issues. His visit to Vietnam in February 2001 showed that erstwhile allies even in distant places like Southeast Asia are not forgotten in this diplomatic strategy. During 2000, the Russian President also visited Mongolia and India and signed new military agreements with both countries.

Russia's new diplomacy in Korea, Mongolia, and Vietnam cannot be music to the ears of Beijing. If through military and political co-operation with China, Russia hopes to obtain some leverage on the United States, its diplomacy in key regions on China's borders, like Korea, Vietnam, and Mongolia, where China would like to be the only big power influence, sends a signal to Beijing that it cannot take Russia for granted, and cannot have the same strategic latitude to its north and south as it did for much of the 1990s.[38] There is concern in Russia's security services that over the longer term a powerful China would be a threat to Russia's Far East.

The year 2000 also saw growing recognition of India as an emergent power, the most important demonstration of it being President Clinton's historic visit. Although India's strategic preoccupations are still largely to its west and north (Pakistan and China), there are signs of renewed interest in Southeast Asia, prompted generally by concerns about the impact of a rising China upon Southeast Asia, and more specifically about the close Chinese links with Myanmar, whose independence and territorial integrity are of vital importance to India. India's traditional strategic interest in Southeast Asia was reiterated by Foreign Minisiter Satwant Singh in a public lecture in Singapore in June 2000. He maintained that "an uninterrupted access to the Malacca Straits and the South China Sea, vital for the economies of the ASEAN region and India, needs to be ensured ... India has never encroached on the strategic space of ASEAN while contributing to stability."[39] Meanwhile, in a reversal of its previous policy of support for the Myanmar opposition, great efforts have been made by India in the past few years to mend relations with the military junta in Myanmar.[40]

There were signs of emerging informal security co-operation between India, Japan, and Vietnam (Indian Defence Minister George Fernandez visited both countries in 2000), all three of which also share strategic concerns about China. Though not happy with India's status as a nuclear power, Japan, like the United States, has come to accept it as a fact and appreciates the potential role India can play to protect sea-lanes through the Indian Ocean. Fernandez said in an interview in March 2000 that India and Japan would hold high-level annual defence consultations, while Japanese coastguard and Indian vessels would conduct joint anti-piracy training. Vietnam will train Indian Army personnel in jungle warfare and counter-insurgency, while India will repair MiG aircraft of the Vietnamese air force and train its pilots.

The realization of India's great power aspirations will depend critically on its economic performance and on its ability to safeguard the domestic secular principle in a South Asian environment of entrenched communalism.

Notes

1. *Report of the ASEAN Eminent Persons Group (EPG) on Vision 2000: The People's ASEAN*, <*http://www.aseansec.org*>.
2. *Joint Communique of the Thirty-Third ASEAN Ministerial Meeting*, Bangkok, Thailand, 24–25 July 2000, <*http://www.aseansec.org*>.
3. Ibid.
4. Ibid.
5. See John Funston, "Malaysia: UMNO's Search for Relevance", in this volume.
6. It emerged in early 2001 that secret talks had been taking place since October 2000 between Daw Aung San Suu Kyi and the junta. However, it was not clear if any concrete progress was made.
7. These included Malaysia's announcement that Johor would develop its own water purification facilities instead of buying processed water from Singapore (which, under existing agreements, processes water in Johor and sells part of it to Malaysia); Malaysian leaders' expressions of concern over Singapore's moves to establish bilateral free trade agreements with Japan, the United States and other countries; and Malaysian media analyses of the plight of Malays in Singapore, which were resented in Singapore.
8. Speaking to a group of Indonesians at the Indonesian Embassy in Singapore, and reacting to a perceived slight by Senior Minister Lee Kuan Yew, he accused Singapore of being arrogant and selfish in its relations with ASEAN countries. He even threatened that Indonesia, in concert with Malaysia, might cut the supply of water to Singapore.
9. *Straits Times*, Singapore, 26 November 2000.
10. Ibid.
11. In a public lecture in Singapore in November, Hisashi Odawa, President of the Japan Institute of International Affairs (JIIA) said that "the ASEAN plus Three is an important tool to engage China ... so that she may play a more constructive role in the regional and international context" and he emphasized that co-operation in East Asia should be strengthened in line with rules and standards set by international bodies. See the *Straits Times*, 17 November 2000.
12. Singapore's Senior Minister Lee Kuan Yew, in an address to the Asia Society Australasia Centre, called for a regional sub-group within APEC which would band together ASEAN, Northeast Asia, and Australasia. Calling it "Asean Plus Three, Plus Two", he said it would better advance the common interests of the western side of the Pacific in trade liberalization and help to resist any resurgence of protectionism in North America. Such a sub-group within APEC could bring the United States around "more by persuasion than argument". *Straits Times*, Singapore, 21 November 2000, p. 4.
13. Singapore's Ambassador-at-Large, Professor Tommy Koh, in "East Asia and Europe Have an Important Date", *International Herald Tribune*, 19 October 2000, p. 8. Professor Koh also cited the need for cultural diversity rather than dominance by American culture as another reason for Europe-Asia co-operation, which, by implication, would require "a more united Asia": "Asians and Europeans, do not wish to live in a world dominated by one culture ... they have rich and vibrant cultures of their own".
14. Lee Kuan Yew, in his address to the Asia Society Australasia Centre.

15. *The Economist,* 15–21 July 2000, pp. 20–22. Bergsten gives four basic reasons behind the drive for East Asian regionalism: the Asian financial crisis; the failure of the WTO and APEC to make headway on trade liberalization; the inspiration provided by European integration (especially the common currency); and disquiet with the behaviour of the United States and Western Europe. He goes on to say that "the rest of the world must accept a global role for East Asia, and modify its own institutions with East Asia in mind". East Asian regionalism of the kind Bergsten talks about has yet to arrive, if it does at all. However, there is no doubt that East Asia, and for that matter Asia, because of its importance in the global economy, deserves better representation in institutions like the World Bank, the IMF and the WTO. The appointment of Thailand's former Deputy Prime Minister Supachai Panichpakdi as Secretary-General designate of the WTO is a good start.

16. See, for instance, Barry Desker, Chief Executive Officer of Singapore's Trade Development Board, in the *Sunday Times,* 24 December 2000, p. 42, where he is quoted as saying: "The FTAs we are signing are state-of-the-art FTAs. They go beyond what we have at the WTO ... it is likely that these FTAs will also lead to significant liberalization in several service sectors".

17. See *Business Times,* 9 December 2000, p. 2.

18. *Straits Times,* 17 November 2000.

19. According to various estimates, seventeen of the twenty-one APEC members were involved in negotiations of one kind or another. See Barry Wain "After the Party", *Asian Wall Street Journal,* 24–26 November 2000, p. 10.

20. *Straits Times,* 23 November 2000.

21. David Shambaugh, "Learning to Coexist", *Asian Wall Street Journal,* 13 July 2000, p. 12.

22. Frustration on the Internet with the lack of information provided by China's media on the atrocities turned to anger and outrage when it was learned that China was giving aid to the Indonesian Government (to help Indonesia overcome its financial crisis) rather than using its permanent membership of the United Nations Security Council to call for sanctions and when Beijing municipal authorities refused to allow students to march on the Indonesian embassy. See Christopher Hughes, "China Rides a Nationalist Cyber-Tiger," *Asian Wall Street Journal,* 21 September 2000, p. 8.

23. Shambaugh, op. cit.; and *The Military Balance 2000–2001* (Oxford University Press for the IISS, 2000), p. 186.

24. For example, Francis Fukuyama claimed in an interview with the *Far Eastern Economic Review:* "There is obviously going to be a huge realignment in terms of alliances in Northeast Asia if reunification happens ... the current system (of) parallel alliances with Korea and Japan is probably going to fall apart. The need for an American presence in both countries is going to diminish substantially. Japan I think is going to be pushed almost inevitably towards a more independent defence posture...". *Far Eastern Economic Review,* 10 August 2000, p. 21.

25. Discussion with Kurt Campbell, Senior Vice-President and Director of International Security Programme, Center for Security and International Studies, Washington, D.C., at the 42nd Annual Conference of the International Institute of Strategic Studies on "The Powers in Asia", Manila, Philippines, 14–17 September 2000.

26. See Jim Mann, "Is U.S. ready for an unfettered Japan", *Straits Times,* 15 December 2000, p. 33.

27. The IMF, based in Washington, did not react as fast to the development of the Asian crisis as it did to the Mexican crisis in 1994. One reason was that the latter impinged much more directly and urgently on the interests of the United States than the Thai crisis of July 1997 did. Yet a Japanese–ASEAN proposal of September 1997 for an Asian Monetary Fund which could respond more speedily, and with more capital, to Asian crises, was torpedoed by the United States.

Furthermore, the United States was not in favour of reform of the international financial system, including monitoring of the activities of hedge funds, a topic which aroused much favourable interest in Southeast Asia in the wake of the crisis. East Asian experience of the crisis was to give impetus to East Asian regionalism through the APT process. See also Richard Higgott "The International Relations of the Asian Crisis", in *Politics and Markets in the Wake of the Asian Crisis*, edited by R. Robison (London: Routledge, 2000) pp. 261–282.

28. It is interesting that prior to President Clinton's visit, China pressed the United States to use the visit as an opportunity to roll back India's nuclear programme, and also urged the President to spend more time in Pakistan. Nayan Chanda and Susan Lawrence in *Far Eastern Economic Review*, 16 March 2000, pp. 26–27.

29. *Far Eastern Economic Review*, 23 November 2000, pp. 20–22.

30. "China's Ambitions in Myanmar", *Strategic Comments* 6, issue 6 (International Institute for Strategic Studies, July 2000).

31. Ibid.

32. *Straits Times*, 13 November 2000, pp. A8.

33. See *Far Eastern Economic Review*, 23 November 2000, pp. 20–22.

34. Thai Queen Sirikit's visit to China in 2000 was marked by extraordinary attention at the highest level by the Chinese hosts. The Queen played Chopin on the piano for President Jiang and he sang for her while Chinese officials let it be known to the Queen's entourage that the President wanted to be briefed daily on how the visit was going. Ibid.

35. China claims all the Spratly Islands in the South China Sea, also claimed in entirety or in part by Vietnam, Malaysia, Philippines, and Brunei. However, China's claims are not confined to the Spratlys alone. Beijing has never explicitly disavowed its extensive claims to the South China Sea itself, which are manifested in its well-known U-shaped line which extends almost to the Natuna Islands. China's claims in the South China Sea are a long-term strategic nightmare for ASEAN. It would be extremely difficult for ASEAN to try to have a balance in the influence of the major powers in Southeast Asia when one of them, a potential superpower, not only shares land borders with Southeast Asia but also has extensive territorial claims in the maritime heartland of Southeast Asia.

36. Unless otherwise stated, information in this section is obtained principally from the *Straits Times, The Economist, Far Eastern Economic Review,* and *Asiaweek*.

37. See Yoichi Funabashi, "Japan's Moment of Truth", *Survival* 42, no. 4 (Winter 2000–2001).

38. See June T. Dreyer, Bruce A. Elleman, and Robyn Lim, "Time to Solidify U.S.–Japan Alliance", *International Herald Tribune*, 5 December 2000.

39. Public Lecture organized by Singapore's Institute of Defence and Strategic Studies, Singapore, 2 June 2000. In delineating India's security environment, Foreign Minister Jaswant Singh asserted: "Given its size, geographical location, and EEZ, India's security environment and therefore potential concerns range from the Persian Gulf in the west... Central Asia in the northwest, China in the northeast, and Southeast Asia". This is, in fact, a re-statement of what policy-makers in New Delhi have said from the time of British India.

40. See Bruce Matthews, "Myanmar: Beyond the Reach of International Relief", in this volume.

SOUTHEAST ASIA'S ECONOMIES
Corporate Sector Concerns Return to the Fore

Nick J. Freeman

Introduction

One could almost hear the collective sigh of relief that echoed around the capitals of Southeast Asia in late 1999 and early 2000, as most countries' economic growth rates returned to positive territory, and the *anni horribilis* of 1997–98 began to fade into memory. During the first half of 2000, economists began to talk of a "V-shaped" recovery for the region in the propitious Year of the Dragon. In big picture terms at least, Southeast Asia appeared to be much improved, with most "headline" macroeconomic numbers looking fairly encouraging: positive gross domestic product (GDP) growth; positive current and capital account balances; rising foreign exchange reserves; and so on. Policy-makers probably felt able to relax a little in the first part of 2000, as the region began to show signs of returning to some degree of normalcy. With the notable exception of Indonesia, it was hoped that the region's economies could now strive for the sorts of growth trajectories they had enjoyed prior to 1997. However, news from the corporate sector did not seem to tally with this general impression of growing economic well-being. National and regional business newspapers across Southeast Asia continued to run stories about persistent delays in banking and corporate debt restructuring. De-coupling completely from the GDP growth figures, all the region's main stock market indices declined quite significantly in 2000, while local currencies remained weak and appeared vulnerable to bad news in the political realm (of which there was quite a lot in 2000). Estimates of the scale of aggregate (both public and private sector) debt carried by the region also made for uncomfortable reading. Meanwhile, foreign investors appeared ambivalent towards Southeast Asia as a host for their capital. Little foreign direct investment (FDI) in new production capacity was evident in 2000, and even FDI in existing — but often distressed — businesses was fairly patchy, despite the significantly reduced price tags attached to them (particularly in U.S. dollar terms). The jitters felt by both the currency and equity markets suggested that all was not well with

NICK J. FREEMAN is a Senior Fellow at the Institute of Southeast Asian Studies, Singapore.

the economies of Southeast Asia after all, and doubts began to grow during the latter part of 2000 about the sustainability of the post-crisis economic recovery process in Southeast Asia.[1]

However, not all the causes of concern in 2000 stemmed from problems within Southeast Asia itself. Beyond the region, mounting fears of a less-than-soft landing in the United States, high oil prices, and the Japanese economy's stubborn inability to be revived, all prompted concerns that the benign global economic environment of 1999 and 2000 would not be there to support Southeast Asia's economies in 2001. It is undoubtedly true that a strong global economic backdrop, and robust global trade flows, were the principal *deus ex machina* of Southeast Asia's economic recovery during much of 1999–2000. If so, might a marked deterioration in global growth and trade flows bring the region's economic recovery process to a premature halt? A deleterious change in the electronics cycle could pose problems for those countries in the region (notably Malaysia, the Philippines, and Singapore) with significant exposure to the electronics industry.[2] Persistently high crude oil prices might also pose difficulties for those countries in the region that are substantial net importers of oil products (principally, the Philippines and Thailand). A sharp slowdown in the U.S. economy would also pose problems for those Southeast Asian countries with significant export exposure to the American market (such as Malaysia and the Philippines).[3]

Consequently, the relatively optimistic appraisals of the region given at the beginning of 2000 had been largely replaced by nervous assessments of Southeast Asia's prospects by the end of the year.[4] Worrisome difficulties at the corporate level, and mounting concerns about potential extra-regional developments to be faced in 2001, together prompted a gradual downturn in business sentiment in Southeast Asia as 2000 progressed.

Slow Progress with Corporate Debt Restructuring
While robust global economic growth and trade flows may have come to the rescue of Southeast Asia's economies in 1999–2000, this was only a stop-gap palliative for the region's structural woes. There is little doubt that corporate and banking sector restructuring remains the *sine qua non* of a more sustained economic recovery in Southeast Asia, as this is primarily where the financial crisis took place in 1997–98, where most damage was done, and where recovery efforts need to be focused. A robust regional recovery in Southeast Asia is difficult to envisage unless the banking sector is recapitalized and banks begin to function as financial intermediaries again (that is, in extending credit), and until corporates are able to resolve their debt obligations. Of course, attaining the former is largely conditional upon achieving the latter. Unfortunately, progress in bank and corporate restructuring was generally slow in 2000, and a real sense of momentum was lacking in a number of countries. In Indonesia, for example, only 15–18 per cent of the country's total private external debt had been restructured by late 2000, according to one estimate.[5]

The sheer complexity of the corporate debt restructuring process in Southeast Asia resembles a Gordian knot, with myriad debtors and creditors involved in renegotiating a spectrum of loans, some of which are fairly elaborate syndicated loans. Unpicking this knot of debt requires a level of dedication and focus that was often lacking in 2000. The case of Thai Petrochemical Industry (TPI) was broadly indicative of the corporate debt problem currently faced in parts of Southeast Asia, and the propensity for foot-dragging by debtors unwilling to accept debt-restructuring schemes that would entail some degree of equity transfer or dilution. As far back as August 1997, TPI had announced that it was unable to meet interest payments on its debts, and was one of the region's first major firms to "go under" during the regional financial crisis. By 2000, the company — the largest petrochemical firm in Southeast Asia — was owing creditors roughly US$3.7 billion (including accrued interest). In the words of the *Asian Wall Street Journal*, its debt "workout [was] widely seen as a key test of Thailand's ability to cleanse its corporate sector of billions of dollars in loans that went sour during Asia's 1997-98 financial crisis".[6] In the three years since unilaterally declaring a moratorium on loan repayments, the chief executive of TPI, Prachai Leophairatana, was able to thwart various debt restructuring plans proposed by the company's 140 financial creditors and its court-appointed custodian. The restructuring plan proposed by TPI's creditors largely entailed a debt for equity swap (which would have resulted in them acquiring a 75 per cent stake in the firm), as well as the disposal of most of the firm's non-core assets. It is perhaps not surprising that the restructuring plan was resisted by Mr Prachai, as his share of equity in the company would be diluted from about 60 per cent to just 15 per cent under the plan. The TPI case became an extremely emotive one, with Mr Prachai using the analogy of a daughter being raped to describe what he perceived creditors were doing to his company. In late December 2000, however, it appeared that Mr Prachai had finally been defeated, after three years, as the bankruptcy court placed the company in the hands of the creditors. It is interesting to note how much more media attention the acrimonious TPI case received, compared with the relatively smooth US$2.3 billion debt restructuring of Thai Oil Company, completed in March 2000. While TPI was just one, albeit high-profile case, it was fairly symptomatic of numerous other difficult corporate debt restructuring cases in Thailand and across the Southeast Asian region. Press coverage of the TPI saga acted to deter potential foreign investors, as it underlined the extent to which new reforms have yet to fully take hold in Thailand.

Southeast Asia's NPLs and Debt Burden

As a corollary of the slow pace of corporate debt restructuring, the resolution of high non-performing loans (NPLs) by domestic banks in parts of Southeast Asia has also proved to be a very gradual process. In some cases, the term "debt restructuring" has simply been a politically correct euphemism for lengthening loan tenures (that is, "rolling over" the loan to allow the debtor to pay over a longer period of time), or on-selling and transferring bad loans to "asset management companies" in order to get them off banks' loan books.[7] While numerous NPLs in Southeast Asia are reported to have been restructured, some subsequently became delinquent again — so-called "boomerang NPLs". In the case of Thailand, NPL levels were even rising again at some banks during late 2000. The World Bank estimates that in September 2000, aggregate NPLs in Thailand still amounted to 22.6 per cent of total loans, or 30.6 per cent if one also included NPLs transferred to banks' own asset management companies. In Malaysia, the official figures for NPLs in the banking sector as a whole (based on a six-month classification) suggest that they had declined from about 8 per cent in mid-1998 to 7 per cent by mid-2000 (or about 26 billion ringgit). However, this seemingly comforting figure excludes 37 billion ringgit of bad loans acquired by Danaharta, and a further 46 billion ringgit in NPLs passed to the Corporate Debt Restructuring Committee (CDRC).[8] The World Bank estimates aggregate NPLs in Malaysia to have actually been 16.2 per cent in mid-2000, or 23.2 per cent if loans transferred to Danaharta are included. In the Philippines, aggregate NPLs have been gradually rising in recent years, and made up 15.3 per cent of total loans in August 2000, according to the World Bank.[9] Urban Bank's move into receivership in mid-2000 indicated that the condition of the Philippine banking sector is not particularly rosy. In Indonesia, total NPLs stood at about 40 per cent of total loans in mid-2000, even after discounting 256 trillion rupiah in NPLs transferred to the Indonesia Bank Restructuring Agency (IBRA).[10] Including loans held by IBRA, the aggregate NPL figure for Indonesia in mid-2000 was an astounding 58.7 per cent of total loans, according to the World Bank. By October 2000, IBRA had restructured just 12 per cent of the NPLs that it had taken over.

Such relatively high NPL levels ensured that many domestic banks had little or no incentive to provide new credit to companies in Southeast Asia during 2000, or if so, at high rates of interest. According to one foreign expert on NPLs, Thai banks' "core business has changed from being banks to being asset-management companies", as their primary attention is on rebuilding their existing loan portfolios rather than extending new credit. The alternative is to write-off the NPLs, but the extent of the NPL problem is too large for most banks to endure such a process. One Thai bank that did this was DBS Thai Danu Bank, which wrote off its NPLs at a 72.5 per cent discount.[11] However, this was only possible as a result of substantial capital injected by a new foreign partner. Only four Thai banks have so far enacted merger deals with foreign investors. Consequently, the "bank reform process [in Thailand] has stalled, leaving bad debt at unacceptably high levels. That has coloured the prospects for credit expansion and hampered growth. … Creditors, especially government banks, have been reluctant to write off losses, highlighting how the interrelationship of Thai politics and business is a hindrance to change that has affected investor perception and damaged credibility."[12] In Indonesia, more than 160 of the 237 banks operating before the crisis were still functioning in

2000. Yet more than 75 per cent of the banking sector's assets were held by just eleven of the largest banks, all of which were either wholly or majority owned by the government, primarily through IBRA. It is clear that most, if not all, of the numerous smaller banks in Indonesia need to be closed down, in order that efforts can be focused on rehabilitating the larger ones. Yet the political will to do so has not been apparent. The bill for recapitalizing the banking sector in Indonesia, which was largely completed in 2000, was estimated to be a staggering US$74 billion.

Partly as a result of the slow progress in corporate and bank restructuring, cumulative debt levels in Southeast Asia remain high. In the Philippines and Thailand, aggregate foreign debt levels — both private and public — are equivalent to 75 per cent of GDP; or US$52 billion and US$86 billion respectively. These sorts of debt levels are heavy weights for economies to bear, and make their access to fresh capital relatively expensive. Indonesia is confronted with a very substantial debt overhang: the country is now the world's twentieth largest debtor, with over US$140 billion in external debts alone, approximately half of which is private sector debt.[13] (The country's sovereign foreign debt of US$80 billion is roughly equivalent to the country's GDP.) It is conceivable that Indonesia may seek to securitize at least part of its external debt burden, using a financing instrument that resembles the Brady bonds issued by several Latin American countries following that region's earlier debt crisis. However, such a move would require approval from various external agencies, including the IMF and the Paris Club of creditors. In 2000, Indonesia signed agreements with both the London Club and Paris Club of creditors: the former relating to US$340 million in debts owed to over 100 foreign commercial banks, and the latter relating to US$5.8 billion in sovereign debt owed to foreign governments. While Thailand successfully weaned itself off IMF lending in 2000, ahead of schedule, Indonesia's economy remained hooked up to this life-support mechanism. In December 2000, the IMF withheld a US$400 million loan instalment to Jakarta, having become increasingly dissatisfied with the pace and consistency of economic reform in Indonesia, and the slow pace of corporate restructuring in particular. The IMF's decision also came one month after it was revealed that up to 130 trillion rupiah (around US$13.5 billion) in emergency liquidity credits issued by the central bank to 42 private banks may have been misused in various ways.

Lacklustre Privatization Programmes
In a sense, there were two privatization "streams" operating in Southeast Asia during 2000. The first entailed the divestment of state-owned firms, as part of more general business liberalization and corporate restructuring efforts under way in countries such as Indonesia, the Philippines, Singapore, Thailand, and even Vietnam. (For Indonesia and Thailand, some of these divestments had been agreed as conditionalities attached to recent IMF loan packages.) The second entailed the divestment of formerly private businesses that were taken

over — temporarily "nationalized" — by government-established "asset management companies" and similar bodies, after having become bankrupt during the financial crisis. For countries like Indonesia and Thailand, engaged in both privatization streams, the deal flow in 2000 *should* have been fairly vigorous, but was not. Indeed, privatization deal flow in Southeast Asia during 2000 was fairly anaemic.

In the case of Indonesia, the assets that IBRA has been seeking to divest account for a substantial proportion of the country's entire corporate sector. In September 2000, the aggregate face value of IBRA's assets was estimated to be 420 trillion rupiah (about US$47.5 billion), of which perhaps 30 per cent can be realized in subsequent sales.[14] Yet the sale of assets by IBRA progressed quite slowly in 2000. That said, a 23 per cent stake in Astra, the country's largest car manufacturer, was sold to a Singapore consortium, through competitive bidding, for roughly US$500 million. A further US$600 million was raised from the sale of eleven companies that used to belong to the Salim conglomerate, and US$800 million in restructured loans were sold to various investors (at an average 50 per cent discount). Beyond these deals, however, IBRA failed to generate the sort of divestment deal flow in 2000 that would have improved the sentiment of foreign investors and multilateral lending agencies alike. The sales of Bank Central Asia — "the healthiest bank in the Indonesian banking system", according to one senior IBRA official — and Bank Niaga were also supposed to occur in 2000, but were postponed until mid-2001, in the hope of getting a higher price.[15] In the Philippines, the country's privatization programme also ran well behind schedule in 2000. For example, the sale of a 30 per cent stake in Philippine National Bank, to Lucio Tan — majority owner of the country's national airline — encountered difficulties. In Thailand, a long-awaited share sale by Thai International airline did not proceed in 2000.[16] However, the privatization and US$175 million initial public offering (IPO) of Thailand's 2,645MW Ratchaburi power station went ahead in October 2000 — one of only three IPOs enacted in Bangkok since the onset of the financial crisis.

For countries like Indonesia and the Philippines, these divestment programmes are perceived as fairly essential elements of the government's budget revenues for 2000 and beyond. The Philippines is running a high budget deficit, and has pledged to plug the hole in part with earnings derived from various privatization projects. Similarly, Indonesia is expected to have a US$5.6 billion budget deficit in 2001, and aims to plug at least half this gap with IBRA sales receipts. IBRA has stated that it aims to divest itself of assets cumulatively worth 28 trillion rupiah (approximately US$3 billion) in 2001, compared with the 19 trillion rupiah target set for 2000 (US$2.1 billion). Meeting this target necessitates a marked acceleration in its rate of divestments, and may oblige the agency to approach asset sales on a more wholesale basis than adopted thus far. One option would be to sell stakes in the five holding companies under IBRA's control, in which the various assets are currently bundled.[17] It is presumed that IBRA aims to sell all its assets by 2004, which is when the agency's current mandate runs out.

Putting the two privatization "streams" together, and given the slow progress thus far, it is clear that a very substantial divestment process is in the pipeline for Southeast Asia in 2001 and beyond, with a massive quantity of business assets (distressed and otherwise) expected to be sold to private sector concerns — both foreign and local. With insufficient investment capital available within the region alone, such a process will require a considerable degree of foreign investor participation. For foreign investors to have sufficient appetite for these business assets — where true debt levels are sometimes recorded off the balance sheet, thereby making proper due diligence difficult to conduct — the pricing issue is critical. Yet there remains a substantial gap between what foreign investors and domestic business interests each regard as a "fair price" for business assets in countries such as Indonesia, the Philippines, and Thailand. Given the environment of heightened political risk, it is perhaps not surprising that foreign investors have been unwilling to make bids for Southeast Asian business assets under the auctioneer's hammer, unless they are at marked discounts to their net asset value, commensurate with the perceived risk premium. A paucity of foreign investor involvement in the divestment process is somewhat worrisome, as these sorts of strategic investors, able to provide additional non-financial inputs, are necessary to resuscitate these distressed companies by making them internationally competitive in the long term.

Malaysia Still Going Its Own Way
One country in which privatization activity was much less apparent was Malaysia. Indeed, the general trend may have been more towards the re-nationalization of private sector business assets and some of its debt obligations. For example, the Malaysian Government increased its stake in loss-making Malaysian Airline System (MAS) in 2000, to about 49 per cent, albeit prior to a possible strategic sale to a foreign airline. What surprised observers about this acquisition was the 180 per cent premium to the market value that the government paid for the shares, buying them at the same price that they had sold them in 1994. In December 2000, a government pension scheme also acquired a 9.5 per cent stake in MAS, primarily by buying shares previously held by the Brunei Investment Agency (at half the price paid for the other shares).[18] The Malaysian national sewer system was also re-nationalized in 2000, and state-run oil company Petronas acquired a controlling stake in the Proton car company. Finally, towards the end of 2000, the government announced that it would enact a six billion ringgit (US$1.6 billion) bond issue in order to buy back two loss-making privatized light railway systems in Kuala Lumpur.

It is probably true to say that the general level of corporate restructuring in Malaysia in recent years has been relatively limited, and that a sense of opacity has surrounded some of the decision-making in this process, at least from the perspective of foreign and minority shareholders. In addition to the MAS share sale, other corporate deals that raised some surprise in 2000 included that between the Renong Group and its affiliate, United Engineers Malaysia (UEM). Such deals may explain in part why foreign portfolio investors withdrew funds from the country in the months after Malaysia's return to the MSCI (Morgan Stanley Capital International) index in May 2000.[19] (In late October 2000 the government decided to lift a 10 per cent exit levy on stock market profits repatriated after more than one year.) The largest restructuring process envisaged for Malaysia was a consolidation of the banking sector, merging fifty-four individual banks into ten selected "anchor banks", which was to have been completed by end-2000. However, it appeared that only six of the ten merged entities were successful in meeting the deadline set. Another end-2000 deadline, to consolidate the country's sixty-six brokerage companies into fifteen securities groups, was withdrawn after resistance was shown by some firms in the industry.

Sickly Equity Markets

As portfolio investors tend to look ahead, equity markets can be good leading indicators of general corporate sector and macroeconomic performance "going forward", at least as perceived by the consensus. (The stock market in Bangkok had been flashing a warning light about Thailand's corporate sector ailments for a number of years prior to July 1997, although most observers chose to ignore the signal.) In contrast with the broad macroeconomic recovery trajectories that Southeast Asia witnessed in 2000, the region's equity markets were decidedly sickly during the year. There were some specific reasons for this. First, Southeast Asia's equity markets seem to have become much more correlated to the fortunes of the U.S. equity markets in recent years, and Wall Street also recorded a poor performance in 2000. Secondly, most of Southeast Asia's equity markets have a paucity of electronics and technology-related stocks; instead, they provide portfolio investors with exposure to banks and property companies (sectors hit hardest by the recent financial crisis), and companies perceived by some to be in "sunset industries". Therefore, even if portfolio investors become positive about the macroeconomic prospects for Southeast Asia, the region's equity markets no longer provide an adequate conduit for them to gain exposure to this growth phenomenon.[20] One Thai fund manager recently noted that of the 392 listed companies on the Stock Exchange of Thailand (SET), she only really liked about ten.[21] If this is the view of a Thai-specific fund manager, it is not surprising that many global fund managers decided to dispense with the Thai equity market altogether in 2000, as well as the Indonesian and Philippine markets. Thirdly, as institutional investors have sidelined the region's equity markets, daily turnover levels have dropped to a point where some major portfolio investors now find it difficult to invest in many Southeast Asian listed companies.

In Malaysia, the stock market was helped in the first half of 2000 by the much-anticipated return of the Kuala Lumpur Stock Exchange (KLSE) into the MSCI index.[22] This prompted a run-up in prices, as institutional investors bought the Malaysian equity market in anticipation, causing it to perform in a manner quite unlike other equity markets in the region. However, once back in the MSCI, the KLSE reverted to the regional norm, and began to decline. This stemmed in part from investors' concerns about the fairly opaque corporate restructuring process in Malaysia, and its impact on the interests of minority shareholders in particular. One foreign securities company depicted the problem thus: "Overall, the bail-outs of politically connected companies continue to highlight the ongoing issues of corporate governance and shareholder value. While we maintain that such risks are contained within a select group of companies, the market as a whole remains penalized."[23] A parallel situation was apparent in Thailand, where the performance of the Thai equity market was held hostage to developments at companies like TPI, and disappointing NPL data from the larger banks, which were perceived as barometers of corporate sector health and recovery.

The successful initial public offering of the integrated equity and derivatives exchange in Singapore (SGX) was one bright piece of news for Southeast Asia's equity markets in 2000. With the solitary exception of Vietnam's rather idiosyncratic stock market — which in the five months after it commenced trading in July 2000 was up by over 80 per cent — all of the region's market indices were markedly down on the year. During 2000, the Bangkok equity market declined by 44 per cent, Jakarta fell 38.5 per cent, Manila declined by 30 per cent, and Singapore ended the year with a decline of about 22 per cent. Even the KLSE index, which had enjoyed a sustained rally in the months leading up to its re-inclusion into the MSCI in May 2000, dipped by about 16 per cent by the end of 2000 (see Table 1).

TABLE 1
Regional Stock Markets in 2000

	Index at end-2000	Index all time high	% Change in index during 2000
Bangkok SET	269	1,789	−44.1
Jakarta JSX	416	741	−38.5
Kuala Lumpur KLSE	680	1,332	−16.3
Manila PSE	1,495	3,448	−30.3
Singapore STI	1,927	2,583	−22.3

	Market capitalisation (US$bn) at end-2000	Market capitalisation (US$bn) at end-1996
Bangkok SET	31	105
Jakarta JSX	31	93
Kuala Lumpur KLSE	124	302
Manila PSE	15	80
Singapore STI	197	184
	Total: 398	Total: 764

SOURCES: *Asian Wall Street Journal; Asiaweek; and Far Eastern Economic Review.*

Such poor performance in share prices has resulted in increasingly small market capitalization figures for Southeast Asia's equity markets, exacerbated further by weaknesses in the regional currencies. By end-2000, Bangkok's market capitalization was just US$31 billion, US$31 billion also for Jakarta, US$124 billion for Kuala Lumpur, US$197 billion for Singapore, and a paltry US$15 billion for Manila. Together, the five main equity markets had an aggregate regional market capitilization of US$398 billion by the end of 2000 — roughly half the figure prior to the crisis in 1997. Given the increasing importance of market capitalization figures in the global asset allocation decisions of portfolio investors, it is clear that some of Southeast Asia's equity markets now face a problem. A vicious cycle appears to have developed: major indices — which base their weightings largely according to market capitalization levels — recommend that Southeast Asian equity weightings be reduced, which prompts selling by (increasingly index-oriented) institutional investors, which then drags down share prices, which therefore causes market capitalizations to contract further, which prompts indices to reduce recommended weightings again, and so on. By late 2000, at least one global index recommended zero weighting for all of Southeast Asia's equity markets, with the sole exception of Singapore.[24]

This would not be such an important issue if Southeast Asia did not need fairly robust equity markets for its economic and financial recovery process. With local banks in most countries generally unable or unwilling to lend, and foreign banks still contracting their loan portfolios in the region, this leaves relatively few avenues for companies to raise capital for funding business development, beyond their own cash flows and balance sheets. The same applies to government asset management companies that are seeking to divest themselves of substantial amounts of distressed assets, and various privatization initiatives that are in the pipeline. While the divestment of some assets can be enacted through sales to strategic investors, the equity markets are needed to play a supporting role. Attempts have recently been made to establish tech-oriented "second boards" in a couple of Southeast Asian countries, with listing requirements that are less demanding than the main equity markets, and therefore better suited for relatively new business ventures that seek to raise funding. Thailand unveiled the Market for Alternative Investment (MAI) in 2000, which aimed to list over six firms by the end of the year, but only succeeded to list a single firm in late 2000.[25] Malaysia unveiled its equivalent, the MESDAQ, in 1999, but had just three companies listed by end-2000.

Singapore and Vietnam as the Regional "Outlyers" of 2000?
Only Singapore and Vietnam appeared to buck the fairly dismal regional trend in 2000, and gave tangible reasons for optimism. In the case of Singapore, which recorded 10.5 per cent GDP growth in 2000, various developments in the business and financial sectors indicated that a coherent and forward-looking strategy to provide a competitive business environment is firmly in place. In 2000, the local banks were instructed to begin jettisoning their non-core assets,

and the media and telecommunications sectors were opened to foreign competition for the first time. Beyond the banking sector, merger and acquisition activity was also fairly vigorous, suggesting that a gradual corporate "shake-out" and consolidation process in Singapore is under way. According to one fund manager: "Singapore has stood out over the past year for doing all the 'right' things. It has used the Asian crisis as an opportunity to introduce corporate restructuring, accelerate market reforms and tighten up on governance."[26] Indeed, Singapore is increasingly standing out from its regional neighbours. Having probably become frustrated at the slow pace of corporate sector reform in Southeast Asia, Singapore made moves in 2000 to project itself above and beyond the region, presumably in order not to be constrained by the apparent sloth of neighbours, and perhaps to lead by example. Singapore's Minister of Trade and Industry was quoted as saying: "The world is moving very fast. We can't be complacent. We've got to keep pushing."[27] This policy included efforts in 2000 towards signing a number of bilateral free trade agreements (FTAs) with New Zealand, Australia, Japan, and the United States.[28] Not sharing Singapore's sense of urgency, the reaction of some ASEAN countries to this unilateral action by Singapore was not entirely positive. Some commentators in Malaysia expressed concern at Singapore's initiative, to which Prime Minister Goh Chok Tong replied: "Those who can run faster should run faster. They shouldn't be restrained by those who don't want to run at all."[29]

For Vietnam, the opening of a small stock market in Ho Chi Minh City, and the belated signing of a trade deal with the United States, both in July 2000, suggested that the recent hiatus in the economic reform process may be drawing to an end. A new enterprise law for domestic firms in Vietnam also indicated that some of the tough constraints on the private sector are slowly being eased. However, clearer indications of Hanoi's willingness to liberalize its business environment will need to be forthcoming if the current perception of Vietnam as a hard place to do business is to be overcome. The fairly remorseless contraction in FDI inflows since 1996 stands as a telling indicator of the way sentiment towards Vietnam has declined in recent years. However, just as foreign investors' "bullishness" towards Vietnam was overdone in the early 1990s, it is quite conceivable that the very sombre mood of recent years has also become over-stated, and some form of upswing is now due. Crucially, Vietnam's existing — and fairly demanding — commitments to ASEAN (including the ASEAN Free Trade Area [AFTA] and the ASEAN Investment Area [AIA]) and the United States (normal trading relations status) will act to drive forward the business liberalization process during the next decade, regardless of the leadership's real appetite for economic reforms. Moreover, should China make strides in the field of business liberalization, one could expect Vietnam to largely follow in its neighbour's slipstream.

For the Southeast Asian economies as a whole, China's impending entry into the World Trade Organization (WTO) in 2000 will pose a challenge in key areas, such as electronics and certain other manufacturing industries. Although it is not entirely a zero-sum game, a WTO-compliant China would nonetheless pose a "formidable competitive challenge" to some ASEAN countries in industries seeking to attract FDI.[30] Indeed, this rivalry for foreign investment has become increasingly apparent in recent years, with China appearing to gain the upper hand. Entry into the WTO might be expected to strengthen China's hand, unless ASEAN is able to respond in a convincing manner. While there is some differentiation between China and the ASEAN countries as hosts for foreign investment, as well as FDI flows from a few ASEAN countries into China, there are relatively few ways that Southeast Asia can easily "leverage off" China's potential. For FDI originating from Europe and the United States, China and ASEAN are fundamentally in a state of direct competition to attract and host foreign investment inflows, except in those few industries where cross-border production networks can be established. One business intelligence organization recently depicted the current situation thus: "As Southeast Asia struggles to attract investors, scared off by political instability and ASEAN's half-hearted reform, capital is pouring into China." Consequently, "... Southeast Asia will be forced either to up-grade the value of its exports or be wiped out by China."[31] There is little doubt that FDI inflows to the region in 1999-2000 merit some concern, if only in terms of relatively anaemic growth. Indeed, Southeast Asia's share of the global "FDI pie" has been shrinking consistently since 1996 (see Table 2).

TABLE 2
Southeast Asia's Foreign Direct Investment Inflows, 1994–99
(US$m)

	1994	1995	1996	1997	1998	1999
Brunei	6	13	11	5	4	5
Cambodia	69	151	294	168	121	135
Indonesia	2,109	4,346	6,194	4,677	–356	–3,270
Laos	59	88	128	86	45	79
Malaysia	4,581	5,816	7,296	6,513	2,700	3,532
Myanmar	126	277	310	387	315	300
Philippines	1,591	1,459	1,520	1,249	1,752	737
Singapore	8,550	7,206	8,984	8,085	5,493	6,984
Thailand	1,343	2,000	2,405	3,732	7,449	6,078
Vietnam	1,936	2,349	2,455	2,745	1,972	1,609
SE Asian Total	20,370	23,705	29,597	27,647	19,495	16,189
China	33,787	35,849	40,180	44,236	43,751	40,400
Developing countries	104,920	111,884	145,030	178,789	179,481	207,619
World	255,988	331,844	377,516	473,052	680,082	865,487
SE Asia as % of world total	8.0	7.1	7.8	5.8	2.9	1.9
SE Asia as % of dev. countries total	19.4	21.2	20.4	15.5	10.9	7.8

SOURCE: UNCTAD, *World Investment Report 2000*.

TABLE 3
Performance of Regional Currencies in 2000

	% Change in 2000 (against US dollar)
Brunei dollar	−4
Cambodian riel	−3
Indonesian rupiah	−23
Lao kip	−7
Malaysian ringgit	0
Myanmar kyat	−18
Philippine peso	−19
Singapore dollar	−4
Thai baht	−11
Vietnamese dong	−3

SOURCES: *Asiaweek* and *Far Eastern Economic Review.*

Conclusion

Southeast Asia needs foreign investor participation if it is to fully recover from the financial and economic damage inflicted during 1997-98.[32] Yet foreign *portfolio* investors largely kept away from the region's stock markets in 2000, while foreign *direct* investors were cautious in bidding for distressed business assets up for sale, and few new FDI projects were announced in 2000. Apart from the distraction of China, the primary reason for the lack of appetite by foreign investors was their perception of increased political risk and economic instability that pertained to a number of countries in the region. Indeed, the events of 2000 did little to buoy foreign investor sentiment towards the region: impeachment of the head of state in the Philippines; bombings in the capitals of Cambodia, Indonesia, Laos, and the Philippines; ongoing civil conflict in various parts of Indonesia (including threats against U.S. citizens); persistent human rights concerns in Myanmar; ongoing worries over corporate governance standards in Malaysia; a spate of political scandals in Thailand; and so on. In early December 2000, readers of the *Asian Wall Street Journal* were confronted with a front page that detailed both the impeachment trial of President Estrada in the Philippines, and the ongoing investigations of the Indonesian central bank governor for his part in an alleged US$80 million "slush-fund scam". Such headlines were hardly conducive to presenting a region of low political risk, and hence attractive to foreign investors willing to commit funds to the region. In the case of Indonesia, the bombing of the Jakarta stock market building in mid-September 2000 and a bomb attack on the Attorney General's office in the capital two months earlier served to underline the political risk concerns that many foreign investors had towards parts of the region in 2000. Even in Indonesia's rural areas, foreign investors encountered demands for money from local authorities and citizens, such as the Freeport gold and copper mine in Irian Jaya. In the case of Thailand, just as the long shadow of the TPI case was lifted in mid-December 2000, it was almost immediately replaced by the controversy surrounding the undeclared business assets of Thaksin Shinawatra (winner of parliamentary elections held in 2001). In addition, the impeachment trial of President Estrada cast a shadow over the Philippines during the final quarter of 2000. Likewise, Tommy Soeharto's ability to evade capture by the police sullied further Indonesia's reputation.

Even beyond the pyrotechnics of bombings and political scandal, a lack of clear direction and coherence in political decision-making in some countries also posed a risk factor for investors. There was a general sense of drift by the ASEAN regional grouping itself in 2000, seemingly unable to identify and present a truly convincing agenda of policies to counter those pundits who speculate whether ASEAN has become "an ineffective sunset organization".[33] For example, the manner in which ASEAN members accepted Malaysia's unilateral decision to delay its reduction on car import tariffs until 2005, in order to protect its domestic car manufacturer, Proton, would have been perceived by some investors as the first step towards a diluted AFTA initiative.[34] At least in promotional terms, this single event did much to discount the fairly solid progress made by AFTA in recent years. Right or wrong, perceptions of a dilution in AFTA will disappoint those investors wishing to establish cross-border production networks in the region. Singapore's Foreign Minister noted in September 2000 that "we may not like these perceptions of ASEAN as an ineffective sunset organization ... But perceptions are political facts and can define political reality."[35] In the economic sphere, foreign capital inflows are necessary, but these will be heavily constrained by growing perceptions among the foreign investor community of a region that lost its way in 2000, as evidenced by the erratic political events and reform drift in Indonesia, the Philippines, and Thailand.

One tangible area of progress for ASEAN was an expanded network of bilateral currency swap and repurchase agreements between the ASEAN members and China, Japan, and South Korea. Agreed in May 2000, this arrangement is intended to provide greater financial support for member countries facing short-term balance of payments or liquidity difficulties. However, the swap arrangement was arrived at after a more ambitious regional crisis fund initiative was shelved. In late 2000, Prime Minister Zhu Rongji proposed the establishment of a free trade area between ASEAN and China, but such a notion will take time for ASEAN to study, as will the proposal to formalize the ASEAN Plus Three concept into some form of East Asian Community arrangement.[36]

It can only be hoped that the "reform fatigue" that was witnessed in several parts of Southeast Asia during 2000 is overcome in 2001, and that the region is able to re-focus on the unfinished business of corporate and bank restructuring. If so, it is conceivable that foreign investor sentiment towards the region will be revived in 2001 and beyond, and Southeast Asia can finally achieve some sort of closure on the financial crisis of 1997-98. Once this is done, Southeast Asian economies can focus their attention on regaining some of the international competitiveness that has been lost in recent years, and in so doing, attempt to close the margin that appears to have grown between Southeast and Northeast Asia.

NOTES

1. Given the region's very poor macroeconomic performance in 1997–98, it was to be expected that the same figures for 1999–2000 might appear much improved, if only as a "technical correction" in the statistics, as opposed to a substantial improvement in the fundamental macroeconomic well-being of Southeast Asia.

2. In 1999, electronics exports accounted for 63 per cent of the Philippines' total export earnings, 67 per cent of Singapore's non-oil domestic exports, 46 per cent of Malaysia's exports, and 12 per cent of Thailand's exports. See "Semi-cycles", Strategic Intelligence (<*http://www.strategici.com*>), 8 November 2000.

3. In the first half of 2000, the United States accounted for 14 per cent of Indonesia's exports, 20.5 per cent of Malaysia's exports, 29.5 per cent of the Philippines' exports, 17 per cent of Singapore's exports, and 21 per cent of Thailand's exports. See "Will US Electronics Torpedo Regional Export Growth?", ING Barings, 16 October 2000. See also the ADB's excellent *Asia Recovery Report 2000* (October 2000), pp. 77–84.

4. For a sample of the generally positive perceptions of the region at the beginning of 2000, a special survey of Southeast Asia published by *The Economist* began as follows: "This is supposed to be the "Asian century", and already many people in Southeast Asia are of good cheer. … The doom and gloom of the financial crisis which began to engulf the region in 1997 has given way to renewed optimism." (*The Economist*, 12 February 2000.) Indeed, the first issue of *Asiaweek* in 2000 titled its regional review as "Asia's Big Comeback" (*Asiaweek*, 31 December 1999–7 January 2000, pp. 104–9.) Investment bank strategists were also fairly up-beat about Asia as a whole during the early part of 2000. In January, one regional strategist wrote "Asia has not looked as good as this for well over 10 years" (ING Barings, *AsiaTalk*, 6 January 2000, p. 2.) Yet by the fourth quarter of 2000, the mood was much more sombre. Singapore's *Business Times* ran a story "S-E Asian recovery looks like it could be stalling" (14 October 2000, p. 2.). In late November, the *Australian Financial Review* published an article entitled "Markets Point to a New Asian Crisis" (29 November 2000.) An editorial piece in the *Asian Wall Street Journal* argued that "Asia's post-crisis economic recovery has been uneven and, in many countries, illusory." ("Now You See It, Now You Don't", *Asian Wall Street Journal*, 27 November 2000.) Brokerage reports even began to speculate on the potential for another bout of regional currency contagion in late 2000, this time sparked by weakness in the Philippine peso.

5. Estimate by Kelly Bird, "The Waiting Game: Corporate Debt Restructuring in Indonesia" (Paper presented at the Seventh Convention of the East Asian Economic Association, 17–18 November 2000), p. 12.

6. *Asian Wall Street Journal*, 28 November 2000, p. 1.

7. Making an important distinction, a senior official at the IMF noted: "There is a sense that the rescheduling component has been emphasized a lot more than the restructuring component." See "IMF presses Asia on corporate reform", *Financial Times*, 4 December 2000.

8. Figures cited in "NPLs Rear their Ugly Head Again", *Malaysian Business*, 16 October 2000, pp. 12–14. The CDRC is designed as a vehicle to bring debtors and creditors together to restructure NPLs of viable companies. Danaharta has a remit to purchase, manage and then dispose of NPLs held by banks. Danaharta is primarily funded through bond issues, with repayment of the bonds anticipated to be financed from future disposals.

9. All World Bank figures for NPL levels in this paragraph were sourced from Masahiro Kawai, "Economic Challenges Facing East Asia" (Paper presented at Regional Outlook Forum 2001, Singapore, 5 January 2001).
10. Bird, op. cit., p. 5.
11. Quote and figures taken from "Passing the Burden", *Strategic Intelligence*, 19 October 2000. (<*http://www.strategici.com*>).
12. Quote from Aberdeen Asset Management Asia's Annual Report for 2000, p. 13.
13. One report estimates that, as of June 2000, the corporate sector alone in Indonesia had external debts of US$64 billion, and domestic debts (including NPLs transferred to IBRA) of 488 trillion rupiah (around US$56 billion). Bird, op. cit., p. 4. In terms of Indonesia's domestic debt levels, bank recapitalization bonds issued by IBRA amount to 650 trillion rupiah (around US$70 billion), and the country's private sector also owes 20 trillion rupiah in domestic debt.
14. An earlier valuation of IBRA's assets put the aggregate figure at US$62 billion, of which: 50 per cent was financial assets (mostly bank loans), 24 per cent was equity in banks that the government had recapitalized, 24 per cent was equity in companies ("shareholder assets"), and the rest were properties and other physical assets owned by the 66 banks which were closed down. See *Business Times* (Singapore), 10 October 2000, p. 20.
15. Quote by deputy chairman of IBRA, Arwin Rasyid, cited in "IBRA defends delay of bank sales", *Asian Wall Street Journal*, 10 October 2000, p. 20. A 22.5 per cent stake in BCA was sold in May 2000, through an initial public offering, from which IBRA raised 900 billion rupiah (about US$95 million). The IMF had initially wanted the two banks to be fully divested in the first quarter of 2000.
16. However, an approval for up to 30 per cent of shares to be held by foreign investors was passed in October 2000, paving the way for a partial divestment in 2001, if there are no further delays. Thai International's current ownership structure is 93 per cent government, 3 per cent Thai individuals, and 4 per cent foreign investors. It is anticipated that a further 13 per cent of shares will be listed on the stock market, and a 10 per cent stake will also be sold to another airline, thereby reducing the government's stake to 70 per cent. See *Business Times* (Singapore), 26 October 2000, and 23 November 2000; and *Asian Wall Street Journal*, 13 December 2000.
17. One of these IBRA holding companies, PT Holdiko Perkasa, has ownership of 107 companies formerly operated by the Salim Group alone. Equity in these companies was transferred to IBRA in 1998, as part of an agreement to recapitalize Bank Central Asia. In November 2000, these assets were offered for sale on Singapore-based website, <*http://www.growasia.com*>, the region's first M&A (mergers and acquisitions) Internet site. In the same month, twenty-four oil palm plantations once owned by the Salim Group were sold to a Malaysian firm for US$381 million.
18. See *Asian Wall Street Journal*, 13 December 2000, p. 18.
19. It was reported that foreign portfolio investors remitted US$2.6 billion out of Malaysia between May and December 2000. The country's foreign exchange reserves also contracted in the latter part of 2000.
20. The number of substantial "technology plays" listed in Bangkok, for example, can be counted on the fingers of one hand. Even beyond the technology sector, it can be difficult for portfolio investors to gain exposure to those companies believed to have performed relatively well in recent years, as many are not listed on the region's equity markets.
21. Quote by Sukanda Lewis of Krung Thai Asset Management, cited in *Asiaweek*, 20 October 2000.
22. The KLSE was dropped from the MSCI index in September 1998, after the imposition of capital controls and the freezing of CLOB accounts.
23. Quote from ING Barings, *AsiaTalk*, 27 November 2000, p. 3.

24. Looking ahead, Southeast Asia's equity markets are likely to be impacted by major indices changing their weightings calculations to take into account the number of "free-float" shares in circulation, and not just the raw market capitalization of companies. Where the proportion of shares in companies still closely held by majority shareholders is fairly high, as is common in Southeast Asia, or where complex cross-holdings exist, recommended weightings are likely to be revised downwards.

25. The managing director of MAI aims to have 20–25 firms listed in 2001, and 50 firms listed within three years of opening. See "Thailand's MAI Shows Signs of Life", *Asian Wall Street Journal*, 14 December 2000, pp. 13–14.

26. Comment by Aberdeen Asset Management Asia, in its Annual Report, 30 September 2000, p. 11.

27. Minister George Yeo, quoted in, "Foreign investors desert South-east Asia for China", *Financial Times*, 12 October 2000.

28. See "S'pore Needs to Leapfrog ASEAN: S M Lee", *Business Times* (Singapore), 9 December 2000, p. 2. The free trade agreement with New Zealand was signed in 2000, and negotiations with the United States commenced in December 2000. Negotiations with Japan and Australia are expected in 2001. Singapore is also reported to be studying the notion of FTAs with countries like Mexico, Canada, and Chile. Singapore's FTAs are designed to be WTO-compliant.

29. Cited in "Keeping Up with the Singaporeans", *Asiaweek*, 8 December 2000, p. 22.

30. Quote taken from an ASEAN report. See *Business Times* (Singapore), 28 July 2000, p. 24.

31. Strategic Intelligence Asia (<*http://www.strategici.com*>), "Feeling the Heat", 10 November 2000.

32. Singapore Prime Minister Goh noted in August: "Foreign investments into the region, especially to Indonesia, have slowed down appreciably. If investment inflows do not increase, this recovery will not be sustained." See *Business Times* (Singapore), 14 August 2000.

33. Quote taken from a speech by Singapore Deputy Prime Minister Lee Hsien Loong, and cited in *Business Times* (Singapore), 1 December 2000.

34. Explaining the muted response of ASEAN members to Malaysia's decision, Thai Foreign Minister Surin was quoted as saying: "We don't want to confront the issue ... If we don't have flexibility with this, they might say 'then to hell with AFTA'." But difficulties can arise when flexibility is judged by others to be weakness. The Executive Director of the US-ASEAN Business Council commented that Malaysia's decision was: "clearly ... a backward step." See *Business Times* (Singapore), 28 July 2000; and *Financial Times*, 12 October 2000. Under the new protocol agreed to in 2000, AFTA members will be able to claim compensation from a country that does not meet its commitments under the AFTA agreement, and may even take reciprocal action if agreement is not reached after six months.

35. Quote taken from "Southeast Asia Adrift", *Asiaweek*, 1 September 2000, p. 44.

36. Both suggestions were raised at the Singapore informal summit in November 2000. See "Leaders Push for East Asian Bloc", *Asian Wall Street Journal*, 27 November 2000.

AUSTRALIA AND ASIA
The Years of Living Aimlessly

Mark Beeson

Throughout Australia's relatively brief life as an independent nation, relations with its regional Asian neighbours have been of immense significance. While "Asia" may not always have occupied the place in Australia's foreign policy agenda that its importance has warranted, simple geographical contingency has meant that it was, and is, an unavoidable geopolitical reality that has to be taken seriously. Whether Australian policy-makers like it or not — and often they do not — there has been little choice other than to come to terms with the looming mass of Asia to their north.

The precise style and substance of Australian foreign policy has reflected a complex and shifting amalgam of domestic politics and wider external imperatives. One factor that has made a difference in both the direction and effectiveness of Australian policy-making, however, has been the enthusiasm and purposefulness with which such initiatives have been pursued by the ruling political élites of a particular era. In this regard, what is most striking about Australia's Asia-oriented policies in the last few years under the leadership of John Howard's Liberal-National Party coalition government, has been an apparent ambivalence about the process of regional engagement and a consequent lack of focus and direction in foreign policy. In short, policy has often been ad hoc, opportunistic, and aimless.

In order to understand why this is the case, and why there has been such a noteworthy change in the way Australian policy-makers have approached relations with Asia over the last few years, it is necessary to place contemporary policies in historical perspective. This task is briefly undertaken in the first part of this chapter, before giving more detailed consideration to the political-economic and strategic dimensions of Australian policy in the recent past. The conclusion that emerges from this analysis may be flagged at the outset: even at a time when states are routinely assumed to have lost power as a consequence of "globalization", the actions of national political élites continue to make a difference and profoundly influence the long-term position of individual states. Whether this potential influence is effectively utilized depends on the ability

MARK BEESON is Senior Lecturer in the School of Asian and International Studies, Griffith University, Brisbane, Australia.

of policy-makers to understand the circumstances that confront them, and then develop strategies to realize national goals. As we shall see, that ability and capacity has waxed and waned over the years, profoundly influencing the success with which Australia has "engaged" with the region.

Australia–Asia Relations in Historical Context

Historically, a number of recurring themes have shaped the actions of generations of policy-makers. As a creation of imperial Britain, Australia has always been a long way from "home" and often painfully conscious of its isolation and potential vulnerability. The sense of being strangers in a strange land, surrounded by peoples of whom they knew little other than that they were different, alien, and possibly hostile, shaped much of Australia's early international relations. Indeed, it is still possible to trace the continuing influence of such insecurities and uncertainties in contemporary policies.

This sense of isolationism and vulnerability when combined with a striking lack of desire for autonomy, inaugurated policies that were characterized chiefly by their dependence on "great and powerful friends" — in Australia's case, Britain and then the United States. Remarkably, although nominally an independent nation since 1901, Australia did not even move to establish independent diplomatic relations before World War II, preferring instead to rely on Britain to mediate its external affairs. It required the unambiguous confirmation of Britain's decline, evidenced by its expulsion from Southeast Asia at the hands of the Japanese during World War II, to break the colonial mindset that had prevailed hitherto in Australia. Even then, the net effect of the changing geopolitical balance in the Asia-Pacific was simply to exchange one strategic dependence for another, as the United States replaced Britain in the minds, if not the hearts, of Australia's strategic planners.

Yet, the changing realities of Australia's regional position were apparent even before World War II. Not only had Japan's growing imperial ambitions demonstrated that there was now a major military power in East Asia, but its rapid rise to become Australia's second largest trading partner during the 1930s also revealed the extent of its growing economic importance to Australia. The contradictory nature of Australia's relations with Asia — partly economic opportunity, partly strategic threat — was encapsulated in this increasingly important relationship, and continues to characterize relations with the region to this day. What has differed is the success with which this fundamental paradox has been reconciled by policy-makers in different eras.

At its most egregious, this tension led to abominations like the "White Australia" policy, which was a defining orientation towards the region for much of the twentieth century. Dedicated to preserving not only Australia's strategic integrity, but also its distinctive Anglo-Celtic culture, the enduring effect of the "White Australia" policy has been to provide an excruciatingly embarrassing legacy for subsequent generations of policy-makers keen to embrace "Asia", rather than keep it at arms length. The principal motivating force behind this belated change of attitude towards the region on the part of Australia's political élites was largely a pragmatism borne of economic expediency: the direction of Australia's trade changed profoundly in the post-war period, to a point where its major trading partners and export growth were overwhelmingly concentrated in the Asian region.[1] Yet, despite the possibly self-serving nature of Australia's positive reorientation towards Asia, the nature of the changes they engendered appeared deep-seated and permanent.

Historically, the content and direction of Australia's relations with Southeast Asia in particular has reflected an array of domestic and international forces.[2] One of the most important and influential in the post-war period was the Cold War and the concomitant strategic obligations and orientation Australia embraced. Indeed, the encompassing logic of Australia's alliance commitments culminated in what Stephen Fitzgerald calls "the great post-war symbol of Australia's attitude to Asia"[3] — the failure to recognize, and the attempt to contain, communist China. It was not until the "watershed" change of policy that began with the Gough Whitlam government's recognition of China in 1972 that a more independent stance towards the region emerged. This shift towards a more enthusiastic and independent embrace of the region continued under the government of Malcolm Fraser and culminated in the broader "engagement" initiatives of the governments of Bob Hawke and Paul Keating in the 1980s and early 1990s. This period saw the establishment of enduring regional institutions in which Australia has played a prominent role. Although the Asia-Pacific Economic Co-operation (APEC) forum and the ASEAN Regional Forum (ARF) may not have fulfilled some of the more optimistic expectations of their promoters, they might have been expected to cement Australia's place in the region's emerging institutional architecture. That Australia's status is still in doubt is testimony to the difficulty of unambiguously defining its place and role in the region.

Part of this uncertainty has domestic roots. The current Howard government has displayed rather more ambivalence than its Labor predecessors about the direction and content of the Asian engagement process. The sense of uncertainty that has characterized the Howard government's approach to relations with North and Southeast Asia — by far the most important elements of "Asia" as far as Australia is concerned — has permeated all aspects of external policy. To gain a more detailed sense of how this relative lack of direction and commitment has manifested itself, it is useful to divide the discussion into broadly political–economic and strategic spheres.

The Political-Economy of Australia's Asian Engagement

To understand why the Howard government has been more cautious about the Asian engagement process, and why it has been given far less prominence in Australia's policy agenda than it had been by some of the present government's predecessors, we need to remember the circumstances in which the Liberal–National Party coalition came to power. One of the recurring themes of Howard's successful election campaign was that the government of former Labor Minister Paul Keating was arrogant, "obsessed" with Asia, and out of touch with the interests and concerns of "ordinary" Australians. One of the major lessons that Howard appears to have drawn from his subsequent electoral success is that the old saw about there being no votes in foreign policy holds true, and that there is little to be gained by prioritizing Asian relations as far as domestic political success is concerned. On the contrary, the remarkable rise of Pauline Hanson's nationalistic, insular, and anti-Asian One Nation Party seemed to confirm the political wisdom of concentrating relentlessly on domestic issues, and explained Howard's subsequent reluctance to unambiguously distance himself from her party's policies and attitudes.

However, the diminished enthusiasm evinced by the coalition government in general, and by Howard in particular, has deeper roots than simply a cold-blooded assessment of the electoral mood. Not only was Howard's own record compromised by politically ill-judged remarks in the late 1980s about the need to control Asian immigration, but his self-confessed admiration of Anglo-Celtic cultural traditions has led him to steadfastly obstruct a number of initiatives designed to revitalize Australian political institutions and achieve social reconciliation domestically. Whether it was his skilful derailing of the popularly supported push to make Australia a republic, or his refusal to offer a government-endorsed apology to Australia's aboriginal population, the Howard government has proved itself to be a highly conservative domestic force. It is less surprising, therefore, that such attitudes should influence external policies, too.

The Howard government inherited a distinctive and highly ambitious approach to regional engagement. Foreign policy under former Prime Minister Paul Keating had been based on nothing less than an attempt to win East Asia over to its own increasingly neoliberal policy paradigm, particularly in the area of trade liberalization. That APEC — Labor's preferred mechanism for achieving such a goal — has not fulfilled expectations has not stopped the Howard government from broadly following Labor's lead. What has been distinctive and innovative about the coalition has been its advocacy of strengthening bilateral ties at the same time.[4] The Howard government, in other words, has tried to utilize multilateral institutions like APEC to give some impetus to the broader, long-term process of regional trade liberalization, while simultaneously pursuing increasingly bilateral agreements with specific partners.

This move to embrace bilateral agreements is not entirely new, nor exclusive to Australia. Indeed, of late there has been a rash of such initiatives in the region, partly driven by the failure of the World Trade Organization (WTO) to initiate a new round of multilateral trade negotiations in Seattle. One of the most important developments in Australian foreign policy that has flowed from this changing international situation, and one of its most conspicuous failures in 2000, was its frustrated attempt to link Australia's own bilateral free trade area — the Australia-New Zealand Closer Economic Relationship

(CER) — with that of Southeast Asia. The rejection of the proposed union between the CER and the Asean Free Trade Area (AFTA) was a decisive blow for Australia's economic diplomacy, and highlighted a number of important and continuing difficulties in Australia's relations with the region.

One of the most enduring obstacles to improving Australia's economic and political relations in the East Asian region actually pre-dates the current government. Australia's relations with Malaysia have been difficult since its Prime Minister, Datuk Seri Dr Mahathir Mohamad, came to office. Malaysian sensitivities about supposed criticisms of its domestic policies generally, and of Dr Mahathir in particular, have been at the heart of continuing tensions between the two countries. Whatever the merits of these arguments, the net effect of Malaysian antipathy as far as Australia is concerned has been to lock it out of a number of potentially crucial regional institutions of which it desperately wanted to be a part. Australia's exclusion from the Asia-Europe Meeting (ASEM), for example, is a continuing reminder of the constraints on Australian foreign policy in the region. The recent failure to link the CER and AFTA compounded the sense of policy failure towards the region. Significantly, despite a highly favourable report from the task force charged with assessing the viability of closer CER–AFTA links, Malaysia was effectively able to sabotage Australia's efforts and demonstrate Australia's continuing vulnerability to ASEAN vetoes more generally.[5]

It might be supposed that, given the apparently imminent retirement of Dr Mahathir, one of the most significant obstacles to Australia's closer economic, and by implication, political integration with Southeast Asia will be overcome. However, it is important to remember that this more intimate interaction is a two-way street; engendering a more positive attitude towards Australia in the region will depend as much on Australia itself, as it does on any change of sentiment in the region more broadly. Indeed, generating goodwill towards Australia would seem dependent on the Australian Government projecting the right sort of "image" in East Asia generally. In this regard, there have been a number of mixed messages, both in the political-economic and — as we shall see — in the security spheres, which have made such an improvement in relations more problematic.

The End of Engagement?

Deciding on Australia's status in relation to East Asia is a recurring theme among policy-makers and opinion leaders in Australia.[6] One of the most revealing and unfortunate signals about the way the current government sees its relations with the region was provided by Foreign Minister Alexander Downer in a statement which one influential Australian commentator described as "the most depressing, negative and counterproductive formulation on regionalism by any senior minister in decades".[7] Downer argued that there are two possible forms of regionalism, one "practical" and one "cultural".[8] He further claimed that Australia could only practise a form of practical regionalism as enduring cultural differences between Australia and "Asia" meant that Australia was inevitably prevented from developing closer ties. Apart from demonstrating little appreciation of the disparate and often conflicting identities and positions subsumed under the rhetoric of East Asian regionalism, Downer's remarks effectively excluded Australia from participation in a process in which a putative sense of East Asian identity was and is being actively *created*. The possible expansion of ASEAN to include other nations like Japan, China, and South Korea — countries which seemed to have no "natural" claims to close ties with Southeast Asia — is a potentially highly significant development that a more Asia-oriented Australian government might have been expected to have tried to become a part of, or at least influence. Yet, the lack of a sophisticated strategy for, or understanding of Asia — which Downer's remarks so clearly revealed — means that Australia has been sidelined from what may prove to be a crucial long-term regional development.

It might be argued that the pursuit of "practical" regionalism is entirely appropriate and something other nations practise, too. The growth of bilateral agreements throughout the region seems to confirm such a possibility. Singapore has been at the forefront of this trend, in which it is establishing a series of relations outside ASEAN, and even the region more generally, to hasten the process of trade liberalization. While this may also cause Singapore difficulties with some of its more recalcitrant neighbours, Singapore has the advantage of being unambiguously "of" the region in a way that Australia is not. In other words, Singapore is embedded in a web of institutionalized relations that give a degree of continuity and resilience to its intra-regional relations that Australia simply does not have. When Australia pursues similar strategies it can look rather like making the best of a bad job, especially where the government appears to lack a long-term vision about the role it wants to play in the region. The relative ineffectiveness of Australia's own multilateral initiatives, like APEC, which has been increasingly sidelined by the World Trade Organization, and its absence from other regional fora, mean that Australian policy-makers must secure agreements where they can. The potential problems of this piecemeal and ad hoc approach are compounded by the fact that one of the principal bilateral relations that Australia has systematically attempted to consolidate under the Howard government has been with the United States.

The consolidation of closer economic — and, as we shall see, strategic — ties with the United States leaves Australia vulnerable to the criticism that it is not and never can be a "genuine" and committed member of the region, particularly the more narrowly defined East Asian variety. Whether it is an East Asian Economic Caucus, or — what is effectively the same thing — the proposed ASEAN Plus Three concept, those hostile to Australia in the region can claim that it remains more closely aligned to its traditional, culturally, and politically sympathetic allies, than it does to its more geographically immediate neighbours. This is especially true when one of the possible attractions of creating a stronger

East Asian organization is precisely to make the region less vulnerable to external forces and to the sorts of interventionism the United States practised during the recent East Asian crisis.[9] That the economic gains from a closer relationship with the United States are likely to be marginal and acrimoniously — if at all — realized,[10] is but one reason to suppose that a strategy of trying to align more closely with the United States is likely to fail. More importantly in the long run, the symbolism of Australia moving to identify primarily with an extra-regional power will do nothing to facilitate closer relations with Asia, especially when part of this strategy involves strengthening the strategic dimension of that relationship.

The Strategic Dimension of Australia's Asia Relations

If economic engagement with Asia has been the great potential opportunity that forced a major reorientation of Australian policy during the last couple of decades, the possible strategic threat posed by the region has been its dark flip-side. From Australia's inception, the threat posed by "Asia" has often been poorly understood. In the post World War II period, as Australia gradually took more responsibility for its own foreign policies, as it developed national expertise in defence and international relations, and as it built up a greater capacity for independent judgement, a more sophisticated view of the region and Australia's place in it has emerged. Despite this greater understanding on the part of Australia's policy-making élites, however, a number of enduring tensions continue to characterize security policy in particular.

During the 1980s and early 1990s, successive Labor governments made a determined effort to deepen and institutionalize Australia's relations with the region. The strategic counterpart to the economically-oriented APEC initiative culminated in the establishment of the ASEAN Regional Forum (ARF) in 1994 — a development that Australia's activist regional diplomacy played a large part in realizing. The rapid economic development of both North and latterly Southeast Asia meant that not only was the region increasingly important to Australia economically, but its very economic success also transformed the strategic outlook. In the minds of Australia's strategic planners, this evoked a new set of possible threats as Southeast Asia suddenly acquired the ability to finance military modernization. The ARF offered the prospect of reducing uncertainty, increasing transparency, and generally developing confidence-building measures in a historically volatile region.

A more contentious initiative undertaken by the former Labor government was its own attempt to consolidate Australia's security position through key bilateral relationships. In this case, the most significant bilateral security relationship was the security treaty negotiated with Indonesia in 1995. In retrospect, it is easy to see how this strategy was fraught with potential difficulties. Not only was the inauguration of this agreement under the Keating government conducted in a highly secret and non-transparent manner, but the wisdom of linking Australia's long-term future security to a close relationship with the aging and authoritarian figure of former President Soeharto was always questionable. Just how unsustainable this strategy was became clear with the rapid decline in Australia–Indonesia relations in the wake of the Timor crisis.

The management of the East Timor crisis and its aftermath has in many ways been the defining foreign policy and security challenge for the present Howard government. The history of the crisis and Australia's military intervention has been detailed elsewhere and will not be repeated here.[11] However, it is important to say something about the dynamics that underpinned it and the longer-term influence it has had on strategic thinking in Australia more generally.

Timor and Its Aftermath

The first point to make about Australia's role in the East Timor crisis is that the intervention enjoyed widespread domestic support in Australia itself. Powerful emotional and historical ties dating back to World War II, and the continuing high profile maintained by the Timorese diaspora in Australia and elsewhere, combined to give Timor-related issues a surprising prominence within a public not noted for a deep interest in foreign affairs. Any government would have been tempted to extract the maximum political capital possible from such a fortuitous outcome. Not only did the Howard government take full advantage of such an opportunity with a series of triumphalist receptions for Australian troops involved in peace-keeping operations, but they used the goodwill generated towards the Australian armed forces more generally to inaugurate a more wide-ranging review of its defence policy.

Given Australia's natural strategic advantages and its apparent invulnerability to conventional attack, let alone invasion, national security has always occupied a surprisingly prominent place in the nation's policy priorities. The level of spending in Australia declined somewhat in the post-Cold War period, but historically there has been general bilateral support for substantial defence expenditure. Under the Howard government, older patterns of defence spending are being resurrected. Significantly, defence has been the only area of public spending insulated from swingeing budget cuts. The longer term agenda of the Howard government is to actually boost defence spending despite the popular expectation that such expenditures might fall with the end of the Cold War. In this context, sceptics have argued,[12] the highly professional and successful Timor intervention offered a way of securing public support for what at other times might have proved to be unpopular spending initiatives.

Australian governments have been understandably coy about identifying precisely where any potential threat might come from. However, Australia's "most important long-term strategic objective" — the defence of its "direct maritime approaches" — inevitably centres primarily on threats that emanate from, or through, Southeast Asia.[13] This has been the guiding rationale for Australian defence for a number of years. What distinguishes the approach of the Howard government is the renewed importance and high profile attached to the strategic alliance with the United States. Although the recent defence review is careful to stress the importance of promoting stability in, and co-operation with, Southeast Asia, it is revealing that it is the alliance with the United States that continues to receive the highest priority. Indeed, the report emphasizes that the alliance enjoys "renewed vigour", something it attributes to "the enduring shared values, interests and outlook" that the two countries are perceived to enjoy.[14]

In order to consolidate the alliance with the United States, John Howard has suggested that Australia should, especially in the wake of the Timor crisis, play a much more active and high profile role in maintaining a regional security order centred on continuing American strategic hegemony. This has a number of implications. Most immediately, and in a manner reminiscent of the "forward defence" policy that led to Australia's involvement in wars in Korea and Vietnam, this means that Australia should be prepared to take a "proactive role" and "attack hostile forces as far from our shores as possible".[15] In an even more explicit and controversial exposition of the new policy orientation, Howard suggested that Australia ought to be prepared to act as America's "deputy sheriff" in maintaining regional stability, and acting on behalf of the United States where required.[16] Although Howard subsequently sought to clarify these remarks following sustained domestic criticism, the overall direction of government policy — which the decision to increase defence spending highlights — is one that continues to place greater emphasis on links with the United States and less on those with Asia. The proposed increases in the defence budget at least become more comprehensible in this context; the United States has actively encouraged Australia to boost spending, thus allowing it to play a role as its key regional military ally.

Other consequences of Australia's foreign policy evolution and re-orientation are more immediately obvious, especially in the deterioration of Australia's relationship with Indonesia. Australia's role in East Timor may have been well received at home and provided a template for its envisaged role as the United States' key regional subordinate, but it has damaged Australia's formerly close relations with Indonesia. Although critics have drawn attention to the possibly self-serving nature of Australia's close ties with the former Soeharto government[17] — a situation which allowed both countries to exploit the oil and gas reserves beneath the Timor Sea — nevertheless, the rapid deterioration of the bilateral relationship is a major blow for Australia's immediate security position and has potentially negative implications for its wider relationship with the region. Not only will continuing instability in Indonesia pose a major security threat for Australia, but the rather insensitive way Australia has handled the fall-out from the Timor crisis has clearly upset many Indonesians and provided ammunition for Australia's regional critics. Ironically, the new coolness in relations between Canberra and Jakarta means that one of Australia's principal attractions as a regional ally as far as the United States is concerned — its knowledge of, and links with Indonesia — has now been significantly diminished. While Australia has been at pains to distance itself from independence movements in Aceh and West Papua, President Wahid's continuing refusal to visit Australia demonstrates just how far the relationship has deteriorated and how difficult it may prove to revive.

Difficult as the relationship with Indonesia may be, it is important to recognize that not all Australia's neighbours have been unhappy with its actions. The pivotal strategic role that the United States continues to play as the lynchpin of a stable regional security position is recognized and welcomed by many in Southeast Asia. In this context, Australia's supportive role in this overarching strategic environment is often quietly welcomed. However, the new Bush administration's determination to press ahead with a contentious missile defence system threatens to overturn the existing relative stability, raise the prospects of a regional arms race,[18] and lock Australia into a more controversial alliance framework.

Implications and Prospects

Attitudes towards Asia have undergone a noticeable change in Australia since the Howard government was elected in the mid-1990s. Asia's relative significance has diminished in the minds of a number of key policy-makers over the last few years as enthusiasm for, and doubts about the benefits of, the engagement project emerged. In the wake of the recent East Asian economic crisis, there is a widely held perception that Southeast Asia is simply not as important — either economically or strategically — as it once was. The idea that East Asia in general, and Southeast Asia in particular might have been on an inexorable, even "miraculous" upward spiral has been punctured, with inevitable consequences for both the way the region itself is perceived, and the way other countries are viewed in relation to it. Significantly, one of the conclusions that the Howard government drew from the recent economic crisis was that Australia's relative immunity was a vindication of successive Australian governments' approach to economic management. Consequently — and with an all too familiar lack of sensitivity about the way this might be read in the economically devastated countries of the region — Howard declared that Australia was now the "strong man of Asia".

While such remarks may have been primarily intended for domestic consumption, the very fact that they were offered at all betrays a revealing lack of awareness of, or sensitivity about the increasingly integrated nature of the international and domestic spheres. Given the Howard government's primary concern with domestic issues, and the Prime Minister's own relative lack of interest in foreign affairs, such outcomes are not entirely surprising. Where John Howard has taken an active interest in Australia's external position, it has been to place renewed emphasis on Australia's "traditional" allies. The desire to maintain a close political relationship with Britain by maintaining an institutional link with the monarchy, and the emphasis given to reviving the U.S. strategic alliance, are both in accord with Howard's contention that

Australia does not need to choose between its history and its geography. In other words, as far as the present coalition government under John Howard's leadership is concerned, simply being geographically adjacent to Asia does not mean that Australia needs to either become part of it in some way, or repudiate relationships of longer standing.

At a time when the East Asian region is in the throes of profound and potentially far-reaching change, such an anachronistic and complacent attitude looks short-sighted. Australian political élites cannot assume that Asia will simply reproduce the "Western" historical experience and inevitably or rapidly develop similar political and economic practices to those favoured by Australia or the United States. Expecting that the burden of adjustment will fall exclusively on East Asia as the region comes to terms with a new international economic and political order is wishful thinking. The risk for Australia is that by not playing an active part in any emergent transregional institutional architecture, Australia inevitably becomes less able to influence the course of regional development. For all the claims about not having to choose between geography and history, Australia's future will clearly be profoundly influenced by the region to which it is geographically adjacent. By not having a clearly defined strategy for encouraging closer relationships with its neighbours, one which allows it to play a more effective and influential role in regional affairs, Australia may be increasingly marginalized from a region upon which its long-term military and economic security depends.

NOTES

1. For more details on Australia's changing trade position, see M. Beeson, "Globalization and International Trade: International Economic Policies and 'the National Interest'", in *The Politics of Australian Society: Political Issues for the New Century*, edited by P. Boreham, G. Stokes, and R. Hall (Addison Wesley Longman, 2000), pp. 213–31.
2. See Meg Gurry, "Identifying Australia's Region: From Evatt to Evans", *Australian Journal of International Affairs* 49, no. 1 (1995): 17–32.
3. Stephen Fitzgerald, *Is Australia an Asian Country?* (St Leonard's: Allen & Unwin, 1997).
4. This strategy was first outlined in Commonwealth of Australia, *In the National Interest: Australia's Foreign and Trade Policy* (Canberra: AGPS, 1997).
5. P. Alford, "Asean Blurs Australia's Free-Trade Vision", *Weekend Australian*, 7–8 October 2000, p. 6.
6. For one of the more thoughtful and important contributions, see Fitzgereald, op. cit.
7. G. Sheridan "Inept Downer a Regional Flop", *The Australian*, 28 April 2000 p. 11.
8. A. Downer "China: Asia Leaders' Forum — Mr. Downer's Opening Speech", at: <*http://www.dfat.gov.au/media/speeches/foreign/000423_alf.html*>
9. See R. Higgott "The International Relations of the Asian Economic Crisis", in *Politics and Markets in the Wake of the Asian Crisis*, edited by R. Robison (London: Routledge, 2000), pp. 261–82.
10. See R. Garnaut, "US Free Trade Agreement Would Rock Our Regional Role", *The Australian*, 22 December 2000, p. 9.

11. L. C. Sebastian and A. L. Smith, "The East Timor Crisis: A Test Case for Humanitarian Intervention", in *Southeast Asian Affairs 2000* (Singapore: ISEAS), pp. 64–83.
12. See M. Beeson, "Debating Defense: Time for a Paradigm Shift?", *Australian Journal of International Affairs* 54, no. 3 (2000): 255–59.
13. Commonwealth of Australia, *Defence 2000: Our Future Defence Force* (Canberra: Defence Publishing Service, 2000), p. 30.
14. Ibid., p. 34.
15. Ibid., pp. 47-48.
16. See F. Benchley, "The Howard Defense Doctrine", *Bulletin,* 28 September 1999, pp. 22–24.
17. S. Burchill, "East Timor, Australia, and Indonesia", *Bulletin of Concerned Asian Scholars* 32, no. 1&2 (2000): 59–65.
18. M. Richardson, "Asia-Pacific Fears Arms Race from Bush Policies Toward China", *International Herald Tribune,* on-line version, 25 January 2001.

AUSTRALIA AND ASIA
Yesterday, Today and Tomorrow

Cavan Hogue

Introduction

A hundred years ago, Rudyard Kipling observed that the Japanese were obviously not *natives*, nor were they really *sahibs*. Today, an Asian Kipling might well observe that Australians are obviously not *Europeans*, nor are they really *Asians*. Are Australians really part of the Asian region or are they just ethnic Europeans yearning to be somewhere else? What does it mean to be "part of the region"? What is the region? Are other regional countries willing to accept Australia, or are their attitudes based on racism and outdated post-colonial prejudices?

Australia's relationship with its surrounding region cannot be understood without some examination of what we mean by *Australia* and what we mean by *Asia*. Neither entity has a single, homogenous approach to the other. Nor did today's relationships spring unformed from the ether following the most recent crisis or the last election.

This chapter will first examine the history of Australia's relationship with the region to see how the simple, negative approaches of a hundred years ago have gradually been transformed into the complex and multifaceted ties that exist now. Then it will look at some of the interests and attitudes that various Australians have towards Asia, and at some of the interests and attitudes towards Australia found among different groups and countries in Asia. Against this background, it will finally look at how things stand now and speculate on how they may develop in the future. The emphasis will be on long-term trends.

History

A hundred years ago, on 1 January 1901, six separate colonies federated to create the Commonwealth of Australia. For the first fifty years of Australia's independent existence, Asia was a threat. Cheap Chinese labour which would undermine the pay and conditions of Australian workers had to be kept at bay by the strict application of the "White Australia" policy. The military threat from Japan was to be contained by the mighty British Empire, of which

CAVAN HOGUE is a former Australian diplomat who is now Director of the National Thai Studies Centre, Australian National University, and an adjunct professor in International Relations at the University of Technology, Sydney.

Australians were a proud part. Asia was, for the most part, made up of European and American colonies and took little interest in Australia. When the anticipated Japanese invasion finally came, Britain proved unable to protect Australia, and the United States, for its own reasons, saved Australia from invasion.

Immediately after the war, the Australian Labor Party (ALP) government tried to maintain the *status quo ante bellum*. It sought a peace agreement which would provide U.S. protection for Australia, and it upheld the "White Australia" policy by rejecting the applications to enter Australia of Japanese war brides and of Sgt. Gamboa, a Filipino soldier who had married an Australian woman. (The ALP had always been a stronger advocate of White Australia than the parties representing employers, whose views on cheap labour were understandably less rigid.)

In the negotiations to establish the United Nations, Foreign Minister Dr H.V. Evatt was responsible for Article 2(7) of the Charter which provided that "nothing in the present Charter shall authorize the United Nations to intervene in matters which are essentially within the domestic jurisdiction of any state...".[1] This was designed to protect the "White Australia" policy and is in interesting contrast to the efforts of more recent Labor Foreign Ministers like Gareth Evans to establish the principle that "good international citizens" have a duty to promote universal human rights even where that impinges on domestic jurisdictions. Evatt also began to think about Australia's future relations with its neighbours and what changes Australia would have to face. Although the Labor government ultimately supported Indonesian independence and made statements about freedom for Asian colonies, forward planning still hoped that European powers like the United Kingdom (UK), France, the Netherlands, and Portugal would retain their colonial territories.[2]

The Menzies government, which was elected in 1949, reversed the migration decisions and a new approach to Asia began to develop. The new government showed no less enthusiasm for arrangements to contain Japan, and negotiated the ANZUS (Australia, New Zealand, and the United States) Treaty with the United States as a way of protecting Australia against any future Japanese aggression. However, in a departure from the past, Foreign Minister Richard Casey began to talk about co-operation with Australia's Asian neighbours, and in 1951 paid the first goodwill visit by an Australian Foreign Minister to Asia. The Colombo Plan, which was launched in1951, was designed to improve social and economic conditions in the neighbourhood. Incidentally, it brought considerable numbers of Asian students into Australian homes, which helped to break down the fear of Asians. On the military front, the Southeast Asia Treaty Organization (SEATO), which was set up in 1954, allied Australia with Thailand and the Philippines. In the years 1963–65, Australian troops were part of a Commonwealth force which protected Malaysia from the aggressive behaviour of Soekarno's Indonesia during *Konfrontasi*.

During its long reign (1949–72), the Liberal-Country Party (LCP) coalition government gradually relaxed the "White Australia" policy to the point where the incoming ALP government of Gough Whitlam was able to administer the *coup de grace* in 1973. Both the evolution under the LCP, and the formal abolition under the ALP, were dependent on the acquiescence of the opposition, so that the operation was truly a bipartisan one. The basic outlines of immigration policy have remained bipartisan, and the only opposition comes from some minor parties. Similarly, despite major disagreements over Vietnam and the recognition of China during the 1960s, the basic outlines of foreign policy have also remained essentially bipartisan. The tactics to achieve them might sometimes have been different but the stated aims have been the same. It was R.G. Menzies who, for all his emotional devotion to the British connection, recognized as early as 1939 that "What Great Britain calls the Far East is to us the near north".[3]

From 1973 to the present, successive governments have steadily increased Australia's interaction with the region. As significant numbers of Asian migrants arrived, Asian languages and cultures began to be taught in schools, Asia became an important market, many more Australians travelled to Asia, and Asian food became popular. The old stereotypes were gradually broken down.

At Federation, no Australian doubted that the relationship with Great Britain was the only one that really mattered. Quite obviously, Britain did not give the same priority to its erstwhile colony. One hundred years later, the Howard government's White Paper[4] said that Australia's four most important relationships were those with Japan, China, Indonesia, and the United States. It is perhaps instructive to note that, with the possible exception of Indonesia, none of these countries would count Australia among its four most important relationships. Japan sees it as a serious relationship with real substance, but Australia is well down the list of Chinese and American priorities.

There has, then, been an evolution in Australian policies and attitudes from the hostility in the first half of the twentieth century, through a period of benevolent paternalism, to a time of co-operation and opportunity, albeit mixed with some confusion and uncertainty. As Asia grew steadily in importance for Australian governments, relations tended to become more pragmatic and positive. Asian countries have resented Australian racism but welcomed its aid and technology. As Australia and Asia changed, relationships became more complex, but some misunderstandings remain as legacies of the past.

Australian Approaches

While governments have tended to follow a bipartisan and evolving policy towards Asia, there are a number of different streams of thought in Australia, and lobby groups pressure governments to adopt their views. The aim of what follows is not to comment on the correctness of different approaches, but simply to describe them.

A strong element has always been the missionary approach. One hundred years ago, this was usually concerned with spreading the Christian religion and the benefits of European civilization — which tended to be seen as one and the same. Today, the Christian religion has been largely replaced by the preaching of democracy and universal human rights. However, while the secular faith may now be seen as more important than the religious, the basic element remains the same: the Truth must be delivered to the less fortunate whether they want it or not. As Ramesh Thakur has put it: "Few Australians deal with Asia with a sense of humility; many approach Asia from a sense of innate superiority and arrogance. Nowhere is this more apparent than in the vexed issue of human rights."[5] These latter day missionaries urge Australian governments to "put pressure on" Asian governments or use the threat of cutting off aid as a weapon against those guilty of offences against human rights and democracy. While resisting the more extreme demands, both the Keating and Howard governments have made the promotion of human rights part of their foreign policy.[6]

At the other end of the scale from those who adopt the missionary approach are the appeasers. They include some who feel guilty about what the colonialists did to Asians and therefore want to apologize and not to offend them. This is not a new approach, and Sir Alan Watt wrote in 1967 that "a vocal minority of Australians seems almost to suffer from a guilt-complex towards Asia".[7] They are joined by exporters who are afraid that criticism of Asian governments may adversely affect the sale of their products. Others feel that only governments who are without sin should cast the first stone. The appeasers urge Australian governments not to offend our Asian neighbours and, when things go wrong, they automatically assume it is Australia's fault.

There also exists a rational view that Australian governments have no business interfering in the domestic affairs of other countries but should simply promote Australian interests in a pragmatic way. This is the classic *realpolitik* approach which tends to be stronger among those engaged in the conduct of international relations than among those who talk about it. It rejects both the missionary and the appeasement approaches. It gives importance to Asia for purely pragmatic reasons. (The secular missionaries often accuse this group of being appeasers when they advocate dealing with whoever is in power rather than whoever the missionaries believe should be in power. One must therefore distinguish between people who are really appeasers and those who are unjustly accused of being appeasers.)

The view that Australia's destiny lies with Europe and North America has been in steady decline during the last fifty years, but is by no means dead. The perceived conflict between Australia's history and its geography still exists in the minds of many conservative Australians and, perhaps even more, in the minds of many Asians. The Asian economic crisis, the widely reported atrocities in Indonesia, and the rebuffing of Australian attempts to join some regional bodies, have strengthened the hand of those opposed to greater integration with Asia.

Isolationism remains a minority view although, as will be explained below, Pauline Hanson's One Nation Party has stirred up isolationist and protectionist sentiment among the marginalized.

Some Australians are primarily interested in Asia as a market while others stress the strategic aspects: Asia as an opportunity and Asia as a threat. Others take a cultural interest, and Asian cooking has invaded Australia in a big way. We should not, however, lose sight of the fact that most Australians are normally preoccupied most of the time with domestic matters. Like ordinary people everywhere else in the world, they are more interested in their jobs, hobbies, and pleasures than they are in the mysteries of international relations.

The media play an important role in stirring up and directing public opinion, forcing governments to say publicly what might be better left unsaid, and in focusing public interest on particular issues. There are knowledgeable Australian journalists who write intelligent things about Asia, but they are read by a minority. There are also journalists who see it as their responsibility to ensure balance in anything they write but they may be outnumbered by those who see their primary role as criticism of governments and getting a big readership. The reporting on the East Timor operation, for example, concentrated on the deeds of Australia's "Timor heroes" and the sufferings of their sweethearts back home. The East Timorese, saved by these noble warriors, were the good guys and the Indonesians were the bad guys. This created wider negative feelings about Indonesia, which were extended by some people to Asia in general.

There is, then, no single view on Asia and even less on particular issues. However, except for the isolationists, there is a widespread view that, while Australians may be different, Australia's future lies in Asia. What is really significant is that the Australian public expects political parties to maintain close and fruitful relationships with their Asian neighbours. This said, there has been a temporary turning away by some from Asia. Australian businesses tend to be oriented towards short-term profits and have swung from exaggerated expectations about the "Asian economic miracle" to equally unrealistic views of the "Asian collapse". As mentioned above, public opinion has reacted negatively to events in some Asian countries.

The Asian Side
Australian relations with the region are affected by Asian prejudices towards, opinions of, interests in, and experiences with Australia. Asian attitudes towards Australia can encourage or discourage Australian integration with the region.

Asia is never clearly defined; it can be historical, geographical, racial, cultural, political, linguistic, culinary, and so on.[8] Asian countries differ in their approach to Australia. Australian–Indonesian relations, for example, are close, complex, sometimes turbulent, but always important; relations with Bhutan are cordial but more limited. Within individual Asian countries also, we find different approaches. The Australian intervention in East Timor was strongly supported by the Thai Government and some sectors of Thai society; it was criticized by nationalist, isolationist groups in Thailand.

While racism in Australia has been reduced quite fundamentally over the last fifty years, it remains strong in much of Asia.[9] Many ethnic Chinese migrate to Australia from Southeast Asia to escape racism in the countries of their birth. There have been no anti-Asian riots in Australia for well over a hundred years; they are still going on in some parts of Asia. More importantly for Australian relations with Asia, some Asians take a racist approach to Australia. They claim that Australians can never be part of Asia because they do not look like Asians, thus defining Asia in purely racial terms.

Countries like Indonesia, Malaysia, and Singapore are more aware of Australia because of proximity in one case, and common colonial heritage in the other two. Thailand has grown more aware of Australia. Co-operation with the recently defeated Democrat-led government was very close and, although there may be less convergence of views on human rights issues, there is no reason to believe that a Thaksin government will turn away from Australia. The Philippines resented the "White Australia" policy more than any other country, but with 150,000 Filipino migrants now in Australia that ghost has been laid to rest. In Cambodia, in the early 1990s, Australia was the effective leader of a group of Asian and other countries that brought peace to that country. India thinks Australia is a cricket team. Australian awareness of China is much greater than China's awareness of Australia, and Australia does not want to have to choose between China and Taiwan/USA. Korea has become a major market and Vietnam is growing in importance, especially as its immigrants are coming to play an increasingly important part in Australian society. Japan is the big one both as a trading partner, and strategically. Some Japanese, especially at official levels, see Japan as the big, civilized nation in the north and Australia as the centre of civilization in the south. Therefore, they believe that the two should make a special effort to work together, usually with Australia in the role of younger brother.

While some Asians are prejudiced against Australia's European heritage, many others see it as a source of strength and admiration. Asian students come to Australia to study, and migration from Asia to Australia has grown dramatically since the lifting of the "White Australia" policy in 1973. Many Asians admire Australia's lifestyle, its political and legal institutions, and its egalitarian spirit. Some Australian tourists cause offence but many more make friends.

Asian–Australian trade is less important to Asia than it is to Australia, and most of it is with North Asia. Australian investment in the region lags behind others. Its relative economic position has declined in the last fifty years and it remains to be seen for how long Australia will be perceived as a source of advanced knowledge and technology. Australian education policy has turned foreign students into a source of income instead of a source of influential friends in the region. The education bubble will eventually burst but, in the meantime, it does provide a very important link. Similarly, the growing percentage of Australians of Asian origin provides commercial and personal links. Personal links are also growing among people who meet through sports, hobbies, religion, work, and other activities.

As the colonial generation is replaced by young people with no experience of colonial oppression and no ideological attachment to non-alignment, we can hope for more pragmatic approaches towards Australia from Asian decision-makers. This is also a generation which is more used to an Australian presence, and is therefore more willing to accept Australia as part of the scenery. Hopefully, the old attitudes which have led to the rebuffing of some Australian attempts to get closer to the region will disappear along with the older generation of Asian leaders.

Some Issues

Alliances and Organizations

There is no fundamental conflict between Australia's defence alliance with the United States and its commitment to the region. The fact is that Australia is only one of the countries in the region which has an alliance with the United States and is not the most important of these allies. The latter has alliances with Japan, South Korea, Thailand, and the Philippines.

Despite some irritations, Asians do not necessarily see the U.S. presence as a threat, and many would see it as something positive. Most Asians are more concerned about the potential threat from China than from the United States. Many still harbour concerns about a possible resurgence of Japanese militarism. Others are worried about traditional border problems, and for others internal security is all that matters. China is probably the only country in the region with a real concern about a U.S. military presence, especially in defence of Taiwan. The U.S. alliance did admittedly get Australia into the Korean and Vietnam wars but it remains an insurance policy from which Australia gets some useful intelligence and strategic benefits. In return, the United States gets the use of facilities in Australia, plus an ally which is seen as influential in the Asia–Pacific region.

Australia's engagement with Asia is on many fronts. The Five Power Defence Arrangements between Malaysia, Singapore, the UK, Australia, and New Zealand still exist and Australia has had a long history of defence co-operation with Indonesia and with all other major countries in Southeast Asia. Then there are the official links through more recent regional economic and security organizations. In addition to common membership of various United Nations bodies, Australia is a member of the Asia–Pacific Economic Cooperation (APEC) forum and the ASEAN Regional Forum (ARF) and was the first country to enter into a dialogue relationship with ASEAN. Australian negotiations with the United States for a Free Trade Agreement are likely to be very tricky, and the issue of agricultural markets will be a stumbling block. On trade issues, Australia usually finds itself fighting with its Asian neighbours against Europe and the United States.

That said, President George Bush could create some serious problems for Australia if he stirs up the conflict between China and Taiwan, or demands support for his missile defence system. Australia will need to show the same strength of character in opposing foolish American strategic initiatives as it has in opposing unjust American trade practices.

The Pauline Hanson Debate

In 1996, an independent Member of Parliament caused a furore in the Australian media, and shortly thereafter in the Asian media, when she made a speech complaining that major political parties were out of touch with ordinary people, that Aborigines in Australia were too well treated, and that there were too many Asian migrants. She formed a political party called the One Nation Party, which won some seats in the Queensland State Parliament. Her party then imploded and she lost her seat. However, the party polled about 10 per cent of the votes in the Western Australian State election on 10 February 2001, and this set off the debate again. A week later, the party polled well in the Queensland state elections, but not as well as it had in 1998. Pauline Hanson is now back in the news.

What is interesting is how this success was interpreted in Asia. Her support comes from people outside the major cities who believe that city-based politicians take no interest in rural Australia, and from the urban poor who believe that the traditional political parties have let the little people down. Globalization is seen as Darwinian economics, which puts business before people. People who are poor and unemployed are tired of hearing learned professors and politicians telling them that the economy is doing well. The One Nation Party has exploited this dissatisfaction through simplistic, populist claims. The racist policies that the Party espouses are not a significant element in its success. There have been anti-immigration parties around for many years and even anti-Asian migration parties, but they have had no electoral success.

In most of Asia, Pauline Hanson's anti-Asian statements were given undue prominence and her success was interpreted as resulting from racist attitudes in Australia. The Asian media thundered against the "resurgence of Australian racism" without explaining that racism was not the source of her support.

The danger for Australia lies not in a resurgence of racism but in the possibility that major parties will adopt narrow populist policies to get elected. This could result in damage to Australia's economy and its relative standing in the world. The challenge for Australia, and perhaps others, is to find a way of reaping the benefits of globalization while looking after its domestic victims.

East Timor

The recent East Timor exercise illustrated some important issues. For Indonesia's neighbours, it was a difficult exercise and Australia's willingness to take the lead was probably appreciated by more than those who resented it. Thailand and the Philippines were strong supporters. It is important to note that Australia went in only with Indonesian and United Nations agreement. Many Australians felt that the United States should have done more but the latter's approach was entirely consistent with the doctrine that it applied in Europe where the North Atlantic Treaty Organization (NATO) allies took the running in Yugoslavia with U.S. backing. Those who were worried about U.S. military intervention in the region might have been outnumbered by those who were surprised by U.S. unwillingness to get directly involved.

Much has been made in the Australian media of Prime Minister Howard's acceptance of the view put to him by a journalist in a published interview that in its actions in East Timor Australia was fulfilling its role as a "Deputy Sheriff" for the United States in the region. It would have been wise to have avoided macho talk about Australia "walking tall in Asia", and many Asians no doubt resented the stridency of Australian media and official self-congratulation. However, the concept is not an unreasonable description of how the United States sees things working and is accepted by the ALP. Indeed, the whole East Timor operation was supported by both parties. Disagreements were confined to detail, and the usual political point-scoring.

There has also been considerable criticism within the country of the Australian Government's failure to prevent violence in East Timor and of its perceived destruction of the security relationship with Indonesia. This criticism comes from both the missionaries and the appeasers. The missionaries believe that Australia has a duty to solve all the problems of the region by forcing its neighbours to follow its more civilized practices. The appeasers believe that every problem between Australia and its neighbours is Australia's fault because it offended them. The *realpolitik* approach is that what happened in East Timor was the fault of Indonesia and that Australia had neither the power nor the responsibility to solve this problem; Australia was, however, able to make a positive contribution, which it did. Indonesia's problems are of its own making. While its neighbours can try to help, they should not be blamed for failing to solve Indonesia's problems — that would be patronizing in the extreme. Close neighbours will always have problems and disagreements. Australia and Indonesia have fallen out before and will no doubt do so again, but the relationship has been managed and will be managed in the future.

While the Australian-led INTERFET (International Force East Timor) intervention was successful, there is a danger that some Australians will come out of it with an exaggerated idea of Australia's ability to solve problems through military means. It was well done, but it was a very limited exercise which had the co-operation of the Indonesian Army and the participation of other Asian countries. The lesson may be that Australia can work with other neighbouring countries to help solve regional crises. It might be seen in the same light as Australia's efforts to bring peace to Cambodia, where Australia led a collective approach that worked.

Keating and Howard Governments
There is a perception among some people, both in Australia and in the region, that the Howard government has moved away from Asia in contrast

to the Keating government's promotion of close relations. However, while Paul Keating's rhetoric was stronger than John Howard's, the policies their governments have followed are not that different. Neither Keating nor Howard has ever suggested that Australia should forget the rest of the world, but both have said that the Asia–Pacific is Australia's region of prime strategic interest. Both support the U.S. alliance. Neither has suggested that Australia is "an Asian country". Both have talked about human rights as being an essential part of Australia's approach to the world. When he came to power, John Howard tried to outdo Keating as someone who was close to Asia. It was only when the Asian economies started to weaken and domestic politics started to intrude that Howard modified his rhetoric. It is not possible to say what Keating would have done under the same circumstances.

Neither had any real interest in Asia before coming to office — in most countries, people do not get elected on foreign policy issues, and Australia is no different. Keating probably acquired greater enthusiasm for the cause than Howard did but, to be fair, Howard does not collect French clocks, or wear Italian suits. Neither speaks an Asian language nor has shown any great understanding of Asian history and culture, but both have seen that Australian interests lie in Asia.

A clear difference between the two is the Howard government's preference for bilateral over multilateral diplomacy. Since Howard's stress is put on regional bilateral relationships rather than world ones, it is hard to argue that this policy represents a downgrading of the region.

There can be no doubt that Keating presented a better image in Asia, and public rhetoric can be important as a sign of solidarity and goodwill. However, even if Howard is perceived in Asia — probably correctly — to be less enthusiastic in linking Australia with the region than was Keating, this will all be forgotten in a few years if John Howard is replaced late in 2001 by someone who says the right things. Opposition leader Kim Beazly has a good knowledge of Asia, and his rhetoric should be impeccable. The worry for Australians is that, for narrow electoral reasons, neither party will take on the populists directly and actively promote more Asian-oriented public attitudes.

The Future

The conflict between history and geography, which has been at the centre of Australia's approach to the world, is slowly being determined in favour of Asia. Australia can never be part of Europe or North America because the Europeans and Americans do not want Australia. The strong cultural links that many Australians feel with their ancestral homelands are not reciprocated by those ancestral homelands. Australia may not be "part of Asia" but at least Asians know that Australia exists.

There can be no doubt that Australia has faced reality and moved much closer to the neighbourhood but Australia does not have to be monogamous. Except perhaps for Myanmar and North Korea, no Asian country rejects links with the world outside Asia. All are actively courting European and American investment. Japan is more of a world power than an Asian one. Like everyone else in the region, Australia seeks economic links where money is to be made. Moreover, like others, its strategic focus is on its own region. It is fashionable to claim that globalization is making regionalism obsolete but in Europe and Asia, smaller entities are making a comeback. People want an identity and until such time as the intergalactic aliens invade, a world identity is not good enough.

While, admittedly, rural areas remain more conservative, there have been quite fundamental changes in Australian society in the last fifty years. Even if Australian society still has an identifiably European origin, it has mutated. We might compare Singapore's essentially Chinese cultural origin with Australia's essentially Anglo-Irish cultural origin but see in both places the creation of a new and separate identity under the influence of other cultures and their own internal momentum.

The real question is: what does being part of Asia mean? Asian societies vary enormously among themselves. Koreans are very different from Thais. Even within the same country, Bataks are very different from Javanese, and Cantonese are very different from Manchus. Singaporeans probably have more in common with Australians than they do with Lao. More Australians than Filipinos can use chopsticks. The current concept of Asia arose out of the colonial experience and is defined differently by different people. It carries much emotional baggage. It might be better to talk only about the "Asia–Pacific region", or to find some other neutral term that is purely geographical. Whatever you call it, Australia is as much part of this region as anyone else, and always will be. However, it is not just a question of Australians accepting where they live, but of its neighbours accepting that neighbours do not all have to be of the same race, religion, or cultural background. Australia's neighbours must get rid of outdated racist and colonial attitudes that refuse to accept people of different racial origins. Australians must also realize that they can be part of this region without having to pretend they are something they are not.

The vexed question of "Asian values" has not been addressed here because it can be something of a red herring. To a large extent, it is an Asian response to the Western secular missionaries. There are Australians and Asians who try to force their values on to people who do not want them but let us hope that the future will bring greater tolerance all round. This subject has been dealt with elsewhere.[10] It is sufficient to note here that there are important cultural differences not only between Australians and Asians but also between Asians and Asians.

There have been evolutionary changes in the last fifty years within Australia, within most countries of the region, and in the nature of the relationship between Australia and the world. As trade, defence, and personal links grow, the continuation of these trends is inevitable. How fast things move will depend not just on Australia accepting its place in the region but on its neighbours also accepting its right to that place. The more Australia is rebuffed by Asia, the more it will turn away; the more Australia is welcomed, the faster that process will be.

NOTES

1. Alan Watt, *The Evolution of Australian Foreign Policy 1938–1965* (Cambridge, 1967), p. 90.
2. See, for example, Dr Evatt's Ministerial Statement of 19 July 1944, on "Post-War Planning", in *Foreign Policy of Australia, Speeches by The Rt. Hon H.V. Evatt, M.P., Minister of State for External Affairs*, edited by W. McMahon Ball (Sydney: Angus and Robertson, 1945). The relevant section is on p. 206.
3. Watt, op. cit., p. 364.
4. White Paper, *In the National Interest* (Canberra: Department of Foreign Affairs and Trade, 1997), p. vi.
5. Ramesh Thakur, "Australia's Regional Engagement", *Contemporary Southeast Asia* 20, no. 1 (April 1998): 18.
6. See, for example, the Howard government's White Paper, *In the National Interest*, pp. 13–14, which affirms the universality of human rights and acknowledges that the issue will sometimes cause problems in Australia's diplomatic relations.
7. Watt, op. cit., p. 358.
8. For a more detailed examination of this point, see the author's article, "Perspectives on Australian Foreign Policy, 1999", *Australian Journal of International Affairs* 54, no. 2 (2000).
9. There has been a fundamental change, at least in the cities, which means the great majority of Australians. This kind of change has not taken place in countries like Japan, Korea, and Malaysia, to cite some obvious cases. Also noteworthy is the change from the strict application of the "White Australia" policy to Asians making up more than half the annual intake of migrants. Racism in 1950 was promoted officially; now it is illegal. There were three Chinese restaurants in Dixon Street and a couple in Campbell Street in Sydney in 1950. Now there is a vast Chinatown complex and surveys have shown that the preferred place for Australian families to eat is a Chinese restaurant. The change has been a basic one. It is perhaps less so in the rural areas, which are more conservative. See the author's article, "Racism and Communalism", in *The Asia-Australia Papers*, No. 2, (The Asia–Australia Institute, University of New South Wales, September 1999), pp. 71–78.
10. See the articles cited in notes 8 and 9 above.

ENVIRONMENTAL CHALLENGES

Lorraine Elliott

Environmental degradation is one of the major challenges facing Southeast Asia in the twenty-first century. The ten Southeast Asian governments have committed themselves to a "clean and green" ASEAN by 2020. The goal is admirable but it will be difficult to attain. The Southeast Asian regional ecosystem is diverse. The obstacles are complex. The consequences of continued environmental decline, however, could be severe. Continued high rates of environmental decline and unsustainable development compromise economic growth, individual quality of life, social stability, and, potentially, regional security.

The salience of environmental change as a policy issue for Southeast Asian countries has increased since the early 1990s and environmental issues are now firmly entrenched on the regional political agenda. Events such as the 1992 United Nations Conference on Environment and Development (UNCED) and the thematic sessions and reporting requirements of the Commission on Sustainable Development (CSD) have made it difficult for governments in Southeast Asia to overlook environmental degradation and sustainable development issues. A burgeoning environmental conscience among individual donor countries and within development organizations such as the World Bank has imposed more stringent environmental conditions on development programmes in Southeast Asia. Grass-roots environmental activism and regional networks of non-governmental organizations (NGOs), focusing on the relationship "between rapid economic growth, depleted environments and increasing poverty"[1] have put further pressure on governments to respond to environmental problems.

In its 1994 review of functional co-operation — the *chapeau* under which environmental issues fall — the ASEAN Secretariat openly acknowledged "the importance, if not urgency, of conserving the region's resources and protecting its environment", noting that "any drastic and irreversible reduction in the region's resources or degradation of its environment will ... have far-reaching implications for the region's ecosystem and quality of life".[2] Environmental degradation in Southeast Asia is no longer just a national problem. While the

LORRAINE ELLIOTT is Fellow (Senior Lecturer) at the Department of International Relations, Research School of Pacific and Asian Studies, Australian National University.

immediate economic, social, and ecological impacts of environmental decline are often localized, many of the environmental problems facing Southeast Asian governments are so widespread as to be justifiably identified as common and regional problems. A number also have an increasingly transboundary character, in both cause and consequence. Regional co-operation among the member countries of the Association of Southeast Asian Nations is therefore an important component of effective and efficient policy responses to environmental degradation. The political challenges of responding to environmental degradation and unsustainable development have also become integral to debates about the development of regional identity, the relevance of ASEAN diplomacy and the "ASEAN Way", and the crisis of credibility which bedevilled the Association in the latter part of the 1990s.

The Changing Political Economy of Southeast Asia

Environmental degradation is not simply a biophysical problem or a phenomenon of nature. Its roots lie in unsustainable development and the everyday practices of human economy and society, whether in pursuit of the basic subsistence requirements of life, economic growth, or profit. Subsistence lifestyles in Southeast Asia remain heavily dependent on the exploitation of natural resources and still constitute the basic means of survival for over half of the region's population. Yet the region's poor should not be blamed as the major contributors to regional environmental degradation, even though poverty is often a proximate local cause. The global attribute that the poor cause less cumulative environmental damage than the affluent is repeated in Southeast Asia. The regional political economy of the environment is also characterized by the shadow ecologies of the industrialized world — the richest 20 per cent of the world's population.

The relationship between population growth and environmental degradation in Southeast Asia, therefore, also requires careful scrutiny. Population pressures in the region do figure as a factor in environmental decline, but population growth alone is insufficient to explain the rate and diversity of environmental change in the region. While rates remain high in some countries, population growth rates in Southeast Asia are generally slowing. The average increase in population for all the ASEAN countries now stands at about 1.7 per cent a year, only a little above the world average of 1.4 per cent, and down substantially from the 2.3 per cent growth rate during the period 1960–92. Expectations are that the rate will decline further to about 1.26 per cent by 2005.[3] Yet in countries such as Thailand and Indonesia, where growth rates have stabilized or declined, there is little evidence that the overall rate of environmental degradation is also slowing.

The major cause of environmental decline and resource scarcity in the region has been "the industrialization of Asia within the world economy".[4] This has been characterized by environmentally unsustainable patterns of economic growth, industrialization and urbanization, increasing consumption, and growing demands for energy and resources. The region has seen high economic growth rates since the early to mid-1990s. Malaysia, Indonesia, and Thailand, for example, all experienced average growth rates of close to 9 per cent per annum from the early 1990s to 1997. Per capita gross domestic product (GDP) almost doubled between 1990 and 1995.[5] Demands for food and energy — two key environmental services — are growing faster than supply. Energy consumption in Southeast Asia remains above the global average and continues to grow at the same time as average global energy consumption and energy intensity have been declining. The rapid growth in industrial sectors has been accompanied by an intensification of the agricultural sector, a decline in rural populations, and an increase in urban (rather than semi-urban) populations. Common property resources are being privatized and taken out of the hands of local communities and the poor for whom common ownership often provides better opportunities for environmental management and a sustainable subsistence livelihood. Industrialization and energy demands create further pollution and waste. Every US$1 billion increase in Asian gross national product (GNP) generates about 100 tonnes of hazardous and toxic waste.[6] Resources have been depleted and the environment degraded to the extent that so-called renewable resources and environmental services are being exhausted in much the same way as non-renewable resources. The consequences are that the region has become "dirtier, less ecologically diverse and more environmentally vulnerable".[7]

Environmental Consequences

The environmental challenges facing Southeast Asia have a quantitative and qualitative dimension. They include deforestation, soil erosion, land degradation and desertification; loss of biodiversity and living resources (such as fish stocks) and the related imperatives of species protection and conservation; degradation of terrestrial, river, coastal and marine habitat; air pollution and water pollution; increasing concerns about the management and disposal of hazardous and toxic wastes; and the impact of global environmental problems, particularly climate change. A number of problems stand out as particularly challenging. Those which are characterized as *very severe* in impact (rather than simply severe or moderate) include atmospheric levels of lead, faecal coliforms and lead pollutants in water, a general lack of access to safe water, deforestation, soil erosion, and annual growth rates in energy consumption.[8]

Deforestation provides some of the most extensive evidence of environmental change in the region. Southeast Asia holds about 25 per cent of the world's remaining tropical timber forests. The causes of deforestation include commercial logging and land clearance for agriculture (often plantation and mono-cropping). Cambodia, Burma, and Vietnam still rely heavily on fuel-wood as an energy source. Estimates suggest that the annual rate of deforestation in Southeast Asia could now be as high as 1.8 per cent, increasing from 1.4 per cent in the 1980s, and almost twice the rate of South Asia, tropical Southern Africa, and tropical Southern America.[9] Nearly one-third of the forests of

Cambodia, Vietnam, and Laos have disappeared in the last twenty years.[10] Frontier forests are particularly vulnerable, and a logging ban in any one country has so far simply displaced the problem elsewhere, particularly where illegal logging is involved.[11]

Deforestation and unsustainable agricultural practices are major causes of soil loss, land degradation, siltation, changes in water retention and run-off patterns, and food insecurity. Southeast Asia already has less per capita arable land (0.09 hectares) than the global average of 0.24 hectares, and land-use patterns have changed more quickly than in Asia as a whole.[12] Land degradation has been exacerbated by increased soil salinity and waterlogging as a result of poor irrigation practices. Loss of forest habitat also compromises biodiversity in the region. Regional biodiversity hot spots, those most vulnerable to the loss of tropical forests, include the Philippines, peninsular Malaysia, and northwestern Borneo. Southeast Asia contains over 200 of the world's threatened mammals, almost the same number of threatened bird species, close to 100 of the world's threatened fish species, and almost 30 of the world's most threatened reptile and amphibian species.[13]

Urban air quality is another serious environmental problem facing many countries in the region and one which has been made worse by the growth of the region's megacities — Jakarta, Manila, and Bangkok. These cities exceed or come close to exceeding the World Health Organization's guidelines on safe levels of particulates and lead, although they are only moderately polluted by sulphur dioxide emissions. Air pollution now constitutes one of the major causes of chronic health problems in the region, including respiratory disease, lead poisoning, and slow mental development in children. Air pollution is not confined to national borders. The most prominent of the transboundary atmospheric issues has been the so-called "haze" problem in Southeast Asia, in which particulate-laden smoke from land-clearance fires, mainly in Kalimantan and Sumatra, spread to Brunei, Singapore, Malaysia, and Thailand.

Air pollution is a consequence of increased energy use in the region, particularly through the extraction, transportation, and consumption of fossil fuels, and growth in the transport sector. In general, the growth in primary energy demand has exceeded Southeast Asia's growth in GDP. Energy demands in the region are likely to continue to grow at a time when global energy consumption is falling. Southeast Asia therefore faces a likely decline in energy self-sufficiency together with an increase in energy-related pollution, including carbon emissions and the production of hazardous waste. Cities such as Manila and Jakarta, for example, produce over 8 million tons of hazardous waste each year.[14]

Water resources are vital to the region's people and economies. Regional environmental policy-makers have ranked water pollution and freshwater depletion as the environmental problem of most concern to them.[15] Although the average withdrawal rate is lower than for Asia as a whole, overuse of water is becoming a serious regional problem as irrigation, industrial, and domestic demands outstrip the rate at which groundwater is replenished. Water demands in the region's megacities are expected to continue to rise at rates between 3 and 10 per cent a year. In both rural and urban communities, access to potable water is often limited. Per capita water availability in the region almost halved between 1950 and 1980, and recent figures indicate that this trend has continued. Water pollution compounds the problem of access to clean water. Sewage is often not treated. Water quality is degraded by urban and industrial pollution and run-off from pesticide and fertilizers used in increasingly intensified agriculture. Many of the region's rivers are now suffering the long-term effects of severe pollution and contain high levels of organic material, heavy metals, pathogens and other pollutants.

The maritime region and coastal zones are also crucial to the economies and livelihoods of the region. More than 60 per cent of the population of Southeast Asia live near to or rely, economically and ecologically, on coastal zones. Yet coastal ecosystems are also suffering extensive pollution damage from flood sediments, industrial wastes, and untreated sewage. Serious degradation, including nutrient pollution and the so-called "red tides" caused by algal bloom, has affected the Gulf of Thailand, Manila and Jakarta bays, and the Mekong Delta region. Ecologically-important mangrove habitat are under threat from development and pollution, much of it from land-based activities. Coral reefs are also being degraded. Unsustainable harvesting of fish stocks has resulted in severe over-fishing of much of the region's fisheries, in some cases almost to the point of non-recovery (as in the case of skipjack tuna or penaeid shrimp, for example).

Climate change presents another serious environmental challenge for countries in the region. The problem is a complex one. Although per capita emissions still fall far behind those of most industrialized countries and the ASEAN countries together still contribute less than 5 per cent of global emissions, annual growth of carbon dioxide (CO_2) emissions in Asia is up to six times greater than that of developed countries.[16] Regional carbon emissions can be attributed primarily to increased energy use (including commercial transportation and private vehicle use), energy inefficiency, and decreased forest cover. Southeast Asia is responsible for a much higher proportion of emissions of another potent greenhouse gas, methane, because of the extent of rice paddy agriculture. These are, however, emissions from subsistence and survival practices rather than luxury emissions. The more immediate challenge for many Southeast Asian governments lies not in the reduction of emissions, although that presents its own economic and environmental difficulties, but in managing the impacts of climate change. Many countries in the region, with low-lying islands and economically and ecologically important river deltas and coastal regions, are among those most vulnerable to the ecological and economic impacts of climate change. These include rises in sea-levels, disrupted weather patterns and precipitation, and changes to growing seasons and agricultural output.

Social and Economic Costs

The economic and social consequences of environmental degradation in Southeast Asia are now being widely acknowledged. High levels of economic growth in the region in the 1990s (the financial crisis notwithstanding) came at considerable cost to the environment. In turn, unsustainable development, environmental degradation, and resource depletion impose substantial economic and social costs at the local, national, and regional levels. This includes tangible costs, such as those associated with the impacts of pollution on human (and animal) health or the loss of productivity, together with intangible welfare costs, such as those associated with a reduction in overall quality of life. Environmental costs also undermine the rate of return on project and infrastructure investments and more generally affect overall economic productivity.

There has been no broad-based regional assessment of the total costs of environmental degradation, but sector-specific estimates suggest that the costs could be up to 10 per cent of regional GDP.[17] In Bangkok, for example, almost one in four residents suffers from some degree of respiratory problem as a result of air pollution. Recent studies indicate that reducing air pollutant levels by only 20 per cent would result in savings in health-related expenditure alone of up to US$3 billion per annum (besides the productivity costs that could be reclaimed if traffic congestion were reduced).[18] Conservative estimates on the costs to Indonesia of haze pollution in 1997–98 are at US$1.4 billion in health and lost tourism revenue, and US$3 billion through losses in "timber, agriculture, non-timber forest products, hydrological and soils conservation and ... biodiversity benefits".[19] The health costs of atmospheric particulate pollution in Jakarta have been estimated at over US$2 billion (in 1989 figures) and at over US$1.6 billion (also in 1989 figures) for lead pollution.[20]

Recent reports by the Asian Development Bank demonstrate the longer-term and indirect economic costs of inadequate protection of natural areas, lack of investment in environmental infrastructure, and resource depletion.[21] The important and increasingly scarce resources are those which have for so long been thought of as renewable, or at least non-depletable, and therefore subject to free access regimes — fish, forests, and arable land. The economic costs and loss of income arise through overuse and through lack of effective management regimes which could prevent illegal resource extraction. On fisheries, as one example, the Indonesian Government estimates that the Indonesian economy loses up to US$4 billion from illegal fishing activity (compared with earnings of only US$2.2 billion).[22] On forestry, the ASEAN Secretariat has estimated that virtually all of the region's primary forests could be logged within a decade or two at present rates of extraction.[23] Plantation forests are, on the whole, not well managed and there is little incentive for long-term sustainable forestry practices. The loss of future timber resources could be substantial, particularly for countries such as Indonesia and Malaysia, which are major contributors to the world timber trade, apart from the ecological consequences of deforestation for ecosystem viability or the social and cultural consequences of the loss of forest-lands for indigenous communities.

Although the contribution of agriculture to ASEAN GDP is declining, it remains an important source of income for the region's rural population. Sustainable crop production is important for regional food security and to minimize the reliance on food imports.[24] Yet land degradation is undermining agricultural yield. Increases in food production have not matched those of previous decades and there is little scope for increasing the amount of agricultural land under irrigation.

Environmental degradation and resource depletion undermine quality of life, particularly for the poor, through their impact on human health, loss of income and increased poverty, and food insecurity. Land degradation and water pollution mean that people in rural communities often have to work harder and longer hours to produce food. Daily tasks of collecting water and energy resources, usually the preserve of women and children, become more burdensome. Depletion of fish stocks in freshwater, coastal and maritime environments deprives people of the main source of dietary protein. Pressures on rural land, combined with declining economic opportunities, exacerbate the rural–urban drift and the environmental impact of increasingly crowded and polluted cities, besides the competition for already scarce urban infrastructure and services.

Environmental problems, particularly when they exacerbate already existing tensions, can therefore be politically and socially destabilizing within countries. They can also be a source of diplomatic tension in the region. Within states, the potential for competition over resources and environmental services, between a range of users including farmers, fishing communities, loggers, industry and others, is heightened by environmental degradation and pollution. While it is unlikely that environmental decline or resource depletion will lead to actual inter-state conflict (although the South China Sea could be an exception here), there are many examples of inter-state tensions in which environmental scarcity is or could be a factor.[25] The haze, for example, has been a point of, thus far, polite but sharp difference between Indonesia and its neighbours. Water resources continue to feature in tensions between Malaysia and Singapore. Disputes over cross-border logging and trade have engaged the diplomatic skills of Thailand, Laos, and Myanmar. Illegal fishing is another likely contentious issue between states, and the governments of both Thailand and Indonesia, for example, have sought to deploy naval resources to protect their fishing grounds and fleets.

Regional Policy Responses
Environmental degradation remains a serious problem in Southeast Asia and will continue to have considerable and at times severe economic and social costs. Governments have responded to environmental challenges with policies

which set effluent and emission standards and limits (although technical standards are less common) and which incorporate prohibition, regulation, and incentive structures for better environmental practice. Various degrees of sanctions are now available to local and national authorities, including fines, loss of concessions or licences, and imprisonment. Some form of environmental impact assessment is becoming a more common feature of planning processes, and most countries now have a single centralized agency responsible for environmental policy.

There have been extensive attempts to protect habitat, to improve air quality, to clean up urban rivers and waterways and to curb the degradation and loss of mangrove ecosystems, to implement fisheries management plans, and to establish coastal and marine protection programmes. Many of these programmes have been prepared in conjunction with ASEAN Dialogue Partners, development assistance agencies, the United Nations Environment Programme, and the Global Environment Facility (GEF). The ASEAN/USAID Coastal Resources Management Programme, for example, has helped to establish integrated coastal management plans for important areas in the Philippines, Indonesia, Thailand, and Malaysia. The Asian Development Bank has provided technical assistance to Indonesia on fires and the haze. The GEF has provided funding for a regional project on oil spill preparedness and response.

Regional co-operation has become a significant component of attempts by countries in Southeast Asia to pursue sustainable development, to minimize environmental degradation, and to manage the impacts of already existing environmental change. As Muthiah Alagappa points out, regional institutions are increasingly important to environmental governance and management. Their tasks can include providing a high level forum to "map the regional agenda, articulate regional goals and build relevant regional norms", to facilitate regional input into global conventions and the implementation thereof, to develop regional initiatives on transboundary environmental problems, to mediate disputes, and to harmonize national efforts.[26]

Environmental concerns have been on the ASEAN agenda since the late 1970s. The first phase of regional co-operation focused on sustaining natural resources with the aims of overcoming poverty and improving the quality of life. The emphasis in the 1980s was on conservation, heritage parks, and nature reserves. Co-operative initiatives on pollution, including air, marine, and transboundary pollution, became more prominent in the 1990s. The second phase of co-operation, from the mid-1990s, was marked by a greater declaratory commitment to more specifically ecological principles such as environmental stewardship, a more clearly articulated awareness of the regional dimensions of environmental degradation, and efforts to integrate environmental concerns with economic ones, particularly trade, in the concept of eco-efficiency. Sustainable development has become the *leitmotif* of environmental policy in Southeast Asia, as in the rest of the world. Nineteen ninety-five was declared the first ASEAN Year of the Environment. The first region-wide *ASEAN State of the Environment Report* was released in 1997, and 2000 was nominated as the second ASEAN Year of the Environment under the theme "Our Heritage, Our Future".

In the period since the late 1970s, governments in the region have also become signatories to many of the major multilateral environmental agreements (MEAs) and have been active participants in international environmental negotiations, often under the umbrella of the G77/China grouping. While ASEAN is not a regional economic entity which is entitled to accede to an MEA in its own right, the Association has become more active in providing support for the development and articulation of a common ASEAN position on problems such as climate change, ozone depletion, or forestry management, most recently through the Working Group on Multilateral Agreements.

ASEAN's most recent third phase of environmental co-operation is more ambitious still. The Hanoi Plan of Action, adopted in 1998 to implement ASEAN's Vision 2020, sets out (among other things) a series of measures to protect the environment and promote sustainable development in Southeast Asia. Its goals are now supported by the Strategic Plan of Action on the Environment 1999–2004 (adopted in April 2000), which envisages much more than sharing of knowledge and pooling of resources. It places even greater emphasis on enhanced regional co-ordination and harmonization of environmental standards (particularly on ambient air and river water quality), on the establishment and strengthening of regional centres and networks to address a range of environmental concerns, and greater attention to the challenges of implementation. The agenda of regional environmental concerns has expanded to include issues such as access to genetic resources and water conservation.

Many of the measures are to be fully implemented by the end of 2001, when the Plan will be reviewed. The rest have a 2004 deadline. However, the record suggests that while the goals are admirable, their achievement is unlikely without assertive attention to the institutional and political problems which have to date hindered effective environmental action under ASEAN, and within individual member states. Principles adopted have often not been put into practice and legislative programmes have either been inadequate for the task or marked by inadequate implementation.

For example, the region now has an extensive network of protected forests. Yet, as the ASEAN Secretariat has noted, "few resources are available to effectively protect them on the ground. In many cases these areas are still exposed to timber poaching and agricultural encroachment".[27] Over 8 per cent of ASEAN's land area is now designated as parks and reserves designed to protect areas of outstanding wilderness quality and biological diversity and to conserve habitats of rare and threatened species. However, these conservation efforts have been undermined by lack of resources and inadequate supporting legislation. Many of the areas are, in effect, too fragmented and too small to provide the necessary protection and conservation values. Despite national programmes for river rehabilitation and regulations on waste-water discharge, improvement in water quality has been very slow or non-existent, with the exception of Singapore.

The problem is partly one of material resources. The network of domestic regulations and legislations, and regional environmental initiatives, is often inadequately resourced in both financial and legal terms. State capacity for monitoring and implementation remains a central problem. Attempts to manage environmental problems are hindered by domestic constraints, including poor planning co-ordination, overlapping and conflicting jurisdictions between government departments, weak implementation of pollution regulations, understaffing of relevant agencies, and lack of financial resources. Similar problems are faced by the ASEAN Secretariat, despite the strengthening of professional and technical environmental expertise during the last decade or so. The Secretariat was reorganized and strengthened in 1992, and Functional Co-operation was elevated to a higher plane at the Fifth ASEAN Summit in 1995, but the number of professional staff in the Bureau of Functional Co-operation remains small.

The ASEAN Secretariat also points to a lack of funds as a major reason for the poor record in implementing national environmental laws and regional programmes under the regional Strategic Plan of Action and its predecessors. Lack of funds compromises the implementation and monitoring of environmental legislation and standards. It also reduces opportunities for investment in environmentally-sound infrastructure and less-polluting technologies. Much of the funding for ASEAN initiatives is reliant on Dialogue Partners. However, the programmes funded under these arrangements have focused primarily on generating and exchanging information and expertise rather than on direct remedial environmental action. The economic crisis has reduced even further the funds available to governments and communities for environmental management programmes and the enforcement of environmental law. There is anecdotal evidence that environmentally destructive practices have increased although that may have been offset somewhat by the possible loss of investment in the resource extractive industry.[28]

Problems of policy incoherence and the neutralization of environmental policies by economic strategies, such as subsidies for agricultural pesticides and fertilizers, or pricing policies which favour higher-polluting fuels in the transport sector, have compounded the difficulties. Property rights to open-access resources, such as water or fuel-wood among rural communities, have not been well-defined or secured. Where land tenure for settlers, peasant farmers, and indigenous communities is uncertain, there is little incentive to manage land and resources sustainably. Indeed, the lack of secure tenure, compounded by poverty, often encourages ecologically damaging risk-hedging behaviour, such as further encroachment on forest lands to grow more crops or to establish or support claims to rights of use and ownership. These problems have not been helped by what some commentators have called "misguided or narrowly opportunistic government policies".[29] This is particularly so in terms of the priority often given to corporate and multinational interests. There is also considerable evidence that, in some Southeast Asian countries at least, military or security forces have been closely involved in environmentally destructive activities, including species smuggling, illegal logging and fishing, and the dumping of hazardous waste.

The recent expansion of ASEAN membership to include the countries of mainland Southeast Asia — Myanmar, Vietnam, Laos, and Cambodia — may create further difficulties in giving successful effect to regional environmental co-operation. While ASEAN now covers all ten Southeast Asian countries, the new ASEAN members are also generally the poorer countries within the region. These so-called two tiers of development illuminate once again the problems of reconciling environmental protection and sustainable development with short-term economic imperatives.

The "ASEAN Way", with its emphasis on personal diplomacy, discussion, consultation, consensus, and unanimity, also contributes to the difficulties in achieving successful environmental outcomes. It creates a form of regional decision-making which might be useful for political and security concerns, but which has become too slow and unwieldy in the face of the imperatives of environmental decline. It has discouraged open criticism of member states and their environmental practices, although recent debates within ASEAN about constructive intervention and flexible engagement are modifying the public face of a norm that has always been only partially observed even in private. Indeed, when it has unintended (or even intended) transboundary consequences, environmental degradation is itself a form of intervention, affecting environmental quality in another state, "violating" territorial integrity, and calling into question the issue of policy autonomy. The haze has been a key factor in these recent debates about intervention, the credibility of the "ASEAN Way", and the forging of regional identity. As ASEAN Secretary-General Severino has observed, the haze problem (among others) has "brought home ... the need to forge a stronger sense of unity in ASEAN if [the] most serious problems are to be addressed".[30] Environment ministers have openly encouraged the Indonesian Government to take action to prevent land-clearance fires and have expressed their strong objection to the irresponsible behaviour of plantation companies, most recently at the fifth informal ASEAN Ministerial Meeting on the Environment in April 2000.

The Challenges Ahead

The situation appears bleak, but it does not have to be. Governments have acknowledged that the problem is approaching a critical level. Statements from ASEAN attest to a regional awareness of the ecological, economic, and social costs of resource depletion, pollution, and loss of species, habitat, and environmental services, and the barriers to overcoming these problems. In the introduction to ASEAN's *First State of the Environment Report* in 1997, then

Secretary-General of ASEAN, Dato' Ajit Singh, called for an intensification of efforts under the ASEAN Strategic Plan on the Environment (now superceded by the Strategic Plan of Action on the Environment). Cambodian Minister for the Environment, Dr Mok Mareth, has argued that strategies for regional environmental co-operation and sustainable development should include not only regional agreements but common laws to enforce those agreements, commonly accepted environmental standards, and immediate response capacity for environmental emergencies.[31] This requires more than dialogue and discussion. At both the national and regional levels, it requires political will and substantial resources, better flow of information and more effective public education, the adoption and transfer of environmentally sound technologies, and better training and capacity for developing and implementing environmental law and regulations. These resources can be generated in part within the region, through a reassessment of funding priorities, through the use of pricing and market-based mechanisms to encourage investment in better technologies and pollution reduction. However, much more attention and assistance has to come from developed countries and the international community on equity as well as practical grounds. It has to involve technology transfer, capital assistance for environmentally-sound investment and infrastructure, building human and administrative capacity in environmental management, monitoring, and implementation. The funds presently made available through development programmes and other financial mechanisms are simply insufficient.

Besides material resources, more effective policy management for environmental protection and sustainable development in Southeast Asia requires a deeper commitment from the private sector and more active participation from the local communities. It is important that rights to and responsibilities for resource and environmental management are equitably shared among stakeholders. Finding a balance between local and corporate interests is crucial to managing the region's environmental challenges. Not only is this likely to improve the chances of sustainable development, but it also addresses the security concerns which arise when local communities resist environmental scarcities not of their own making. As Marian Miller observes, "it is futile to attempt to implement international or regional agreements [which] local communities are unlikely or unable to support".[32]

Addressing the institutional failures that cause poverty is central to sustainable development. Land tenure has become a key factor in these debates. Without security of ownership over land, people are reluctant to engage in conservation strategies, and they have less incentive to manage the land in an environmentally sustainable way. More secure property and land rights do not necessarily have to be based on individual or corporate rights. There is good evidence that strategies which define community rights along with common management strategies can be more beneficial in managing resource use and minimizing environmental impact than policies which rely on price signals, market-based instruments, or command-and-control regimes alone. Meeting the challenges of sustainable development and preventing further environmental decline is therefore no longer (if it ever was) just about better environmental regulation. Improving financial, technological, and human capacity for environmental management is a necessary but not sufficient condition for sustainable development in Southeast Asia. A "clean and green" ASEAN by 2020 also requires giving greater priority to local communities, encouraging and if necessary imposing stricter rules on corporate actors and investment practices, and integrating environmental policy with economic and social policy, and intensifying regional co-operation on the environmental challenges which will, in both the short and long-term, affect all countries and peoples in Southeast Asia.

NOTES

1. Jayant Lele, "Introduction: Searching for Development Alternatives — Class, Gender and Environment in Asian Economic Growth", in *Asia — Who Pays for Growth? Women, Environment and Popular Movements*, edited by Jayant Lele and Wisdom Tettey (Aldershot: Dartmouth Publishing, 1996), p. 20.
2. ASEAN Secretariat, *From Strength to Strength — ASEAN Functional Cooperation: Retrospect and Prospect* (Jakarta: ASEAN Secretariat, 1994), p. 33.
3. ASEAN Secretariat, *First ASEAN State of the Environment Report* (Jakarta: ASEAN Secretariat, 1997), pp. 64–65.
4. Aat Vervoorn, *Re-orient: Change in Asian Societies* (Oxford: Oxford University Press, 1998), p. 157.
5. See Teranishi Shun'ichi and Oshima Ken'ichi, "Accelerated Industrialization and Explosive Urbanization", in *The State of the Environment in Asia 1999/2000*, edited by Japan Environmental Council (Singapore: Institute of Southeast Asian Studies, 1999), pp. 5–6.
6. Cited in Mohammed Arif, "Environmental Policies of the OECD and their Implications for ASEAN", in *OECD and ASEAN Economies: The Challenge of Policy Coherence*, edited by Kiichiro Fukasaku, Michael Plummer, and Joseph Tan (Paris: Organisation for Economic Cooperation and Development, 1995), p. 124.
7. Asian Development Bank, *Emerging Asia: Changes and Challenges* (Manila: Asian Development Bank, 1997), p. 199.
8. Ibid., p. 203.
9. ASEAN Secretariat, *First ASEAN State of the Environment Report*, pp. 4–5.
10. "Biologists issue warning over deforestation in Indochina", Agence-France Presse, 24 March 2000 [via SEA-SPAN, *http://www.icsea.or.id/sea-span*].
11. Cross-border trade in illegal logs between Cambodia, Thailand, and Laos is a case in point, despite attempts by the Thai Government to maintain border controls and commitments by the Cambodian Government to crack down on illegal logging.
12. United Nations Environment Programme (UNEP), *Global Environmental Outlook 2000* (London: Earthscan, 2000), p. 76; and ASEAN Secretariat, *First ASEAN State of the Environment Report*, p. 2.
13. UNEP, op. cit., pp. 80; 82.
14. Asian Development Bank, *Asian Environmental Outlook 2001* (Manila: Asian Development Bank, 2000); see executive summary at *<http://www.adb.org>*.
15. Ibid., p. 209.

16. See Ian Townsend-Gault et al. "Transboundary Ocean and Atmospheric Pollution in Southeast Asia: Prospects for Regional Cooperation", in *New Challenges for ASEAN: Emerging Policy Issues*, edited by Amitav Acharya and Richard Stubbs (Vancouver: UBC Press, 1995), p. 32.
17. See, for example, partial estimates provided in Asian Development Bank, *Asian Environmental Outlook 2001*, p. 223.
18. Nagai Susumu, Shibata Tokue and Mizutani Yoichi, "The Accelerating Car Culture", in *The State of the Environment in Asia 1999/2000*, p.10.
19. James Schweithelm, *The Fire This Time: An Overview of Indonesia's Forest Fire in 1997/98* (Jakarta: WWF Indonesia Programme, 1998).
20. Asian Development Bank, *Asian Environmental Outlook 2001*, p. 223.
21. See ibid., pp. 224–27.
22. "Indonesia loses 4 billion in lost revenue every year", *Jakarta Post*, 1 November 1999 [via SEA-SPAN, archived at *http://www.icsea.or.id/sea-span*].
23. ASEAN Secretariat, *First ASEAN State of the Environment Report*, p. 5.
24. Food security is defined as existing "only when all people, at all times, have physical and economic access to sufficient safe and nutritious food to meet their dietary needs and food preferences for an active and healthy life" (Angelina Briones and Charmaine Ramos, "Market Forces and Food Security: The Case of Developing Asia", in *The Global Environment in the Twenty-first Century: Prospects for International Cooperation*, edited by Pamela S. Chasek (Tokyo: United Nations University Press, 2000), p. 223.
25. See Lorraine Elliott, "Environment, Development and Security in Asia-Pacific: Issues and Responses", in *Beyond the Crisis: Challenges and Opportunities*, edited by Mely C. Anthony and Mohamed Jawhar Hassan (Kuala Lumpur: ISIS Malaysia, 2000).
26. Muthiah Alagappa, "Environmental Governance — The Potential of Regional Institutions: Introduction", in *The Global Environment in the Twenty-first Century: Prospects for International Cooperation*, p. 257.
27. ASEAN Secretariat, *First ASEAN State of the Environment Report*, pp. 7–8.
28. See Peter Dauvergne, "Environmental Crisis", *Far Eastern Economic Review* 162, no. 28 (1999): 27.
29. Lim Teck Ghee and Mark J. Valencia. "Introduction", in *Conflict over Natural Resources in Southeast Asia and the Pacific*, edited by Lim Teck Ghee and Mark J. Valencia (Singapore: Oxford University Press, 1990), p. 6.
30. Cited in Peter Eng, "Transforming ASEAN", *Washington Quarterly* 22, no. 1 (1999): 55.
31. H. E. Mok Mareth, "Environment as a Catalyst for Asia Pacific Cooperation", in *Conference Report: Environmental Change and Regional Security*, edited by Kent Hughes Butts (Carlisle Barracks, PA: Centre for Strategic Leadership, 1997), p. VII–9.
32. Marian Miller, *The Third World in Global Environmental Politics* (Buckingham: Open University Press, 1995), p. 152.

EAST TIMOR'S FUTURE
Southeast Asian or South Pacific?[1]

Hal Hill

Introduction

Following on from the tragic events of September 1999, East Timor will shortly become the world's newest nation. Presumably, in time it will also become a member of the Association of Southeast Asian Nations (ASEAN). As it charts its way forward, one of the key challenges it faces will be to define its international economic orientation. Indonesia and Australia will always be East Timor's major trading partners and diplomatic focus, in addition to its membership of the Portuguese-speaking world.

However, there is a broader question of whether its world-view, and its political, economic and social institutions, will be predominantly "Southeast Asian" or "South Pacific". This is meant not simply in a geographic sense, since a case could be made for the fact that it belongs to either region. Nor is it addressing the issue of whether an independent East Timor will join both ASEAN and the Pacific Islands Forum (or whether it might even be forced to choose between them). Rather, it is the more fundamental question of whether its economic performance will more closely resemble that of its neighbours to its northwest or east. That is, will it be an outward-looking, growing and increasingly prosperous country, or a mendicant, aid-dependent state, with a bloated public sector and stagnant living standards. The latter, unfortunately, characterizes many of the Pacific Islands.[2]

In many respects, after the immediate task of rehabilitation is completed, East Timor will resemble a typical Pacific Island economy, albeit at the poorest end of the spectrum. It will be a large aid recipient, dependent also on remittances. Its institutions are weak, and its human capital resources rather limited. It is small, both in a geographic and a demographic sense, and rather isolated.

With its history of neglect and oppression, it is difficult to be optimistic about the future. The challenges might appear insuperable. Much of its physical infrastructure is shattered, while the supply of public utilities is most inadequate.

HAL HILL is Professor in the Division of Economics, Research School of Pacific and Asian Studies, The Australian National University.

More than 80,000 of its people are still located in squalid refugee camps across the border in West Timor, and in other parts of Indonesia. It does not possess a constitution, a political system, or a functioning bureaucracy. Much of its commercial expertise has fled the country — for example, its small ethnic Chinese community in 1975–76, and the Bugis traders from South Sulawesi in 1999. Many of its teachers and senior civil servants returned hastily to Indonesia in the second half of 1999, never to return. More than half the urban population does not have regular employment. The 22 per cent of the population who voted for autonomy (that is, against independence) still harbour deep resentment and fear. Some of these people, the so-called militia in particular, combined with disaffected elements of the Indonesian armed forces, threaten to disrupt peace and order.

However, there are some rays of hope. Unlike Portugal's former colonies in Africa, there are at least some prospects for stability and peace, both internal and external. Although pressures will emerge as political activity intensifies in the run-up to the inaugural general election (especially with more than ten political parties across the political spectrum vying for votes), the key elements of the East Timorese leadership appear to be reasonably united around the three major figures associated with the achievement of independence. They are its likely inaugural president, Xanana Gusmaõ, a long-time guerrilla leader and head of the National Council for Timorese Resistance (CNRT); the likely prime minister and foreign minister, José Ramos Horta, the movement's principal international spokesman for the past quarter century; and the spiritual leader and head of the Catholic Church (East Timor is about 95 per cent Catholic), Bishop Carlos Belo. Notwithstanding widespread bitterness in Indonesia, the administration of Abdurrahman Wahid, which came to power two months after the referendum and signalled a major break with the Soeharto era, has indicated a desire to develop a co-operative relationship with the new nation. Owing to its tragic history, the world is well disposed towards East Timor, and in consequence, international aid flows are large. As a new nation, there is much to learn from the mistakes of others in the realm of economic policy and public administration. Moreover, unlike other countries obtaining their independence in the wake of bitter conflict, East Timor's recent economic history and its resource base are fairly well documented. Finally, there is a substantial East Timorese diaspora abroad, many of whom have much to offer by way of expertize and investment.

The country is also not without commercial potential. A mini resource boom is in prospect, offering considerable medium-term revenue flows. Oil and gas could loom very large, and within a decade government revenues could be equivalent to as much as 50 per cent of current gross domestic product (GDP). The exact magnitude of these revenues will depend on negotiations with Australia concerning the demarcation of the Timor Gap, international oil prices, the Timorese's oil tax regime, and future explorations. Coffee also has good prospects, with annual exports of US$50 million or more considered feasible. The East Timor product commands a price premium in international markets, owing to its quality and the fact that it is certified to be free of pesticides. Already the U.S. coffee chain, Starbucks, features East Timorese coffee in some of its outlets. Tourism is another sector of great potential. East Timor is a region of great scenic beauty and superb beaches. Air services between Dili and the two major adjacent cities, Denpasar (Bali) and Darwin (Australia), have already resumed, and as the infrastructure is rebuilt, tourism can be expected to develop into a significant export industry. An obvious prerequisite for its expansion is the restoration of peace in the border regions with West Timor. Public health programmes, particularly malaria eradication, are also crucial.

It is important to emphasize just how low East Timor's starting point is. Its per capita income of about US$300 is one of the lowest in the world. Even if rapid economic growth of, say, 5 per cent per capita is achieved (approximately comparable to the record under the "normalization period" of Indonesian rule), it would take about twelve years to catch up with Indonesia's *current* income level. Slower growth, of 2 per cent per capita, would extend this period to fifty-five years.

Recent Developments
It is impossible to estimate with any precision the economic cost of the massive dislocation which occurred in September–October 1999. Some 70–80 per cent of buildings were destroyed, modern-sector commerce came to a halt, for several months there was no functioning government, and agricultural cycles were disrupted.

By late 1999, following pacification, an international rescue effort was mounted under the auspices of the United Nations, which established the United Nations Transitional Administration in East Timor (UNTAET). Initially, the relief effort focused on ensuring adequate food supplies, basic humanitarian assistance, and the most urgent infrastructure rehabilitation priorities. By early 2000, and with independence looming, the focus began to shift to medium-term issues associated with the foundation of a new state, including establishing a functioning bureaucracy, adopting monetary and exchange rate arrangements, and a fiscal policy framework.

Table 1 provides some rough indicators of economic activity and external support during the transition period. Growth in the last two full years of Indonesian rule slowed down as a consequence of the country's economic crisis, although the deceleration was not as marked as in other parts of Indonesia. There was then a calamitous decline in 1999, followed by economic recovery. It will take several years for a return to 1997 levels of economic activity. Per capita GDP estimates are impossible in the absence of reliable population figures. The data also indicate that living standards did not fall as sharply as GDP, since the share of consumption in GDP rose by about 50 per cent between 1999 and 2001. This in turn was facilitated by a large increase

TABLE 1
East Timor: Short-Term Economic Indicators

	1997	1998	1999	2000	2001
GDP ($ million)	383	375	228	263	303
GDP growth (real, %)	4	–2	–38	15	15
Consumption (% of GDP)	72	74	93	114	111
External savings (% of GDP)	25	21	21	52	55
Fiscal balance (% of GDP)	–67	–29	–36	–55	–35
Current account I (% of GDP)	–33	–29	–23	–52	–55
Current account II (% of GDP)	–6	–4	–2	–52	–55

NOTES: All figures are very approximate. Those for 2000 are estimated projections, while for 2001 they are simply projections. The data on fiscal balances refer to fiscal years 1997 to 1997–98, etc. Current account "I" and "II" refer to estimates excluding and including official transfers respectively.
SOURCES: Data provided by the East Timorese authorities.

in external savings, to over 50 per cent of GDP. Both fiscal and current account deficits were very large during the Indonesian period; they continue to be as international donors have quickly replaced the aid flows from Jakarta.

The civil service during Indonesian rule numbered approximately 33,000 persons. Initial estimates of the minimum requirements by the joint UN/World Bank Assessment mission in late 1999 suggested a total of about 12,000. With the imposition of a fiscal framework, including defined expenditure targets, and the CNRT's belief that the proposed civil service wages were too low, this number was reduced further to around 10,000. Whether such a figure, just 30 per cent of the pre-independence total, can be sustained in the face of international commitments and the powerful pressures for public sector employment — motivated by a desire for much-needed public programmes or simply patronage — remains to be seen. More recently, there are indications that the size of the civil service will expand.

The budget deficit initially proposed for FY 2000/01 was about 54 per cent of GDP, similar to that in the late (pre-crisis) Indonesian period and, likewise, entirely grant financed. This deficit will fall quickly as short-term humanitarian assistance begins to taper off. Revenue is projected to be about 6 per cent of GDP in 2000/01. In the first half of 2000, a number of revenue measures had already been introduced, or announced. These included a 5 per cent across-the-board import duty, various excise taxes, a 5 per cent sales tax, a 5 per cent tax on hotels, restaurants, accommodation, and vehicle rentals, a 5 per cent presumptive tax on coffee sales, and a 10 per cent wage tax.

Major Development Challenges

The task of nation-building is complicated at the best of times, but East Timor has to grapple with daunting challenges of physical reconstruction, reconciliation, the development of political institutions, and virtually every conceivable development policy issue. The focus of this section is the latter, but it is impossible to ignore the political and social backdrop — that is, a constitution has to be drafted, political parties are in the process of being established, peace in the country-side (and especially along the border with West Timor) has to be restored, and an inaugural general election has to be conducted.

A national language policy has to be decided. This is proving to be a particularly complex issue, with four languages being considered. There is Tetum, the *lingua franca* of East Timor, but considered to be insufficiently "scientific" for formal education and legal purposes. Secondly, there is Portuguese, which is spoken by just 5 per cent of the population, but it is preferred by much of the political élite, which has strong emotional ties to Portugal, viewing it as the only significant nation-state which sustained their struggle against Indonesian rule. The Portuguese-speaking world is making a determined effort to support the introduction of the language, including an offer to place a teacher in every secondary school. The nascent national university in Dili has a programme which plans to use Portuguese entirely as the language of instruction within a decade. The major international language is actually Bahasa Indonesia (diplomatically referred to as "Malay" in some circles), which is spoken by practically everybody under the age of 40 years, since universal primary education was introduced to the then province from the late 1970s. However, for obvious reasons, there is widespread political resistance to its adoption as an official national language. Finally, there is English, which is now quite widely spoken in Dili, given the large international presence, and also the returning East Timorese diaspora (the majority of whom lived in Australia in the period 1975–99).

Free of political constraints, a national language policy might recognize Tetum (and various regional dialects) as an informal social language, Indonesian/Malay as the national language, and English for the small educated élite and the international connections it confers. However, it appears that the pressure to adopt Portuguese as the official language may well be unstoppable. For a country with such limited educational and commercial resources, such a strategy may be costly.

Returning to development policy, the following are among the key challenges that the new nation is grappling with.

Macroeconomic Policy
This is obviously a critical policy area. Unless macroeconomic stability can be achieved, and "institutionalized", there is little prospect of rapid economic development. Here at least, there are some promising signs. In the case of monetary and exchange rate policy, it makes little sense for a tiny economy lacking basic financial institutions to attempt to run an independent policy regime. UNTAET has adopted the U.S. dollar as the Territory's legal tender during the interim period. Beyond this, there are reasonable prospects that a

similar arrangement will be adopted by an independent East Timor, perhaps in the form of a currency board (CB) system, under which the local currency will be pegged to a foreign currency, or basket of currencies.

The case of fiscal policy is more complicated and challenging. How quickly should East Timor aim for fiscal autonomy? How should it manage potentially large oil and gas revenues? And how should it fund its civil service, and what size should it be?

As the International Monetary Fund (IMF) and donors correctly emphasize, it is crucially important to develop a framework for expenditure and revenue flows, to educate the community not to expect across-the-board subsidies (especially to better-off urban dwellers), and to inculcate the expectation that taxes are necessary and have to be paid. This is especially so since, first, subsidies were a part of life during the Indonesian period; secondly, donor fatigue could — and probably will — set in quickly; and thirdly, the framework needs to be intact before the large oil revenue flows commence.

Conversely, within a coherent fiscal framework, there is a case for running a very large short-term (for example, in this and the next two or three financial years) fiscal deficit, and a significant one for the medium-term (the three or so financial years beyond this). This is provided the deficit can be aid-financed and relies minimally (if at all) on oil, and any subsidies are transparent and earmarked as short-term.

The rationale for such a strategy includes the following:

- There is a large task of national reconstruction, especially the stock of dwellings. Moreover, up to 80,000 refugees across the border may have to be re-absorbed into East Timorese society and its economy.
- It takes time to adjust from a period of large subsidies, of the type applicable during the Indonesian period. Moreover, while one would want to avoid as much as possible aid dependence à la the Pacific Islands, it is a reality that tiny, very poor countries do receive considerable long-term aid flows.
- There is a massive public sector adjustment to be made. The civil service has been cut by almost one-third from 1997 (about 33,000 persons down to 12,000; this figure includes also teachers and police). This group now has to run an entire nation, rather than function as a sort of distant "post office", as was more or less the case during the period of highly centralized rule from Jakarta. Ninety per cent of public servants are in the low-pay categories, but they are now expected to work a full working week, in contrast to the widespread moonlighting prevalent during the Indonesian period.
- In the transition period, major policy and institutional challenges have to be sorted out, and national institutions established. These include, for example: defining the legal system, including land and property ownership; developing institutions to deal with the rest of the world

(not least a diplomatic corps); and setting up a national statistical agency. There is also the major problem of dealing with so many aid agencies and programmes. (Donors are cooperating in principle, and no doubt substantially in practice, but they all want to have their own programmes recognized. They all have a tendency to favour capital works over maintenance, and they all want access to the top echelons of the over-stretched, tiny, internationally-educated East Timorese élite.) These will all involve much expense.

- In a country with a particularly traumatic recent history, deficiencies in core areas such as basic education and health need to be addressed more quickly than is usually the case, as the basis for constructing a viable civil society and achieving sustainable economic development.
- It takes time to establish effective tax collection procedures.

It is therefore not surprising that fiscal policy issues are among the most difficult and hotly debated. The general principles of fiscal prudence and caution, user-pays for most public services, a lean civil service remunerated at market levels, and as broad a tax net as possible are critical. However, much revolves around the question of how long the transition period can and should last, and how large the subsidies and hence the deficit should be in the next three to five years. This in turn requires some assessment of the capacity of the emerging political system to get off the "subsidy drip" after the transition period. The more pessimistic the assessment of this issue, the stronger is the case for pushing quickly for a tough fiscal stance to be in place by independence.

On the horizon, as noted, oil and gas are likely to loom large in the East Timorese economy, with revenue flows perhaps equivalent to as much as 50 per cent of government revenue within a decade. It is impossible to overstate the importance of effective management of these resources. They provide undreamed of wealth, and if used wisely could provide the basis for rapid and sustained development. However, the experience with resource booms in so many countries has been disastrous — that is, widespread corruption, enrichment of a tiny, politically connected élite, government waste and inefficiency, and the familiar "Dutch disease" impact on the non-oil tradeable sectors. It will be imperative to keep most of the oil revenue outside the government's routine budget. Placing them in some sort of offshore escrow account would appear to be the best solution.

Trade and Openness
East Timor has very little choice other than to maintain an open trade regime. Its sea and land boundaries with the rest of eastern Indonesia are so porous that high trade barriers would almost certainly be circumvented by smuggling. By late 2000, it was already clearly evident that there was extensive, unofficially sanctioned trade across the East–West Timor land boundary, even though in principle this boundary was officially sealed off.

International transport networks have been restored, as noted, though there may be problems with monopolies. Informal small-scale shipping networks are thought to be developing again. Domestically, there is the question of whether the extensive road network constructed during the Indonesian period can be maintained by an Independent East Timor. There is also the question of how to re-establish shipping networks to the isolated enclave of Oecussi.

The trade regime thus far is clear and open — that is, a 5 per cent across-the-board import duty, plus a fairly widespread 5 per cent surcharge. Customs procedures are now simple and straightforward. As with tax policy, it is important to keep duty exemptions to an absolute minimum. *Yayasan* (non-governmental organizations or NGOs) loom as a potential problem in both cases. Understandably, an administration in urgent need of revenue has turned to these duties as a quick and simple source of funds. However, notwithstanding the difficulties, it would seem desirable to shift towards some sort of turnover tax as quickly as possible, so as to avoid the temptation of using duties as protective devices.

Property Rights and the Legal System

Land titling is a complex issue in all societies in which there is an ill-defined blend of traditional and modern commercial legal systems. However, there is evidence to suggest that, owing to East Timor's turbulent history, the problem is particularly daunting there. Currently, land in East Timor can be claimed under four bases: underlying traditional interests, Portuguese-era titles, Indonesia-era titles, or occupation since the 1999 vote for independence. Most land title offices were apparently destroyed by the departing militias and troops in 1999, and in the process most records were lost. Before that, during the Indonesian period, land under Portuguese control or in Fretilin-sympathetic areas was apparently appropriated by the military. In addition, the sizeable population exodus of 1975 and 1999 have meant that there is an international East Timorese community with outstanding land title claims. Resolving these claims will be a protracted and complex issue, but one which deserves the highest priority. Land disputes and illegal squatting are already widespread. Since a functioning judiciary is barely in place, it may make sense to adopt a lease system in the transitional period, under which land subject to dispute — or likely to be — can be leased for a specified time period (perhaps 5–20 years, depending on the activity), subject to a clear medium-term resolution.

Competitiveness

A major problem of competitiveness seems to be emerging in East Timor. As would be expected, the "expatriate economy" operates on the basis of Darwin (North Australia) plus prices. However, the East Timorese economy is also expensive, partly, the result of cost-push pressures resulting from the international presence. Even for East Timorese markets, goods are highly priced. Dili was always expensive in Indonesian times (with at least a 20–40 per cent differential compared to Java). Impressionistic evidence suggests that this differential may now be as much as 100 per cent for many simple consumer goods. This is obviously serious, and will build in a high cost structure. Already, minimum daily wages in the public sector are at least US$4, and these set the benchmark for the tiny "formal" private sector. In the coffee estates, apparently daily wages are about US$3, which is two to three times those in Indonesia.

Related to this is the challenge of public sector wage policy. Wage scales are compressed, with maximum monthly wages of US$800, and approximately a 5:1 differential between top and bottom (excluding the five East Timorese Cabinet members who each receive US$2,000 per month). For a US$300 per capita economy, the minimum is rather high. However, conversely, wages at the top are too low to attract the necessary skills, a problem especially complicated since the "supply price" among the qualified pool — mainly the "diaspora", since the higher echelon Indonesians have returned home — is more or less what they were earning or at least could earn abroad (most now have foreign passports). Some in addition have commitments abroad (for example, children's education) which effectively rule them out from the civil service.

There is, in addition, a general problem of acute skill shortages. This may become less serious when the United Nations departs, but it will certainly remain. To avoid relying on the expensive North Australian labour market, East Timor will need to tap into more competitive East Asian labour markets. Barring Indonesia, the Philippines is the most likely alternative (as has occurred, for example, in neighbouring Papua New Guinea).

Perhaps these are transitional problems, and as expatriates depart, transport networks and commercial relations with Indonesia improve, prices will fall. Meanwhile, a regular shipping service between Surabaya and Dili has been operating for several months, and the impact has not yet been felt. There may be a broader problem of international transport networks, in that all the providers are monopolists, although in principle the markets should be contestable. For example, in the case of air transport, the operators are Merpati (Denpasar-Dili) and Air North, an Ansett subsidiary (Darwin-Dili). Tickets for both are very expensive by international standards. For sea transport, there is one shipping line each from Surabaya and Darwin. In addition, and perhaps partly eroding monopoly rents, there is, as noted, considerable cross-border (that is, East–West Timor) illegal trade.

These cost issues raise the broader question of who will want to invest in the country. The potential should be considerable, especially from among the approximately 80,000 East Timorese diaspora abroad. Currently, not surprisingly, most investments are going into the quick-yielding construction, hotel, and restaurant sectors. Among the problems investors face are:

- Highly insecure ownership arrangements, especially for land.
- Higher cost structures than potential competitors (that is, competitors for footloose investment), such as Indonesia and Vietnam. Wages are much higher in East Timor, as are utilities charges.

- While the use of the U.S. dollar is sensible as a means of securing macroeconomic policy objectives, East Timor is linked to a strong currency, and will most likely have a fairly rigid labour market. Thus, the option of boosting competitiveness via a nominal depreciation which "sticks" (that is, a real effective depreciation) is not available.
- Acute shortages of skilled and semi-skilled labour (for example, electricians, mechanics) for which Darwin prices (which are in turn high by Australian standards) apply.
- Poor infrastructure, including uncertain power supplies (generator back-up is essential). Most businesses use the (expensive) Telstra mobile telephone network.
- Inevitable uncertainty about post-independence policy directions.
- The absence of a modern financial sector. The foreign banks now present — BNU from Portugal, and Australia's Westpac — are obviously reluctant to accept any local collateral in connection with loan applications.
- The absence of a legal code, and any effective form of legal protection.

Social Policy and Urban Bias

East Timor's social indicators are understandably very poor, notwithstanding considerable educational advances during the Indonesian period. Here, priorities matter enormously. Resources allocated to one activity represent forgone opportunities elsewhere. Already, there is the danger of an emerging urban bias, particularly around the capital, Dili, fostered by labour market and social policies, and in consequence of very large aid flows (and oil revenue in prospect).

In education, for example, on both equity and efficiency grounds, it makes sense to concentrate subsidies at primary and junior secondary levels (as was broadly the case under Indonesian rule). For higher levels, it makes sense to invoke the user-pays principle since the gap between the social and private returns to education narrows. However, fear of student protests, and a view that a national university is an important symbol of nation-building, has already begun to result in a reallocation of resources from the primary to the tertiary sectors.

Similarly, in the case of public health expenditures, the highest social returns are likely to be achieved through, for example, public programmes of disease eradication, the provision of potable water supplies, the provision of basic community health services throughout the country, and mass inoculation campaigns, rather than in investments in expensive, high-tech public hospitals. There appears to be an emerging — and probably inevitable — "Dili bias". This refers not just to the expatriate presence, but more fundamentally to key elements of the emerging policy regime, elements which are supported as much by East Timorese as U.N. officials. Examples include: (a) a relatively high minimum wage in the public sector, pushed up in part by high prices, as noted above; (b) the danger that some public utilities will be subsidized; and (c) the provision of middle-class social subsidies.

Conclusion

East Timor is a new nation quite literally being reconstructed "out of the ashes".[3] In more normal circumstances, this would be an exciting challenge — writing a constitution, developing political, legal and educational institutions, and charting the way forward on economic policy.

However, times are anything but normal. The East Timorese people are very poor, and they have lived under very harsh conditions in the last two years. Before that, they experienced a quarter century of troubled rule from Jakarta, and centuries of neglect from Lisbon. Everything is urgent, from holding an election to rebuilding schools and ensuring adequate food supplies. Aid supplies and international commitments are currently plentiful, but this window of opportunity may be fleeting. There will be other crises around the world which will divert international attention, and donor fatigue is a problem everywhere, especially when the inevitable domestic (East Timorese) political squabbles erupt, and tales of corruption and waste in government surface. The Portuguese world is currently very supportive, but it is distant, small, and unlikely to have the resources available to make a durable commitment to East Timor's development.

Against this backdrop, these are crucial times in East Timor. If it is able to lay the foundations for political cohesion and stability, social harmony, and good economic policy, it could in time emerge as a prosperous state, at peace — and integrated — with its neighbourhood, in which its citizens enjoy steadily rising living standards. That is what most of the people of Southeast Asia have come to expect, at least prior to the recent crisis. The alternative scenario is the "South Pacific" one, of socio-economic stagnation, political division, and regional instability. The next few years will give us important clues as to which path East Timor is likely to travel.

NOTES

1. This chapter draws on the author's ongoing collaborative research on East Timor with members of the East Timor Study Group, which included fieldwork in November 2000 and January 2001. Some of the issues mentioned here are examined in more detail in the author's forthcoming paper, "Tiny, Poor and War-torn: Development Policy Challenges for East Timor", *World Development,* July 2001. See also Helder Da Costa, "Building East Timor's Economy: The Roles of Foreign Aid, Trade and Investment" (Ph.D. dissertation, University of Adelaide, Adelaide, 2000).
2. For a detailed recent analysis of South Pacific development issues, see R.S. Duncan, S. Cuthbertson, and M. Bosworth, *Pursuing Economic Reform in the Pacific,* Pacific Studies Series No. 18 (Manila: Asian Development Bank, 1999).
3. This borrows the phrase from J.J. Fox and D.B. Soares, eds., *Out of the Ashes: Destruction and Reconstruction of East Timor* (Adelaide: Crawford House Publishing, 2000).

BRUNEI
DARUSSALAM

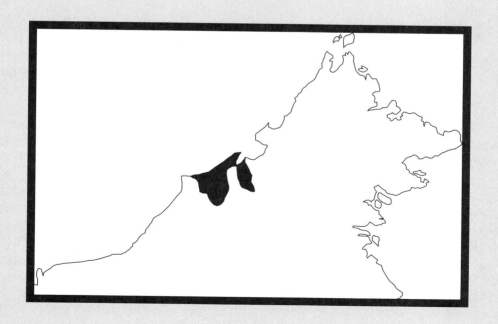

NEGARA BRUNEI DARUSSALAM
Economic Gloom and the APEC Summit

A.V.M. Horton

During 2000, the seventeenth year of Negara Brunei Darussalam's full independence, there were two main themes, namely, concerns about the economy, and the Asia-Pacific Economic Co-operation (APEC) summit. To these may be added a rift within the royal family, which at the time of writing (December 2000) has not been completely healed.

Royal Family Rift

His Royal Highness (HRH) Prince Jefri Bolkiah, a younger brother of His Majesty (HM) the Sultan, has held vizier rank (as *Pengiran Digadong*) since 1979. When the sultanate regained full independence at the beginning of 1984 he became Minister of Culture, Youth and Sport, doubling as Deputy Minister of Finance. After the death of the Seri Begawan Sultan in September 1986, he was promoted to Minister of Finance, a post he held from 20 October 1986 until 23 February 1997. Even thereafter, he played an important role in state affairs, continuing, for example, as Chairman of the Brunei Investment Agency (BIA) until mid-1998. Then two major internal scandals erupted in quick succession. First, the Amedeo Development Corporation, a company associated with Prince Jefri, collapsed in 1998, allegedly leaving debts of B$6,000 million; winding up procedures commenced in July 1999 but as at November 2000 creditors were still awaiting repayment. Secondly, in late February 2000 the Negara Brunei Darussalam (NBD) government began legal proceedings against Prince Jefri for alleged improper use of BIA funds during his tenure at the agency. The prince, who had been spending long periods in exile since 1998, denied any wrongdoing and vigorously contested the charges. At length, in May 2000, a settlement was reached out of court. Under the agreement, personal assets said to have been acquired using BIA funds were to be resumed by the state. The essential thing now is for the royal brothers to close ranks; according to one analyst, however, "the saga of the feuding royal family looks set to continue".

A.V.M. Horton is an Honorary Fellow of the Centre for Southeast Asian Studies, University of Hull, England.

Associates of Prince Jefri were energetically pursued by the authorities. In late November, for example, Haji Awang bin Kassim, 51, a former Deputy Managing Director of the BIA, was released on bail of B\$50 million. He was ordered to surrender his passport and to report twice daily to the Anti-Corruption Bureau. The case was then adjourned until 31 January 2001.[1]

Prince Jefri's fall from grace notwithstanding, the existing political establishment has survived remarkably unscathed. The continuing commitment of the *rakyat* to the MIB (Melayu, Islam Beraja) project was amply demonstrated on National Day (23 February 2000) and again on *Hari Keputeraan* (15 July 2000), the latter occasion marking the fifty-fourth birthday of HM the Sultan. The monarchy has been firmly rooted in the national soil for centuries; but even an institution as resilient as the NBD royal family would be unwise to risk any further waves. Sterling work is done by HM the Raja Isteri, by HRH the Pengiran Isteri, by HRH the Perdana Wazir (who published an autobiography, *Time and the River*, in August 2000), and by HRH Princess Masna, Ambassador-at-large. The younger generation also shows promise: HRH Crown Prince Al-Muhtadee Billah (installed on 10 August 1998) has been taking on an increasing workload of public duties in preparation for his future role as leader of the country. His Royal Highness is already trusted to act as Deputy Sultan when His Majesty travels overseas. Another emerging royal is HRH Prince Abdul Qawi, son of the Perdana Wazir, who is Deputy Executive Director of QAF Brunei Group, one of the largest commercial concerns in the sultanate.

Governmental stability has been maintained. There has been no free election nor party political activity worthy of the name (since 1962), and, despite the occasional reshuffle, no new blood in the Cabinet (since 1989). It might be noticed here, however, that two new permanent secretaries were appointed on 12 May 2000: Dato Zakaria Noordin at the Ministry of Development, and Haji Abdul Rahman Ibrahim at the Ministry of Industry.

In late March, plans were announced for a "transformation of governance" involving greater transparency and less regulation. Meanwhile, His Majesty pays unannounced visits to government departments in order to keep civil servants on their toes.

Economic Gloom

The priority for 2000 was economic recovery. NBD's economy grew by 2.5 per cent in 1999, compared with 4 per cent negative growth in 1998. In January 2000, 3 per cent growth was forecast for the year 2000. The price of crude oil continued its ascent, a matter of no small importance to a country whose hydrocarbon sector contributes perhaps half of national gross domestic product (GDP) and the overwhelming bulk of export value. On 1 October 1999, Brent crude stood at US\$23.59 per barrel on the London market, the Shell share price at £4.54; by the start of trading on 1 December 2000, the indicators were US\$32.45 and £5.56 respectively, peaks of US\$34.26 and £6.27 having been attained in the interim.

Within the sultanate, leaded petrol was removed from sale on 1 March 2000. Then, on 28 September, the Brunei Shell Petroleum Company (BSPC) began a drilling programme at the onshore Seria oilfield with the aim of doubling production there to 45,000 barrels per day.[2] A new market for NBD oil was found in China (see the foreign affairs section, below); and in July, India expressed a vague interest in purchasing NBD hydrocarbons. A contract for a masterplan study on downstream oil and gas industries was signed with the government on 13 April 2000 by Dover Consultants Pty Limited of Australia in co-operation with a local firm (Syed Muhammad and Hooi) of consulting engineers. On 29 July, Petroleum Geo-Services of Houston and Oslo won a contract to conduct an offshore seismic survey, due to be completed by the end of 2001. With regard to company news, it emerged in October 2000 that Shell had made a bid to take over Fletcher Challenge Energy, a New Zealand company with interests in NBD; at the time of writing, one or two obstacles remained to be cleared before the deal could be finalized.[3] Elf-Aquitaine, a French multinational whose assets include the Maharaja Lela field in the South China Sea, merged with TotalFina during 1999–2000, thereby creating the fourth-largest energy conglomerate in the world.

The buoyant oil market has not solved all the sultanate's difficulties. The ordinary government budget (excluding investment income) showed a deficit of B\$500 million in 1998, and a shortfall of B\$1,000 million was predicted for 1999. The deficit for 2000 was expected to be half of that of the previous year.[4] Taxation authorities became more strict in collection, and welfare services were trimmed. Although government fiscal worries should have eased as the year progressed, there will certainly be no return to the halcyon days of 1979–80: in real terms, oil is still worth only one-third of what it was then. Conversely, the NBD government needs to restrict its own spending because of recent budget deficits. Worst hit in the "ailing economy" has been the service sector, especially the construction, retail, and hotel trades. There is a glut in the property market. Thousands of foreign workers have been repatriated. About six thousand local people continue to be registered with the Labour Department as looking for work. Youth unemployment is particularly severe: even graduates returning from an expensive university education overseas find few jobs waiting for them. The after-effects of the collapse of the Amedeo Corporation in 1998 are still being felt; the sultanate is littered with abandoned construction projects; and some of those which had been completed are white elephants.

The longer-term outlook for hydrocarbons may not be very bright either. In an interview published in the *Sunday Telegraph* (London) on 25 June 2000, a former Saudi oil minister, Sheik Yamani, warned that "after five years there will be a sharp drop in the price of oil" because of excessive supply, coupled with lower demand caused by the introduction of new technologies, such as cell-fuel cars;[5] and within thirty years there would be "a huge amount of oil" but "no buyers". The Stone Age did not come to an end because of a shortage of stone. The implications of these views for NBD are serious, confronting the sultanate with a nightmare scenario which nobody had envisaged hitherto. The logic of Sheikh Yamani's position was that, instead of conserving reserves, NBD ought to pump out its oil as quickly as possible while there remains a market for it.

The Brunei National Economic Council (BDEC), chaired by HRH the Perdana Wazir, held its first meeting on 5 August 1998 to consider a programme of economic reform. According to the Council, the current position is simply unsustainable: "Income growth is unable to keep up with population growth, a budget deficit has reduced the government's ability to provide direct employment, and the private sector is weak". Since 1985, NBD's economy had been growing at an average rate of only 1.25 per cent a year whereas the population had been expanding twice as fast; hence, there has been a continuing slippage in gross national product per capita. Higher economic growth, the diagnosis ran, depended upon economic diversification away from the hydrocarbon sector; an estimated 2,500 new jobs a year were needed, and private sector employment would have to double by 2011.[6]

The Council's Report, released in February 2000, envisaged a two-stage approach. First, there would be an immediate "stimulus package" of B$200 million in order to inject liquidity into the economy and restore confidence. The money would be directed towards small businesses. The BDEC recommended that government housing projects be accelerated and that the relevant authorities identify within one month one hundred small-scale tourism facilities for APEC 2000. The Ministry of Communications should be required forthwith to implement plans for extending information technology into public services, schools, and homes. Three thousand job seekers should be trained in hospitality skills for deployment during APEC 2000. Banks should be mobilized to provide easier financial assistance to entrepreneurs.

Secondly, there was to be a longer-term "strategy for sustainable growth". Privatization was recommended as a means to control government expenditure, eliminate waste, and reduce the size of the public sector. Suitable targets for sell-off included telecommunications, water supply, and electrical services, together with the Employees' Trust Fund, the Muara Container Terminal, the Meragang Hatchery, and the Department of Stores, Supplies and Information Technology. Tax reform and removal of subsidies were urged.

The Perdana Wazir, who seems to have been the principal beneficiary of Prince Jefri's downfall, was himself appointed to implement the policy; and on 20 March, a secretariat was established. The action plan notwithstanding, six months later bankruptcies reached a disturbing level and business confidence remained low.

Despite the minus factors just outlined, a sense of balance needs to be retained. In reality, as analysed in greater detail later, Negara Brunei Darussalam remains one of the most blessed countries on the planet, and overall its inhabitants enjoy an enviable standard of living. Many Chancellors of the Exchequer elsewhere in the world would be delighted to be harassed by the "problems" facing a sultanate still able to provide work to more than eighty thousand foreigners.

In July-August, plans were unveiled for the establishment of a Brunei International Financial Centre, designed to make NBD a centre for banking, securities, and insurance. High priority was placed on the development of a niche market in Islamic financing and the prevention of money-laundering. The sultanate was co-operating with Malaysia and Bahrain in the founding of an Islamic Financial Market. It was also announced that the Brunei Development Bank was to be renamed the Islamic Development Bank of Brunei; His Majesty officially opened the bank's headquarters at Kiulap on 11 November 2000.[7] Finally, a new regulation was introduced that will require all companies in the sultanate to use International Accounting Standards (IAS) for their financial statements by 2002.[8]

The APEC summit certainly helped to alleviate the unemployment problem in the short term by providing work in the service sector; and it is possible that at least some of these jobs will be sustained during Visit Brunei Year (VBY), 2001. Hotels were less empty during the summit, but an anticipated retail boom failed to materialize; one reporter gathered the impression that "foreign delegates are not scrambling to pour money into the local economy".[9]

Plans for VBY 2001 preceded the BDEC report, but they certainly reflect the thirst for diversification (which actually dates at least as far back as the 1950s). A vigorous "kingdom of unexpected treasures" promotion is under way, designed to sell the sultanate around the world. It is hoped to attract one million visitors and income of B$225 million. The country could offer "pristine rainforest, top-class resorts and crime-free streets"; it would be promoted as a family destination as well as a gateway to Borneo and the world of ecotourism. Target markets were the ASEAN countries, Japan, Hong Kong, Taiwan, Australia, Germany, and the United Kingdom. The VBY programme includes an international Islamic arts exhibition, a *silat* festival, a gastronomic event, and the sixth ASEAN Science and Technology Fair. The large Ulu Temburong National Park was advanced as another pole of attraction.

As long ago as 1995, HM the Sultan had stated: "In an effort to diversify the national economy, my government is committed to the development of a tourist industry in this country". At present, however, tourism contributes less than one per cent of the sultanate's GDP. Sheikh Jamaluddin, Director of Tourism Development, warned that the oil and gas industry had a finite lifespan. "We want to ensure that employment is always there for our people, and tourism will ensure that". NBD did not wish to compete with other Southeast Asian destinations, but sought to add to the tourism value of the region as a whole. Sheikh Jamaluddin noted that some facilities in the sultanate needed to be improved, such as night-life, taxi services, souvenir shops, and resort hotels.[10]

On 28 June, it emerged that His Majesty's Government had approved a six-month study by a local firm of consultants, who were to prepare a Strategic

Plan designed to increase the involvement of Brunei Malays in economic activity.

APEC Summit

The eighth APEC Leaders' Summit was chaired by His Majesty the Sultan in Bandar Seri Begawan, on 15–16 November 2000. Founded eleven years ago, APEC is an international body comprising Pacific Rim economies dedicated to trade and investment liberalization. Following the accession of Vietnam, Russia and Peru in 1998, the organization encompasses twenty-one states, contributing 40 per cent of the world's population, 45 per cent of world trade, and a combined GDP in 1996 of US$16 trillion. During the Bogor summit of November 1994, APEC members agreed to work towards the establishment of a free trade zone by 2020; developed economies were expected to reach the target ten years earlier. Individual Action Plans were adopted by each country at Manila in 1996.[11]

The 2000 informal summit, which had been given the theme "Delivering to the Community", drew to Bandar Seri Begawan the leaders of the twenty-one member states, including Presidents Clinton, Jiang Zemin, and Putin. Some six thousand visitors were anticipated. It was undoubtedly the most high-profile event ever to have been staged by the sultanate and a severe test of a small country's logistical capabilities. The test appears to have been passed with flying colours. There were none of the disorderly scenes which had marred recent international conferences at Seattle and Prague.

In a twenty-three-page declaration released at the end of the summit,[12] APEC leaders reaffirmed their "commitment to the Bogor goals of free and open trade and investment". Signs of recovery after the recent Asian economic crisis were most encouraging; but oil-price volatility remained a threat. Later sections of the document were devoted to "Managing Globalisation", "Creating New Opportunities", "Strengthening the Multilateral Trading System", and "Making APEC Matter More". There were also several annexes.

Cynics tend to regard APEC as merely a "talking shop"; but President Clinton claimed that developing economies within the organization had fared much better during the 1990s than non-members. Malaysia's Trade Minister, Dato' Rafidah Aziz, stressed the importance of APEC's Economic and Technical Co-operation initiative, designed to bring the group's work closer to the Asia-Pacific people through information technology, youth, and women's issues. Besides the main conference agenda, there was much activity at the fringe: Presidents Clinton and Putin had a 75-minute working lunch, for example, at which they discussed arms control and strategic stability; similarly, President Kim Dae-Jung and Prime Minister Mori met privately to consider the North Korea issue. Singapore and New Zealand signed a comprehensive bilateral free trade agreement.[13]

The summit marked the conclusion of a series of meetings which had been taking place in NBD (and elsewhere) throughout the year. Many of the less-wealthy member-states complained, indeed, about the cost of having to send representatives to the various meetings. There were, for example, no fewer than three gatherings of senior foreign ministry officials during 2000. The needs of women and small businesses were addressed in June. Hence, the fifth meeting of the Women Leaders Network (founded in 1996) was held in Bandar Sri Begawan on 17–20 June 2000;[14] similarly, a Small Business Forum (including a ministerial meeting) was held in the sultanate on 20–24 June. The APEC Business Advisory Council (ABAC), on which each member-state has three representatives, advised leaders of the concerns of the private sector.

State Visits

The APEC summit was framed by state visits to the sultanate by President Kim Dae-Jung of South Korea (immediately before), and President Jiang Zemin of the People's Republic of China (immediately afterwards).

At a state banquet on 13 November, His Majesty noted that the visit by Nobel-laureate Kim offered "a unique opportunity to reaffirm ties and explore new areas of cooperation between NBD and the Republic of Korea". The sultanate looked forward to developing contacts with South Korea at government-to-government and private sector levels. Technology transfer and assistance in the education and training of the people would be welcome. As a first step, an agreement concerning the reciprocal protection of investments between the two countries would be signed on 14 November. The Korean President noted that the importance of NBD was growing by the day as a source of energy supply. In bilateral discussions, the two leaders also touched upon the problems faced by Hyundai, a Korean company.[15]

Diplomatic relations were established between NBD and China on 30 September 1991, although Chinese links with Borneo actually stretch back well over a thousand years. HM the Sultan had visited Beijing in November 1993 and August 1999. During President Jiang Zemin's state visit (17–18 November 2000), the first by a Chinese head of state to the sultanate, three economic agreements were signed. The most important MOU (memorandum of understanding) was a one-year renewable Sale of Oil Agreement between the Brunei Shell Petroleum Company and the China International United Petroleum and Chemicals Company (UNIPEC) for ten thousand barrels per day of Champion Export Crude Oil. This was the first time the sultanate had secured a presence in the Chinese market, whilst for UNIPEC, the agreement represented a further step in its efforts to secure supplies of high quality crude oil from a variety of sources. The second MOU involved the encouragement and reciprocal protection of investments. The third aimed to establish NBD as an "official tourism destination", thereby enabling Chinese tourists to visit the country in greater numbers. A number of approved travel agencies had been nominated for use by tour groups of no fewer than five people; independent travellers were not affected.

Earlier in the year (31 January to 2 February), a State Visit was paid to NBD by HM the Yang Di-Pertuan Agong of Malaysia, Sultan Salahuddin Abdul Aziz Shah Al-Haj of Selangor.[16] Other eminent visitors to Bandar Seri Begawan included President Abdurrahman Wahid (27 February), General Pervez Musharraf (31 March to 2 April), Xanana Gusmaõ of East Timor (late May), Kate Carnell, Chief Minister of the Australian Capital Territory (mid-July), Hun Sen (19–21 August),[17] the Earl and Countess of Wessex (25–27 October), Dr Mahathir Mohamad (late October), Lee Kuan Lew (early November), and Chelsea Clinton (accompanying her father during the APEC Summit). His Majesty's birthday guests on 15 July ranged from long-standing family-favourite Princess Basma of Jordan to newcomers such as Lord Powell of Bayswater.

Diplomatic relations were established during the year with Lesotho (30 March), Kazakhstan (14 June), Latvia (14 July), El Salvador (28 August), Tanzania (6 October) and Malawi (11 October). NBD now maintains links with well over one hundred countries and, as at July 1999, had thirty-two permanent missions abroad. HM the Sultan has quickly established a close rapport with the new monarchs of Jordan, Morocco, and Bahrain. Ties with Africa were further upgraded by the exchange of state visits with President Rawlings of Ghana. Working visits were paid to Canada and to existing friends in Southeast Asia and the Middle East. His Majesty graced the United Nations Millennium Summit with his presence in early September, and on 30 June was awarded the President's Gold Medal by the Royal College of Surgeons of Edinburgh.

NBD and Vietnam signed an MOU on the formation of a joint commission for bilateral co-operation on 14 June 2000.[18] An "open skies" agreement was reached with the United States on 15 November; and on the same day, NBD and Russia concluded a "bilateral consultation protocol" designed to strengthen co-operation between the two countries in various fields of mutual interest. On 24 November, HM the Sultan attended the fourth ASEAN Informal Summit in Singapore; the main event was the signing of an e-ASEAN Framework Agreement.[19]

Military

The Brunei Malay Regiment was founded on 31 May 1961 and granted the prefix "Royal" four years later. The organization was renamed Angkatan Bersenjata Diraja Brunei (ABDB or the Royal Brunei Armed Forces) upon the attainment of full independence at the beginning of 1984. A re-organization in 1991 resulted in the establishment, under the ABDB umbrella, of the Royal Brunei Land Forces, the Royal Brunei Navy, and the Royal Brunei Air Force. There are various other military units, including the Company of Women Soldiers (Kompeni Askar Wanita), founded in 1981.

Major-General Shari Ahmad has commanded the ABDB since 31 August 1999. On 7 April 2000, Pehin Colonel Mohammad Yusof bin Abu Bakar formally assumed duty as Officer Commanding (OC) Royal Brunei Armed Forces

Services, one of the "other military units" just mentioned. His predecessor, Pehin Colonel Mohd Jaafar bin Haji Abdul Aziz, had long since been appointed OC Royal Brunei Land Forces (October 1999).

In the fourth quarter of 1999, there were two developments worth mentioning. First, "Maju Bersama", a joint NBD-Singapore exercise, was held in *ulu* Tutong and Belait on 8-14 October. Secondly, at Bukit Agok Range on 9 November, the Royal Brunei Air Force revealed its latest purchase of hardware, namely, a French-made anti-aircraft guided-missile system. An Air Regiment had been formed at the beginning of 1999 under the command of Lieutenant-Colonel Hamid Nayan specifically to manage the new weapon, which has a range of four miles.

During 2000, Negara Brunei Darussalam continued to foster its military links with long-standing allies and friends, both within the region (notably Singapore and Malaysia) and further afield. Military visitors also trooped to the sultanate from Indonesia, the Philippines, and Thailand. Regular military exercises were staged with Singapore, Australia, and the United States. A ten-day joint NBD-Singapore military exercise, "Latihan Rintis Bersama II", ended on 27 March 2000. Then, on 21–26 July, the Royal Brunei Navy and the Royal Australian Navy co-operated in the "Penguin 2000" exercise. This was reportedly the tenth such exercise since the series commenced in 1980. CARAT (Cooperation Afloat Readiness and Training), a five-day military training exercise involving 750 personnel of the Royal Brunei and U.S. navies, began on 7 August.

The sixth meeting of the NBD-Malaysia Defence Cooperation Committee was held on 31 July at Berakas. The committee was established following an MOU between the two governments signed on 14 February 1992.

On 12 July, HM the Sultan visited the British Army Garrison at Seria in order to bid farewell to the Second Battalion of the Royal Gurkha Rifles. The unit was to be replaced by the 1,000-strong First Battalion Royal Gurkha Rifles, which was expected to arrive from the United Kingdom early in September following peace-keeping duties in Kosovo.

Police and Law and Order
The Brunei Police Force was founded on 1 January 1921 and granted the "Royal" prefix on 23 September 1965. Dato Paduka Seri Haji Yaakub bin Pehin Zainal has been Commissioner since 11 March 1997. On 4 May 2000, Haji Abdul Rahman Johan, acting Deputy Commissioner, was confirmed in the substantive office.

Various manoeuvres were staged. For example, the seventh "Brusing", a joint NBD-Singapore police training exercise, was held in the sultanate on 7-20 October 1999. "Latihan Sembilang Siri 1/2000", an exercise involving the Royal Brunei Navy and the Marine Police, was held on 15–17 May 2000. There were also security exercises prior to the APEC Summit.

The total number of reported crimes in the country increased from 2,750 cases in 1998 to 3,085 in 1999, equivalent to an annual rate not far short of one infringement per hundred inhabitants. Offences against the person (such as murder, child abuse, rape) totalled 401 cases in 1999, a fairly sharp jump from the 338 incidents during the previous year. Misdemeanours involving property (such as burglary) increased from 1,230 to 1,281. (By November 1999, the Neighbourhood Watch Scheme, initiated ten years earlier, had almost ten thousand participants). The incidence of commercial crime (such as currency forgery) rose from 357 reports to 388. "Law violation activities" soared from 825 cases in 1998 to 1,015 in 1999. The principal offence under this heading is drug abuse: 286 arrests were made in 1990, 508 in 1994, 510 in 1997, and 558 in 1999. In mid-April 2000, the dangers of *dadah* were emphasized in Friday sermons throughout the sultanate and in a special broadcast by RTB (Radio-Televisyen Brunei). International Anti-Narcotics Day was observed on 26 June 2000; and a bilateral meeting was held at BSB on 17 August between the Narcotics Control Bureau of NBD and its Malaysian counterpart.[20] At the thirty-third meeting of ASEAN Foreign Ministers, held in Bangkok on 24–25 July, the deadline for a drug-free ASEAN was brought forward from 2020 to 2015.

There were 14,680 breaches of traffic regulations during 1999. This was despite repeated efforts made by the government to spread its road safety message. No fewer than 2,782 road accidents happened in 1999, involving sixty-four serious injuries and forty-five fatalities. It was announced that the government would re-examine the driving school curriculum. Yet in January-August 2000, there were another 1,894 accidents causing twenty-six deaths, and resulting in damage estimated at more than B\$13 million.[21]

Fire is a continual hazard in the sultanate, with Kampong Ayer (BSB's "water village") appearing to be particularly vulnerable to serious conflagrations. Islamic charitable organizations quickly come to the support of victims. Hence, on 24 March 2000, the Sultan Haji Hassanal Bolkiah Foundation donated alms of B\$39,100 to thirty-three families from Brunei-Muara and Tutong districts who had recently lost their homes. Similar presentations were made on 30 June and 1 September following further blazes.

Islam

Pehin Mohd Zain Serudin continued as Minister of Religious Affairs throughout 2000, and Pehin Abdul Aziz Juned remained in office as Government Mufti. Pehin Salim Besar has been Chief Kadi since 1 January 1995.

In line with the Melayu Islam Beraja (Malay Muslim Monarchy, or MIB) concept, all Islamic festivals were faithfully observed. At the start of the year, most members of the royal family were in Saudi Arabia to fulfil the *umrah*. Soon after their return home 57,090 persons streamed through the Istana Nurul Iman (the principal palace) during the three days of the Hari Raya Aidilfitri festival. During the *haj* season, there were to be eight flights for approximately 1,400 pilgrims. One senior religious official warned that going on pilgrimage was not an excuse to take a holiday or have a rest but was, rather, a spiritual journey in fulfilment of the fifth pillar of the faith.

A *titah* by HM the Sultan marking Hijrah 1421 (Islamic New Year) was broadcast by RTB on 5 April 2000. On the next day, His Majesty presented Hijrah 1421 awards to three *tokoh agama* (religious leaders), namely, Awang Hj. Abdul Hamid bin Perali, 73; Pengiran Hj. Yussof bin Pengiran Sabtu, 74; and Dato Paduka Awang Hj. Abdul Wahab bin Mohammad, 87.

On *Maulud* (15 June), the (lunar) anniversary of the birth of the Prophet Muhammad (PBUH), more than thirty-five thousand of the *ummah* took part in a procession in BSB, with HM the Sultan and other members of the royal family taking the lead. In Kuala Belait, the attendance was more than nine thousand; forty-four contingents (3,091 persons) marched in Temburong District; and the turn-out in Tutong was more than fifteen thousand.

On 9 November 2000, HM the Sultan officially opened the permanent campus of the Sultan Haji Hassanal Bolkiah Tahfiz Al-Quran Institute in Jalan Tutong, BSB. The Institute was founded on 1 January 1993 to train pupils to memorize the entire Quran; thus far, it has produced twenty-two such *hafiz*. Some graduates proceed to prestigious institutions of Islamic learning overseas.[22]

The final of the National Quran-Reading Competition, attended by senior members of the royal family, was held at the International Convention Centre, Berakas on 14–15 August 2000. Mudim AH Metassim bin Haji Metussin was crowned champion, whilst the women's section was won by Dayang Siti Nur Zuhairah binti Haji Damit. Pehin Salim Besar, chairman of the panel of judges, declared, however, that the standard attained by the participants was not yet satisfactory.[23]

Foundation stones were laid for new mosques at Mentiri (13 March), and at Lorong Tiga Selatan in Seria (21 June). An Islamic religious school with 297 pupils was officially opened at Police Headquarters (Gadong) on 27 March 2000.

With regard to publications, 11 May 2000 saw the appearance of *Penyembelihan Binatang dan Pengendalian Daging* [Slaughtering Animals and Meat Preparation], which comprised seventy *fatwa* on *halal* food preparation promulgated by the Government Mufti between 1962 and 1999. On 10 August, Bismi Trading Company was awarded the contract to print and distribute two more books of *fatwa*. Meanwhile, on 2 February, Dato Professor Mahmud Saedon Othman, Vice-Chancellor of Universiti Brunei Darussalam, signed a contract with the university for the publication of his 236-page book on Islamic family values.

Conversion efforts proceeded apace: three hundred people adopted Islam between January and July 2000, bringing the total to about ten thousand in the past thirty years. HM the Sultan sometimes personally witnessed Islamization ceremonies.[24]

Education and Communications

NBD's own university, Universiti Brunei Darussalam (UBD), was founded in 1985. Thus far, no fewer than 3,962 students have graduated. The 2000–01 intake was 1,156, lifting the total number of students above the three thousand level. The university is to establish an Institute of Medicine.[25] On 14 June, it was announced that the Language Unit in the Faculty of Arts and Social Sciences was to be raised in status to become the UBD Language Centre, and it would offer courses on Japanese, Mandarin, and French, in addition to the existing Malay, English, and Arabic. On 8 November 2000, the university published the first issue of *Southeast Asia: A Multidisciplinary Journal.*

The highlight of the third quarter in the education field was the tenth *Hari Guru* (Teachers' Day), celebrated on 23 September every year in honour of the late Seri Begawan Sultan. The theme this year was "Teknologi Info-Komunikasi Pemangkin Pendidikan Berkualiti" (Info-Communication Technology: Catalyst for Quality Education). HM the Sultan announced plans for the unification of the national education system. Religious and general academic education, currently separate entities, were to be streamlined under the Ministry of Education. The Islamic Education Department at the Ministry of Religious Affairs (KHEU) would be transferred to the Ministry of Education; and the Institute of Islamic Education, currently under the aegis of the KHEU, would be absorbed by the UBD to become the Sultan Omar Ali Saifuddin Islamic Studies Institute. Meanwhile, the KHEU had been seeking for some time to reduce its reliance on foreign lecturers. In another statement on *Hari Guru,* Pehin Md Zain Serudin, Minister of Religious Affairs, revealed that His Majesty's Government had allocated B\$11.3 million to supply computers to all schools in the country.

BruNet, the sultanate's Internet Service Provider (ISP), was established by the Telecommunications Department in September 1995. By the end of that year nearly one thousand subscribers had been recruited. The number of users increased to 12,000 by 1999 and was expected to reach 22,000 by 2000. In early April 2000, however, Pehin Zakaria Sulaiman, the Minister of Communications, announced an end to its monopoly: ISP licences would be issued to a local company, Data Stream Technology (DST), and to three other concerns in an attempt to create healthy competition and greater efficiency. DST planned to begin its service before the APEC summit. On 4 September 2000, the Department of Telecommunications introduced its Netkad service, a joint venture with a local company (KPF Comserve) which will provide an alternative means of gaining access to the Internet. It was disclosed in mid-October that a Brunei Information Technology Council was to be formed with the purpose of facilitating "the strategic development and diffusion of the state-of-the-art IT for the entire nation".[26]

On 5 October 1999, all port operations at the BSB wharf ceased; henceforth, Muara was to be used instead. A passenger vessel, *Seri Anna,* was launched at Muara on 27 November 1999; the boat will ply between Muara and Labuan. Plans were afoot in 1999–2000 to transform Muara into the leading port in the "East ASEAN Growth Area". A B\$11 million contract was signed on 10 April 2000 for the dredging of Muara Channel to make it deep enough to accommodate the latest generation of container ships.

Conclusion

In the short-term, it is not an entirely trouble-free sultanate which approaches the commencement of the twenty-first century on 1 January 2001. There are certainly some reasons for optimism, but many intractable problems remain.

Viewed from the perspective of a hundred years, by contrast, Negara Brunei Darussalam ends the century on a *glittering* note. On 1 January 1901, the country's very existence was at stake. Vast swathes of territory had already been lost; and, pressed from the southwest by Rajah Charles Brooke of Sarawak and from the northeast by the British North Borneo Company, Sultan Hashim (r. 1885–1906) depended upon a protector (the United Kingdom) which was by no means committed to his realm's continued survival as a separate entity; indeed, the UK-Brunei Protectorate Agreement of 1888 had been worded specifically to allow the sultanate's complete obliteration from the map of nations. The sultanate was undoubtedly in dire straits: poor, weak, declining, sparsely-populated; nor was there any really valuable economic product to underpin the wealth and power necessary to enable the country to take control of its own destiny. The population was largely illiterate (as recently as 1950 the sultanate lacked even a single secondary school) and susceptible to decimation by disease.

At the end of the twentieth century, by contrast, matters could hardly be more different, symbolized by the fact that the capital city and the country itself were given new names in 1970 and 1984 respectively. There is no doubt that the sultanate is now firmly back in control of its own affairs. For better or worse, it has established its own system of government (the MIB concept) and its inhabitants enjoy an excellent standard of living. The sultanate is a respected player in regional affairs.

Brunei had been saved by the introduction of the British residential system in 1906. Its prosperity was assured by the discovery of the Seria oilfield in 1929 and boosted by fresh finds offshore (from 1963 onwards) and hikes in the oil price (especially during the 1970s). The liquefaction of natural gas, also dating from the early 1970s, helped to fill the national coffers to overflowing, as did increasing investment income. The second half of the century, coinciding with the reigns of Sultans Omar Ali Saifuddin III (1950–67) and Hassanal Bolkiah (1967–), has been a golden age unprecedented in the country's long history. Indeed, since 1 January 1996 Negara Brunei Darussalam has been officially ranked as a "developed nation".[27] The sultanate enjoys great stability, on the surface at any rate. Viewed from this angle, the setbacks of 1998-2000 are comparatively trivial. The onset of the twenty-first century may be welcomed with pride and confidence.

Notes

1. It might be mentioned here that in December 2000, the BIA sold seventy million shares in Malaysian Airlines; the purchaser of the 9 per cent stake, worth RM280 million, was believed to have been the Malaysian Government (*New Straits Times*, online, <*http://www.nstp.com.my*>, 4 December 2000).
2. *Pelita Brunei*, 27 September 2000, p. 3. Most of NBD's production has long since been derived from offshore wells.
3. *Pelita Brunei*, 19 April 2000, p. 12; *Pelita Brunei*, 9 August 2000, pp. 6, 7; *Daily Telegraph*, 11 October 2000, p. 38; *Daily Telegraph*, 13 October 2000, pp. 34, 35; <*http://www.fcl.co.nz*>, news releases dated 18 October 2000, and 17 November 2000.
4. *Borneo Bulletin*, 27 September 2000, p. 1; *Borneo Bulletin*, 9 November 1999, p. 1; *Borneo Bulletin*, 4 February 2000, p. 1.
5. By way of confirmation, *The Sunday Times* (London) reported on 29 October 2000 that ZeTek Power was about to commence production of fuel-cells at Cologne.
6. *Borneo Bulletin*, 18 February 2000, p. 1; *Borneo Bulletin*, 21 February 2000, pp. 1–2; *Borneo Bulletin*, 8 March 2000, p. 1.
7. *Borneo Bulletin*, 9 February 2000, p. 1; *Business Times* (Singapore), 5 July 2000, pp. 1, 17; *Pelita Brunei*, 19 July 2000, pp. 2,6; and *Pelita Brunei*, 22 November 2000, p. 12.
8. APEC 2000 website (<*http://www.apec2000/gov.bn*>) report dated 14 August 2000. On IAS, see Dieter Ordelheide, ed., *Transnational Accounting* (London and Basingstoke: Macmillan, 1995), pp 1661–804.
9. *Borneo Bulletin*, online at <*http://www.brunei.gov.bn*>, 14 November 2000:h17.htm; *Borneo Bulletin*, 16 November 2000:h32.htm.
10. *Pelita Brunei*, 20 August 1997, p. 13; *Pelita Brunei*, 28 July 1999, p. 11; *Pelita Brunei*, 6 November 1999, p. 1; *Pelita Brunei*, 10 November 1999, p. 15; *Borneo Bulletin*, 11 February 2000, p. 1; *Pelita Brunei*, *Aneka* section, 2 August 2000, p. 1; *Borneo Bulletin*, 17 October 2000; *Borneo Bulletin*, 16 November 2000.
11. APEC 2000 website (<*http://www.apec2000.gov.bn*>); *Borneo Bulletin*, 16 November 2000:h1.htm; *Pelita Brunei*, 18 November 1998, p. 16; *Pelita Brunei*, 11 October 2000, p. 3; *Statesman's Year-Book 1996–97*: pp. 52–53; *Statesman's Year-Book 2000*.
12. <*http://www.apecnews.org.bn*>, "Leaders' Declaration - Brunei Darussalam. Delivering to the Community. Bandar Seri Begawan 16 November 2000, 1710hrs" (23pp).
13. *Borneo Bulletin*, 14 November 2000; *Borneo Bulletin*, 16 November 2000; *Financial Times* (London), 15 November 2000.
14. *Pelita Brunei*, *Aneka* section, 19 April 2000, p. 2; *Pelita Brunei*, 26 April 2000, p. 12; *Pelita Brunei*, *Aneka* section, 10 May 2000, p. 2; *Pelita Brunei*, *Aneka* section, 7 June 2000, p. 2; *Pelita Brunei*, 21 June 2000, pp. 3, 12; *Pelita Brunei*, 28 June 2000, p. 3.
15. Earlier, in mid-October, His Majesty had travelled to Seoul in order to attend the third Asia-Europe Meeting. Government of Brunei Darussalam Official Website, on-line news, found at <*http://www.brunei.gov.bn*>, 19 October 2000; *Borneo Bulletin*, 14 November 2000; *Borneo Bulletin*, 18 November 2000; *Pelita Brunei*, *Aneka* section, 22 November 2000, p. 9.
16. HM Sultan Hassanal Bolkiah paid a working visit to Malaysia on 5 April; and on 17 April he was back in the Peninsula to attend the funeral of HM the Raja of Perlis.
17. On 19 August, NBD and Cambodia signed two agreements, the first dealing with trade and investment, and the second with air services. NBD now has air service agreements with all ASEAN countries and thirty-six others beyond the region (*Pelita Brunei*, 30 August 2000, p. 5).
18. Vietnam News Service, 15 November 2000 (<*http://vietnamnews.com.vn*>).
19. *Pelita Brunei*, 6 December 2000, p. 5.
20. *Pelita Brunei*, 26 April 2000, p. 11; *Pelita Brunei*, 5 July 2000, p. 6; and *Pelita Brunei*, 30 August 2000, p. 11.

21. *Pelita Brunei*, 15 March 2000, p. 10; and *Pelita Brunei*, 20 September 2000, p. 16, and editorial, p. 2.
22. *Pelita Brunei, Aneka* section, 13 January 1993, pp. 1–2; *Pelita Brunei*, 11 February 1998, p. 10; *Pelita Brunei*, 25 March 1998, p. 12; *Pelita Brunei*, 20 September 2000, p. 1; and *Pelita Brunei*, 15 November 2000, p. 1.
23. "Prestasi bacaan peserta belum memuaskan", *Pelita Brunei, Aneka* section, 6 September 2000, p. 9.
24. *Pelita Brunei*, 31 May 2000, p. 6; and *Pelita Brunei*, 7 June 2000, p. 1.
25. *Pelita Brunei*, 4 October 2000, pp. 8–9, 13; and *Pelita Brunei, Aneka* section, 9 August 2000, p. 6.
26. *Borneo Bulletin*, 26 February 1996, p. 1; *Pelita Brunei, Aneka* section, 1 September 1999, p. 1; *Borneo Bulletin*, 4 April 2000, p. 1; and *Borneo Bulletin*, 19 October 2000.
27. Even the principal causes of death are now cardiovascular disease and cancer.

CAMBODIA

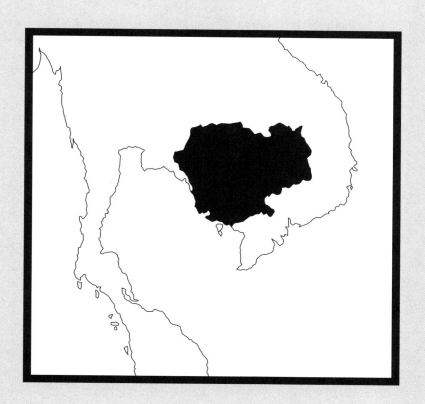

CAMBODIA
Democracy or Dictatorship?

Caroline Hughes

Political Issues

In 2000, the political situation in Cambodia remained relatively stable for the second year in a row, which was an important achievement, given the country's tortuous history. This stability itself begs important questions regarding Cambodia's political trajectory, however — questions which are answered differently by activists and analysts on different sides of the ongoing political divide. This overview of events in the year 2000 will suggest that the current period of political stability is contingent and liable to relapse into turmoil, but that even contingent stability in itself generates forces for further change.

The current period of political stability coincides with the early and middle phases of the electoral cycle. In this respect, among others, the second electoral cycle since the promulgation of the 1993 Constitution contrasts significantly with the first. The first electoral cycle was marred throughout by a continued, overt power struggle between the two major parties of the governing coalition. On one side stood the possessor (by a narrow margin) of the 1993 electoral mandate, the royalist Front Uni Nationale pour un Cambodge Independent, Neutral, Pacifique Et Cooperatif (FUNCINPEC), led by First Prime Minister Prince Norodom Ranariddh. On the other side stood the junior coalition partner, the Cambodian People's Party (CPP), led by Second Prime Minister Hun Sen, the successor to the 1980s one-party state and continued near-total monopolizer of operational bureaucratic power.

Analysis of the first electoral cycle focused on the relationship between these two men, their central party organizations, and the military units loyal to them, as the key to Cambodian stability and reform. This power struggle deteriorated into long-predicted violence in July 1997, with the ouster of Ranariddh and much of FUNCINPEC's leadership, and the defeat of FUNCINPEC forces in a military battle in Phnom Penh and, subsequently, on the Thai border.

The coalition that emerged between the CPP and FUNCINPEC following new elections and protracted protests and negotiations in 1998 has provided

CAROLINE HUGHES is the Leverhulme Trust Special Research Fellow, School of Politics, University of Nottingham, United Kingdom.

the basis for the current period of relative stability. The CPP gained only a slim and contested majority in the National Assembly in the 1998 elections, but this has served to align the *de jure* distribution of power within the government with the *de facto* distribution of bureaucratic and military power on the ground. FUNCINPEC's ability to mount a political challenge to the CPP has been significantly undermined, and rumours of splits and discontent within FUNCINPEC were rife throughout the year. Similarly, the disarming of FUNCINPEC, together with the defection to the government of the insurgent National Army of Democratic Kampuchea, also known as the "Khmer Rouge", most of whose former commanders are now to a greater or lesser degree aligned with the CPP, entails that the CPP presently enjoys a near-monopoly over the political loyalties of the military.

As a result, few imminent threats to the position of the Hun Sen government are apparent. The current period of stability is the direct result of this recent consolidation of power. What remains unclear is whether this stability is engendering a transfer of power from effective partisan networks to fragile non-partisan political institutions, and whether Cambodia should in consequence be categorized as an emerging democracy or as a congealing dictatorship. The signals offered during the year were mixed, in this respect.

Elections

This question will become more urgent over the next two to three years, as the current electoral cycle spins to a close. The concentration of military power in the hands of the CPP poses a potential problem for the ability of other political parties to campaign for support. While the problem is latent, midway through the electoral cycle, opposition parties can be expected to lobby vigorously over this issue, at home and abroad, in the lead-up to the commune elections, tentatively scheduled for 2002, and the general election in 2003. The commune elections are particularly important as an indicator of the distribution of power between non-partisan political institutions and partisan party networks operating within them. They will not only test the extent to which Cambodia's fragile democratic institutions are capable of disciplining CPP responses to strong opposition challenges, but also the extent to which the CPP can discipline its own local cadres.

The significance of the commune elections emerges from the nature of the Cambodian state, and the relationship between political parties and the bureaucracy. Cambodia's constitution commits the country to a regime of liberal democracy. However, the Kingdom of Cambodia in 1993 emerged from the 1980s State of Cambodia, following a United Nations–sponsored peace process that left the politicized "existing administrative apparatuses" of the 1980s intact. In particular, the commune authorities, appointed in the early 1980s and presumed to be loyal to the CPP, have been largely unaffected by the political transition.

The commune level of administration is crucial for the control of local politics in Cambodia. Opponents view the use of local authorities by the CPP as a mainstay of CPP power. During the 1998 elections, it was alleged that commune authorities across the country had contributed to the CPP's victory, firstly, by mobilizing the three million voters to register as CPP party members and pressuring and exhorting them to vote accordingly, and secondly, through their domination of the Commune Election Committees charged with organizing the elections. Success in organizing commune elections, to break this monopoly, thus contributes significantly to Cambodia's democratization process at the national level also.

First scheduled for 1996, commune elections have been repeatedly delayed, but already, the leaders of both FUNCINPEC and Cambodia's third party, the opposition Sam Rainsy Party (SRP), have alleged that political violence has been perpetrated against party members who were being groomed to contest the commune elections.[1] As ever in Cambodia, the lack of hard evidence in these cases of alleged political killing, and the intense partisanship of all those involved, precludes an authoritative assessment of this claim, and the associated question of involvement of senior party figures in ordering the alleged abuses. Past experience suggests that once the date for commune election has been set and preparations begun in earnest, greater international attention may have a deterrent effect, particularly to the extent that international funding is sought for the commune election process, and that conditions are attached to that funding. The impressive ability of the CPP leadership to discipline the lower ranks of the party has been demonstrated before, in particular following then second Prime Minister Hun Sen's call for calm in the aftermath of the July 1998 national elections.

It is important to note, however, that the interests at stake in national elections are primarily those of the party leaders, who are the most immediate beneficiaries of international approbation and aid. Whether the same level of intra-party discipline is possible during election processes where the future of the local party cadres hangs in the balance remains to be seen. Until this is demonstrated, the current level of political calm must be seen as politically contingent — resting upon the current interests and capabilities of the ruling party leadership — rather than as politically necessary, emerging from a common and cross-party commitment to the consolidation of democracy, embedded at all levels of the political apparatus.

Security is not the only concern attending discussions of the commune elections. Other major concerns are the integrity of the election process, and the implications of the elections for the development of the Cambodian party system. These concerns translate into two hotly debated provisions in the draft commune election law, approved by the Council of Ministers on 18 August 2000, and currently awaiting the attention of the National Assembly. These provisions concern the question of reform of the National Election Committee (NEC); and the form of commune leadership and the election system to be used to select it.

The question of reform of the NEC is contentious, because of a lack of consensus over the NEC's performance in organizing the 1998 elections. Those who believe that the 1998 elections represented an adequate reflection of the will of the people consider the hard-won technical experience of the existing committee structure as too valuable to lose. Those who view the 1998 elections as a complex and cynical mechanism for manipulating international concerns believe that root and branch reform of the NEC — the alleged overseer of this elaborate charade — is necessary. In January 2000, Hun Sen expressed the opinion that the NEC should remain unchanged until nine months before the next general election. The SRP and FUNCINPEC, who claim that they are unrepresented on the committee, demand reform, together with non-governmental organization (NGO) observers.

With regard to the electoral system, there are two contending options for commune leadership, with associated implications for the contending parties. The first option is for the popular election of an individual commune chief from a number of candidates, including both party-sponsored and independent candidates. Once elected, the chief could either appoint a council, or work with a full-time, permanent secretariat. The second option is for collective leadership by means of a council, elected by a system of proportional representation from party lists. Once elected, the council could choose a chief from amongst themselves.

These options are contentious because of the drastic implications for the influence of political parties over this vital level of administration. Both the CPP and FUNCINPEC are confident of their electoral appeal in the countryside — the CPP because of its formidable organizational ability, and FUNCINPEC because of the broad appeal of royalism — and thus can be expected to favour a party-based system that increases their influence over local politics. The SRP, by contrast, is a largely urban party and has an interest in the emergence of independent commune leaders who are likely to permit greater space in the rural areas for opposition party proselytizing.

The party list system forms the basis of the current draft law, and its approval by the Council of Ministers was viewed by some NGO representatives as the prelude to a carve-up of local power between the coalition partners.[2] The draft law has yet to be debated in the National Assembly, and a date for elections is unlikely to be set until each of the coalition partners believes that the situation is favourable to them. The form and conduct of the commune elections will offer a new opportunity to examine the ways in which partisanship, rather than statesmanship, affects decision-making over the framework for Cambodia's future democratic development.

Reform of the State

The form and functioning of the state apparatus moved in 2000 to centre stage in Cambodia's relations with international donors, as well as in relations between parties. The May 2000 meeting of the Consultative Group of international donors generated a working group for public administration reform, with a remit to promote good governance in Cambodia.

The government's reform plan, presented at the donors' meeting, covered "a number of areas of governance reform deemed critical to Cambodia's development over the near- and medium-term, including judicial and legal reform, public finance, civil administration reform, anti-corruption, natural resource management, and military demobilization."[3] Reform of the public service had already taken some first steps in the form of censuses of both the bureaucracy and the military, conducted in 1999/2000, designed to facilitate the removal of "ghosts" from both apparatuses, and to serve as a baseline survey upon which policies for change could be based. In the case of the civil service, the census was to be followed by a "functional analysis" aimed at identifying key roles, to which appropriate expertise and resources could be targeted.

The CPP-led government, and Prime Minister Hun Sen, have repeatedly reiterated their commitment to the process of reform. However, significant obstacles stand in the way, notably the vested political interests and power bases that had been built during the one-party regime of the 1980s, and consolidated during the early years of the 1990s. Rampant corruption and patronage within the bureaucracy was officially sanctioned at that time as a means to secure official loyalties, as evidenced by measures such as the infamous Article 51 of the Civil Servants Law, which prevented prosecution of bureaucrats or soldiers charged with crimes, except with the express permission of their superiors in the civil service or armed forces.

Article 51 was amended in 1999, and an ambitious reform agenda has been embraced, in the context of CPP dominance in the government. The test of the reform policy is whether the CPP is prepared to loosen its grip on the political loyalties of the military and bureaucracy to the extent that the party's ability to exercise power outside the context of the democratic mandate is threatened. The signs are not all positive. In early 2000, the *Phnom Penh Post* reported that foreign investors were disappointed with the progress made in an anti-corruption drive announced in late 1999.[4] Several months later, Prime Minister Hun Sen defended the record of the military from (well-documented) accusations of illegal land confiscation and human rights abuse, stating that such accusations "affect the dignity of the military and I can't accept it."[5]

Other unwelcome portents included the decision to transfer control of village militias, currently under the Ministry of Defence, to the Ministry of Interior.[6] The village militias have long been viewed by the CPP's opponents as the armed wing of the party, a key means by which the CPP controls political dissent in rural Cambodia, and a major source of human rights abuse. The SRP and international human rights activists have long called for the militia to be disbanded, and its transfer from one ministry to another suggested that this course of action is not imminent.

While a discourse of public sector reform has been embraced at the behest of donors, the implementation of such reforms is constrained by the weight of vested political interests, and the ways in which these support the CPP's political dominance. Politicized patronage networks within the bureaucracy undermine the emergence of a broad ethos of public service, permitting partisan use of the state to further party aims. Throughout the war years, state and party interests had been viewed as inseparable, by both sides, and this perception continues to be a significant force determining the functioning of political institutions.

The key material barrier to the emergence of a more professional bureaucracy is the paltry remuneration offered to public servants. Low public sector salaries continue to mandate partial and rent-seeking behaviour on the part of cliques of public officials. Since 1998, public sector salaries have been raised by 30 per cent, but still remain inadequate to meet the cost of living. Further pay increases have been ruled out until rationalization plans are finalized in 2001.[7]

If wages are raised significantly, removing the justification for corruption as an economic necessity for impoverished civil servants, then the space would open for a radical reorientation of allegiance and competence within the Cambodian state. This would permit the cultivation of a commitment to efficiency and effectiveness, rather than to patron and party. Significant pay rises within the bureaucracy, judiciary and military, not to mention the education and health services, are vital to movement towards good governance in Cambodia, and remain the most important test of the government's will to reform in that direction.

State-Society Relations

A significant departure since 1998 has been the opening of political space for the expression of grievance from society at large, in response, arguably, to the relative lack of acrimony between Cambodia's politicians. This was illustrated throughout 2000 by a series of demonstrations and strikes, mostly located in Phnom Penh, but often comprising discontented constituencies from rural Cambodia. The SRP has frequently associated itself with these protests, but there is little evidence that it has orchestrated them. Rather, the party has adopted an advocacy role, facilitating and channelling protest, rather than provoking it.

The emergence of aggrieved and vocal protestors must be regarded as an important step for Cambodian democracy. The increasing confidence of Cambodian citizens in expressing concern and demanding redress from the government reflects the lessening of tension between the senior party leaders and, crucially, their associated military units. While the consolidation of military power in the hands of the CPP in 1997 is problematic for the electoral prospects of the opposing parties, it has also permitted a transfer of the main site of day-to-day political contention away from the military sphere and into the civil domain.

A move towards political contention in the form of civil rather than military action permits greater participation by ordinary citizens, and an expanding view of citizens as legitimate participants in political affairs, rather than merely as victims of political turmoil. This view is also taking hold within the sector of internationally-funded non-governmental organizations in Cambodia. Two political campaigns organized by NGOs in 2000 — a campaign to promote public input into the shape of commune election legislation, and a campaign to elicit views on a trial for the leaders of the Democratic Kampuchea (DK) regime — saw the mobilization of citizens to participate in public forums, petitions, and public rallies for change.

These campaigns are ground-breaking in that they represent attempts by NGOs to mobilize the power of public opinion in order to promote transparency and accountability regarding highly sensitive and contentious political issues. Previous examples of public rallies and protests by NGOs have been relatively scarce. A notable early instance was the series of public forums organized by the NGO network, Ponleu Khmer, to facilitate public discussion of the constitution, coterminous with debates within the Constitutional Assembly in 1993. The advocacy campaigns seen during 2000 attempt to recapture the early democratic optimism of the Ponleu Khmer forums, by once again facilitating specifically public discussion and ownership of issues basic to the future of Cambodian democracy. In this sense, they reflect the growing perception of ordinary citizens as powerful political actors in their own right.

Yet the civil protest that occurred in Cambodia during the year has had limited impact on the government. This was evident when the Council of Ministers in August approved a draft commune law which exhibited almost total disregard for public opinion, as mobilized by the election networks. *Ad hoc* groups of demonstrators have found the government similarly immovable. A series of demonstrations was held early in the year by market traders at the O'Russei market, protesting the requirement that traders buy back at high prices from private developers customary rights to stalls in a newly redeveloped market building. The campaign failed to elicit significant concessions or support from the government.[8] A major campaign of industrial action by garment workers elicited only minimal wage rises, and widespread abuse of the labour law continues within the garment industry. Protests by squatters placed under an eviction order by the Phnom Penh municipality have also been limited in their impact on government policy. While space for civil protest has opened in Cambodia, and has been used creatively and courageously by citizens in pursuit of their rights and interests, this has not yet been matched by greater accountability on the part of the government.

Two events at the end of the year raise a note of concern, in this respect. In late November, fighting broke out in Phnom Penh as a group of armed men attacked a television station, the Council of Ministers building, and the Ministry of National Defence with AK47s and grenades. A fire fight with security forces ensued, leaving eight dead, and subsequently, hundreds of people were detained for questioning in relation to the attack. Within a fortnight, further violence occurred in the form of a bomb blast in the centre of Phnom Penh.

The government laid responsibility for these attacks at the door of a supposed U.S.-based terrorist group called the Cambodian Freedom Fighters, and commentators suggested that the attacks were intended to prevent a visit from the Vietnamese Prime Minister to Cambodia, scheduled for late November. While few concrete facts have emerged, political accusations were quick to fly, as the opposition SRP accused the government of manufacturing the original incident as a pretext to arrest opposition party members. Other commentators suggested that the attack was connected to internal power manoeuvres within the CPP.

While the precise causes and implications of the violence remain unclear, it reflects the lingering polarization within Cambodian society and a continued belief that peaceful political contention within the bounds of the constitution is ineffective. In particular, to the extent that the attack was connected to the impending official visit, it reflects a continued belief in the CPP's subordination to Vietnamese "hegemony" — a theme that has long been a staple of opposition party rhetoric. It is fuelled, at least in part, by continued inflexibility and lack of responsiveness of government to popular concerns. This both increases frustration among citizens suffering from very real social and economic hardship, and encourages their suspicion that, as the Cambodian Government does not appear to them to be acting in the interests of the Cambodian people, it is perhaps operating in the service of a foreign power.

Social Issues

Service Delivery and Policy Implementation

In this political context, a number of serious social problems were addressed during 2000, although opinion remained sharply divided on how much of the rhetoric translated into action. A particular concern has been the continued failure of the state to guarantee, even minimally, the basic rights of ordinary people, or to respond in an efficient and equitable fashion to a series of social and environmental crises. These issues reflect, in part, a lack of infrastructure for service delivery. However, a sharp difference lingers in the effectiveness of state action in pursuit of party objectives, as opposed to broader objectives of governance, suggesting that the politicization of social objectives, and the harnessing of these to party fortunes, is a continuing political strategy used by the Cambodian leaders.

The persistent impoverishment of health services is a good example, in the light of the continued emergence of evidence regarding the rapid spread of the HIV virus in Cambodia. A United Nations report released in February 2000 commented that the prevalance of HIV in Cambodia was "alarmingly high", reaching 42.6 per cent among commercial sex workers, and estimated at 1 in 70 among the total Cambodian population.[9] The report also highlighted the increase in mother-to-child transmission of HIV, as a result of increased prevalence among married women (2.4 per cent in 1998).[10] Intensive activities by NGOs and international organizations have promoted education and awareness of the issue, and recent moves to decriminalize commercial sex and to promote the use of condoms within the commercial sex industry have been positive in terms of promoting the health of sex workers.[11] However, a lack of availability of affordable health care means that people living with HIV in Cambodia remain largely without access to treatment designed to prevent the onset of AIDS. This not only has an impact upon the quality and expectancy of life for those affected, but also imposes a heavy burden upon families to cope with the crisis, thus inhibiting social acceptance of people living with HIV.

In communications with international donors, the Cambodian Government has prioritized the issue of increasing spending on social services, while reducing the proportion of the budget devoted to defence spending.[12] This aspiration is closely related to the question of depoliticization of the state, since manipulation of defence funding has been closely linked to the consolidation of political party influence throughout the 1990s. Yet few concrete moves towards the stated goal have been noted. The disparity between social services and defence expenditure has actually increased since 1996, according to some estimates, with health spending occupying little more than 5 per cent of government expenditures in 1999 — a 1 per cent increase from the previous year — compared with more than 40 per cent devoted to defence. The International Crisis Group notes World Bank concerns that whereas the Health and Education ministries often cannot "make full or efficient use" of the minimal resources they are awarded, the Ministry of Defence regularly overspends its budget.[13] Continued tolerance of this situation in the face of, among other problems, an HIV epidemic that the United Nations describes as "alarming" once again suggests a deprioritization of non-partisan issues, and an almost exclusive focus upon political party fortunes.

The year 2000 did see some action on longstanding plans to reduce the size of the armed forces through the demobilization of soldiers — a plan intended to release money for the social sector. Overall, the government, with international prompting, plans to demobilize 30,000 soldiers out of a total defence force of 133,817, by the year 2003. If the demobilization of soldiers is successful in prompting a broader demilitarization of society, it will not only permit greater investment in social service infrastructure and delivery, but will also tackle the most serious source of social violence in Cambodia, namely, the presence and dispersion of ill-disciplined, poorly paid and heavily armed soldiers across the country.

Early evidence suggests, however, that the reintegration of former soldiers into society has been poorly managed. A pilot project, demobilizing 1,500 soldiers, gave rise to criticism during the year, as the International Crisis Group called it "a magnet for new forms of corruption",[14] and journalists reported that soldiers had been left with few opportunities to engage fully in civilian life, and often remained clustered around bases, looking to their former commanders for support. This prompted fears that, rather than demobilizing, the military was merely moving soldiers off the official payroll, while individual commanders unofficially retained their services in the broad and unregulated sector of military entrepreneurship and violence.

Similar problems are evident in the government's management of environmental protection — a crucial policy area in a country where the overwhelming majority live off the land. In a commentary on the National Environment Action Plan, for 1998-2002, the Asian Development Bank stated that the Cambodian "institutional framework is weak, and operating guidelines and practices yet to be developed and internalized. The number of people who have received suitable and sufficient training in environment-related disciplines is still low."[15]

A series of episodes, including the discovery of toxic waste emitted from garment factories in the Tuol Kok district of Phnom Penh,[16] an outbreak of fish poisoning in Siem Reap province,[17] and the dispossession of fishermen of their fishing rights,[18] suggest that the government controls neither the private sector nor its own officials adequately, with profound consequences for the lives and livelihoods of citizens. In the forestry sector, similarly, the environmental watchdog Global Witness commented in May 2000 that the government had "by and large, failed to suppress illegal activities by timber concessionaires, both in terms of detection and punitive actions."[19]

With regard to these, and a variety of other serious social issues that continue to threaten the quality, and even the possibility, of life for the Cambodian citizen, the problems of low levels of competence within the bureaucratic machinery of the state remain intertwined with political questions. Failures apparent in the management of crisis and reform cannot be placed solely at the door of material and technical constraints. Responsive and highly effective informal chains of command are apparent in cases where mobilization to protect party political interests is necessary. The massive CPP operation in 1998, which saw three million voters enrolled into the party and rewarded with centrally-allocated gifts, is a case in point, exhibiting impressive organizational skills reaching across the country and down to the village level. Yet these organizational capacities break down regularly and irretrievably in cases where a non-partisan and even-handed approach to reform is required, and particularly where powerful vested interests are challenged. This pattern suggests a continued tendency on the part of many officials to elevate partisan loyalty to the party above non-partisan loyalty to the state. This is a failure which is likely to be exacerbated rather than relieved, at least in the short term, by the continued incumbency of the dominant party as the party of government, as this continuity of itself stabilizes and secures the vested interests upon which political fortunes rest.

Impunity and the Trial of the DK Leaders
Continued failures to implement policy effectively are mirrored by a continued arbitrariness in the judicial system, another key item on the reform agenda

agreed with donors. One hundred individuals acquitted of crimes by the courts were arbitrarily rearrested in December 1999 on the orders of Hun Sen, in response to complaints of court corruption, and remained in jail without trial in July 2000. Meanwhile, a vicious acid attack on a young woman during the same month, allegedly perpetrated by the jealous wife of a high-ranking CPP official, evoked little response from the government. Although an arrest warrant was issued by the court, it was not implemented. Cabinet spokesman Khieu Thavika described the attack as a personal matter "for the first and second wife to resolve."[20] Subsequently, the official whose wife was implicated in the attack was selected by the government as an official observer at a meeting of a U.N.-sponsored Asia-Pacific Forum of National Human Rights Institutions in New Zealand.[21]

The question of impunity has been viewed as lying at the heart of issues over the proposed international tribunal for former leaders of the DK regime, which presided over the atrocities of the late 1970s. Overthrown in 1979, these leaders enjoyed international support throughout the 1980s, allowing them to build an insurgent army which continued to threaten stability and development in Cambodia into the mid-1990s. This army came to be viewed by the contending parties of the early 1990s as a key prize in the political power struggle that followed the U.N.-sponsored peace process of 1991–93.

From 1996, a series of defections to the government led to the demise of the insurgency, with the arrest of the last man standing, the so-called Ta Mok (or "Grandfather" Mok), in 1999. Mok is at present in jail without trial, awaiting the outcome of protracted negotiations between the Cambodian Government and the United Nations over the possibility of international participation in a tribunal to try him. This issue has been at the centre of much international comment and analysis of Cambodia's political developments during the year, frequently presented as a test of the government's commitment to reform.

The question of an international tribunal is an illuminating example of the way in which Cambodia's political leaders prioritize the retention of discretionary powers in dealing with political and social issues. Differences regarding the broad philosophy underlying the trial have seen the Cambodian Government positing peace and justice as opposing values in this context, to which international negotiators respond that peace without justice is an oxymoron. More specific questions at issue between U.N. negotiators and the Cambodian Government have been the location of the trial, the ratio of Cambodian to foreign judges, and the procedures for deciding disputes between them.

All these differences, arguably, reflect the mismatch between U.N. concerns to promote a procedural and impersonal form of justice, familiar to Western liberal publics, and Cambodian Government concerns to promote a highly personal form of justice embedded in local political power realities. U.N. negotiators fear that for the Cambodian Government, the tribunal is not viewed as an opportunity to create judicial precedents, which empower the notion of principled treatment of citizens according to the law. Rather, it is feared that the Cambodian Government views the tribunal as an opportunity to wreak vengeance on its erstwhile enemies, while protecting those who have defected, thus exhibiting and confirming the importance of loyalty and patronage, over justice and right, in providing personal protection in post-war Cambodia. If this is achieved, the international tribunal will serve to embed impunity even more thoroughly into Cambodian governance.

Viewed as an ill omen, in this respect, is the acquittal in June this year of Chhouk Rin, a former National Army of Democratic Kampuchea (NADK) commander charged with the kidnap and murder of three foreign tourists in 1994. Chhouk Rin subsequently defected to the government and was awarded an amnesty, which formed the basis of the judge's decision to acquit him. U.N. negotiators have insisted that any international tribunal should work unhampered by both amnesties awarded in the past and the prospect of royal pardons in the future. Yet a policy of judicious amnesty and pardon has been central to the CPP's exercise of power in the 1990s. The amnesty, together with the pardon, is a key political tool in Cambodia, where the judicial system is habitually manipulated, and used as a foil in order to demonstrate the power of individuals to punish and protect.

Low levels of competence among the Cambodian judiciary, as noted by U.N. experts seeking to justify international control of any tribunal for the DK leaders, assist such manipulation. Not only are courts non-assertive and easily pressured, in cases where powerful officials or army commanders are accused of crimes, but they are also open to ridicule by the Executive branch, as demonstrated by Hun Sen's order in December 1999 that the one hundred suspects acquitted by the courts be rearrested and held in jail. As such cases illustrate, the Executive has retained discretionary control over crime and punishment in Cambodia, and has used this control to make flamboyant gestures of vengeance and forgiveness towards political enemies. Such flamboyance is anathema to the legalistic approach of the U.N. Group of Experts planning the tribunal for the former DK leaders. Consequently, many of the negotiations throughout the year focused on the margins of discretion awarded to the Cambodian judges who will constitute a majority on the tribunal.

The outcome negotiated is a "supermajority" system, in which a decision obtained by a simple majority of all the Cambodian judges voting unanimously requires the concurrence of at least one foreign judge, in order to be carried. Promoters of international control argue that this provision is too slender a guarantee, and that in the highly charged political atmosphere of Phnom Penh, the possibilities of undue influence being brought to bear on foreign judges are infinite. Promoters of Cambodian control argue that the implicit requirement of a foreign sanction for Cambodian justice is an invasion of Cambodia's hard-won sovereignty. Such polemics continue to surround a process of painstaking negotiations aimed at finessing fundamentally divergent perspectives on justice into ever-finer print on the agreement.

Economic Issues

While the impact of forces for democratization within the Cambodian state and polity is at present ambiguous, the current period of stability is constituting and empowering forces from the wider society, which will affect Cambodia's political trajectory in the future. Foremost among these is the development of the economy, which continues to represent an arena of change with profound effects for society and politics over the long term.

Cambodia saw continuing economic growth in the first six months of the year. Tourism arrivals in Phnom Penh increased by 21 per cent in the first quarter, year on year, and arrivals in Siem Reap rose by more than 100 per cent. Surveys among urban workers found that wages had increased for most sectors, some sharply. Growth of real gross domestic product (GDP) was forecast in June at 5 per cent for the year 2000, similar to the growth figure for 1999, with the industry and service sectors expected to expand by 9.8 and 7.7 per cent respectively. Garment exports in the first quarter increased by 47 per cent from the first quarter in 1999.[22] Exchange rates remained stable throughout the year, while inflation fell to an annual average of 4 per cent in June, reflecting falling food prices in the first half of the year.[23] Nevertheless, investor confidence — badly shaken by the political upheaval of 1997–98 — has not yet been restored. Foreign direct investment was projected at US$120 million for the year 2000, showing no change from the levels reported for 1998 and 1999, and significantly less than the 1996 level of US$294 million.[24]

This performance was praised by Cambodia's international donors. In particular, the government's imposition of value-added tax (VAT) in 1999, leading to an increase of two percentage points in tax revenues as a proportion of GDP, was viewed as a positive step by donors. Increased control over forestry and customs was viewed by International Monetary Fund staff as contributing to the improved performance in revenue collection, and as constituting a "break from Cambodia's past record of inconsistent policy implementation and poor governance."[25] However, other analysts saw these apparent improvements in governance as arising from contingent developments, rather than structural changes. The International Crisis Group reported that it was unclear whether the extra revenue "can be attributed to the VAT imposed on external sources of cash or to selective crackdowns on particularly lucrative industries or wealthy individuals."[26]

Devastating floods in October and November were predicted to take at least one percentage point from the estimated growth figure.[27] The floods — recorded as the worst in Cambodia in thirty years — affected twenty-one provinces and three million people, causing 252 deaths, with the most severe damage located in the southeastern provinces of Kandal, Kompong Cham, Prey Veng, Takeo and Svay Rieng. About 1.3 million people were displaced, and almost half a million hectares of crops were lost. Also destroyed were health centres, schools, and clean water supplies. The government estimated the total cost of rehabilitation and reconstruction in the wake of the floods at US$79 million.[28]

Apart from bad weather, the relative recent health of Cambodia's economy has already spawned new social and political forces in the shape of trade unions, which have emerged at the forefront of the newly empowered social movements in Cambodia. Located in the garment factories which provide Cambodia with the major part of its export earnings, the trade unions have expanded in membership and increased in activism since the first stirrings of industrial unrest were felt in 1996. The unions are unusual among Cambodian non-governmental organizations in that they have emerged in response to local action, rather than in response to internationally promoted values and funding.

Throughout the year 2000, spontaneous walk-outs and demonstrations by factory workers protesting ill-treatment and poor pay and working conditions preceded the unionization of factory after factory. The high point of the year's activism occurred in June, when 29 of Phnom Penh's 179 factories went on strike, demanding legislation to increase the minimum wage. The unions have become embedded in transnational networks, including the Clean Clothes Campaign in the United States, which encourages American retailers to check working conditions in suppliers' factories, and have participated in training programmes with American trade unions and with the International Labour Organization. Unions also hold classes for workers on provisions of the Cambodian Labour Law, in temples in the industrial districts of Phnom Penh and Ta Khmau.

While reports have emerged of union officers in factories being persecuted, the spread of unionization appears to be inexorable, as workers interviewed offered tale after tale of successful strikes to demand the reinstatement of union officials.[29] While conditions within factories remain deplorable, and wages pitiful, the organization of workers is proceeding apace, and the activism of the unions reflects a new energizing force among the pressures for greater democratization of Cambodia's political system.

Conclusions

The current political stability enjoyed by Cambodia comprises the stabilization of both pro-democratic and anti-democratic forces within the country. Whilst the greater concord currently observable at the level of high politics permits a greater openness for civil action by citizens in pursuit of their rights and grievances, it also reflects a stronger hold by the dominant party over the reigns of power. Commentators are divided on whether the increasingly co-operative attitude of the CPP towards the demands of donors reflects a genuine desire for reform stymied by material factors, or the cynical use of reformist rhetoric to mask policies aimed at the stabilization of vested and politically partisan interests. Either way, the key indicators of state effectiveness, such as responses to social crises and the implementation of the long-standing reform agenda for demobilization and promotion of the rule of law, suggest an uneven development of the state's capacity or willingness to act promptly, effectively, and impartially.

The failure of the CPP-dominated government to act decisively and unequivocally to promote professionalism within the bureaucracy feeds suspicions of a continued concern within the CPP to make use of bureaucratic partiality for electoral ends. From this perspective, it appears that the increasing stability of formal political arrangements is contingent upon a continuing perception on the part of the CPP, that such arrangements can assist, rather than significantly hinder, the CPP in retaining power.

Stability has wider effects, however, which over the long term will produce marked changes to the structure of Cambodian society and politics. Early industrialization has already produced trade unions with a powerful mobilizational capacity locally, and a strong transnational network. Similarly, the student movement and internationally-sponsored NGOs are becoming more vocal in Phnom Penh. Increasing political confidence, in conjunction with the tensions produced by the transition to the free market, for example over the issue of land ownership and access, has led to the constitution of constituencies of interest, who are forging transnational links, and staking a claim to government attention and concern.

Rapid moves towards consolidated democracy are not to be expected in Cambodia in the near future, and the next elections may engender a new period of instability. However, for this war-weary nation, stability in itself offers a range of new opportunities for as yet unacknowledged political constituencies to coalesce, to find their voices and to project their concerns. The success of the CPP in consolidating power *vis-à-vis* its political party opponents, and the contingency of democratic arrangements upon the degree to which they assist in this, suggest the use of formal democracy in the service of single-party dominance. However, the CPP has by no means won the consent of the population to this style of rule. Moreover, rapid economic changes are likely to prompt a concomitant restructuring of interests in society in the future, which will require a response from the state that goes beyond personal benefaction. The strikes of garment workers, together with demonstrations by landless farmers, suggest that a thickening of state–society relations as a consequence of political stability has offered citizens a chance to make their complaints heard. Sooner or later, a convincing response from the government will be required, or violent incidents, of the sort seen in Phnom Penh in November and December, may become a more frequent occurrence.

Notes

1. Stephen O'Connell, Lon Nara, Vong Sokheng, "Rainsy Activists Target of Violence", *Phnom Penh Post,* 1–14 September 2000; online edition, *<http://www.phnompenhpost.com>*.
2. Vong Sokheng, "Two-Party Hijack of Commune Elections Feared," *Phnom Penh Post,* 1–14 September 2000; online edition, *<http://www.phnompenhpost.com>*.
3. Royal Government of Cambodia, "Cambodia: Supplementary Memorandum of Economic and Financial Policies for 2000", Phnom Penh, 31 August 2000; online, *<http://www.imf.org>*.

4. Phelim Kyne, "Investors Question PM's Anti-Corruption Initiative", *Phnom Penh Post,* 18 February–2 March 2000; online edition, *<http://www.phnompenhpost.com>.*
5. Phelim Kyne, "RAC Booted, RCAF Boosted, by Hun Sen", *Phnom Penh Post,* 7–20 July 2000; online edition, *<http://www.phnompenhpost.com>.*
6. Stephen O'Connell and Vong Sokheng, "Militia: Armed, Untrained and Transferred", *Phnom Penh Post,* 21 July–3 August 2000; online edition, *<http://www.phnompenhpost.com>.*
7. Royal Government of Cambodia, "Supplementary Memorandum of Economic and Financial Policies for 2000", Phnom Penh, 31 August 2000; online, *<http://www.imf.org>.*
8. Personal interviews, O'Russei Market, Phnom Penh, June–July 2000.
9. UNAIDS Cambodia, "The HIV/AIDS/STD Situation and the National Response in the Kingdom of Cambodia," 3rd ed. (Phnom Penh, Feburary 2000), p. 7; Stephen O'Connell and Bou Saroeun, "National Security Crisis Feared from AIDS", *Phnom Penh Post,* 12–25 May 2000; online edition, *<http://www.phnompenhpost.com>.*
10. UNAIDS Cambodia, op. cit., p. 34.
11. Phelim Kyne, "Prostitution Gets Government Okay", *Phnom Penh Post,* 10–23 November 2000; online edition, *<http://www.phnompenhpost.com>.*
12. Royal Government of Cambodia, "Supplementary Memorandum of Economic and Financial Policies for 2000", Phnom Penh, 31 August 2000; online edition, *<http://www.imf.org>.*
13. International Crisis Group, "Cambodia: The Elusive Peace Dividend," ICG Asia Report no. 8 (Phnom Penh/Brussels, 11 August 2000), p. 12.
14. Ibid., p. 23.
15. Asian Development Bank, "Cambodia: Country Performance Assessment", online edition, *<http://www.adb.org>.*
16. Bou Saroeun, "Factory Waste Sickens Villagers", *Phnom Penh Post,* 28 April–11 May 2000; online edition, *<http://www.phnompenhpost.com>.*
17. Bou Saroeun and Phelim Kyne, "Poison Fish Outbreak in Siem Reap Baffles Authorities", *Phnom Penh Post,* 4–17 August 2000; online edition, *<http://www.phnompenhpost.com>.*
18. Bou Saroeun, "Fisheries Reform Seems All Talk and No Action", *Phnom Penh Post,* 8–21 December 2000; online edition, *<http://www.phnompenhpost.com>.*
19. Global Witness, "Chainsaws Speak Louder than Words", May 2000, p. 3.
20. "Cambodia Vice", *Straits Times,* 14 December 1999; *Camnews,* at *<camnews@lists.best.com>,* 14 December 1999.
21. Phelim Kyne, "Svay Sitha Picked for Human Rights Forum", *Phnom Penh Post,* 4–17 August 2000; online edition, *<http://www.phnompenhpost.com>.*
22. "Economy Watch — Economic Indicators", *Cambodia Development Review* 4, no. 2 (2000): 16.
23. International Monetary Fund, "Cambodia: 2000 Article I Consultation and First Review Under the Poverty Reduction and Growth Facility — Staff Report" (Washington D.C., Oct. 2000), p. 6; online edition, *<http://www.imf.org>.*
24. Ibid., Table 6.
25. Ibid., p. 5.
26. International Crisis Group Asia, op. cit., p. 13.
27. "Holiday Interrupts Flood Relief", *Phnom Penh Post,* 29 September–12 October 2000; online edition, *<http://www.phnompenhpost.com>.*
28. Susan Postlethwaite, "Floods Affect Nearly 3 Million Cambodians", *Phnom Penh Post,* 13–26 October 2000; online edition, *<http://www.phnompenhpost.com>.*
29. Personal interviews, Phnom Penh, July 2000.

DEALING WITH CRIMES AGAINST HUMANITY
Progress or Illusion?[1]

Stephen R. Heder

Introduction

In 1999, Cambodia's Prime Minister Hun Sen and the United Nations had locked horns over proposals from the latter for an international tribunal to try "those persons most responsible for the most serious violations of human rights" when Cambodia was ruled as "Democratic Kampuchea" (DK) by the late Pol Pot's Communist Party of Kampuchea (CPK) from 1975 to 1978. Their confrontation followed the disintegration since 1996 of armed opposition to Hun Sen by DK remnants. The highlights of this disintegration had been the defection and *de jure* amnesty for the DK-era crimes of former DK Foreign Minister Ieng Sary; the detention of Pol Pot by his erstwhile DK comrades and his death in their custody; the submission to Hun Sen's authority of Kae Pok, a former CPK Central Committee member, Nuon Chea, Pol Pot's former deputy, and Khieu Samphan, the former DK chief of state; and the arrest of Ta Mok, a former member of the CPK Standing Committee who was the last active leader of insurgent opposition to Hun Sen, and of Kang Kech Iev (commonly known as "Duch"), the former chairman of the CPK's central extermination centre, S-21 (commonly known as Tuol Sleng).

In welcoming the surrender of Sary, Pok, Nuon, and Samphan, Hun Sen had declared a policy of forgetting their pasts. He had retreated from a request he had made in 1997 for United Nations assistance to set up an international criminal tribunal to try alleged CPK criminals, and had rejected an early 1999 proposal by three U.N.–appointed legal experts on how to organize one. Instead, he called for a "Cambodian-style" trial with some international participation. He clearly had in mind something like the show-trial that had been organized under Vietnamese auspices in Cambodia in 1979. Pol Pot and Ieng Sary were convicted *in absentia* of genocide in this Vietnamese-scripted event that focused exclusively on them, and was dressed up with the participation of fellow-travelling foreign jurists. Its selectivity reflected a Vietnamese policy of granting impunity from prosecution to all former CPK members who were prepared to

STEPHEN R. HEDER teaches politics in the Department of Political Studies, School of Oriental and African Studies (SOAS), University of London, and is the Cambodia Consultant of the War Crimes Research Office of the Washington College of Law.

work with them against the DK regime. Those protected included Hun Sen himself, who had been a junior CPK military cadre, and a number of others who are now senior officials in Hun Sen's ruling Cambodian People's Party (CPP).

Hun Sen's behaviour in 1998 and 1999 continued the originally Vietnamese policy of protecting long-term CPP members from legal scrutiny. It promised the same exemption to Ieng Sary, Kae Pok, Nuon Chea, and Khieu Samphan. It envisaged a thinly-disguised remake of the 1979 trial, with Mok and Duch in the dock instead of Pol Pot and Ieng Sary, but again hopefully legitimized by the presence of friendly foreign jurists who would not contradict Hun Sen's script for the proceedings. These continuities rendered implausible Hun Sen's attempts to claim he was pursuing a "Cambodian" solution to the problem of DK accountability.

Moreover, throughout 1999, the United Nations' guardians of international standards of accountability for crimes against humanity and of fair trial procedures had steadfastly demanded a trial ensuring that these norms were met. They were certain that this would require a trial free from the control that Hun Sen exercises over the contemporary Cambodian judiciary. This meant a trial conducted by a majority of international judges and an independent international prosecutor, all appointed by the United Nations, in a court separated from the Cambodian judiciary, with Cambodian judges involved but vetted by the United Nations, all operating according to the procedural standards being used by existing international tribunals. The gap was starkly revealed during negotiations in August 1999 between the United Nations Office of Legal Affairs (OLA) and a Task Force appointed by Hun Sen, at which the two sides exchanged vastly different drafts on what a tribunal should look like.

In late 1999, the United States injected itself between Hun Sen and the United Nations as a broker of political deals and inventor of new legal mechanisms to implement those deals. This intervention followed the failure of U.S. attempts since 1997 to achieve international-standard accountability for DK-era crimes, pursuant to its stated policy goal of replacing "the Cold War ... with the War Against Atrocities."[2] The United States had tried to obtain a Security Council mandate for an International Criminal Tribunal for Cambodia, and also to snatch senior CPK suspects from hideouts along the Thailand-Cambodia border in order to whisk them off to a foreign court where they could be tried under the doctrine of universal jurisdiction. The Security Council route was actively obstructed by the DK's onetime close ally, China, and more subtly by Cambodia's former colonial overlord, France, which was eager to please Hun Sen. The snatch operations failed because of a lack of co-operation from friends of the DK among Thai military officials, and also because of difficulties in finding a foreign court prepared to handle the case.

Thus, starting in October 1999, the United States began putting its own ideas to the United Nations and Hun Sen about how to proceed, and then attempting to pressure or induce both to accept these ideas, relying on its superpower status *vis-à-vis* the United Nations and offering to reward Hun Sen with a lifting of the U.S. congressional restrictions on aid to Cambodia which was imposed following Hun Sen's *coup de force* of 1997. The U.S. strategy was to convince the United Nations to lower the bar while offering to pay Hun Sen to jump over it. Supported more or less strongly by Japan and France, the United States was able during the first half of 2000 to overpower the United Nations, forcing it into making the greatest concessions. However, these remained insufficient to satisfy Hun Sen, who also made accommodations but repeatedly stalled progress towards a final deal. In this, he continued to enjoy the support of China and the encouragement of France.

During 2000, Hun Sen marshalled two arguments to buttress his position. They aimed to replace his earlier contention that he was pursuing some uniquely Cambodian path, and also his claim that he was acting in defence of Cambodian sovereignty. The latter had been punctured in 1999, when Cambodia's King Norodom Sihanouk pointed out that the government had every sovereign right to co-operate with such a court.

Instead, Hun Sen and his spokesmen argued, first, that proceeding with an international trial would provoke a violent reaction from rallied DK remnants and disrupt the country's political stability and economic development; and, secondly, that opening up the issue to a public democratic debate, as would be required for passage of a tribunal law in parliament, would result in the obstruction of the legislation by "hardline" elements within the CPP. However, both arguments were discredited by the end of the year. The first claim was contradicted by mounting proof that no DK remnants were about to resume armed struggle. The second was contrary to evidence that many in the CPP were in favour of a more international trial; that this was also the predominant view in the CPP's usually but not entirely supine junior coalition partner in government, FUNCINPEC; that, furthermore, this was the preference among ordinary Cambodians and the informed public opinion within Cambodia's nascent civil society; and that Hun Sen's *bete noire*, the opposition Sam Rainsy Party (SRP), was attempting to capitalize on all this to attack him. The great lengths to which Hun Sen went precisely to prevent free and open discussion of how a trial should be conducted indicated that his fear was not the bogus threat of a ragtag ex-DK uprising, but the real danger of the emergence of a coalition of dissident CPP elements, FUNCINPEC, the SRP, civil society organizations and public opinion in favour of so much U.N. involvement in a trial that Hun Sen would lose political control of it.

By year's end, with Hun Sen's arguments and stalling tactics exposed and bankrupted, he decided to appear at least to have given the latter up. Suddenly, the threat of hardline CPP opposition evaporated, and a tribunal law that provided for U.N. participation in a domestic trial but fell short of what the United Nations had hoped for earlier in the year sailed through the CPP-dominated national assembly, with FUNCINPEC members falling back into line. Many observers believed, however, that Hun Sen would continue to duck and weave, alternatively to sweet-talk, double-talk and stiff-arm both the United States and the United Nations in order to maintain such *de facto* control over a trial process as to be able to predetermine its outcome, or to come up with new ways to sabotage progress towards a trial with U.N. participation if he feared he would be unable to do so. They feared that the trial could still turn out to be what one perceptive Asian diplomat had called "an optical illusion. You think it's there but it's not."[3]

The United Nations Non-Paper of 5 January 2000

In October 1999, a major U.S. interjection in the negotiation process had proposed that a trial should take place in an "extraordinary" court within the Cambodian judiciary and with a majority of Cambodian-appointed judges, but operating according to a "super-majority" arrangement. This meant that judicial decisions would have to be made by more than a majority of judges, so that at least some international judges would have to agree with them. This was coupled with a suggestion that the court's prosecutorial jurisdiction should be severely limited to cover only former "senior" CPK leaders, plus Duch, who because he had not been a member of the CPK Central Committee did not fit this definition but had somehow to be included. Finally, the United States suggested to the United Nations that it should leave itself in a position to opt out of a trial if, once it began, the proceedings were too outrageously political and unfair.

In December 1999, Hun Sen's Task Force produced a new draft tribunal law, which incorporated the super-majority concept, but left him with enough channels of influence to exert his political control. It put forward language aimed at ensuring impunity for CPP members and leaving open the possibility of trying only certain "top-level" DK leaders plus Duch, while giving Hun Sen wide latitude with regard to who among the leaders would be prosecuted. The Cambodian majority judges were all to be appointed by the Hun Sen-dominated Supreme Council of the Magistracy. Although the draft allowed the United Nations to propose foreign judges, the Council would also have to approve all nominees, and it could alternatively accept judges nominated by governments friendly to Hun Sen. Provisions for a Cambodian and a foreign "co-prosecutor" taken from Hun Sen's August draft similarly empowered the Council to appoint the Cambodian and approve the foreigner. Moreover, to give Hun Sen a veto over prosecutions, it retained a clause from the August draft that did not allow indictments without the agreement of the Cambodian prosecutor. Furthermore, it specified that the court would operate according to Cambodian procedures, that had been widely criticized as being unfair or ill-defined. In addition, while it promised that the government itself would not request amnesties for those convicted, it did not prohibit others from doing so, and it left in place Ieng Sary's existing amnesty. It did, however, take up the U.S. suggestion of paving the way for a U.N. exit from the whole affair by providing for the court to be financed by a voluntary Trust Fund, which if not subscribed by governments convinced that supporting a trial was worthwhile, would leave the United Nations unable to participate.

Still, this new draft was significantly short of what the United States wanted and far below United Nations standards. The United Nations OLA lawyers responded with a confidential "non-paper" that highlighted the gap. Implying doubt that a super-majority could prevent a Hun Sen-directed sabotage, it insisted that all court personnel must be totally free from political influence, asked for an increase in the proportion of international personnel, and demanded that the United Nations must appoint all of them together with an independent foreign prosecutor. It also wanted the United Nations to be able to reject Cambodian judges, and for the court to be a "special" one, which would be *outside* the existing judicial system. It insisted that the prosecution process must not be politically "selective", and that "the principle of accountability be given comprehensive interpretation". This meant that no one among those responsible for the serious violations should be excluded for any reason. Finally, the "non-paper" pointed out that for the United Nations, the usual first step in such situations was not the passage of a law, but a U.N.– government agreement on their binding mutual obligations to conduct a trial conforming to international standards of accountability and fairness, which the government should then incorporate into domestic legislation.[4]

To avoid discussion of the "non-paper" within his own Cabinet, Hun Sen rushed it into approving the December draft without having seen the U.N. document. He also blocked a proposal from Sok An, the head of his own Task Force, that parliament be allowed to see what OLA had to say, and insisted that he would not talk with the United Nations about the issues of judicial independence and fairness. The United States immediately began pressuring the United Nations to compromise legal principles to make a political deal, promising that it would, however, get Hun Sen to allow an international prosecutor to indict without being vetoed. This U.S. pressure undermined the position of Cambodian human rights non-governmental organizations (NGOs), whose lack of faith in the independence and fairness of the existing Cambodian judiciary led them to demand almost total U.N. control over any tribunal, and complete adherence to international norms and procedures.[5]

In spite of these domestic objections, the draft law was submitted to the Legislative Commission of the National Assembly, before which the government normally provides explanations of bills it initiates, for what was supposed to be quick adoption by Parliament. However, there were two problems. First, the passage of the law without further changes would provoke an open confrontation with the United Nations and would be a blatant snub to the United States, and Hun Sen recognized that this might adversely affect Cambodia's aid prospects.[6] Secondly, the FUNCINPEC Chairman of the Legislative Commission wanted to consider calls for changes by the United Nations and Cambodian NGOs. This reflected the underlying unhappiness with Hun Sen's position within FUNCINPEC, including in the eyes of the Party's leader, National Assembly President Prince Ranariddh. It also reflected popular sentiments in favour of a trial that specifically denied that Hun Sen could be trusted to hold one[7] and desired a largely international trial.[8] In this context, Hun Sen threatened that if things went further than he wanted, local unrest or armed insurrection would occur, but this was belied by reports that neither ordinary people nor current military commanders in the former DK areas had the stomach for such actions.[9]

Delaying Tactics and Corell's March Visit
Although Hun Sen was more than powerful enough to ride out popular views, FUNCINPEC dissidence and the threat of dissent within his own party, all this combined with the danger of a diplomatic crisis, led him to dissemble and buy time. This he could do with the discrete support of China, Russia, and France, which all remained opposed to a predominant role for the United Nations in a trial, although the latter were prepared to accept some U.N. participation.

Thus, at the end of January, Hun Sen switched to the tactic that he pursued for most of the remainder of 2000: refusing to sign any agreement with the United Nations until parliament had passed a trial law, and delaying the passage of any law that would not give him the degree of control over a trial that he wanted, while all the while continuing to negotiate with a United Nations pushed into ever more concessions by the United States.

However, for the moment, U.N. Secretary-General Kofi Annan continued mostly to follow the legal advice of the OLA rather than the political counsel of the United States, Japan, France, and Russia. His position was expressed in a letter to Hun Sen on 8 February 2000, which demanded a court meeting "international standards of justice, fairness and due process of law" and operating in "freedom from interference of any kind," with a majority of U.N.–appointed international judges and a U.N.–appointed prosecutor able to indict without obstruction by a Cambodian co-prosecutor. A major concession, however, was made with regard to whom the prosecutors would be free to indict. Although Annan demanded that Ieng Sary's amnesty not be honoured, he dropped the "non-paper's" more general insistence on non-selective and comprehensive prosecution.[10]

Hun Sen immediately responded quite rightly that the United Nations was asking for more than any of his U.S., French, Russian, or other diplomatic interlocutors were demanding. Although the United States, Japan, and to a lesser extent France were also asking Hun Sen to make further concessions, the balance of diplomatic forces advising the United Nations to be "flexible and creative" in defining minimum standards for judicial independence and fairness[11] was in Hun Sen's favour. Thus, after further urging from the United States, Kofi Annan dropped his call for a majority of international judges and for the application of international procedural standards. However, he still insisted on the exclusion of amnesties, past and future, and on freedom of action for a U.N.–appointed prosecutor, at least within the reduced parameters of the court's personal jurisdiction.[12]

These were the scaled-down demands included in the negotiating brief given to a U.N. delegation dispatched to Phnom Penh in March. Although the team was headed by OLA chief Hans Corell, it was politically guided by Shashi Tharoor, the Director of the Office of the Secretary-General, who was there to ensure that political considerations overrode legal ones.[13]

In closed-door talks with Hun Sen's Task Force, the Corell-Tharoor delegation offered to drop the U.N. demand for a majority of international judges and accept the super-majority formula if Hun Sen would accept an international prosecutor whose indictments could not be blocked, guarantee that no past amnesties would be honoured or future amnesties given, and that everyone indicted would be arrested. On this last issue, the United Nations accepted as sufficient a Task Force undertaking that the government would reiterate assurances about arrests in an international agreement with the United Nations. However, the Task Force stuck to Hun Sen's position that the two co-prosecutors must agree on indictments, and refused to void Ieng Sary's amnesty, or give airtight guarantees against future amnesties. The result was that although the bargain the United Nations had put on the table remained on offer, it was not agreed to.[14]

To preclude further negotiations, the Task Force claimed that discussions with the United Nations had to be suspended until Parliament could debate and pass a domestic law on the trial, and Corell acquiesced in this. However, although the United Nations had called for Parliament to be informed of what it had proposed, and National Assembly President Ranariddh said he would be happy to do so right away, Hun Sen was not about to allow any parliamentary action that might move the legislation significantly forward. Task Force chairman Sok An told the Assembly's Legislative Commission that there was still nothing further to discuss, since nothing had been agreed with the United Nations. Then, after just one meeting during which he formally briefed the Commission on a few articles in the draft law that had been presented to it in January, Sok An repeatedly found excuses for not continuing this process, thus scuttling any immediate prospect of the matter being debated in Parliament.

The United States tried to push things ahead by declaring that the only outstanding issue was overcoming the Cambodian co-prosecutor's veto on indictments. It portrayed the underlying problem not as one of political bias in the Cambodian judiciary, but as one of building "political trust" between Hun Sen and the United Nations, and the solution as setting up an arbitration panel to resolve disputes between the two prosecutors. Working through a U.S. Senator, Democrat John Kerry, it suggested a panel comprising three Cambodian and two international judges from the court, who would have to vote by super-majority against an indictment in order to prevent it from going forward. The United Nations was very sceptical that the formula was either workable or in line with legal principles, and it was roundly condemned by human rights experts, but the United States continued to push both sides to accept this "customized model" fit for Cambodia's "national situation."[15]

The 18 April Draft Memorandum

Hun Sen initially tried to sidestep the idea, egged on as ever by China and France, but with the United States dangling the prospect of a lifting of congressional restrictions on aid, he declared he would accept the panel if the United Nations dropped all its other demands. However, on 18 April, the United Nations instead forwarded to Hun Sen a draft bilateral memorandum of understanding through which it proposed to accept an arbitrating "pretrial chamber" as part of an overall comprise package that included its residual ongoing demands.

The text confirmed how much the United Nations had already conceded or was prepared to concede. The court would indeed be an "extraordinary" part of the existing politically-influenced judicial system and operate according to the existing substandard procedural code. Although the text suggested that judges and prosecutors might "seek guidance" from international standards and propose amendments to procedure, these provisions were toothless.

Moreover, the personal jurisdiction clause in the 18 April text was extremely restrictive, limiting prosecution only to "senior leaders of DK responsible for serious violations of Cambodian and international law". This excluded both lower-level officials regardless of the seriousness of their crimes and the highest leaders if their crimes were not serious. This phrasing was so limiting that it would, if interpreted literally, even exclude from prosecution former S-21 chairman Duch. Moreover, the clause on investigations also restricted these to "senior leaders", suggesting that those at lower levels could not be investigated even if this was only in order to build up a case against those higher up.

On the other hand, the United Nations reiterated its insistence that the Secretary-General appoint all international judges and prosecutors, and it called again on Hun Sen to guarantee both no amnesties for those convicted by the court, and that the amnesty granted to Ieng Sary should not be a bar to his prosecution.[16]

Within the U.N. legal and human rights machineries, there were grave misgivings about the extent to which the United Nations was offering to negotiate away principles to accommodate the United States, and thus Hun Sen. However, the United Nations had not gone far enough to satisfy Hun Sen's desires for control over any trial, and he therefore rejected the bargain implicit in the U.N. text with a counter-attack that reinforced his delaying tactics. He withdrew his support for the U.S. arbitration panel concept. This forced another intervention by Senator Kerry in late April to get Hun Sen to recommit himself to the arbitration panel concept and to try to get him finally to put the matter before Parliament and proceed to a formal agreement with the United Nations. With the lifting of congressional sanctions again as bait, the former was achieved but not the latter.

Thus, although the United States put forward a target date of 15 June for the passage of a tribunal law and signing of the agreement, Hun Sen defied this deadline, while maintaining that he was in favour of quick movement but was unable to get Parliament to move or approve anything.[17] To buttress this, he hinted that despite the United Nation's promise that no CPP figures would be prosecuted or even touched by investigations, he faced stiff opposition from those within the Party who still felt threatened. However, even if some did, their opposition was a minority position within the CPP, or at least only one of several positions in the Party.[18]

Nevertheless, Hun Sen's assertions sufficed to ensure that donors attending an international aid conference for Cambodia in France in May did not publicly raise the tribunal issue. They certainly did not challenge his declaration that political stability and economic development should be much higher priorities than a trial, which could reasonably be delayed while he concentrated on these more important matters.

Cambodians remained less convinced. Amidst further confirmation of the spuriousness of Hun Sen's threats that proceeding with the kind of trial that the United Nations wanted would provoke uprisings,[19] it emerged that the public believed that if anything happened, it would be staged by Hun Sen himself.[20] This was accompanied by simmering public anger at Hun Sen for his blatant horse-trading[21] and foot-dragging over the tribunal.[22] Fear of reprisals from Hun Sen prevented this from being expressed except by the stridently oppositionalist party led by the outspoken Sam Rainsy, which had from the beginning challenged Hun Sen to hold a popular referendum on the issue, and by the more vocal among local human rights organizations, which now also pointed to the loss of credibility that the United Nations was inflicting on itself by the concessions it was making.

Corell's July Visit

Nevertheless, faced with continual U.S. prodding, the United Nations gave the negotiations another try, and Corell arrived back in Phnom Penh on 5 July. He hoped finally to reach consensus on the contents of an international agreement specifying the government's commitments to the United Nations and how they would be expressed in a domestic law.

Despite protests from Cambodian human rights organizations that they and the public were being kept in the dark, Corell's discussions with the Task Force were shrouded in greater secrecy than the previous round. Thus, it only emerged three months later that at the initial meeting, Corell retabled the still unpublished draft memorandum of understanding of 18 April, modified by provisions for rejigging its already restrictive personal jurisdiction clause to more clearly guarantee impunity to CPP members, while also fitting in Duch.[23] How it might do so was laid out in a marked-up version of the text of the government's draft law, which included U.N.–proposed amendments. However, among these were also clauses tightening qualifications for the appointment of both Cambodian and foreign judges, asking the government to consider appointing non-civil servants as court staff, and slightly widening the theoretical scope for modifying existing judicial procedures to make them fairer. On the other hand, it now added to the United Nation's opt-out clause a provision that the trial could then proceed with United Nations personnel replaced with foreigners contributed by friendly governments or with CPP-approved Cambodians. Thus, if the United Nations could not raise the funds necessary to participate in the trial, Hun Sen could go ahead with an all-Cambodian process completely under his domination.[24]

The Task Force responded to this with proposals for massive changes in the draft memorandum that reduced to an absolute minimum government commitments to the United Nations, even suggesting the elimination of the government's undertaking to arrest indicted suspects.[25] After what the United Nations described as "frank and comprehensive discussions",[26] Corell presented slightly revised versions of the draft memorandum[27] and marked-up draft law[28] that he left behind without further discussion to "memorialize" an "understanding on the basic parameters of the relationship" between the United Nations and the government.[29] The United Nations thus rejected all the Task Force's suggested guttings of government commitments, and stuck to its other demands.

The fact was that the U.N. texts still had enough in them to give pause to Hun Sen about the extent to which he would be able to manipulate the proceedings, even though they contained far from enough guarantees against that manipulation to promise a genuinely independent, fair and impartial court. Corell was clearly concerned that the pause would only give rise to further delay. He warned the Task Force that the United Nations would not wait forever, and indicated a deadline of September for signing an agreement.

It soon became apparent that this was having no impact, and by mid-July even the United States was beginning to show public signs of impatience with Hun Sen's delaying tactics. However, France, and above all China, were sticking to the opposite tack, and Hun Sen reassured the latter that despite his talks with the United Nations, he would adhere to his original policy of "forgetting the past" of ex-DK leaders.[30] Thus, Sok An abruptly cancelled a scheduled meeting with the Legislative Commission in August. When Kofi Annan reported that month on Corell's talks, he carefully avoided claiming that any agreement had been reached.[31]

Then, as U.S. attempts to remain upbeat and find someone other than Hun Sen to blame for the problems wore increasingly thin,[32] he decided to throw it a scrap of progress just before he left Phnom Penh for New York in early September to attend a U.N. summit and the General Assembly. Sok An finally showed up to give a short briefing, but no new documents, to the Legislative Commission, claiming that this was proof of the government's determination to move quickly. However, this was contradicted by suggestions that if a trial were to take place, it should not happen for several more years.

In New York, Hun Sen refused to discuss the issue, although he did reiterate that Ieng Sary should not be indicted and that CPP members should be immune from prosecution. Meanwhile, Sok An again became unavailable to the Legislative Commission, and Parliament and the public were still being kept ignorant about what had transpired in July. This situation was partially corrected in mid-October, when documents from the meeting finally leaked out. This precipitated the formation of an informal alliance of junior FUNCINPEC politicians and non-governmental organizations, backed by student groups and trade unions, to push for progress towards a proper trial.[33]

Diplomatic pressure was also rising. In early November, a U.N. General Assembly resolution, backed by the United States, called on Hun Sen to stop foot-dragging and expedite the passage of domestic legislation in line with what the United Nations had demanded in July.[34] This was countered at mid-month by the visit to Phnom Penh of an aid-bearing Chinese President, Jiang Zemin. Although public protests compelled Chinese officials to deny that Jiang was asking Hun Sen not to allow U.N. involvement, they clearly stated their opposition to it.[35] However, the United States fought back at the end of the month when Senator Kerry visited Cambodia on the coat-tails of President Clinton's fanfare tour of Vietnam. Making sure that Hun Sen understood that Cambodia was falling behind Vietnam in its relations with the United States, Kerry reiterated that he stood to gain development aid and diplomatic status from co-operating with a trial. It was left clear that if he did not, a new Congress and administration might put Phnom Penh into a semi-pariah status not far above Yangon, Pyongyang, and Kabul.

The Law Passes

In the face of this, everything that had supposedly stood in the way of the passage of the draft law magically melted away. After months of pretending that the National Assembly might have a mind of its own, both Hun Sen and Ranariddh promised to deliver a passed law without problems by early January 2001, and so they did. With Sok An made available to brief the Legislative Commission, it was able in early December to pass on to the Assembly floor a draft that incorporated many but not all the amendments suggested by the United Nations in July. It was then adopted without change and unanimously after "debates" on 29 December and 2 January, during which neither CPP nor FUNCINPEC parliamentarians raised any serious points. The SRP's position was that although it was not entirely happy with the law, it did not want further delay, and so voted in favour.[36] This left confirmation of the bill by the Senate and its signature by King Sihanouk as next steps.

The United Nations' reaction was cautious. It was no doubt disappointed that the law failed to specify that Ieng Sary's pardon was no bar to his prosecution, and that it watered down possibilities that the court might incorporate international standards into its procedures and drop other safeguards for fairness. Feeding this disappointment was the realization that it had been manoeuvred into a deal it did not want by the Clinton Administration, only to be confronted with a much less U.N.–friendly George W. Bush Administration. It was left stuck facing Hun Sen's ongoing manoeuvres to find a path that would promise enough U.N. involvement to get U.S. aid but deliver so little impartiality and fairness as to allow him to determinate what would happen to Ta Mok, Duch, Ieng Sary, Khieu Samphan, Nuon Chea, and Kae Pok. Almost all observers agreed that the hardest parts were yet to come: getting the new U.S. administration and other governments to pay for U.N. involvement in a trial that falls significantly short of international standards, and getting Hun Sen to co-operate with the tribunal sufficiently well to keep the funding flowing long enough for a trial with U.N. participation to be completed. Moreover, even if in the end it proves possible for the United Nations to live with a trial that serves as much to certify that Hun Sen and other current CPP figures were neither "senior leaders" nor among those "most responsible" for CPK crimes as it is to bring those who were fairly to justice, the aura of his control over the trial will leave many Cambodians wondering whether the certification is valid. They would also wonder why the international community would be willing to give its stamp of approval to such a trial.

NOTES

1. This chapter includes references to both public and internal U.N. documents. Citation is given where possible, but where the documents cited are not publicly available, the reference is simply noted as a "U.N. document".
2. David J. Scheffer, Ambassador-at-Large for War Crimes Issues, "Perspectives on the Enforcement of International Humanitarian Law", 3 February 1999.
3. "China and Cambodia: What's at Stake for New Pals", *Phnom Penh Post*, 10–23 November 2000.
4. "Non-Paper on Khmer Rouge Trial", U.N. document, 5 January 2000.
5. Cambodian Human Rights Action Committee, "Khmer Rouge Draft Law Cannot Bring Justice to Cambodians", 6 January 2000.
6. "Cambodia: The Price of Justice", *Far Eastern Economic Review*, 17 February 2000.
7. Laura McGrew, "The Thorny Debate on Justice for Pol Pot's Madness", *Phnom Penh Post*, 18 February–2 March 2000.
8. "Public Forum on Khmer Rouge Trial Opens in Capital", *Kyodo* (Phnom Penh), 24 February 2000.
9. "Cambodians Enjoying Stability Under Hun Sen", *Nation*, 3 March 2000.
10. Letter from Kofi Annan to Hun Sen, U.N. document, 8 February 2000.
11. "UN Pressured Over Cambodia Tribunal", Associated Press, 14 March 2000.
12. "The Secretary-General Briefing to the Security Council on Visit to Southeast Asia", U.N. document, 29 February 2000.
13. Interview with a senior U.N. official, 9 August 2000.
14. "UN Hopes for Agreement on Genocide Tribunal Framework Fade", *South China Morning Post*, 21 March 2000.
15. Interview of U.S. Ambassador Kent Wiedemann, *Phnom Penh Post*, 28 April–11 May 2000.
16. "Articles of Cooperation/Memorandum of Understanding Between the UN and the RGC Concerning the Prosecution under Cambodian Law of Crimes Committed During the Period of Democratic Kampuchea", U.N. document, 18 April 2000.

17. Documentation Center of Cambodia, "Comments of Samdech Hun Sen, Prime Minister of the RGC, regarding the Khmer Rouge Draft Law", 3 May 2000.
18. Craig Etcheson, "End of the Road for the Khmer Rouge — or Travesty of Justice", *On the Record* 13, no. 2 (17 July 2000).
19. Interview with U.N. human rights official, 7 July 2000.
20. "From the Editorial Desk," *On the Record* 13, no. 9 (10 August 2000); and "What Cambodians Want from a Process", *On the Record* 13, no. 9 (10 August 2000).
21. "Cambodia's Terrible Legacy", *On the Record* 13, no 1 (14 July 2000).
22. "Cambodians Pray on Day of Anger", Associated Press, Choeng Aek, 20 May 2000.
23. "Draft 5 July 2000", U.N. document.
24. "Phnom Penh, 5 July 2000 at 6:00 PM", U.N. document.
25. Task Force text, "Amendments Proposed for the Draft Memorandum of Understanding/Articles of Cooperation (as distributed by the U.N. delegation, 5 July 2000)", U.N. document.
26. U.N. Press Release, "Statement Attributable to the Spokesman for the Secretary-General", 6 July 2000.
27. "Draft 7 July 2000", U.N. document.
28. "Phnom Penh, 7 July 2000 at 3:00 PM", U.N. document.
29. U.N. Press Release, "Press Statement by Mr Hans Corell, Pochentong Airport, Phnom Penh, 7 July 2000".
30. *People's Daily*, 30 August 2000.
31. U.N. General Assembly, "Situation of Human Rights in Cambodia: Report of the Secretary-General" (A/55/291), 11 August 2000.
32. Barry Wain, "Breaking Gridlock with Phnom Penh", *Asian Wall Street Journal*, 8 September 2000.
33. "KR Tribunal Secrecy Denounced", *Phnom Penh Post*, 27 October–9 November 2000.
34. U.N. General Assembly, "Situation of Human Rights in Cambodia" (A/C.3/55/L.39), 8 November 2000.
35. "China Says It Didn't Support Khmer Rouge's Policies", Associated Press, Phnom Penh, 13 November 2000.
36. "Trial Law Sails Through Assembly", *Phnom Penh Post*, 5–18 January 2001.

INDONESIA

INDONESIA
The Trials of President Wahid

Arief Budiman

Introduction

The year 2000 was a trial year for President Abdurrahman Wahid (popularly known as Gus Dur). In August there was a People's Consultative Assembly (Majelis Permusyawaratan Rakyat or MPR) annual meeting that evaluated his performance after ten months. When Wahid was elected as President, in October 1999, there was a high expectation that he would lead an effective government and take Indonesia out of its deep trouble. However, that hope is fading rapidly. Many people, including Wahid's supporters, have become uneasy with his erratic behaviour. Therefore, during the MPR session, there was growing pressure to impeach Wahid in order to allow Vice-President Megawati Soekarnoputri to take over the presidency. How was the situation at the end of 2000? What are Wahid's chances of survival as President until the end of his term in 2004 when the next presidential election will be held?

The restoration of democracy to the country brought contradictory results. On one hand, it gave power to the people to control the government. On the other hand, the new power gained by a wider political élite has been used to attack the executive and in many cases enhance personal interests, which has made it difficult for the existing government to work effectively. In a sense, democracy has brought a sort of political anarchy which has contributed to the economic difficulties.

The economic condition was stable, albeit operating at a low base. There were problems of unemployment or under-employment, although many people still managed to make a living. An economic recovery to the pre-crisis level still seems unlikely owing to the lack of investment. In 2000, local and foreign business people were still reluctant to invest significantly because of the fragile political condition and the lack of the rule of law.

The weak rule of law is a major concern for Indonesia. In 2000 there were many cases in which people took the law into their own hands. Petty criminals have been killed on the spot (often burnt alive) when caught by mobs. In many cases, they were not handed over to the police, because many have lost

---

ARIEF BUDIMAN is the Foundation Professor of Indonesian Studies, Melbourne Institute of Asian Languages and Societies, University of Melbourne, Australia.

faith in the police to deliver justice.[1] In addition, the police seemed reluctant to take action against the Muslim militia groups that destroyed many night-clubs in Jakarta, and in other big cities, in the name of Syari'ah (Islamic Law). In Solo, Central Java, the Muslim militia harassed American tourists in November because of the perceived pro-Israel policy of the United States in dealing with the conflict between Israel and the Palestinians. If the law is not enforced, Indonesia could descend into civil anarchy.

The greatest achievement of the Wahid administration has been his success in restoring democracy, even if it is a very fragile one. People can freely express their opinion in public without getting into trouble with the government, which is a marked difference from the situation under Soeharto. People are also free to organize themselves into associations.

Wahid has been applauded for his commitment to democracy and pluralism. So far he has proven himself consistent in following these ideals. His political opponents can criticize him openly, his approach in solving problems is always through political dialogue (such as in dealing with the independence movements in West Papua and Aceh), he seeks to protect the Christian and Chinese minorities, and he keeps trying to revoke the ban on communism. Other leaders may not be as liberal as Wahid.

The Leadership of President Wahid

Wahid was elected by the MPR as President in October 1999. The MPR is the highest constitutional body of Indonesia. It consists of all the 500 members of the legislative DPR (Dewan Perwakilan Rakyat or Parliament) and another 200 special members (appointees and regional representatives) of the MPR. The 700 members, *inter alia*, elect the President and also have the power to impeach him or her.

President Wahid's erratic behaviour did not really create serious problems when he was the head of Nahdatul Ulama (NU), Indonesia's (and the world's) largest Muslim organization. In NU circles, this behaviour has been considered as proof of his advanced logic, which is supposed to be one step ahead of the logic of the common people. He is perceived as a *wali*, a saintly person who gets revelation directly from God. The fact that he is nearly blind and that his party only controls 8 per cent of the MPR seats, but yet he has managed to become President, has strengthened the belief among his followers that he possesses something approaching super-human power.

Soon after his inauguration as President, in a meeting with Members of Parliament who had criticized him, he uttered in Javanese "*prek*" (get lost). Then he accused Parliament of being a "kindergarten" after an intense debate.[2] Unnecessary statements like these, linked with accusations of corruption against high public employees (sometimes resulting in unprofessional dismissals), have become quite common during the Wahid administration.

In addition to his erratic public comments, Wahid has continued with his well-known predilection for travelling. As the head of NU, he had travelled extensively throughout Java, visiting many *pesantren* (Islamic religious schools) in the villages, and made a number of visits to overseas destinations. Now as President, he continues to travel to an impressive number of countries. At first, the general population thought these visits were useful. However, after these trips became excessive, many were cynical about their utility. Within five months of becoming President, Wahid had visited more than fifty foreign countries, which has made him the world's most travelled head of state within such a short period of time. At one point he even wanted to buy a private presidential airplane for his travels. In September, he went to Seattle to visit the U.S. airplane manufacturer Boeing. He dropped the idea after much criticism.[3]

Wahid's erratic behaviour has also spilled over into the international arena. The most serious incident occurred in November when Wahid reacted to a perceived slight by the Senior Minister of Singapore, Lee Kuan Yew, concerning the longevity of his administration. In front of a group of Indonesian expatriates at the Indonesian Embassy in Singapore, Wahid accused Singapore of being arrogant in its relations with other ASEAN countries and "only looking for profit".[4] Singapore, Wahid also explained, looked down on the Malay people. For this, he issued a threat to Singapore that Indonesia, acting in concert with Malaysia, may consider stopping the supply of fresh water to Singapore. The Indonesian press was largely critical of Wahid for the way that he had expressed these views. The Indonesian Foreign Minister, Alwi Shihab, tried to play down the incident by likening the relationship of the two countries to that of husband and wife: "There may be anger within the relationship from time to time, but things always improve."[5] He also commented that the incident was unnecessary and hurt both countries. This type of behaviour from Wahid could create problems with the international community.

After Wahid's election, he set up a coalition Cabinet of political parties that had supported him during the presidential election. Knowing that his party, the PKB, got only 8 per cent of the MPR seats, the Cabinet was based on a multiparty compromise. Named the "National Unity Cabinet", he invited other parties to join. He also courted General Wiranto to become the Co-ordinating Minister for Political and Security Affairs in order to obtain military support.

However, this Cabinet failed to work as a team. He then started to criticize some of his ministers in public (which is not normal practice in most countries) and removed some Cabinet ministers under controversial circumstances. For instance, Wahid allegedly dismissed the Co-ordinating Minister for Social Affairs and Welfare, Hamzad Haz, but told the public that Haz had resigned voluntarily. This was later denied by Haz and to this day it is not clear what really happened. Later, again during one of his foreign visits in February, he asked General Wiranto to resign, because his name was associated with the violation of human rights in East Timor. Wiranto refused and Wahid repeated his call several times. When the President arrived back in Indonesia, Wiranto met him and a statement by the President was issued saying that the resignation would be postponed until the human rights violations case was cleared. However, later in the evening of the same day, the President dismissed him, leaving Wiranto somewhat at a loss as to what had happened.

On 24 April, Wahid removed two more ministers, Laksamana Sukardi (Partai Demokrasi Indonesia–Perguangan or PDI-P), and Jusuf Kalla (Golkar). First, they were accused of not being able to work in harmony with the other economic ministers. However, this was denied by the other ministers. Later, he accused these two ministers of corruption. The difficulty here is that Laksamana Sukardi was well known as an able and "clean" official, and many refused to believe Wahid on this issue. To make matters appear more suspicious, Sukardi was replaced by Rozy Munir, one of Wahid's close confidants. Munir's reputation is at best doubtful.

However, the most unprofessional "dismissal" was that of the Governor of Bank Indonesia, Syahril Sabirin, at the end of June 2000. According to the law, the President had no legal power to do this. In order to achieve his purpose, Wahid asked the Attorney General, Marzuki Darusman, to give Sabirin two options (according to Sabirin's press interviews): (1) to resign and be appointed as Indonesian ambassador to a foreign country; or (2) to be arrested for corruption. As he refused to resign, he was arrested. After about six months in jail, he was released and resumed his position as Governor of Bank Indonesia. This was possible because Sabirin continued to enjoy the support of the chairman of the DPR, Akbar Tanjung. It was obvious that Akbar's support for Sabirin, a Golkar Party member, was in the strategic interest of Golkar. However, Sabirin is still a suspect and his case has not yet been dropped.

After realizing that the National Unity Cabinet did not work, in August Wahid set up a new Cabinet consisting only of persons closely affiliated to the President or his party. He did not even consult Vice-President Megawati (who also leads the largest party in Parliament), who then expressed her anger by finding an excuse not to attend Wahids' announcement of his new Cabinet before Parliament. Megawati's PDI-P members were totally excluded from the new Cabinet. When asked about Megawati's absence during the announcement, Wahid flippantly remarked that Megawati went home to take a shower, and one could not do anything when a woman wanted to take a shower.

There are two controversial figures in the new Cabinet: the Minister of Defence, Mahfud M.D., and the Minister of Finance, Prijadi Praptosuhardjo. Mahfud was a lecturer in an Islamic private university in Yogyakarta, teaching law. He is completely inexperienced in military affairs but has found himself as the Minister of Defence. His sole qualification for the position is his long association with Gus Dur. He provoked a strong reaction from the international community when he suggested that Indonesian intelligence reports had confirmed that the East Timorese were tired of the United Nations and wanted to be part of Indonesia again. The Minister of Finance, Prijadi Praptosuhardjo, has also been a close friend of the President. When he was a branch director of a state bank, he provided easy financial credits for some projects run by Nahdatul

Ulama. Under his leadership, the branch was reported to have suffered from substantial bad loans. He also failed to be promoted to a higher position because he did not pass the "fit and proper" test conducted by Bank Indonesia.

After only several months in office, Wahid's changing behaviour is clear for all to see. Among those who know him, this is not something new. A top cleric in Nahdatul Ulama once described Wahid as a driver who never gave a signal when he wanted to put on the brakes or make a turn. This erratic behaviour has become more evident after he suffered two strokes that have also affected his eyesight.

Corruption and Scandals

Six months after Wahid took office, in May 2000, he was accused of having used state money improperly. His private "masseur", Suwondo, went to the State Logistics Body (Bulog, or Badan Urusan Logistik) to "borrow" Rp 35 billion (about US$4 million). The money was then passed to several people: Suwondo's wife; a businesswoman named Siti Farika; a deputy chairman of PDI-P; as well as to an airline company in which Wahid and Suwondo were involved.[6] At the end of 2000, this scandal, known as "Buloggate", was still a problem for Wahid, and has the potential to lead to his impeachment if evidence of his direct involvement is forthcoming. Then, there was another scandal in which Wahid was said to have received US$2 million from the Sultan of Brunei, which he failed to report to the state treasury. Wahid claimed that it was a personal gift, and that the money was spent on humanitarian projects in Aceh. This scandal, known as "Bruneigate", has also refused to go away. By early 2001, these scandals had provoked substantial criticism in Indonesia and caused Parliament to pass a motion of censure.

A third scandal was "Borobudurgate", in reference to Hotel Borobudur in Jakarta where Wahid met with the notorious son of Soeharto, Tommy, who was about to receive a jail sentence for corruption. Tommy was trying to arrange a pardon from the President. Although at first Wahid denied that there was such a meeting, in the end he admitted that there was some discussion. However, he denied that there was a bargain struck on how much Tommy had to pay to get the pardon. In any event, Tommy disappeared when the jail sentence was about to be pronounced and remains at large.[7] It was unwise in the extreme for Wahid, as President, to have had this meeting. Related to the issue of bringing justice to bear on the Soeharto family for its past corruption, in November former President Soeharto was freed from all allegations by the court because of his poor health. This ruling was later challenged by a higher court after Wahid commented negatively on it.

Another scandal of a different kind was with regard to the President's alleged past affair with a woman named Aryanti. The woman has now come forward to tell her story. A picture of the woman sitting on Wahid's lap was circulated widely in Parliament and among the general public. There had also been rumours that Wahid had had an affair with Siti Farika, the woman who received Rp5 billion in the "Buloggate" scandal. However, this scandal has not been pursued by Wahid's opponents. According to rumours circulating, the main reason is that many of the political élite do not wish to set a precedent for this sort of thing — as it may rebound on more than a few.

All these scandals are surely damaging to the image of Wahid. Whether or not he can ride these scandals out may be the key to his political survival.

The Political Survival of Wahid

Whether Wahid can survive depends also on the political élites that support and oppose him. The MPR, constitutionally Indonesia's most powerful body, has the authority to both elect and impeach the President. Of the total of 700 seats, the PDI-P (under Megawati), the biggest party, controls 185 seats (27 per cent of the total seats), while Golkar (Akbar Tanjung) controls 182 seats (26 per cent). Wahid's own party, the PKB (Partai Kebangkitan Bangsa) controls only 57 seats (8 per cent). Amien Rais' party, PAN (Partai Amanat Nasional) forms a bloc (Poros Tengah, or Central Axis) with a small Islamic party PK (Partai Keadilan), and together they control 49 seats (7 per cent).[8]

Wahid's political position is thus very weak. He won the presidency because of the support of the coalition of Islamic parties (mobilized by Amien Rais) and much of Golkar — all of whom found Wahid the better alternative to Megawati Soekarnoputri. After he became President he persuaded Megawati to be his Vice-President. Wahid now depends on the support of Megawati, who supports him in spite of Wahid's tendency to neglect and even harass her. Megawati has remained loyal to Wahid, although slowly she seems to be distancing herself.

Wahid does not seem to dwell on his weak political position. He seemingly ignores the power composition of Parliament, namely, the MPR and the DPR, which are controlled by members of other parties. Thus, the Wahid administration is subject to much turbulence, because it is constantly being attacked by the political forces that control the legislature.

Faced with a hostile political élite, will Wahid survive? The answer is not simple for the following reasons. If Wahid were to leave office, Megawati would be the next President. There are three reasons why people have strong reservations over this alternative scenario. First, Megawati is perceived by many people as either having no ability to lead the country, or as being too nationalistic and potentially prone to solving political problems by using the military. Her inaction in dealing with the problem in Maluku, for which she has been given special responsibility, has been perceived as indicative of her inability to deal with the general problems of the country. In many instances, when the country was in crisis, she remained largely silent. If she made any comments, her remarks usually either reflected a sense of reactionary nationalism, or were very general and had little or no substance.

Secondly, some Muslim opposition to Megawati derives from the fact that she is a woman. According to one interpretation of Islamic belief, a woman cannot hold a position of leadership over men. However, opposition by the Islamic parties has declined. For example, Amien Rais, in a statement in November, said that he would be prepared to become the Vice-President if Megawati became the President. However, in general, opposition to a female leader is still strong among conservative Muslims, and this will remain an obstacle. Thirdly, Megawati's husband, Taufik Kiemas, is known to be linked to some conglomerate businessmen, and has also been accused of corruption. Therefore, if Megawati becomes President, there is no guarantee, on current evidence, of a cleaner administration.

Another problem is the timing. If Megawati steps in now, she would immediately become subject to the scrutiny and strong criticism currently directed at Wahid. Her silence and general inaction would be exposed openly. So far, these characteristics have not been exposed to any great extent. This situation may not remain if she becomes the President. Therefore, for Megawati it seems wiser to wait and learn as much as possible about the art of leadership from her experience as Vice-President, if necessary until 2004. In this way, her quietism could ultimately be seen as "silence is golden", making her more popular rather than being thought of as incompetent. When Wahid's popularity is at its lowest ebb, she can step in and be welcomed as a saviour.

Another potential challenger for the position of President is Akbar Tanjung, the head of the Golkar party. Akbar is more skilful in politics than Megawati, as well as an effective bureaucrat. He also controls a party that, as the former ruling party, has a nation-wide political machinery, with an abundance of financial resources. The only thing he lacks now is political legitimacy. He is seen as part of the Soeharto administration and the masses do not seem to be ready to accept Golkar back in the driving seat. People believe that if Akbar becomes the head of state, he would not be able (or willing) to take action against his old friends and colleagues — the Soeharto family and their associates. So, it seems unlikely that Akbar can become President at present or in the near future.

It seems more realistic for Akbar to contend for the vice-presidency. This could be done if Megawati assumes the presidency, and the PDI-P and Golkar come to some political arrangement. Megawati, as the symbol of the opposition against Soeharto, could compensate for Akbar's lack of political legitimacy, and Akbar's management skills could make up for Megawati's managerial shortcomings. In addition, Megawati's strong nationalism, together with Akbar's old patronage links, might protect many generals from prosecution by international tribunals for human rights violations, and this would therefore attract the support of the military. There are two possible problems with this scenario. Firstly, it seems that Megawati still feels uneasy about Akbar. Wahid has annoyed her several times, but she still seems to see him as her erratic elder brother, as expressed in her repeated exclamation: "*Terserah Mas Dur Saja*" ("it is up to Brother Dur"). During the difficult time when she was politically harassed by Soeharto, the only political leader who dared to show his sympathy and friendship in public was Wahid, then the chairperson of Nahdatul Ulama. This special relationship between Megawati and Wahid has proved enduring. Secondly, as noted earlier, the conservative Muslims within Golkar may still oppose Megawati's bid for the presidency on the grounds that she is a woman.

Akbar is very much aware that Golkar is still deeply unpopular. He is working very hard to recreate the image of Golkar, and so far he has been quite successful. However, he needs more time for his party to be ready to step back into a leading position of power without widespread public opposition.

Amien Rais, the chairman of the MPR, continues to promote himself as a future Vice-President. At one point, he was at the forefront of the opposition figures because of his strong stand against Soeharto during the events of early 1998. However, he has changed his political position so often that many now question whether he is genuine, or simply an opportunist. Many people still believe that he supports the Laskar Jihad (a radical Muslim group involved in the Maluku conflict) after he publicly attended a mass rally of this organization in Jakarta. Amien Rais is the only contender who is visibly trying hard to gain power as soon as possible. He keeps tarnishing the Wahid administration, and is now pushing Megawati to assume the presidency, offering himself as her Vice-President. This is a change from his previous position of opposing Megawati because she is a woman and his stated desire to be President himself. His change of heart is understandable, because the longer he has to wait, the more likely he is to engage in risky political manoeuvres, which may discredit him even more in the eyes of his supporters.

The absence of a credible alternative to Wahid strengthens the hand of the incumbent President. Wahid is also seen by the political élite as a better alternative to a power vacuum that could be filled by the military. At least, Wahid is committed to democracy and pluralism. However, in view of his erratic behaviour, the patience of the parliamentarians and the masses could also be running out.

The Military

When Wahid was elected President in October 1999, the military was still powerful, although its power was much reduced compared with what it had been during much of Soeharto's time. The military institution was still there, entangled with the complex structure of government.

After taking office, the first thing Wahid did was to appoint Dr Juwono Sudarsono, a civilian, as Minister for Defence — the first civilian to hold the position since Soeharto came to power. (Juwono Sudarsono was later replaced by another civilian, Mahfud M.D.) Four months after Juwono's appointment, on 14 February, General Wiranto, the powerful general who had been close to Soeharto, was replaced by Admiral Widodo (from the Navy) as the Commander-in-Chief of the Armed Forces. In the history of the Indonesian military, this position had hitherto always been held by a general from the army.

Following the replacement of Wiranto, many strategic positions were also given to the President's allies within the military. Two weeks after the dismissal of General Wiranto, 74 officers were replaced on 28 February. By March 2000, many of the key positions within the military were occupied by generals who were close to Wahid. It appeared that Wahid had put the military firmly under his control.

However, some events seem to contradict this assumption. In Aceh, killings and kidnappings continued, carried out by both the Free Aceh Movement (GAM) and the Indonesian military (mostly the latter). Jakarta gave orders to the military to stop the killing, but to no avail. This also happened in Maluku, and the conflict between Christians and Muslims there could not be stopped. It has been reported that the police and the military have been involved in the killings, and at times have taken sides with, respectively, the Christian and Muslim belligerents. In addition, when the radical Muslim militia group Laskar Jihad went to Maluku, it was not stopped, even though Jakarta had ordered the police and the military to intercept them. The order was simply ignored, and the civilian authorities seemed powerless to do anything. There is a widespread belief that these radical Muslim militias have connections with some faction of the military which wants to destabilize the Wahid administration. This may explain why the police have been very cautious about taking any measures against such groups. In Jakarta, bombs exploded several times in September. It would seem that these explosions were warnings to the government not to put Soeharto or his family members on trial. The explosions could not have happened without the use of military ordnance.[9]

At the beginning of September, a dramatic event shocked the United Nations Millennium Meeting in New York, which President Wahid was attending. Three U.N. humanitarian workers in Atambua, West Timor, were murdered brutally by the Indonesian military-backed militia. The U.N. Secretary General Kofi Annan, President Bill Clinton, and a number of other world leaders expressed their disappointment. Wahid openly stated that these killings were meant to humiliate him internationally, and were perpetrated by those who opposed his government.

By the end of the year, the inability of the President to control the military became more obvious, as shown by two other incidents. The first one was the case of General Agus Wirahadikusuma, whom Wahid had appointed to be the Commander of Kostrad (Army Strategic Command). The general tried to crack down on a major corruption scandal involving about 190 billion rupiah of Kostrad's funds which implicated its previous commander, the powerful General Djadja Suparman. He leaked some information on the case to the press.[10] The military headquarters denied the allegations, and Wirahadikusuma was dismissed only four months after taking office. In this case, Wahid was not able to protect Wirahadikusuma.

The second case involved the arrest of five leaders of the Papua Independence Movement just before they celebrated the anniversary of the day they consider to be their day of independence — 1 December. On 5 December, Wahid ordered that these leaders be released, but the Irian Jaya police chief, Brigadier General Sylvanus Wenas, ignored the President's orders. Wahid was again unable to do anything.[11]

By the end of 2000, Wahid had not succeeded in controlling the military. On the contrary, he seemed to be losing overall command. It is likely that not only is Wahid in danger but further democratization is also in peril.

Regional Independence Movements and Regional Issues

The strongest independence movements are in Aceh and West Papua (previously known as Irian Jaya). During the Soeharto administration, Aceh and West Papua were valuable economic cash cows for the regime. Rich in natural resources, the government exploited these regions heavily and most of the profits went to Jakarta while few returns went to the local people. Regional protestations were viewed as treason and dealt with severely by the military. Having experienced this for years, many in Aceh and West Papua have reached a point where they consider it better to become an independent state. They view Indonesia as a colonial country, exploiting them economically and repressing them politically. In the new freedom of the post-Soeharto era, the cries for justice from the two regions have been transformed into a more intense struggle for independence. Unlike the Soeharto regime, the Wahid administration has dealt with this problem (at least in the beginning) politically through negotiations, rather than through military repression as a first resort.

In Aceh, negotiations have been conducted since Wahid became President. While negotiations are in progress, a truce known as the Humanitarian Pause (Jeda Kemanusiaan) has been launched. Unfortunately, the military continues to conduct an agenda of kidnapping, torture, and killing in Aceh, in particular against those viewed as being members of the Free Aceh Movement. It must also be noted that some members of the Free Aceh Movement have been provoking the military in order to create social unrest and thus draw more support from among the Acehnese for their struggle. Many innocent people have been victims in this conflict as a result of the tactics used by elements on both sides.

In West Papua, a similar thing has happened. At first, Wahid dealt with the problem politically, not militarily. He let the people adopt the name West Papua for their province, instead of the old name Irian Jaya. He also let the Papuan people raise their own flag, the Morning Star flag, as long as it is raised together with the Indonesian national flag. Moreover, Wahid contributed one billion rupiah for the meeting of the Papua Council (Dewan Papua) in June. The Council called for an acknowledgement that West Papua had legally gained independence from the Dutch in 1961, and therefore, the case for its inclusion into Indonesia may be null and void. The declaration drew angry responses from a number of elements in the Indonesian Parliament.

The government has told both the Acehnese and the West Papuans that it is ready to grant them a large measure of autonomy, but not independence. On 19 December, Wahid specially went to Aceh to again offer this option for autonomy, but this time in a public manner. However, both the Acehnese and the West Papuas seemed to reject the offer.

Meanwhile, the Wahid administration is set to implement the regional autonomy provisions decided by the former B.J. Habibie administration. The regional autonomy laws, designed to take effect during 2001, devolve authority to Indonesia's districts and regencies — of which there are more than 350 — not to the provinces. Districts and regencies will become responsible for key governance issues such as health, education, roads and transport, aspects of economic management, and so on. However, the seriousness of the administration on this issue was questioned when the minister in charge, Dr Ryaas Rasyid, announced his intention to resign because of the lack of support from the President for his portfolio's responsibilities — and finally did so in early 2001.[12]

Sectarian Conflicts

Religious conflicts were more prominent in the year 2000, namely, between the Muslims and the Christians in certain areas. The most debilitating sectarian conflict took place in the Maluku islands. This conflict (which started in August 1999) was still ongoing at the end of 2000, albeit on a smaller scale. Several thousand lives have been lost.

Although predominantly religious, the conflict in reality is a complex one involving also class and ethnic issues. The Muslims are mostly transmigrants from outside Maluku. There are also sub-ethnic groups in Maluku that have been divided along religious lines, and there has been political conflict relating to the position of the local governor.[13] There are indications that some ex-cronies of Soeharto, working together with rogue military generals, are involved in the prolonged conflict in this area.

In the middle of 2000, the Maluku conflict seemed to be fading away, but was dramatically revived when thousands of members of the Jihad Command (Laskar Jihad) went to the islands to help their fellow Muslims. Jihad Command was a paramilitary organization that was set up in Yogyakarta and received paramilitary training in Bogor, a small town 60 km from Jakarta. The President's instruction to the police and the military to stop the Jihad Command from entering Maluku was not obeyed.

There were some efforts to expand this religious conflict to other parts of Indonesia. In Mataram, Lombok, a conflict between the Muslim and Christian communities broke out at the end of January 2000 and some churches were set on fire, forcing many Christians to flee the island. Then in Medan, there were bomb explosions in some churches in May,[14] while at the same time pamphlets were circulated in the city calling upon the Muslims to emulate the courage of their brothers in Maluku and to attack the Christians. In Bali, too, it was reported that there was some effort to create a conflict between the

Muslim and Hindu communities, but to no avail. However, a bomb exploded in front of a church in Padangbulan, Bali, on 20 August.

On 24 December (Christmas Eve), several bombs exploded in front of churches in Jakarta, including the Jakarta Cathedral, and in other cities. About fifteen people were reported dead.[15] However, rather than being provoked, Christian and Muslim leaders together condemned this practice of terror. The youth organizations of both religions then agreed to work together to safeguard the Idul Fitri (the Muslim New Year, which fell on 27 December).

To conclude, the biggest religious conflict has occurred in Maluku. The government has only been moderately successful in dealing with this conflict. Efforts to spread the conflict to other places have so far failed. On the contrary, the Christmas Eve bombings in Jakarta have seen Muslim and Christian organizations drawing closer together.

The Economy

According to the *Wall Street Journal*, the Indonesian economy will grow at 4 per cent for the year 2000.[16] This annual growth rate is far from sufficient, and constitutes "a bounce back after the crisis", as the newspaper put it. However, the *Journal* continued: "With more than 200 million people, it needs to grow at 8% per year just to absorb the 30% to 40% of the workforce that is currently underemployed or unemployed, in addition to a massive 3% annual growth in available workers."

Investments, both domestic and foreign, are still very low. Australian economist Ross McLeod has argued: "The economy has been growing modestly, but investment spending — the most basic indicator of confidence in Indonesia's near-term economic prospects — remains far below pre-crisis level."[17] The *Wall Street Journal* further stated that: "Before the Asian crisis, in 1997, investment was $17 billion. In 1999, the figure was $9 billion. This year it's up about 16% — but it's only the percentage that's big and far short of Indonesia's needs."[18]

Investment is very much related to the confidence of investors, and this confidence is based on political stability, the rule of law, projections of the future, and so forth. The non-economic factors that create business confidence are crucial, but the present government has failed to provide these conditions. Even the then Co-ordinating Minister for the Economy, Kwik Kian Gie, said in May: "If I were a foreign investor, I wouldn't come to Indonesia. The law enforcement is not there, but not only that, the whole thing is so confusing."[19] Thus, in the end, the Indonesian economic problem has been compounded by its political problems. Without new investments, recovery will be very slow.

Fortunately, at the Tokyo meeting of the Consultative Group on Indonesia (CGI) on 18 October 2000, Indonesia was granted new loans amounting to US$4.8 billion for the year 2001, and an extra US$540 million in technical grants to support the Indonesian non-governmental organizations (NGOs).[20] This will keep Indonesia afloat for a while.

The effort of the Indonesian Banking Restructuring Agency (IBRA) to recover state loans given to many banks and large businesses during the Soeharto administration has so far not succeeded because of the weaknesses of Indonesian law on this issue, and the corrupt nature of the judiciary. Here, IBRA is dealing with about Rp 207 trillion and approximately 170,000 debtors. However, 82.8 per cent of the sum is owed by 1,339 corporate debtors (0.8 per cent of debtors).[21] IBRA has a giant task, and given the present conditions, analysts are sceptical that IBRA can perform this task successfully. If these loans can be recovered, they will contribute significantly to the state budget, and Indonesia could then make a start with a new, healthy banking structure.

Presently, the economy is stable at a low level but there is no sign that it will recover in the near future. This is due to the continuing crisis in the political arena, which discourages investments.

Conclusion

Based on what has happened in the year 2000, the following conclusions can be drawn.

There are two factors that have created the difficult situation in Indonesia: the Soeharto legacy and Wahid's leadership. The socio-political and economic legacy inherited by the Wahid administration is quite bad and would challenge even the most able leader. However, Wahid is a leader with serious shortcomings, and this is evidenced by his erratic behaviour and lack of managerial skills.

Some parliamentarians (mostly from Wahid's party, the PKB) tend to think that Wahid has to be defended as President, at least until 2004. Given the difficulty of the situation, whoever replaces Wahid will face the same problems and will probably do no better. Those who think that the leadership factor is more important are likely to work hard to replace the President with somebody they think is better. With a better leadership, they believe, Indonesia will perform better. Which group is stronger? By the end of 2000, those who opposed Wahid seemed to be gaining strength. However, if Wahid can improve his performance and does not make any fatal mistakes, and can retain the support of Megawati, he should last until 2004, his health permitting.

Should Wahid step down from the presidency before 2004, the successor government may well be a coalition between the PDI-P and Golkar, with the support of the military. Together, the two leading political parties control the majority of votes both in the DPR and the MPR. They probably would be able to provide a stable government, but they may not be able to implement some important agenda of the "*reformasi*" movement.[22] The question is: outside the circle of some militant students, do people still remember and care about the "*reformasi*" agenda? This is an especially pertinent question when economic conditions are not improving.

Thus, at the end of 2000, even though Wahid was formally the President, his power was weak. As has been discussed earlier, he failed to help his appointee, General Agus Wirahadikusuma, fight against corruption in Kostrad.

Wahid also failed to stop Syahril Sabirin from resuming his post as the Governor of Bank Indonesia.[23] Moreover, when Wahid ordered the police to release the five leaders of the Papua Independence Movement, his request was ignored.[24] In view of this, the question is whether Wahid, if he continues to be President until 2004, can rule effectively alongside an increasingly hostile DPR and MPR.

NOTES

1. See "Indonesian Justice Run Amok," *Los Angeles Times*, 21 December 2000.
2. *Tempo Interaktif*, 18 November 1999.
3. *Tempo*, 17 September 2000, p. 18.
4. *Asian Wall Street Journal*, 26 November 2000.
5. *Straits Times*, 28 November 2000; and *Tempo*, 10 December 2000, pp. 16 and 28.
6. Ross H. McLeod, "Survey of Recent Developments", *Bulletin of Indonesian Economic Studies* 36, no. 2 (Canberra: The Australian National University, July 2000): 5.
7. *Tempo*, 3 December 2000.
8. Harold Crouch, "Indonesia: Democratization and the Threat of Disintegration", *Southeast Asian Affairs 2000* (Singapore: Institute of Southeast Asian Studies, 2000), p. 117.
9. See *Tempo*, 18–24 September 2000, p. 2.
10. *Tempo*, 6 August 2000; and 13 August 2000.
11. Agence France Presse (AFP), 11 December 2000.
12. See interview with Ryaas Rasyid in *Tempo*, 10 December 2000, pp. 38–42.
13. Tamrin Amal Tomagola, "The Bleeding Halmahera of North Moluccas", in *Political Violence: Indonesia and India in Comparative Perspective*, edited by Olle Tornquist, SUM Report No. 9 (Oslo: University of Oslo, 2000), pp. 21-29. For a concise and comprehensive report on the tragedy of Maluku, see *Indonesia: Overcoming Murder and Chaos in Maluku*, ICG (International Crisis Group) Asia Report No. 10 (Jakarta/ Brussels, 19 December 2000).
14. See *Tempo*, 4-10 September 2000, p. 30.
15. See *Tempo*, 14 January 2001.
16. *Wall Street Journal*, Interactive edition, 18 October 2000.
17. McLeod, op. cit., p. 5.
18. *Wall Street Journal*, Interactive edition, 18 October 2000.
19. Dow Jones Newswires, 11 May 2000, cited in McLeod, op. cit., p. 14.
20. *IFI's Update*, No. 9 (October 2000). IFI is published by "Down To Earth", the International Campaign for Ecological Justice in Indonesia, London, England.
21. Hadi Soesastro, "The Indonesian Economy under Abdurrahman Wahid", *Southeast Asian Affairs 2000* (Singapore: ISEAS, 2000), p. 137.
22. The important items of the "*reformasi*" agenda, as popularly understood, are democratization under full civilian rule, and the trial of Soeharto, his family, and his cronies.
23. *Asian Wall Street Journal*, 7 December 2000.
24. Associated Press, 9 December 2000.

Southeast Asian Affairs 2001

INDONESIA
Violence and Reform Beyond Jakarta

Michael Malley

In Jakarta's troubled relations with its regions, events that failed to occur in 2000 nearly overshadowed those that did. In 1999, politicians and pundits had warned shrilly that communal violence was contagious and would cause the country to disintegrate unless the government swiftly decentralized political power and redressed the injustices many regions had suffered under Soeharto. However, by the end of 2000 the government still lacked a coherent approach to regional issues, yet ethnic and religious conflict had not engulfed the country and new separatist movements had not even emerged let alone succeeded.

Although Jakarta's inability to devise and pursue effective policies did not cause the country to crumble, it encouraged regional challenges to grow. During 2000, separatist movements in Aceh and Irian Jaya strengthened, communal conflict in Maluku sharpened, and demands for greater regional autonomy multiplied throughout the country. These developments led President Abdurrahman Wahid to warn the People's Consultative Assembly in August that a "wave of disintegration is threatening the existence of the unitary state and national unity".[1]

Many Assembly delegates agreed, but they were not moved either to endorse his policies or to take firm action on their own. Rather than support Wahid's efforts to negotiate with Aceh's rebels or approve his recommendation to change Irian Jaya's name to Papua as separatists there demanded, delegates directed his government to grant "special autonomy" to those provinces by May 2001, but did not even sketch the sort of provisions they would find acceptable. Furthermore, they offered no guidance regarding communal conflicts and failed to consider a proposed constitutional amendment to accommodate regional interests by creating a House of the Regions alongside the existing House of Representatives (DPR). The Assembly did amend the constitution to guarantee regional governments "autonomy as broad as possible", but attached a condition that allowed the national government to legislate limits on that autonomy.

MICHAEL MALLEY is Visiting Assistant Professor of Political Science at Ohio University in Athens, Ohio, USA.

The People's Consultative Assembly (MPR) session demonstrated that the lack of co-ordinated action on regional policy stems from much deeper problems than the weakness of Wahid's leadership. It reflects the nature of the country's ongoing political transition, particularly the indecisive outcome of the 1999 elections. Wahid's mandate is weak, since three parties won more legislative seats than his own. Legislative leaders cannot compensate for his weakness, since no party gained a majority of seats in either the Assembly or the House, and more than a year after the elections none has managed to forge a majority coalition. In these circumstances, political rivalry has flourished and the military has retained a high level of independence even as its formal political roles have shrunk. As a result, Wahid's government has been forced to divert political resources from handling regional and other challenges to ensuring its own survival, and this suggests that Indonesia will continue to confront separatist, communal, and autonomist pressures in the coming year regardless of who its president is.

Separatism

Aceh

The revival of the Acehnese separatist movement following Soeharto's resignation in May 1998 poses the most significant regional threat to Indonesian national unity. At its core are two main groups. The Free Aceh Movement (GAM) has an armed force of several hundred soldiers whose titular head is Hasan di Tiro, who has lived abroad since the 1950s. He founded the movement in 1976, and declared Aceh's independence on 4 December that year. Jakarta easily suppressed the movement in the late 1970s, but the GAM regrouped during the 1980s and launched a rebellion in 1989. By 1993, the Indonesian military had quelled that rebellion, but its brutal tactics strengthened anti-Jakarta sentiment. As many as 5,000 people are believed to have died in the crackdown, and the uncovering of mass graves in 1998 refuelled public animosity towards Indonesian troops and sparked fresh violence.

In the more open political climate since 1998, another group has emerged. Under the leadership of university students in Banda Aceh, the Aceh Referendum Information Center (SIRA) was established in February 1999. It loosely unites a broad range of non-governmental organizations behind a demand that Jakarta permit the province to hold a referendum on independence. On 8 November 1999, just two weeks after Abdurrahman Wahid was elected President, SIRA organized a public demonstration in the provincial capital, Banda Aceh, that is commonly estimated to have attracted nearly one million people out of the total provincial population of just over four million.

Both groups have a common set of grievances, which the majority of Acehnese appear to share. One is the sense that ever since the 1950s, successive governments in Jakarta have broken promises to grant Aceh autonomy commensurate with its status as a "special region", rather than a mere province. In particular, they seek authority over religious and educational affairs. A second grievance arises from Jakarta's exploitation of the region's economic resources, especially its natural gas. Thirdly, they resent Jakarta for the widespread human rights abuses that occurred in the military's anti-insurgency campaign during Soeharto's last decade in power.

At the beginning of his presidency, Wahid adopted a two-pronged approach towards Aceh. On the one hand, he attempted to isolate Aceh from international support. In late 1999, he secured pledges of support for Indonesia's territorial integrity from countries that had backed East Timor's independence, following the August 1999 ballot in the territory, such as the United States and Australia, as well as predominantly Muslim countries that might sympathize with predominently Muslim Aceh. On the other hand, he signalled a desire to accommodate Acehnese demands in order to reduce their support for independence. On 25 January 2000, the President visited Aceh. He avoided the mainland, where security forces clashed regularly with rebels, in favour of Sabang, a port city on the Singapore-sized island of Weh. Since Soeharto withdrew the city's duty-free status in the mid-1980s, the island has lost nearly half its population. To many Acehnese, Sabang's fate symbolized the negative impact of national policies on the provincial economy. During his visit, Wahid announced that he had issued a Presidential Decision (No. 2 of 2000) that returned the port's free trade status, and ordered his Cabinet to co-ordinate the development of the island's infrastructure. However, progress was slow. Not until 22 December, during a visit to the island, did Vice-President Megawati Soekarnoputri officially reopen the port and announce government funding to construct a new pier to handle ships of 10,000 tons, ten times larger than the existing pier can accommodate.

Despite Wahid's efforts, the level of violence between Indonesian security forces and the GAM intensified. Human rights groups estimated that 350 people died in the first two months of the year, compared to 273 during the whole of 1999.[2] During the same period, Wahid was engaged in a struggle with General Wiranto, his Minister of Political and Security Affairs, to limit military influence in national politics. After Wiranto resigned, the military's influence in national politics appeared to wane, thereby creating an opportunity for Wahid to pursue a more accommodating approach towards Acehnese demands.

In March, Wahid sent State Secretary Bondan Gunawan to Aceh to meet the GAM's military chief, Teungku Abdullah Syafi'ie, whom the military had earlier claimed to have killed. Bondan travelled without security to the GAM headquarters in Pidie for the meeting, but about a month later security forces swept the area where the two men had met, making clear their opposition to direct negotiation with the GAM. In April, the government put on trial twenty-four soldiers and one civilian whom it charged with involvement in the massacre of a religious teacher, Teungku Bantaqiah, and fifty-six members of an Islamic boarding school in West Aceh in July 1999. On 17 May they were sentenced to between eight and a half and ten years in jail. Although these are among the harshest sentences ever given to military personnel, human rights activists criticized the government for bringing only low-ranking officers and soldiers to trial. Not only was the officer who led the attack, Lieutenant Colonel Sudjono, called as a witness rather than charged as a suspect, but he also disappeared shortly before the trial began. By December he had not been found.

The most significant breakthrough occurred on 12 May when representatives of the Indonesian Government and the GAM signed an agreement in Geneva to initiate a three month-long "humanitarian pause". The agreement took effect on 2 June, but in September it was extended until 15 January 2001. The agreement committed both sides to refrain from violence in order to allow humanitarian aid to be delivered to the tens of thousands of people living in refugee camps. In a statement accompanying the agreement to extend the pause, both sides even agreed "to enter exploratory talks in order to arrive at a lasting and comprehensive political solution for Aceh."[3] However, each side continued to launch attacks on the other. Human rights groups based in Aceh reported that more than 200 people were killed during September and October. They estimate that during the first eleven months of the year between 524 and 841 people died in the conflict.[4]

Several prominent people were assassinated. The Malaysian-based leader of a rebel faction that favoured negotiations, Teungku Don Zulfahri, was killed in Kuala Lumpur on 1 June. In September, the body of human rights worker Jafar Siddiq Hamzah was found in North Sumatra, and Safwan Idris, a member of an official commission to investigate human rights abuses, was killed in his home in Banda Aceh.

The lack of progress during the humanitarian pause increased tensions ahead of two key anniversaries at the end of the year. Both dates acquired additional significance because they surrounded scheduled talks between the Indonesian Government and the GAM in Geneva. The civilian movement for a referendum on independence (SIRA) planned a rally for 10–11 November, and hoped to attract several hundred thousand participants as it had the previous year. However, government troops blocked sea and land routes into Banda Aceh and killed dozens of people who tried to reach the city. In protest, the GAM withdrew from the planned peace talks. Despite the military's efforts, tens of thousands of people managed to gather for a two-day rally, and as many as 100,000 gathered a week later for a public prayer that SIRA organized for those who died trying to reach the first rally. On 22 November, SIRA's leader, Mohamad Nazar, was arrested and charged with fomenting public disorder. On 4 December, the anniversary of the GAM's founding in 1976, hundreds of rebels gathered at thirty locations throughout the province, including the Baiturrahman mosque in central Banda Aceh just across the river from a government military command post. Although the ceremonies passed off peacefully, clashes later in the day claimed at least fifteen lives.[5]

In the face of these challenges, divisions within the national government sharpened during the last several weeks of the year. Top defence officials, aligning themselves with the Vice-President, warned sternly that the humanitarian pause would not be renewed and suggested that a state of emergency could be declared if the GAM did not engage seriously in negotiations. However, leaders of the DPR took a more cautious approach, and a meeting between the two groups of officials on 26 November produced a statement that urged the government to avoid declaring a state of emergency and to open dialogue with a broad range of Acehnese independence groups, not just the GAM.

Wahid himself made another visit to Aceh on 19 December in which he acknowledged making mistakes. He called on the armed forces to treat the Acehnese as "brothers not enemies" and pledged to resolve the conflict through dialogue if the rebels returned to the negotiating table. He also offered the province more than US$10 million to cope with monsoon-induced floods, and signalled support for the adoption of Syari'ah law in the province. However, the serious security threats that greeted him indicated the magnitude of the challenge that loomed as the year ended. More than 2,000 additional troops were deployed prior to his arrival, but despite their presence, bombs exploded outside two government office buildings two days before he arrived, and just hours before his plane touched down a grenade exploded at the local police chief's residence, located just 500 metres from the Baiturrahman mosque where the President was scheduled to speak. In addition, police also defused a bomb that was planted along the road between the airport and the mosque. In view of these threats, Wahid wore a bullet-proof vest, delivered a thirty-minute address to 500 carefully selected guests, and remained in Aceh for less than three hours.

Irian Jaya/Papua

In Irian Jaya, as in Aceh, a longstanding rebel movement has been joined by a more recent civilian organization to press for independence from Indonesia. The Free Papua Organization (OPM) was founded in 1965, shortly after the United Nations transferred the territory from Dutch to Indonesian control in 1962-63. The OPM declared the formation of a Government of West Papua in 1971, two years after Soeharto staged an "Act of Free Choice" in which his government organized about 1,000 tribal elders to ratify union with Indonesia. In the late 1970s and early 1980s, the rebels and Indonesian troops engaged in periods of intense military conflict, but since then violence has been very limited. In large part, the movement's lack of military success is attributable to demography, geography, and economics. The province's population of about 2.5 million is spread over a mountainous terrain nearly eight times larger than Aceh. Moreover, as a result of migration from other parts of Indonesia, indigenous Papuans account for only about two-thirds of the province's population and immigrants dominate most of the leading economic sectors.

During the two years since Soeharto's fall, hundreds of public figures in Papua have co-operated to build an increasingly well-organized independence movement. In mid-1998, they established the Forum for the Reconciliation of Irian Jaya Society, which called on the government to open discussions about the territory's political status, but allowed that the outcome could be less than full independence. In February 1999, Soeharto's successor, President B.J. Habibie, was persuaded to hold a National Dialogue with one hundred Papuan leaders, but their blunt demand for independence soured further chances for dialogue and led to a crackdown on independence supporters. In February 2000, about 500 Papuans attended a four-day meeting at which they elected a thirty-one-member Papuan Presidium Council to prepare a transitional government. From 29 May to 4 June they held a week-long Papuan People's Congress at which 2,700 registered participants established a 501-person legislature to complement the Executive Council. In addition, a loosely organized militia, known as the Papuan Task Force, sprang up across the province and has perhaps 15,000 members. Although some elements have ties to members of the Council and enforce law and order in the absence of Indonesian control, most are organized along tribal lines and some engage in criminal activity. One of its main units is controlled by the son of the Council president.[6]

The Papuans' grievances are much the same as those of the Acehnese. They resent Jakarta's control over the exploitation of their natural resources, particularly as symbolized by the enormous Freeport copper and gold mines. They also resent the transfer of their land to hundreds of thousands of government-sponsored migrants, mostly from Java, and decry a long line of human rights abuses by Indonesian armed forces. Other Papuan complaints mirror those of the East Timorese. Unlike the Acehnese, who can claim an important role in the Indonesian revolution against Dutch rule in the late 1940s, Papuans say that they were excluded from talks about their own future in the 1940s, when the Netherlands was able to keep control of the territory, and again in the 1960s when Indonesia gained control. Moreover, under Indonesian rule they felt unfairly excluded from positions in local government.

Until the middle of 2000, Wahid took an accommodating approach towards Papuan demands. In late 1999, he released independence leaders whom his predecessor Habibie had jailed and permitted the Papuan flag to be flown on condition that it be flown alongside but not higher than the Indonesian flag. In addition, he spent New Year's eve in the provincial capital, Jayapura, where he announced his agreement that the province's name be changed to Papua (a change that did not occur, and consequently resulted in much confusion).[7] Ahead of the Papuan People's Congress in May 2000, he donated Rp 1 billion (about US$120,000 at the time) to the Papuan Presidium to cover one-third of the event's estimated cost.[8]

The theme of the Congress was "Straightening Out West Papua's History", and participants used their version of history in diplomatic fashion. They referred to the meeting as "Papuan People's Congress II", to link it to a previous congress held in the last days of Dutch colonial rule. They claimed that there was no need to declare independence in 2000, and thereby invite arrest by Indonesian authorities, because the first Papuan People's Congress had done so on 1 December 1961. However, they directly challenged Indonesia's claim to sovereignty by calling for a review of the limited referendum Indonesia had staged in 1969. In addition, the Congress established an executive committee and assigned it responsibility for creating an electoral commission and drafting a constitution.[9]

The Congress marked a turning point in Indonesian policy towards the Papuan independence movement. During the Congress, security forces did nothing to disrupt the proceedings, even though independence flags were flown and the participants clearly advocated secession. Indeed, the participants chanted "*merdeka*" (meaning freedom, or independence, in Indonesian) when a coterie of top officials entered the meeting hall. The Jakarta-appointed Governor, who had arrived to deliver an address, was accompanied by the regional military and police commanders, as well as the Speaker of the provincial legislature.[10] These events deeply disturbed Wahid and his Cabinet. Afterwards, the President claimed that the organizers had reneged on their promise to allow all Papuans, including those who opposed independence, to attend, and suggested that additional military forces might be sent to the province.

As the anniversary of Papua's declaration of independence approached, Jakarta toughened its approach and the level of conflict in Irian Jaya rose. Early in October, the new national police chief announced that Papuan flags could no longer be flown, a view reiterated by the Cabinet Secretary and the provincial police chief. In early November, the Presidium Council and the provincial police reached an agreement to allow the flags to be flown during daylight hours on 1 December, but to prohibit any activities other than a public prayer gathering. In mid-November, the army sent two strategic reserve (Kostrad) battalions to the province, bringing the total number of army and police personnel there to about 10,000. Thus strengthened, the police abrogated their agreement with the Council at the end of the month and arrested the Council's President, Theys Eluay, and its Secretary General, Thaha Al Hamid, as well as three other members of the Council, and charged them with subversion.

The anniversary itself passed off quietly, but a series of clashes in early December resulted in at least 18 deaths and more than 150 arrests. Flag-flying incidents sparked most of these incidents, but others resulted from attacks by OPM rebels. In late November, OPM leaders held a meeting in Papua New Guinea at which they sought to strengthen themselves organizationally, establish stronger links to civilian independence groups, and devise new political and military strategies. They took credit for at least one attack in early December.[11] President Wahid attempted to reduce the level of tension by calling on the police to release the separatist leaders and celebrating Christmas in Jayapura. However, during that visit he warned that he would take firm action if independence was declared, and said that he "respected" the arrest of pro-independence leaders.[12]

Riau

The only significant independence movement to emerge since the fall of Soeharto is an inchoate one in Riau. Its leaders organized a people's congress along Papuan lines and tried to forge ties with Free Aceh and Free Papua separatists, but have failed to transform "Free Riau" from an idea into an organization. Their principal grievances are quite similar to those of Aceh and Irian Jaya: paltry local benefits from the exploitation of local natural resources, particularly petroleum and timber, and lack of local political control. However, in contrast to those regions, Riau has never mounted an armed rebellion against Jakarta. Consequently, it has never suffered Indonesian military operations and the extensive human rights abuses that have fuelled separatist sentiment in Aceh, East Timor, and Irian Jaya.

Riau's independence movement originated in the student-led protests that caused Soeharto to resign in 1998. After his resignation, the movement turned its sights on Governor Soeripto, a retired Javanese army general who had overseen Soeharto's policies in Riau for nearly a decade. In November that year, a broad coalition that included leading provincial politicians won President Habibie's support to replace Soeripto a month before his term ended with a native-born general, Saleh Djasit. From that point, Riau's reformists began to push even more aggressively to acquire a share of the province's oil wealth. In March 1999, amidst this struggle, a leading figure in Riau's reform movement declared a "Sovereign Riau" (*Riau Berdaulat*). A prominent medical doctor and frequent commentator on political affairs, Tabrani Rab cultivated the support of student activists by staking out more radical positions than other senior public figures, most of whom depended on the bureaucracy for their livelihoods.

Like the Papuans, Riau's independence supporters organized a "second" people's congress in 2000 that harked back to one held during the Soekarno years. In 1956, Riau politicians had held a congress to demand the creation of their own province. At that time, the territory of Riau was part of the province of Central Sumatra, which was dominated by Minangkabau politicians and bureaucrats from West Sumatra. The national government only assented to Riau's request in 1959, after Central Sumatra's leaders rebelled against Jakarta.

Originally scheduled for early December 1999, the Riau People's Congress II was held in Pekanbaru from 29 January to 1 February and attended by approximately 2,000 people. Organizers delayed the gathering in order to muster material support from, and secure the participation of, leading politicians and bureaucrats who opposed a declaration of independence. During the Congress, the delegates engaged in marathon debates regarding three alternative political frameworks for the province. Of the 623 delegates who remained until the meeting ended in the early morning hours of 1 February, 146 voted for federalism, 199 for enhanced autonomy, and only 270 for independence, while 8 abstained.[13] Although less than half of the delegates supported independence, they dominated the Working Body that the Congress established to continue its work. In late June, they hosted delegates from the Acehnese and Papuan separatist movements. In a joint statement, known as the Pekanbaru Declaration, they pledged to co-operate to achieve independence, but Riau's separatist leaders continued to reject the violent means their counterparts employed.

The Congress revealed a deep ambivalence among Riau's élite which the national government was able to exploit. Since Indonesia's political transition began in 1998, Riau's reformers have demanded a greater share of the province's oil output, which amounts to half the country's total. In 1999, Habibie had pledged to grant the province 10 per cent of the province's oil output, but later that year Wahid offered to let Riau retain 75 per cent of the earnings from all its natural resources. After the Riau People's Congress in February 2000, Wahid's government treated the issue more seriously. On 30 April, the President visited Pekanbaru and agreed in principle to allow the provincial government to take over an oilfield that produces about a tenth of the province's oil after a private company's rights to operate that field expire in August 2001.

As the year wore on, the independence movement appeared to lose momentum and the provincial government's bargaining position weakened. In July, Tabrani Rab accepted the provincial legislature's nomination to serve on the national government's newly created Regional Autonomy Advisory Council despite having argued vociferously that Riau could achieve its goals only through independence, not enhanced autonomy. Some independence activists took to calling him the "former President of Free Riau."[14] In early December, the national government rejected Pekanbaru's demand for a 70 per cent share in the oilfield, and allocated it just a 20 per cent share. While many separatist supporters viewed this as a defeat, provincial officials generally accepted that they lacked sufficient capital to afford a larger role in the project.

Communal Conflict

Violence in the Maluku islands has claimed more than 5,000 lives and driven more than 500,000 people from their homes since it first broke out in January 1999.[15] Until the end of 1999, Maluku's troubles were serious, but confined to two distinct areas. Initially, the violence was concentrated on the island Ambon, particularly in Ambon City, the capital of Maluku province. Traditionally, Christian Ambonese comprised a majority of the island's inhabitants and dominated the provincial bureaucracy. Over time, Muslim immigrants evened the balance, and in the 1990s President Soeharto appointed Muslims to the position of governor of Maluku, and Muslims gradually displaced Christians in the bureaucracy, threatening the networks of patronage that reached into local society. By the time of Soeharto's fall, tensions were running high. However, for reasons that remain unclear, security forces were unprepared for an outbreak of violence.

During the second half of 1999, a separate set of local conflicts resulted in fighting among Christians and Muslims in the northern Maluku islands after Jakarta decided to remove them from Ambon's control and create a province of North Maluku. This touched off a struggle between the Muslim Makian and the predominantly Christian Kao, who had competing land claims. The Makian linked their demand for the creation of their own subdistrict (*kecamatan*) to a provincial level struggle between two royal families for dominance within the new province. In October, the Kao destroyed a number of Makian villages and drove the Makian to neighbouring Ternate and Tidore islands. In response, Muslims in Ternate drove Christians out of that city.

A turning point occurred during the last week of 1999, when Kao villagers attacked a Muslim subdistrict, killing more than 500 people and turning more than 10,000 into refugees. This incident received widespread attention in Indonesia and motivated the formation of Muslim militias elsewhere in the country to protect Muslims in Maluku. In early January, more than 100,000 people marched in Jakarta to demand a holy war on behalf of Maluku's Muslim communities. Leading politicians, including the chairman of the People's Consultative Assembly, Amien Rais, addressed the rally. Within weeks, militias began to arrive in Maluku, but they did not make a significant impact until mid-year when members of the well organized Jihad militia (Laskar Jihad), arrived.

In April, the Laskar Jihad announced publicly that they were training at least 2,000 members at a base near Jakarta and intended to send as many as 7,000 members to defend Muslims in Maluku. The organization's leaders even met with Wahid on 6 April to inform him of their plans.[16] Although he angrily dismissed them, he was unable to prevent them from sending their forces to Maluku in May. After establishing control over local militias and gaining access to sophisticated weaponry, the militia launched a devastating attack on a Christian village located between two Muslim villages in Halmahera. The attack was intended as a response to the Christians' attack the previous December, and illustrated their strategy of clearing Christians from predominantly Muslim areas. There was widespread evidence that regular army units co-operated with the Laskar Jihad.

Amid worsening violence, Wahid declared a civilian state of emergency in Maluku and North Maluku on 27 June. This was effectively a declaration of martial law, but with provincial governors rather than military commanders as the chief authority in their regions. In addition, Wahid replaced the Christian regional military commander with a Hindu and increased the number of troops in the region. By the end of the year, nineteen battalions were stationed in the islands.[17] Still, no effort was made to control the Laskar Jihad, let alone remove them from the Maluku islands, and the violence persisted for the remainder of the year, particularly in Maluku province. In late December, after receiving a report from an inter-religious investigative team, the province's governor acknowledged that some Jihad units had forced Christians to convert to Islam at gunpoint. Ambon's Catholic bishop alleged that more than 600 Catholics and Protestants had been forced to become Muslims, and appealed to the United Nations to intervene.[18] In North Maluku, a tense peace replaced violence as Christians and Muslims were increasingly isolated from one another.

Major outbreaks of communal violence occurred in at least three other parts of Indonesia during 2000, but unlike the conflict in Maluku, these did not elicit support from elsewhere in the country or result in a continuing cycle of violence. In Lombok, a protest on 17 January against attacks on Muslims in Maluku turned into a riot in which several people were killed, more than a dozen churches burned, and thousands of people displaced from their homes. In Poso district, Central Sulawesi, Muslims and Christians attacked one another in April and May, resulting in as many as 300 deaths and turning nearly 70,000 people into refugees. Although the causes remained murky, many attacks appeared well co-ordinated, and security forces were unable or unwilling to intervene. However, in December the government put alleged ringleaders of both religions on trial.[19] In late October, fighting between Madurese and Malays in Pontianak, the capital of West Kalimantan, claimed twenty lives, but police were able to contain the violence and prevent a repetition of the massive conflicts that had occurred in 1997 and 1999 when hundreds died and tens of thousands were displaced.[20]

Regional Autonomy and Decentralization

Less dramatically than in Aceh, Irian Jaya, Maluku, or even Riau, politicians across Indonesia have worked to loosen Jakarta's influence over them since Soeharto's fall in 1998. Typically, they have demanded the right to elect their own district heads, mayors, and governors without interference from Jakarta, and to create new provinces and districts in which they can exercise influence. Depending on the kind and amount of economic resources within their borders, they have sought either greater control over their own economies or larger transfers of resources from Jakarta. In both cases, they have sought greater authority over how they may use those resources.

In response to these pressures, as well as the fear of national disintegration, Habibie's government had passed a pair of landmark laws in April 1999 to decentralize political authority and fiscal resources to district governments. Habibie and his civilian advisers recognized that the highly centralized system developed during the Soeharto years had become untenable. At the provincial and district levels, branch offices of national government ministries and regional army commands sharply limited the power of the local governments. In late 1998, without consulting regional politicians or interest groups, a small team of bureaucrats hurriedly drafted new laws on regional government and centre–region fiscal relations. The incumbent House of Representatives, elected in 1997 during Soeharto's last term, passed the laws less than two months before the historic elections of 1999 in which most of the members lost their seats.

The first law grants district-level governments a broad range of rights. Only authority over defence, foreign affairs, justice, religion, and monetary policy remain solely with the central government. Most importantly, the law eliminates the district's status as an administrative unit of the national government. This has two practical implications. One is that regional chief executives (*bupati* and mayors) no longer serve simultaneously as heads of the regional government *and* chief representatives of the national bureaucracy in their regions, but only as heads of the regional government. Accordingly, the national government has surrendered to district legislatures the right to elect these officials. Secondly, the law provides that all district-level offices of national government ministries shall be transferred to district governments or eliminated. As a result, the central government's administrative reach will extend only to the provincial level, where most of its authority is preserved in the new law.

The second law revamps the fiscal relationship between the central and regional governments to give the latter greater autonomy in managing their own finances. It makes two key changes. For the first time, the central government has committed itself to share revenues derived from natural resource production with the regions in which the resources are produced. Thus, regional governments will be entitled to 15 per cent of after-tax revenues from oil, 30 per cent from natural gas, and 80 per cent from forestry, fisheries, and general mining. The law's second key change is the introduction of a requirement that the central government should distribute to the regions in the form of block grants at least 25 per cent of its domestic revenues (namely, all revenue excluding receipts from foreign aid and loans).

Sluggish Preparations
The laws call for radical changes, but have left the government little time to prepare for their implementation. For the Habibie government, demonstrating its commitment to regional reform ahead of elections was more important than devising a realistic timetable to achieve that reform. However, the Wahid government chose not to delay the laws' implementation for fear of worsening its relations with regional governments, and by mid-year it became clear that adequate preparations could not be made before the laws took effect in January 2001.

Both of the new laws provide general frameworks for reform, not blueprints, and assign the task of writing detailed regulations to the national government. This has created three problems. First, it has placed the task of interpreting the laws in the hands of national bureaucrats, who are precisely the people whose powers the laws are intended to erode. Secondly, the vagueness of the laws has left tremendous room for interpretation. For instance, the law on regional government reserves to the central government a broad range of "other authority", such as the development of human and natural resources. In May, Wahid issued a Government Regulation (No. 25 of 2000) that listed, but did not define, the issues over which the national government and its provincial administrators would retain authority. The document runs to approximately twenty pages. Its provisions range from exceedingly general ones, such as "regulation of the national telecommunications system" to quite specific: the government claims not just the right to set educational standards, but to determine the school calendar and number of hours of instruction, and not just the right to regulate the supply and price of energy, but to set economy class transportation fares.

Thirdly, the laws have placed an enormous burden on a government whose capacity is quite limited. Although Wahid managed to issue Regulation No. 25 in May, he did not issue another one until late September, then issued several at once in mid-November, and delayed others until after the laws have taken effect in 2001. The serious extent of the government's unpreparedness has been reflected in its deteriorating relationship with the International Monetary Fund (IMF). In a revised Memorandum of Understanding signed on 7 September, the government acknowledged that it still had not prepared regulations on such critical aspects of decentralization as "(i) transfers of civil servants, assets, and spending to the districts; (ii) fiscal transfers and shared revenues required to finance transferred functions; (iii) guidelines for local government borrowing; [and] (iv) accountability of local government and financial management by adherence to budget process." The continuing lack of progress led an IMF official in Jakarta to call on the government in late November to review both laws, particularly their ambiguous provisions enabling regional governments to borrow money on foreign markets. In mid-December, these concerns contributed to the IMF's decision to delay the scheduled disbursement of US$400 million until February or March 2001.[21]

The government's inability to prepare adequately stemmed in large part from Wahid's decision to reshuffle his Cabinet in August in order to placate his legislative rivals. Not only did he replace his Finance Minister, who had been deeply involved in planning for decentralization, but he also eliminated the position of State Minister for Regional Autonomy, which had been held by Ryaas Rasyid, one of the chief architects of the decentralization strategy. Ryaas had advocated this move as long as a separate agency was created to oversee decentralization. Instead, Wahid folded Ryaas' responsibilities into the Department of Home Affairs, the body primarily responsible during the Soeharto era for monitoring and controlling regional governments, and placed a conservative retired army general, Surjadi Soedirdja, at the head of that department. Rather than take responsibility for the delays, Surjadi suggested that districts that were unprepared to undertake a full range of responsibilities under the new law could simply yield them back to the provincial or national government, as Regulation No. 25 of 2000 provides.[22]

Likely Sources of Conflict

The new laws promise far-reaching changes in the distribution of authority and power between the central and regional governments, yet they leave major pieces of Soeharto's centralized political system in place. As a result, they have created many opportunities for conflict.

The army's territorial command structure, which parallels the country's administrative structure, remains unchanged. Although many district heads welcome their new autonomy from higher placed bureaucrats, they now confront military commanders who can still count on support from a centralized command structure, and this structure is unlikely to change soon. In December 1999, the army's most outspoken advocate of reform, General Agus Wirahadikusumah, sparked a public debate when he recommended that the army should abolish its territorial commands. By the end of 2000, the prospects for such reform appeared slight, especially since October when Wirahadikusumah's rivals prevented Wahid from installing him as army chief. One of these rivals is the army's head of territorial affairs, General Agus Widjojo, who had said earlier in the year that the territorial commands could be phased out, but only over 7–10 years. Like most senior officers, he believed the commands were necessary to prevent the country's disintegration, and after Wirahadikusumah was sidelined, Agus Widjojo openly criticized Wahid for failing to use the military to control unrest in Irian Jaya and Aceh.[23]

A second set of conflicts is likely to arise from tensions between provisions in the new regional finance law and the existing practice of public finance. For instance, the new law promises revenue-generating regions a larger flow of resources, but neither it nor other legislation provides a mechanism that will allow Jakarta to return more revenues to relatively wealthy regions while maintaining the current flow to resource-poor regions. Transfers from the national government typically have provided about three-quarters of provincial budget resources and 80 per cent of district receipts. In mid-December, just after the government announced the amount of money it would grant each regional government during the coming year, the Finance Minister acknowledged that the amounts were insufficient for some provincial governments outside Java.[24]

Yet another set of conflicts stems from a tension between the new regional finance law and an unchanged 1997 law that assigns specific taxes to national, provincial, and district governments. The new law gives natural resource-rich regions access to lucrative sources of revenue, but it does not provide any new ways for other regions to increase their revenues. As a result, districts such as Kediri, a major cigarette-producer in East Java, and Sanggau, which hosts a large state-owned palm oil plantation in West Kalimantan, are unable to extract revenues from the major economic activity within their borders.[25] The government is aware of these problems and had planned to submit a new tax law to the House of Representatives until mid-year when Wahid became embroiled in a conflict with the legislature and reshuffled his Cabinet.[26]

Although conflicts among regional governments, and between them and the central government, are inevitable, the new regional government law devotes little attention to dispute resolution mechanisms. Indeed, it says simply that interregional disputes will be resolved by the national government through consultation (*musyarwarah*), and that if any region is dissatisfied with the government's decision it may appeal to the supreme court. Thus, Jakarta not only has the power to write the rules by which it will share power with the regions. It also claims the right to adjudicate disputes that arise from conflicting interpretations of those laws and rules.

A major test of the new laws during 2000 suggests that the national government is likely to yield authority to the regions even when the laws do not require it, but that regional governments are likely nonetheless to look to Jakarta to help resolve local disputes. Although the new regional government law does not take effect until 2001, district legislators across the country have demanded and won the right to implement one of its key provisions — the election of district heads without interference from Jakarta — before then.

Despite its long tradition of telling regional legislators whom to select, the Department of Home Affairs remained relatively aloof from the elections of 185 district heads and mayors, that were held in 2000. However, defeated candidates and their supporters frequently alleged that the victor had paid legislators for their votes. Rather than lodge a complaint with the local police or prosecutor, legislators typically took the matter to the Department of Home Affairs. For the most part, the Department refused to involve itself in those cases, and they ended peacefully. However, in a small number of cases discontented supporters of defeated candidates engaged in extreme acts of violence, ranging from violent protests to burning down legislative buildings.[27] Their discontent often stemmed from the ease with which bureaucrats who lacked popular support but enjoyed access to financial resources were able to perpetuate their influence by bribing newly elected legislators.

These election-related incidents illustrate a larger problem that many observers fear will snowball in 2001. In the absence of centralized, bureaucratic oversight, regional politicians are free to behave as they like. They are no longer accountable upward to the Department of Home Affairs, but electorates and interest groups are not yet able to hold them accountable downwards. For this reason, some Indonesians favour a shift towards the direct election of district heads and governors. Although the new regional autonomy law does not permit regional governments the freedom to determine how they will select their leaders, legislators in the province of South Sulawesi began to draft a regulation to implement direct elections during the coming year.[28]

Conclusion

Despite growing weakness at the centre and continuing crises in certain regions, at the close of 2000 the risk of national disintegration appeared lower than political rhetoric suggested. Prospects for peace and the restoration of Jakarta's authority in Aceh, Irian Jaya, and Maluku dimmed during 2000, but none of these conflicts threatened to envelope other regions. Moreover, Maluku remained the only region in which a new, persistently violent conflict emerged since Soeharto's fall in 1998. This could change, of course, but in the coming year such conflicts seem less likely to erode national government authority than the combined impact of official decentralization policies and growing demands for regional autonomy. Thus far, such demands have been relatively costless, while demands for independence have elicited harsh military responses. Increasingly assertive regional governments are more likely to press a fragile civilian government in Jakarta to share more political authority and fiscal resources than rush for the exits.

NOTES

1. *Kompas*, 8 August 2000.
2. *Kompas*, 4 March 2000.
3. *Jakarta Post*, 26 September 2000.
4. *Jakarta Post*, 2 October 2000; *Tempo Interaktif*, 31 October 2000; *Jakarta Post*, 9 December 2000; and *Waspada*, 15 December 2000.
5. *Jakarta Post*, 6 December 2000.
6. *Far Eastern Economic Review*, 16 November 2000.
7. *Kompas*, 18 August 2000.
8. *Kompas* (online), 27 May 2000.
9. *Suara Pembaruan*, 29 May 2000; and *Sydney Morning Herald*, 5 June 2000.
10. *Van Zorge Report*, 5 June 2000.
11. *Sydney Morning Herald*, 1 December 2000; and Agence France Press, 12 December 2000.
12. *Kompas* (online), 25 December 2000.
13. *Suara Pembaruan*, 3 February 2000.
14. *Riau Pos*, 16 July 2000.
15. For extensive coverage of the conflict in Maluku, see the International Crisis Group report, "Overcoming Murder and Chaos in Maluku" (Brussels and Jakarta, 19 December 2000); and the Van Zorge Report's "War in the Malukus" (18 July 2000).
16. *Kompas*, 7 April 2000.
17. *Suara Pembaruan*, 29 December 2000.
18. *Sydney Morning Herald*, 23 December 2000; and 26 December 2000.
19. *Far Eastern Economic Review*, 6 July 2000; *Suara Pembaruan*, 1 December 2000; and *Jakarta Post*, 2 December 2000.
20. *Kompas*, 17 November 2000.
21. *Kompas*, 22 November 2000; and *Straits Times*, 16 December 2000.
22. *Jakarta Post*, 30 September 2000.
23. *Tempo*, 2 July 2000; and *Far Eastern Economic Review*, 9 November 2000.
24. *Bisnis Indonesia*, 19 December 2000.
25. *Kompas*, 30 November 2000; and 1 December 2000.
26. *Kompas*, 20 July 2000.
27. *Kompas*, 22 December 2000; and *Suara Pembaruan*, 19 December 2000.
28. *Jakarta Post*, 29 November 2000.

LAOS

LAOS
Signs of Unrest[1]

Bertil Lintner

Introduction

By most accounts, 2000 was not a good year for Laos. The economy continued to suffer from the effects of the 1997 Asian financial crisis. The Lao currency, the kip, depreciated in value, and inflation remained high. Almost no new foreign investment came into the country in 2000, and local business people suffered because of the weakened purchasing power of the population at large. Less business meant less revenue, and a shortage of funds in the central coffer forced the government to backtrack on its promise to let the provinces keep more of locally collected revenue, and to decentralize the decision-making process.

Politically, Laos got its first, rare lesson in dissent. On 26 October 1999, a group of students had tried, but failed, to stage a peaceful democracy demonstration in Vientiane. Some of them managed to escape to Thailand, and were later granted asylum in the United States, from where they spoke out more openly against the government and in favour of political reforms. Even a former minister, Khamsay Souphanouvong, sought political asylum in New Zealand. He had lost his position as Finance Minister in March 1995 and was dropped from the 49-member Central Committee a year later. The reason for his dismissal was not entirely clear, nor why he decided to defect to New Zealand with his entire family. Khamsay was more than an ordinary ex-minister; his father, the late Prince Souphanouvong, or "the Red Prince", was one of the leaders of the Lao revolution and the first president of the new communist government that took over in December 1975.

Laos' entry into ASEAN in 1997 brought an intial ray of hope that the country would merge into the harmonious family of nations in the region. However, the regional economic crisis crushed those expectations, and relations with fellow ASEAN-member Thailand remained tense as the two countries were unable to resolve the question of ownership of several disputed islands in the Mekong river, which separates the two countries. Laos also accused

Bertil Lintner is a Senior Correspondent (based in Thailand) for the *Far Eastern Economic Review*.

Thailand of harbouring anti-government rebels — and decided to move closer to its long-time political and military ally, Vietnam, and China.

All these developments did not go down well with the international donor community, without whose support the country would collapse economically. The donors, led by Japan, Sweden, and Australia, did not mince words in a report on the situation in Laos for the year 2000, and their own obligatons: "There is a need to move out of the niceties and to get some clear answers from the government," said one representative.[2] The World Bank has announced that future assistance would depend on changes in Laos' authoritarian political system.

Domestic and Social Issues

Throughout the 1990s, the Lao Government was guided by efforts to encourage a free-market orientated economy while maintaining centralized political control under the strict one-party rule of the Lao People's Revolutionary Party (LPRP). Laos' basic philosophy became known as *jintanna kan mai* ("a new way of thinking"), which could be best described as *perestroika* without *glasnost*.

In the wake of the economic crisis of the late 1990s, however, yet another entirely new way of thinking began to take root. Laos had become the only member of ASEAN to suffer triple-digit inflation and the kip fell from 1,080 to the U.S. dollar to as low as 10,000, which was the biggest depreciation in the region, even surpassing Indonesia's. According to the International Monetary Fund (IMF), annual inflation rose from 26 per cent in December 1997 to 142 per cent a year later, before peaking at 167 per cent in March 1999.[3] The fall of the kip meant that private savings were wiped out, and government employees lost up to 80 per cent of their purchasing power.

The situation was brought somewhat under control in late 1999 and early 2000 by a wide range of austerity measures, including salary caps and high interest rates. However, all the country's fundamental problems remained, including low productivity and heavy dependence on foreign aid. The kip rose to 7,500 to the U.S. dollar in early 2000, but then began to slide again, and hit 8,250 in early 2001.

When new economic policies were launched in 1986 to replace the old, planned socialist economy, businessmen from neighbouring Thailand — where the culture is similar and people speak a language which is closely related to Lao — were the first foreign investors to arrive. Thai goods soon accounted for an estimated 45 per cent of Laos' total imports, 37 per cent of total exports, and 42 per cent of the US$5.7 billion in total committed foreign investment in the 1980s and 1990s. However, the Thais were the first to pull out when the crisis hit their own country in 1997, leaving behind an economic vacuum that few other investors were willing to fill. Since 1997, nearly 300 foreign companies have closed down, and most of them were Thai-owned. Plans to develop a string of hydroelectric power stations, and to export the electricity to Thailand and, to a lesser extent, Vietnam, had to be scrapped in the wake of the crisis.

For years, Laos had pinned its hopes on the construction of a number of such stations.

In addition to the existing plants at Nam Ngum north of Vientiane, with its 150 MW capacity, and the 45 MW station at Xexet in the south, only one new plant has been opened in recent years: the 220 MW station at Nam Theun-Hinboune, which went into operation in April 1998. Sales of electricity were expected to add 7 per cent to Laos' gross domestic product (GDP) annually, but the Electricity Generating Authority of Thailand had by then begun to reassess its energy needs. Thailand, it was announced, would not need more energy for the next few years, which, in effect, killed the main 900 MW, US$1.4 billion mega-project called Nam Theun-2.

The only business that seemed to be booming was the cross-border trade with China. Laos sold, officially and unofficially, timber and minerals to China, and, in return, cheap Chinese consumer goods flooded the country. The exact value of this trade remains unknown, as much of it is done informally and without official revenues being paid.

As a direct outcome of the country's economic woes, there were signs in 2000 indicating that at least some of the LPRP veterans felt that capitalism had failed them. Economic controls were re-introduced, including attempts at forcing private firms to give the state part ownership, and restrictions on imports and exports imposed. The situation was further exacerbated by the fact that Laos' rigid political system was never liberalized. The lack of transparency, combined with a weak legal system, undermined investor confidence, and fewer investment projects led to worsening economic conditions for the population at large. Unemployment, and problems which usually come in its wake, such as drug abuse, prostitution and petty theft, rose dramatically in the wake of the crisis.

A string of mysterious bombings also hit the capital Vientiane and other towns in 2000, and there was an increase in attacks by ethnic hill tribe insurgents in the north, as well as signs of growing factionalism within the ruling LPRP. The first bomb exploded on 30 March 2000, at a well-known restaurant in Vientiane which was popular with expatriates and tourists. At least six people were injured, including some foreigners. Two weeks later, another bomb exploded in a small restaurant near Vientiane's old market, where many Vietnamese guest workers congregate. A third bomb exploded outside the state-owned Lane Xang Hotel on 4 May, but caused no injuries. This was followed by a more powerful bomb in Vientiane's morning market in late May, and a bomb in the nearby bus-station a week later. Yet another bomb was found near the Vietnamese embassy, and an explosion rocked the General Post Office somewhat later. On 11 September, a bomb exploded outside the Asian Pavilion Hotel in central Vientiane.

In early July 2000, a group of armed anti-government rebels attacked the border-crossing point of Chong Mek near the Thai border in southern Laos and hoisted the old pre-1975 royal flag over the customs post. At least five people were killed in the attack — which caused relations with Thailand to deteriorate as Laos accused the Thais of having sheltered the armed men. A Thai TV crew was also there to film the attack, which made the Lao authorities even more convinced that there had been Thai complicity in the raid.

Outside observers trying to assess developments in Laos have focused mainly on identifying those responsible for the bombings and the attack on Chong Mek. The government blamed it all on U.S.–based ethnic Hmongs, perhaps allied with lowland Lao supporters of the now-exiled royalty that had ruled the country before 1975. In an interview with the *Far Eastern Economic Review* in July 2000, Foreign Minister and Deputy Prime Minister, Somsavat Lengsavad, attributed the bombings to "business conflicts", or even "love affairs".[4]

The allegations of "outside agitators" seem misplaced when it comes to the bombings in urban areas, but in the case of the hill tribes there is considerable sympathy for their plight among exiled communities primarily in the United States, where the pre-1975 Hmong leader, General Vang Pao, resides. However, conditions in Laos itself are likely to have fuelled grievances among the Hmongs as well, including government corruption, poorly executed resettlement programmes for hill tribes moved to the lowlands, ethnic marginalization, and the absence of democratic means to address their problems.

Furthermore, the bomb attacks in the cities may not be the work of any single group. More likely, they are the outcome of widespread desperation among the population at large over deteriorating economic and social conditions. However, the crisis is also internal within Laos' ruling elite. "It's purely a case of brute-power politics," said a Vientiane-based analyst in mid-2000. "It's a very Byzantine ploy: One group inside the party is trying to demonstrate that the present ruling elite doesn't have a grip on security and hence it's time for change."[5]

Very broadly speaking, southerners have traditionally been closer to Vietnam, while northerners have usually looked to China for support and inspiration. The President, Khamtay Siphandone, is a native of Champassak in the south, but, as head of state and also party chief, he has to balance the various forces in the intertwined party, government, and army apparatus. A more outspoken pro-Vietnamese official is Defence Minister General Choummaly Sayasone from Attapeu, also in the south, as well as Saysomphone Phomvihane, former Finance Minister and ex-Governor of the southern province of Savannakhet.

Moscow-trained Saysomphone is the son of Kaysone Phomvihane, the half-Lao half-Vietnamese founder of the Lao communist government and first *de facto* leader of the post-1975 regime. Although no longer a government minister, Saysomphone remains a member of the Central Committee of the LPRP, and, mainly because of his family background, a rallying point for pro-Vietnamese individuals in Laos.

A central figure among the more pro-China elements is Foreign Minister Somsavat. At 55, he is one of the youngest and most dynamic figures in the government. A native of the old royal capital of Luang Prabang in the north, he is also ethnically Chinese and fluent in Mandarin. He has the closest connections with Beijing of any government and party official. He is also Laos' face to the outside world, both within ASEAN and with the international donor community, whose continued support is vital for the survival of the present regime.

Other influential northerners include Minister of Communications, Transport, Posts and Construction, Phao Bounnaphonh, and Justice Minister Kham Ouane Boupha (who represents Savannakhet in the south, but is a native of Luang Prabang). However, divisions are not always very clear. Prime Minister Sisavat Keobounpanh comes from Houa Phan in the far north of the country, and was for several years president of the Lao-China Friendship Association, but recent intelligence reports from Vientiane indicate that he has shifted to the pro-Vietnamese faction.

The northerners among the ruling élite are generally more dynamic and outward-looking than the more conservative southerners, but there are no signs that either group is interested in substantial political reforms. In fact, they share a deep suspicion of the exiled royalist movement, which in the past year has won audiences with lower-ranking representatives of the governments of France, Australia, New Zealand, and Canada.

The royalist movement is centred on Prince Soulivong Savang, the eldest grandson of the last king, Savang Vatthana, who was deposed by the new regime in 1975 and later died in a prison camp in Houa Phan. The role of the prince goes back to August 1981, when he, then only 18, crossed the Mekong river into Thailand on a bamboo raft together with his younger brother, Dhayavong Savang. The two princes went to France, where Soulivong obtained a law degree. In July 2000, the now 37-year-old prince toured the United States with his uncle, Prince Sauryavong, and met lowland Lao exiles as well as Hmong community leaders and a number of U.S. politicians, including the Governor of Minnesota.

Although a rising star among the exiles, it is impossible to ascertain the degree of support Soulivong's movement has inside Laos, or if pro-democracy activists, such as those who took to the streets of Vientiane in October 1999, were even aware of its existence. However, with communist ideology fading in everything but name, a deepening political and economic crisis, and the country now a member of ASEAN, the question of a more suitable system of government is being discussed even in government circles.

The fact that the rebels who attacked Chong Mek in July were carrying the royalist flag must also have caused alarm in government and party circles. The royal family from their exile in France vehemently denied any involvement in, or prior knowledge of, the attack. It coincided, nevertheless, with Soulivong's visit to the United States and enabled him to tell his supporters that there was an armed anti-government movement inside the country.

By mid-2000, the situation had become so confusing that the country's former President and now Senior Adviser, octogenarian Nouhak Phoumsavanh, had to hold several crisis meetings with individual government officials. Nouhak warned that the country risked disintegration especially if rival factions within the government did not come to terms with each other. In a meeting with his successor Khamtay, the ex-President reportedly said that Laos may even have to consider radical reform of its rigid political system "to reflect today's economic and political realities".[6] Exactly what that meant was not clear, and no major political decisions are likely to be made before the Seventh Party Congress, which is scheduled to take place in March 2001.

However, there seems to be little doubt that the aborted demonstrations, the bombings and other signs of dissent reflect overall frustration with the present, authoritarian system. Lacking normal outlets to vent their various grievances, other Lao resorted to more extreme acts. In January 2000, ethnic hill tribe insurgents from the Hmong minority attacked the town of Khoun on the Plain of Jars, killing six people and burning several buildings. Skirmishes were also reported from the Saysomboun area just south of the plain, and in the mountains near the Vietnamese border to the east. Eyewitnesses observed military cargo planes and convoys of ground troops heading for the affected areas.

The Lao authorities may be able to dismiss the exile movement, and even play down growing discontent at home, but it will find it much harder to ignore the frustration of crucial foreign donors such Japan, Sweden, and Australia, which for years have contributed to Laos' economic development, and now want to see a more pluralistic system in place in Vientiane. Assistance from abroad accounted for 16 per cent of Laos' GDP in the late 1990s, and 59 per cent of its fiscal budget.

The Economy

Laos, one of Asia's poorest countries, continued its slide deeper into economic malaise throughout the year, and, according to World Bank reports, social indicators reflected a state of affairs similar to that of many least developed countries in Africa. Laos' present, and still unresolved, crisis derives from economic problems that began three years ago with the financial crash in Asia. At first, many foreign observers believed that Laos with its small, mainly agricultural economy, would be shielded from the worst effects of the crisis. It was not only a question of the Thais pulling out.

Mismanagement, excessive government spending, and a huge trade deficit made matters even worse, and economic decline, combined with lack of political flexibility, set the scene for the social disorder that hit Laos in the year 2000. The renewed crisis prompted international monetary experts and foreign diplomats to question the very fundamentals of the Lao economy.

The Asian Development Bank estimated that Laos' exports, including timber, textiles, tin, coffee, and electricity totalled US$310 million in 1999, a decline from US$341 million the year before. Imports stood at US$524 in 1999, down only slightly from US$553 in 1998. The trade and fiscal deficit were covered by foreign aid, primarily from Japan, Australia, and Sweden. Foreign exchange reserves at the end of 1999 amounted to US$123 million, or three-and-a-half months of imports.[7]

The predicted GDP growth rate had to be adjusted several times, owing to economic stability and signs of hyperinflation. According to the most optimistic estimates by the foreign donor community in the capital Vientiane, the economy might have grown by 7 per cent in 1999, while the World Bank put the figure at 5.2 per cent and the Asian Development Bank (ADB) anticipated 4 per cent. Annual inflation rose from 26 per cent in December 1997 to 142 per cent a year later, before peaking at 167 per cent in March 1999. By mid-2000, inflation had levelled out at 31 per cent, which, although a considerable improvement, still is one of the highest figures in the region.

By mid-2000, foreign investment was also down to a trickle: foreign direct investment dropped to US$150 million in 1997 from US$1.2 billion in 1995, and has fallen further since. A government attempt to attract foreign tourists — and the foreign currency they bring — by declaring 2000 "Visit Laos Year" looked promising at the start. However, the spate of bombings at bus-stations, restaurants, and hotels, which was highly publicized in the foreign media, hurt the campaign.

As a consequence, many Lao have come to rely on remittances from overseas. In the wake of the communist take-over in December 1975, some 350,000 Lao left the country, almost 10 per cent of the population at the time — which, in per capita terms, is a bigger exodus than that from Vietnam and Cambodia during the same period. According to a U.N.–sponsored survey, 56.5 per cent of the population in Vientiane said they had relatives overseas, and 48.1 per cent of respondents said they received money from them. A December 1999 report by the State Planning Committee lists "remittances from abroad" as the single most important source of income in the Vientiane valley, representing 28 per cent of all household earnings, compared to 25 per cent from agriculture, 22 per cent from wages, and 18 per cent from business.[8]

Such social safety valves may prevent more social unrest among the population at large, but will not satisfy the increasingly frustrated international donor community, and without foreign assistance, even the modest growth in 1999–2000 would not have happened. Weak macroeconomic management and a lack of decisive decision-making on the part of the government are bound to prolong the crisis in Laos — and convince international donors that they have to push harder for substantial economic and political reforms.

Foreign Policy and the Future of Foreign Aid

Laos' entry into ASEAN in 1997 does not seem to have brought the country any nearer to the notion of belonging to a harmonious family of nations in the region. Relations with Thailand remained tense as the two countries were unable to resolve the question of ownership of several disputed islands in the Mekong river, which forms most of their common border, especially in the wake of the 3 July 2000 attack on the Chong Mek border post in southern Laos.

The state-controlled media in Vientiane accused the Thais of complicity in the attack, and the Lao Government demanded that Bangkok extradite the rebels who survived the clash and then sought refuge across the Thai border. Both sides, however, sought to downplay the political element in the attack, attributing it to pure banditry. The fact remains, however, that the rebels hoisted the old royal flag over Chong Mek, and stated that their goal was the overthrow of the country's communist government.

The question of the disputed islands also continued to mar Thai–Lao relations to the point that an open conflict seemed imminent in September 2000. Lao militia and village guards confronted Thai farmers, who had grown maize on three islands opposite Thailand's Chiang Rai province. All three islands lie just off the Thai side of the river, but the Lao Government argues that under the 1926 Siam-Franco Treaty, all islands in the Mekong belong to Laos, no matter how close they are to the Thai bank. As far as the Thais are concerned, most of the frontier, including the water border, remains to be demarcated.

There were also other reasons for frictions between the Thai and Lao governments. When the Hmongs launched their offensive in early 2000, it was evident that the Lao army had insufficient means to suppress the renewed insurgency. Intelligence sources reported that Laos received much-needed support from its long-time political and military ally, Vietnam. In exchange, Vientiane granted Hanoi preferential trade treatment, waiving import tariffs on Vietnamese goods and taxes on Vietnamese investment, much to the chagrin of competing Thai business interests.

The exact number of Vietnamese military personnel that took part in the operation is not known. Intelligence sources said that they provided logistical support and acted as advisers, but did not engage in combat. However, the very presence of Vietnamese units in Laos was enough to set off alarm bells in Bangkok and other capitals in the region. It also caused the long-simmering and largely dormant rivalry between pro-Vietnamese and pro-Chinese factions within the leadership to resurface.

That China also has become a major player in Laos' domestic affairs became evident during the currency crisis of 1999. China provided generous export subsidies and interest-free loans that helped stabilize the kip. Moreover, in celebration of the twenty-fifth anniversary of the communist takeover in Laos, China donated 60 million renminbi (US$7.2 million) to help build a mammoth cultural centre in downtown Vientiane that opened in February 2000.

Given the political and economic problems that Laos encountered in 2000, it may have been only natural that the country's leaders came to rely more on Vietnam and China rather than, as during the economic mini-boom of the mid-1990s, Thailand and the other capitalist members of ASEAN. However, this was not a development that pleased the donor community, which wants to see more openness and bolder free-market reforms.

Significantly, the donors, who usually meet every few years in Geneva to discuss aid for Laos, held their meeting in late 2000 in Vientiane. "The meeting should not be perceived as pledging conference, but rather as a forum for exchange of government-donors views," said a survey conducted by the United Nations Development Programme (UNDP) before the meeting. It added that "the burdensome government decision-making process and the lack of transparency" are "matters of serious concern."[9]

One such concern was the question about "military expenditure, and which proportion of the domestic income is diverted to military use or to benefit the military leadership ... if internal resources and income is diverted to the military, why should the money of taxpayers from foreign countries be utilised?"[10]

Another point of criticism was the failure to implement the decentralization programme. On 4 October, just a few weeks before the donors' meeting, the National Assembly passed a law that required the local authorities in the provinces to give a bigger, not smaller, portion of their revenue to the central government. Under the social and economic plan for the fiscal year 2000/2001 each of Laos' eighteen provinces are obliged to hand over 57 per cent of its income, an increase from 43 per cent in 1999, to the government in Vientiane.[11] Besides having less to spend, the provincial governments will, for the first time, see their hold on power curbed as the new law spells out their responsibilities. Until the new law was passed, the Prime Minister's decrees served as loose guidelines for local administrators. It was widely feared within the donor community that the move, apart from undermining the authority of provincial governments, would most probably hamper the government's rural development programmes.

The same National Assembly session also set a target for economic growth of 6–6.5 per cent for the fiscal year 2000/2001, and a US$400 target for per capita income for the next fiscal year, an increase from US$350. Whether these targets will be met remains to be seen, but the situation did look promising as 2000 drew to a close. Some foreign economists have begun to argue that perhaps the solution would be to abandon attempts to build up labour-intensive and highly competitive sectors, such as the garment industry — until recently a major foreign-exchange earner — and to concentrate on what small countries usually do best: to find niches in the market where Laos has the skills, and outside competition is minimal.

Dr Hans Luther, a Vientiane-based economist, argues that a Lao company that wishes to compete in the international rice market would stand little chance. Laos, compared with Thailand and Vietnam, has no comparative advantage in the large-scale production of rice. A possible "niche" would be to produce "red rice" as health food. Bottled spring water, farmed rainbow trout, chemical-free coffee, orchids, and other fresh flowers, certain types of fruit and mushrooms are other possible areas where a country such as Laos, with its lack of industrial and agricultural development and with a population of only five million, could compete.[12]

While many policy-makers would dismiss such suggestions as small and trivial, many economists would argue that the road to renewed progress has to begin at a very basic level. For Laos, there seems to be no way back to the high hopes and aspirations of the 1990s, when various industrial projects and plans to develop hydroelectric power schemes for export dominated the debate. Those days are over, and with donor fatigue setting in among those countries that have so far assisted Laos in development, radically new, and more down-to-earth, solutions are needed — and without economic development, it will be impossible to avoid further social and political unrest.

Conclusion

The main problem in Laos is that the leaders fear they will lose power if they change their policies. However, if they do not change, the economy is bound to get worse, and they may lose support even from within their own ranks. With donors breathing down their necks, it will become increasingly harder for the Lao Government to resist reform, even if most analysts agree that any fundamental change will take time — and that the most important players may not be the fledgeling opposition movement, or leaders in exile. Given the government's tight grip on power, change is likely to come from within the present ruling élite, but only if the present rulers can find a way to retain power, or at least to dominate any future, possibly more pluralistic system of government.

NOTES

1. Some of this material is based on two other publications by the author: *2001 Asia Yearbook* (Hong Kong: Far Eastern Economic Review, 2001); and "Unrest in Laos", *Strategic Comments* (London: International Institute of Strategic Studies, September 2000).
2. United Nations Development Programme (UNDP), *Round Table Meeting VII: Lao PDR, Summary of Perspectives* (2000), p. 8.
3. Ngozi Okonjo-Iweala, Victoria Kwakwa, Andrea Beckwith, and Zafar Ahmed, "Impact of Asia's Financial Crisis on Cambodia and the Lao PDR," *The International Monetary Fund: Finance and Development* (September 1999).
4. The interview was never published in the *Far Eastern Economic Review*, but reproduced in the *Vientiane Times*, 28–31 July 2000.
5. Interview with Vientiane residents, July 2000.
6. Sourced from a Western intelligence report, August 2000.
7. These and other statistics are supplied by Western embassies in Vientiane.
8. See also "1997–1998 Vientiane Social Survey Project" (Vientiane: Institute for Cultural Research, Ministry of Information and Culture).
9. UNDP, op. cit., p. 1.
10. Ibid., p. 9.
11. "Laos backtracks on decentralisation", *Nation*, 5 October 2000.
12. Dr Hans U. Luther et al., *Niche Markets* (Vientiane: National Organisation for the Studies of Policy and Administration, May 2000).

MALAYSIA

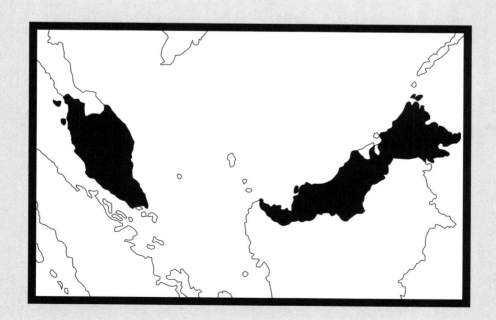

MALAYSIA
UMNO's Search for Relevance

John Funston

To many observers, Malaysia at the beginning of 2000 appeared a rare case of stability in a turbulent region. Just a month earlier, Dr Mahathir Mohamad had led his government to secure 148 of 193 parliamentary seats in a general election. Political uncertainties had receded, declared a leading financial house.[1]

Government electoral success, however, came from the support of non-Malays on the peninsula and indigenous groups in Sabah and Sarawak, while Malays deserted it in droves. The United Malays National Organization (UMNO), the dominant party in the governing Barisan Nasional (BN) coalition, had perhaps its worst election ever. Its parliamentary seats declined from 94 to 72. Four ministers and five deputy ministers were defeated, and many others experienced a massive reduction in their majorities. Parti Islam SeMalaysia (PAS) was the main beneficiary, tripling its representation to 27 seats, becoming leader of the parliamentary opposition, and scoring massive majorities in Kelantan and Terengganu state assemblies. The new Parti keADILan Nasional (National Justice Party, or keADILan) led by Wan Azizah, wife of ousted former Deputy Prime Minister Anwar Ibrahim, gained 5 seats and some 12 per cent of the vote. About half the Malay vote went to the opposition — indeed, some UMNO leaders put the party's share at less than 40 per cent.[2] That removed the basis of governmental legitimacy in Malaysia hitherto, which had rested on UMNO having overwhelming Malay support.

What were the reasons for UMNO's setback? The main cause was the Anwar factor, with government handling of this issue perceived as in conflict with traditional Malay norms against shaming opponents, and being cruel (*zalim*). Islamic issues also played a part, as both sides defined the Anwar issue in these terms. Secondly, it reflected Malay identification with the major themes of *reformasi* — justice, democracy, transparency, accountability, and opposition to *korupsi, kronyisma* and *nepotisma* (KKN).[3]

The initial reaction of most UMNO leaders was to acknowledge that UMNO and the government needed to reform. Dr Mahathir, however, rejected this analysis. He explained the result in terms of lies — spread by Anwar, other

---

JOHN FUNSTON is a Senior Fellow at the Institute of Southeast Asian Studies, Singapore.

Barisan Alternatif (BA) leaders, the Islamic clergy (*ulamak*), the PAS newspaper *Harakah*, and the Internet — PAS' bribery in promising heaven to its supporters, factionalism in UMNO caused by Anwar, and Malay ingratitude. There were no fundamental shortcomings, Dr Mahathir argued, though the opposition had taken advantage of the government's generosity to convince people otherwise. Having diagnosed the illness, the doctor's prescribed medicine was restoration not reformation. Rather than pursuing reform, the government should counter lies by clamping down on or discrediting opposition parties. UMNO must unite around the leadership and be re-energized to reclaim its rightful position as the natural party of the Malays. Both UMNO and the government needed to improve public relations, so that people would appreciate Malaysian exceptionalism and understand that there had been no cruelty in dealing with Anwar.

Countering the Opposition

Moves against the opposition began shortly after the general election, with pressure on the pro-opposition media. *Harakah* was initially threatened with tough measures if it continued selling to non-PAS members, then after complying with this, was instructed in February to reduce publication from twice a week to twice a month. Its editor and printer were charged with sedition in January, for an article on Anwar's sodomy trial that had appeared on 2 August 1999. The annual publishing licence for the fortnightly *Detik* was not renewed, and after an uncertain stand-off for a few weeks, the Ministry of Home Affairs advised in March that it would not be allowed to resume publication. *Wasilah*, from the same publisher as *Detik*, was closed in August. Popular weekly tabloid *Eklusif*, which divided coverage between pro-government and opposition equally, also met the same fate when its annual permit expired in June. New Internet daily *Malaysiakini* (established just prior to the general election), often critical of the government but measured in its reporting, was denied media accreditation, ostensibly because it did not have a permit for publication.

Blunter instruments were employed as well. As Dr Mahathir flew out for an overseas visit on 12 January, three senior opposition members were arrested for sedition, and a fourth was arrested the following day under the Official Secrets Act, all for offences dating back to August/September 1999. Most controversial was the sedition case against Democratic Action Party (DAP) leader Karpal Singh, for raising in court the possibility that Anwar had been poisoned in prison. This was the first occasion in the Commonwealth that a lawyer had been so charged for representations made in court, and the previous October Dr Mahathir had acknowledged that Karpal enjoyed legal immunity. Having previously maintained that all such prosecutions were decided on by the Attorney General without political interference, Dr Mahathir noted that the government had wanted to act earlier but desisted so as not to be accused of preventing the opposition from contesting the general election.[4] Scores of other opposition members or supporters were arrested throughout the year, most charged with illegal assembly. In a controversial December case, opposition party leaders who intercepted buses carrying government supporters on the day of a by-election (presumably "phantom voters") were charged with rioting.

The police also maintained a restrictive policy against public gatherings of any kind. Applications for small rallies (*ceramah*) were often denied, or turned down at the last moment when preparations were well advanced. Public demonstrations were disallowed, with strong public warnings against assembly and the use of massive force — including helicopters and water trucks laden with chemically-laced water — to prevent or disperse them. Opposition attempts to mobilize a major protest on the first anniversary of Anwar's sentence on corruption charges (billed as the Black April protest) were met with a full-scale blockade of Kuala Lumpur. In the end, only one to two thousand were able to assemble, and 48 arrests were made. A similar show of force was employed for the verdict on the sodomy trial in August, and aided by a last-minute change of time for handing down judgement, the opposition was kept off balance. Crowds of 500 and 2,000 did gather on the scheduled and actual judgement days (4 and 8 August), but with members of the new Human Rights Commission in attendance, only a few arrests were made. Police approached the year's final major demonstration on 5 November with a commitment to "total denial and domination", and arrested five of the organizers on the day before. In this case, however, the best police efforts failed to prevent a gathering in excess of 50,000. Another 122 were arrested, and two weeks later photographs of 90 wanted by the police for questioning appeared in the media (including a two-year-old boy).[5]

At the same time, the government moved to cut the identification between Islam and the opposition. In Selangor, then other states, mosque committees elected by the local congregation were replaced by state appointees. Government leaders warned repeatedly that only sermons prepared by state authorities could be read at Friday prayers, and that mosques should not be used for political purposes. For months, government leaders debated the banning of the word "Islam" in political party titles, never ruling out the possibility of doing so. In November, Dr Mahathir warned that the government was making plans to take drastic measures against those misusing Islam under the Penal Code.[6]

Both state governments under PAS control found themselves under financial pressure from the central government. Kelantan was refused a loan to improve its water supply — proof, Dr Mahathir warned voters at a by-election, that the government would not seek to wean away opposition strongholds by financial inducements. More dramatically, in September, the federal government withdrew petroleum royalty payments from Terengganu, even though these were guaranteed under legal agreements in 1975 and 1987, and had been paid since 1978. Worth over RM810 million in 2000, it was the largest component of state revenue, and widely viewed as a resource that could be used to entrench and expand PAS influence. The federal government took over distribution of this sum (after the first instalment of RM405 million), describing it as a "welfare payment" (*wang ehsan*) rather than royalty.

Additional steps were taken to reduce opposition finances and financial benefits to the opposition and its supporters. Curtailing the circulation of *Harakah* deprived PAS of a useful money-spinner. Entrepreneur Development Minister Datuk Mohamed Nazri Abdul Aziz announced in May that BN supporters would henceforth have priority for educational loans. Malacca state terminated the services of pro-BA doctors and lawyers, withdrew money from banks whose staff had supported the BA, and banned official visits to Kelantan and Terengganu.

Government leaders, with assistance from the party and state-controlled media, embarked on an intensive campaign to discredit the opposition, particularly Anwar. Dr Mahathir repeatedly accused Anwar of sodomy and other sexual misdemeanors, in Malaysia and abroad, before and after the August court ruling. UMNO's new Internet website conveyed the same message. In May, a video-cassette entitled "Truth and Justice for Anwar" (*Kebenaran dan Keadilan untuk Anwar*) — previously distributed just prior to the general election – was reportedly circulated to mosques throughout the country. By October, it was out in VCD (video compact disc) format, dropped at bus stops and other locations in Kuala Lumpur, and later more widely. This professionally produced video purports to provide details of ten of Anwar's sexual partners (six men, four women), and gives explicit details on the nature of the partnership. It also hints at a conspiracy between Anwar and foreigners, a common theme in most government attempts to discredit the opposition. It also includes recorded "confessions" (subsequently retracted) given to the police by two of Anwar's alleged homosexual partners — clear evidence that the VCD could only have been made with government approval. A detailed information circular conveying the government position on the Anwar trial was sent to all students in the United States in October.

The government also sustained a prolonged campaign against PAS. In addition to Dr Mahathir's claim that PAS leaders had offered heaven to its supporters in return for their vote, PAS was said to have branded UMNO supporters as unbelievers (*kafir*), notably in a speech by Terengganu leader Ustaz Hj Hadi in 1981 (described as *Amanat Hadi*). Other claims were that: PAS had endorsed a book on Islamic political parties that had labelled UMNO secular and devilish; PAS spiritual leader and Kelantan leader Nik Aziz had insulted Islam by saying that God blasphemed, and had insulted women by holding them responsible for inciting rape; and that PAS and other opposition groups were trying to foment a Palestinian-style *intifada*. PAS leaders were described as fanatical extremists, and held largely responsible for the atmosphere of "hatred" directed against the government, and activities of the Al-Ma'unah sect. (In July, Al-Ma'unah was implicated in an arms heist against two army camps and a shoot-out with security forces in which two hostages and one gang member were killed.) KeADILan received less attention than PAS, but became the main target in late October when Youth chief Mohd Ezam Mohd Noor was denounced as a "traitor" for criticizing Dr Mahathir overseas.

Repositioning UMNO

Efforts to reposition UMNO involved both house-keeping issues designed to revitalize, reunite and streamline the party, and initiatives on Islam and Malay "rights" designed to win back broader Malay support. Shortly after the general election, Dr Mahathir announced plans to hold meetings of the party's top executive body, the Supreme Council, every fortnight instead of every month. He also promised to hold these in different locations — providing more opportunity to meet with the rank and file — rather than confining them to Kuala Lumpur. Public relations activities were intensified, with local publicity officials brought to Kuala Lumpur to receive briefings from senior leaders, the UMNO newspaper re-launched, and a new Internet website established, initially as e-umno then changed to umno-online. Plans were also developed to strengthen UMNO's involvement in social welfare activities — addressing public needs in such areas as employment, consumer protection, and other legal problems. A special office for this purpose, modelled on a successful Malaysian Chinese Association (MCA) example, was opened in Selangor in October.

Efforts to reunite UMNO focused on a General Assembly in May, which involved the election of office bearers. This is normally a three-yearly event, but was postponed almost a year to avoid divisions before the general election. Previous assemblies had been public relations opportunities — much of it shown live on TV — to endorse the actions of the party president and present an image of cohesion and strength. Dr Mahathir has typically shone on such occasions, never failing to elicit enthusiastic ovations for his "summing up" speech. He was anxious to ensure that this Assembly followed the usual script.

Arguing that Malays and UMNO were too weak to endure a divisive contest for power, on 3 January Dr Mahathir persuaded the UMNO Supreme Council to "advise" the party that only he and Deputy Prime Minister, Abdullah Badawi, be nominated for the top two posts (President and Deputy President). Despite reports of rank and file dissatisfaction, and public opposition from veterans such as Musa Hitam, Ghafar Baba, and Tengku Razaleigh Hamzah, the party complied. Sidelined by this, Tengku Razaleigh belatedly allowed himself to be nominated for a Vice Presidential post. Needing seventeen nominations under new rules passed in December 1998 (previously it was only two nominations), he was rejected on a technicality when his own division was adjudged not to have followed correct nomination procedure. Further measures to reduce politicking included a restrictive code of conduct, and eventual agreement by all the contestants to swear off vote buying and campaigning.

Dr Mahathir's opening address to the Assembly on 11 May set the tone for much of the three-day meeting. He was bitterly critical of ungrateful Malays, lazy Malays, corrupt Malays, insincere Muslims, excessive democracy, the West and foreigners in general, the international media, and globalization. He also warned of the deceitful opposition, and the alleged moral and other shortcomings of Anwar. UMNO had to go back to its pro-Malay origins, the struggle for *agama, bangsa dan negara* (religion, race and nation). For the first time ever, Dr Mahathir ended his speech with a prayer (in Arabic), and his close ally and head of Wanita (women's section of UMNO), Dato' Rafidah Aziz, publicly donned a head scarf for the first time and proclaimed it part of UMNO Women's official wear henceforth. Observers categorized the meeting as reflecting the pursuit of a new Malay Agenda.

The Assembly left UMNO with at least a superficial unity, and a new direction. There were, however, several discordant notes, including critical reactions to Dr Mahathir's presentation on Anwar and money politics (murmerings intended to convey that rhetoric was not matched by action). Comments from the floor were unusually critical, directed at the lack of democracy within the party, and the tendency of the Supreme Council to leave everything to the President. Some of Dr Mahathir's supporters were sidelined in the election for senior party office bearers.[7]

The final act of house-keeping undertaken by UMNO involved revising the party constitution. In the lead-up to an Extraordinary General Assembly for this purpose, a special committee chaired by party Vice President Tan Sri Muhyiddin Yassin toured the country to gain input from the rank and file. This revealed strong public support for two proposals — direct election of top positions such as the party president by some 30,000 party members, and dropping requirements for a high percentage of divisional nominations for office bearers. When these went forward to the Supreme Council, not only were they scrapped, but a proposal for the election of office bearers only every parliamentary term (about five years) was added. In the event, popular opposition to the five-year proposal resulted in it being withdrawn. In a few cases, amendments adopted did address a popular concern to make the party more relevant to its members and the public, such as requiring consultation on election candidates with divisions, and establishing a more independent disciplinary committee comprising party veterans who no longer held senior party positions. A youth wing for women members was also agreed on. Overall, however, the changes were conservative in nature. Notwithstanding the defeat of the five-year proposal, party elections could still be delayed for four and a half years (eighteen months beyond the scheduled three years), and as President, Dr Mahathir gained approval for two more appointments to the Supreme Council (totalling 15 out of 47).

Besides internal reforms, UMNO also sought to strengthen its position by focusing on the issues of Islam and Malay interests. Dr Mahathir and other leaders spoke often and passionately about the tragedy of a divided Muslim brotherhood (*ummat*). Several initiatives were adopted both by the government and the party in a bid to outshine the opposition, and in particular PAS. Religious leaders (*ulamak*), state religious officials, and the

Sultans as head of religion in their respective states, were repeatedly urged to promote unity among Muslims behind the government. In April, a National Islamic Action Council, comprising ministers, UMNO officials and government agencies, chaired by Deputy Prime Minister Abdullah, was established to co-ordinate efforts to provide a correct understanding of Islam. In the same month, Perlis state approved a new law providing drastic rehabilitation measures against Muslims found to have strayed from correct teachings, though by year's close, this had still not been gazetted. A similar bill almost made it to the federal parliament in September before widespread protests caused second thoughts. Compulsory Islamic classes of two hours a week for all Muslim public servants were announced in June. In October, UMNO appointed twenty *ulamak* with specific responsibility to oppose PAS. In the same month, the party held a special conference on Islam in Johor, where UMNO leaders promised the full implementation of an Islamic state, including the controversial *hudud* (a part of Islamic criminal law), though this would be achieved gradually.[8]

The first post-UMNO Assembly chance to pursue a more robust defence of specifically Malay interests came somewhat strangely after Dr Mahathir spoke at the MCA annual assembly in mid-June, when in a conciliatory mood he expressed confidence that one day a Chinese or Indian could become prime minister. This did not go down well with some in UMNO, and a few days later Dr Mahathir claimed he was really warning Malays that they could lose their supremacy: "If the Malays have become so weak, poor, begging from others and they are being bought with money to support the non-Malays, it is then possible that a non-Malay may hold the position."[9]

On 14 August, the UMNO-linked Malay newspaper *Utusan Malaysia* led with the provocative headline: "Destroy Malay special rights". The article featured an interview with David Chua, Vice Chair of the government-appointed National Economic Consultancy Council, who had spoken of reducing economic affirmative action for Malays in an interview published a week earlier in the *Far Eastern Economic Review*. In the days that followed, *Utusan Malaysia* played up the alleged threat to Malay rights, relating this particularly to "17 points" drawn up by the Malaysian Chinese Organisations Election Appeals Committee (Suqiu) and accepted in principle by the Cabinet just prior to the 1999 elections. Suqiu protested in vain that it was not opposed to the Malay "special position" provided for in the Constitution (there is no provision for "special rights"). On 17 August, an emotional Dr Mahathir promised not to budge "even one step" in defending Malay rights, and the following day UMNO Youth demanded an apology from Suqiu during an unruly demonstration in front of the Selangor Chinese Chamber of Commerce. On 19 August, a newly appointed 35-year-old Selangor Mentri Besar promised any sacrifice, "even bloodshed", to defend Malay rights. In a bitter 30 August (independence day eve) address, Dr Mahathir targeted extremist Chinese (Suqiu), who, he said, were just as dangerous as Al-Ma'unah and communists in the past.

In the months that followed, Chinese unwillingness to integrate Chinese-medium schools into the newly promised "Vision Schools" (placing government-assisted Malay, Chinese, and Tamil primary schools together within the same facilities, and unifying some administration) led to strong criticism from UMNO leaders. In the run-up to a by-election in November, officials warned the Chinese press not to play up the "Vision Schools" issue. Just prior to the election, Dr Mahathir lashed out at Chinese "extremists" who had forgotten the assistance provided during the economic crisis, and now assisted the opposition in the election campaign.[10] *Utusan Malaysia* was then quick to blame the government's defeat on extreme actions by the opposition, and warned that Chinese voters could not be trusted. Dr Mahathir again reiterated his opposition to Chinese educational extremists, who "want everything to be segregated. Chinese schools to be separated from other schools to the extent of Chinese schools becoming foreign schools and not schools within Malaysia".[11] In Parliament a little later, he said that the Cabinet had earlier accepted Suqiu's 17-point memorandum only because otherwise it would have lost votes in the general election. This provided an opening for the Malay alumni group, Gabungan Pelajar Melayu Semenanjung (GPMS), led by middle-ranking UMNO members and under Dr Mahathir's patronage, to launch another campaign against Suqiu and its alleged threat to Malay special rights. GPMS, together with a broader Malay Action Front (MAF, Barisan Bertindak Melayu), pushed the communal agenda ever further. In early 2001, UMNO Youth reached an uneasy *modus vivendi* with Suqiu, and in February, the MAF held a public rally that unexpectedly focused more on criticizing Dr Mahathir than on attacking non-Malays. UMNO, for its part, ended the year trying a different tack, agreeing to an academic's proposal that it attempt to discuss Malay unity with PAS and keADILan — an apparent concession to the opposition, but one they showed little willingness to embrace.

Sisyphean Efforts

Malaysian leaders' attempts to recapture the initiative for the government and in particular UMNO were intense and wide-ranging. In addition to matters covered already, they included also a systematic attempt to convince Malaysians that they had the best system of governance conceivable, one that had delivered outstanding economic performance, democracy, and exemplary justice. Entering his twentieth year in office, 75-year-old Dr Mahathir, the world's longest ruling Prime Minister, maintained the hectic pace that has been a hallmark of his rule. But, as with the mythical Greek god condemned to push uphill a stone that rolled down again as soon as it reached the top, these efforts made little headway.

Attempts to clamp down on and discredit the opposition encountered numerous problems. Some of the opposition media were closed, but many reappeared on the Internet. *Harakah* and *Detik* both appeared there in a daily version. Other *reformasi* sites waxed and waned, but in total put out a vast amount of anti-government material. Independent *Malaysiakini* gained over

100,000 hits a day, similar to the circulation of most leading daily newspapers. *Reformasi* stalls continued to do a flourishing trade in cassettes, video cassettes and VCDs, showcasing the latest *ceramah* and protest rallies.

Legal actions failed to act as the deterrent they once had. Civil disobedience became entrenched as a form of opposition to what were perceived as unjust laws. Several opposition leaders had multiple charges brought against them, but they appeared unconcerned about the possible sentence, including a ban from political office for five years (where the sentence was for two years or a fine of RM2,000). The slow progress of charges through the courts perhaps strengthened opposition resolve — none had completed passage before the end of the year. Civil disobedience reached a new level in November when PAS Youth head Mahfuz Omar and two colleagues opted for a month's jail rather than pay a RM1,500 fine over participation in an illegal rally against a visiting Israeli cricket team three years earlier. The sight of such leaders jailed for an act of peaceful opposition to Israel undoubtedly strengthened the opposition cause.

Tough police action against the opposition did have some success in limiting major demonstrations, such as those planned for the anniversary of Anwar's corruption sentence in April, and his sentencing for sodomy in August. However, these did little to change basic sympathies, as the large turnout for the 5 November rally demonstrated. Photographs distributed by opposition supporters of heavily protected police, backed by water trucks carrying chemically-laced water, dispersing peaceful crowds, may well have provoked further resentment. Opposition parties also continued with a programme of *ceramah*, in many cases without regard for whether a police permit was issued or not.

The ending of royalty payments to the Terengganu government, and other measures, such as limiting sales of *Harakah*, undoubtedly reduced funds available to opposition parties. The withdrawal of the royalty was widely perceived as unfair, and likely to entrench resentment against UMNO in Terengganu and elsewhere. The opposition were also able to mobilize vast numbers of people who provided services free of charge, and did not rely on funds to the same extent as government parties.

Attempts to discredit Anwar, and the BA more generally, made little progress. Repeated assertions of Anwar's guilt, and the distribution of steamy video-cassettes, appeared to have little effect. A number of developments in Anwar's court case also worked against the government. These included two prosecution change of dates, the conviction in unrelated cases of the two star prosecution witnesses for, separately, bankruptcy and *khalwat* (close proximity between unmarried couples), and Dr Mahathir's refusal to participate after he had earlier claimed "incontrovertible proof" of Anwar's misdemeanors, and professed a willingness to testify. UMNO lost further moral high ground in August when the Selangor Mentri Besar was forced to resign over allegations of sexual impropriety. Dr Mahathir's view that this was a "personal problem" and should not be linked to UMNO, contrasted notably with his earlier stand on Anwar.

To many Malays, the continuing denigration of Anwar remained *zalim*. So also was his predicament in October, when allowed to visit his ailing mother only after threatening to go on a hunger strike. His return to hospital in late November for chronic back problems was widely perceived — rightly or wrongly — as linked to his assault by the former head of police during his first night in captivity. That his assailant had yet to spend a day in jail, and was received with notable deference during a court appearance in December, was not helpful to the government's cause.

Other efforts to discredit BA parties also appeared to have limited impact. Little by way of proof was offered to substantiate various claims against PAS. Attempts to link the party with the extremist Al-Ma'unah foundered on a quite unconvincing government explanation of the Al-Ma'unah affair. Even the police and army accounts of the incident differed markedly, and an account in *Aliran Monthly* documented discrepancies in accounts offered by the government or pro-government media in relation to fifteen separate items.[12] Remarkably, the government found itself on the defensive, and widely accused of having staged the incident itself (a *sandiwara*). Generally, the alternative media were able to deflect most efforts to discredit the opposition, and in cases like Al-Ma'unah put the government on the defensive.

UMNO's own changes did result in a rejuvenated party, for a while, but the fortnightly Supreme Council meetings soon slipped to monthly or longer. Only one meeting was held outside Kuala Lumpur (at Ipoh in July). Party meetings at different levels often found it difficult to attract a quorum, and even some of Dr Mahathir's functions required intensive preparation to ensure a respectable audience. UMNO's machinery had "spluttered to an untimely halt" wrote Karim Raslan, a lawyer and writer close to the party, in late August.[13] Attempts to reunite and reinvigorate it proved impossible with rank and file resentment at leadership manoeuvres to entrench their positions at the General Assembly in May and through constitutional changes in November, and unhappiness over the handling of the Anwar case.

After the BN lost the Lunas by-election in November, Dr Mahathir came in for direct public criticism. The main reason for the loss, Supreme Council member Shahrir Samad said, was "the character of our leader, Dr Mahathir".[14] In an interview with *Mingguan Malaysia*, deputy UMNO Youth leader Datuk Abdul Aziz Sheikh Fadzir — controversial leader of an anti-Suqiu demonstration in August — also faulted Dr Mahathir for the Lunas defeat, and for several other shortcomings. UMNO must change, he declared, but it does not seem to want to; it appeared concerned only with protecting its leaders. "The Youth will no longer protect the leadership".[15] Two emergency meetings of top UMNO officials were convened after the Lunas defeat, with media reports claiming that both included calls for Dr Mahathir to resign.[16] Party problems were, Dr Mahathir conceded in late December, "quite serious".

UMNO efforts to reinvent itself as a defender of Islam and Malay rights also made little impact. In one implicit acknowledgement of this, the minister in charge of Islamic affairs in the Prime Minister's Department, Datuk Seri Abdul Hamid Othman, was sacked in a minor Cabinet reshuffle implemented in January 2001. Unlike former times when a cry to protect Malay rights quickly isolated any who did not join in, efforts this time were strongly opposed. BA Malays refused to join UMNO in demonstrating against Suqiu in August, and indeed, declared they would defend the Chinese. For a moment in December, UMNO appeared to have won a victory, when pro-opposition webmasters declared their support for Dr Mahathir against Suqiu's alleged opposition to Malay "special rights". This, however, was quickly rejected by BA leaders, and the webmasters soon followed suit.

Nor did a range of other developments help the government's cause. The economy grew rapidly in 2000, but this held little attraction while the jewels of Malaysia's acclaimed privatization programme were being bailed out with billions of ringgit of public money, and lower income earners were increasingly pressed. In the global arena, an increasingly critical international community extended fewer and fewer of the accolades once used to demonstrate Malaysia's superiority to the rest of the world. (See sections on Economy and Foreign Policy.)

Above all, a range of legal issues, many related to the prosecution of Anwar, cast Malaysia in an unflattering light. In April, four high-profile international legal groups issued a critical report on the Malaysian judicial system, entitled "Justice in Jeopardy".[17] The following month, the minister in charge of legal affairs, Datuk Dr Rais Yatim, started a storm when he commented adversely on the Chief Justice socializing with a prominent lawyer. (Photographs related to this had been placed on the Internet much earlier.) The Chief Justice responded strongly, claiming that the meeting had been a chance one, but then did not refute information carried by Internet newspaper *Malaysiakini*, which provided detailed evidence that the Chief Justice and the lawyer had indeed holidayed together. Nonetheless, the government extended the Chief Justice's tenure for another six months at the height of this controversy. The final stages of Anwar's sodomy trial saw a protracted legal battle in which Dr Mahathir resisted attempts to call him as a witness, in spite of a subpoena requesting his attendance. Dr Mahathir was further embarrassed when a defence witness, a former head of the Anti-Corruption Agency, testified that the Prime Minister had ordered him to stop an investigation into a top civil servant — a similar type of "corruption" for which Anwar had been convicted in his first trial. The guilty verdict, and the ruling that Anwar's nine-year sentence be served consecutively with the six-year corruption sentence, provoked strong domestic and international criticism. "Rightly or wrongly", observed political scientist P. Ramasamy, "this will be interpreted as a political trial".[18] A survey on legal systems by the Hong Kong-based Political Economic and Risk Consultancy (PERC) in early June rated Malaysia eighth out of twelve Asian countries, below even the Philippines and Thailand. In December, the appointment of a well-regarded judge, Tan Sri Mohamad Dzaiddin Abdullah, as Chief Justice, reportedly at the insistence of the Council of Rulers and against Dr Mahathir's wishes, and the appointment of a new Attorney General, ended the year on a hopeful note. However, the elevation of the former Attorney General to the country's highest court a few weeks later raised concerns anew.

The sum of these events was a massive loss of trust in the government and the UMNO leadership. On a visit to Kuala Lumpur in August, Singapore's Senior Minister Lee Kuan Yew was "bewildered" and "perplexed" by the extent of cynicism and scepticism towards the government, sentiments he picked up from members of the mainstream media. That same media was boycotted by many on the opposition side, with sales of papers such as *New Straits Times, Berita Harian* and *Utusan Malaysia* declining by 30 per cent from two years earlier. Nearly all government actions were probed to see if they were a *sandiwara*.

By-elections, contested with extraordinary vigour and mobilization of resources by the government, tracked public unease. The first in April for the state assembly in Pahang saw UMNO retain the seat owing to the non-Malay vote, but it made no inroads against a majority Malay opposition vote in the 1999 elections. The next in June, for a parliamentary seat in Negri Sembilan (Teluk Kemang), cut the government's majority from 9,694 to 5,972. Both Chinese and Malay votes declined, and the BA won a majority of postal votes (from army camps).[19] The Kedah assembly seat of Lunas, which became vacant as the result of a (still unresolved) assassination, appeared to have an impregnable government majority of 4,700, but was won by the BA with a 530 vote majority. Increasing numbers of Chinese and Malays voted for the opposition, as did more than 80 per cent of new voters (those not on the roll in 1999). While by-elections are no guarantee of results in future general elections, the extent of the swing was remarkable, and upset assumptions that the government was always safe in seats where a little over half the voters were non-Malays. Adding to the government's embarrassment was the fact that it occurred in Dr Mahathir's home state, and deprived the state government of a psychologically important two-thirds majority.

The Economy

Economic growth rates accelerated in 2000 to about 8 per cent, marking a return to levels achieved before the economic crisis of 1997. Billion-dollar mega-projects were again regularly announced, in an apparent indication that the Malaysian economy was back to normal. In November, a multi-sectoral Second National Economic Consultative Council proposed the replacement of the National Development Policy with a Vision Development Policy (2001–2010), promising more of the same but with a greater emphasis on a knowledge economy.

The high growth rate was, however, largely attributable to two fortuitous factors: a boom in the international demand for electronic goods (60 per cent of Malaysian exports), and a dramatic increase in oil prices. Behind the rapid growth, Malaysia's corporate sector remained mired in a sea of debt. Foreign sentiment turned increasingly negative, as the government ignored its professed commitment to improving corporate governance, and intervened increasingly in ways that were perceived as giving an unfair advantage to politically-linked businessmen. Malaysia's standing on a range of economic freedom indicators plummeted.

The year started positively. With Malaysia scheduled to return to the Morgan Stanley Capital International (MSCI) Index on 31 May, investors turned bullish. They sent the Composite Index of the Kuala Lumpur Stock Exchange (KLSE) soaring to 1021 on 18 February, up 20 per cent for the year, before a gradual decline. In late February, Malaysia finally resolved the dispute with Singapore over the RM17 billion shares formerly traded on Singapore's Central Limit Order Book (CLOB) (albeit in a manner that caused some concern to foreign investors), allowing their gradual release onto the Kuala Lumpur Stock Exchange (KLSE) over 56 weeks beginning on 3 July. The following month, the government approved a Code of Corporate Governance, based on voluntary compliance, covering disclosure on a range of activities from director's salaries to the composition of company boards. Deputy Prime Minister Abdullah reinforced this by speaking often on the importance of governance, and promising not to bail out mismanaged companies again. Other encouraging signs over the year included removal of a 10 per cent tax on repatriated portfolio profits held for more than one year, and some progress towards consolidating the financial sector.

The early euphoria did not last, however. The stock market finished 33 per cent down on its February high, despite strong intervention from local (mostly government-linked) funds, and corporate Malaysia remained in the doldrums. By late October, Danaharta, set up in June 1998 to relieve banks of bad loans and debts, had bought RM46.8 billion for the year, a hefty 60 per cent more than a year earlier.[20] One after another, large Malaysian corporations failed to meet repayment obligations, and had to be bailed out by Danaharta or other government-linked agencies. High-profile privatized projects had to be re-nationalized — sewerage operations in May, the Malaysian Airlines System (MAS) and two light rail operations (LTR) in December. Notwithstanding massive debts run-up by these operations, the government bought all back on terms highly favourable to politically well-connected owners. Sewerage operators were paid RM200 million, and the government assumed debts of RM800 million. The Managing Director and 30 per cent owner of MAS, Tajudin Ramli, had his shares purchased at RM8 (for a total cost of RM1.7 billion) when the market price was RM3.62. Dr Mahathir justified this by saying that the government could not allow MAS to be taken over by foreigners, although a little earlier he had said that the government would consider giving up its controlling interest if that were necessary to attract a foreign partner. No independent valuation was conducted, and no discount incurred for RM8.6 billion in losses sustained under Tajudin's stewardship. The LTR rescue cost RM6 billion, the biggest such exercise hitherto.

The most complicated corporate problems centred on Renong-United Engineers Berhad (UEB), UMNO-linked companies with debts of over RM24 billion. Early in the year, Renong had sought to ease its debt burden by selling a share in its telecommunications interests to Singapore's state-linked Singtel for RM2.2 billion. This was ditched at the last moment for political reasons, but the state investment agency Khazanah was brought in instead (at a slightly less generous price). In June, a Renong subsidiary (Hottick) lost virtually all its investments in a Philippine steel company. Danaharta stepped in to take over the companies for RM4 (RM1 to each lending bank), then instructed the banks to write off loans of RM3.1 billion.

In November, UEB came to the rescue of Renong, by purchasing assets valued at RM6.73 billion, through issuing new UEM shares and commercial paper. Analysts saw this as similar to a manoeuvre three years earlier, when UEB purchased 32.6 per cent of Renong and caused a melt-down of the KLCI. They put Renong's worth much lower, and saw no benefits for UEB. The move freed Renong of a great deal of debt, left it with about 54 per cent control of UEB, and gave politically well-connected owner Halim Saad a chance to exercise the "put option" (repurchase of shares at cost plus interest, due in April 2001) promised to UEB following the 1997 manoeuvre. Notwithstanding this generosity, two weeks later UEB extended Halim's put option by fifteen months. Shares for Renong and UEB plummeted around 40 per cent.

Other developments added to the perception of a lack of transparency and political intervention in economic affairs. New privatization projects were regularly announced, without any details on how decisions had been taken. These included a RM1 billion deal to provide a computer network linking six hospitals, a budget plan to allow Employees Provident Fund (EPF) members to withdraw money for buying computers, but only from one designated supplier, and a RM30 billion Kedah development plan. Several mega-projects were of questionable economic and environmental value, including a RM2 billion dam in Selangor, and the resumed RM9 billion Bakun hydro-electricity dam in Sarawak. The September appointment of an UMNO parliamentarian, Dr Jamaluddin Jaris, to replace the respected manager of the privatized electricity company Tenaga also caused concern, particularly as Dr Jamaluddin had been an active player in the energy field up to his appointment.

Such developments alienated Malaysians and foreigners alike. UMNO leader Shahrir Samad predicted that the MAS deal would lose UMNO more votes. A sympathetic analyst in Singapore who in November had urged the West to put its money on UMNO and Dr Mahathir, one month later described the situation as depressing for investors:

> The country's biggest — and most debt-laden companies — are going to find it difficult to break the debt gridlock without a healthier stock market. But the Catch-22 situation is that the market is unlikely to break out of its trading range until international investors see major breakthroughs in debt resolution — and on terms which are fair to minority shareholders, and dare we say, taxpayers too.[21]

Foreigners who had joined the rush into the KLSE at the beginning of the year cashed out. In the six months to September, they withdrew RM7.2 billion, compared with RM1.4 billion a year earlier.[22] Foreign direct investments (FDI) also went down by 71 per cent in the first five months, compared with 1999.[23] Government figures showed an increase in FDI applications and approvals, but 80 per cent of this figure was accounted for by one RM7.4 billion natural gas project. Net foreign outflows reportedly increased from US$7.9 billion in 1999 to US$10.2 billion.[24]

Besides the corporates, it was also a bad year for other sectors of Malaysian society, with sharp drops in agricultural prices — for palm oil, rubber, and rice. At year's end, rice farmers demonstrated against low prices in Dr Mahathir's home state of Kedah. Poorer Malaysians were also hit by increases in petroleum prices, and follow-up increases in areas such as bus fares (up by as much as 33 per cent). The government Employees Provident Fund reduced its death payments from RM30,000 to RM2,000 without warning or explanation.

There was, however, some good news in December. About 4 million Malays holding shares in the government-run Amanah Saham Bumiputra received a generous dividend of 11.75 per cent, while the Amanah Saham Nasional for all Malaysians paid 8 per cent (against a fixed deposit maximum interest of 4 per cent). About 800,000 civil servants received a 10 per cent salary increase and a bonus of half a month's salary, after being told two months earlier that a bonus was not possible. Politicians gained a pay rise after a three-year freeze, with ministers' salaries increasing by 15–22 per cent.

Foreign Policy

Domestic politics drove foreign policy throughout 2000. On almost a daily basis, Dr Mahathir and others called for unity behind the government because of the dangers of Western colonialists. Western governments, business, and the international media were seen as involved in a conspiracy to cause unrest in the country and ultimately topple the government. Some accounts even blamed the Jews. An *Utusan Malaysia* article linked Western hostility to Zionist plans for a third World War, and claimed Zionists already controlled Indonesia through their influence in banking and the International Monetary Fund (IMF).[25] UMNO's Internet website described *Time, Asiaweek*, and *CNN* as tools of the Jews to divide Islam.[26] Contrarily, however, Malaysian leaders also sought to project themselves as open to foreign investment, and committed to a moderate approach on Islamic matters, unlike alleged extremists led by PAS.

As the government sought to outpoint the opposition, relations with neighbours were also subordinated to the importance of demonstrating Malaysian exceptionalism. Regional countries that had come under the IMF were depicted as having lost their sovereignty, and unable to develop as quickly as Malaysia. Demonstrations and violence in Indonesia were constantly highlighted, linked to this loss of sovereignty and the excesses of *reformasi*. Singapore was frequently cited as an example of how Malays had suffered under meritocracy, and a warning of what might befall Malaysia were it to embrace opposition policies. Senior Minister Lee Kuan Yew's nostalgic visit to Kuala Lumpur in August focused on a package of issues that has defied resolution for years (including the supply of water to Singapore and the development of Malaysian-owned land in Singapore), but did nothing to lower the general temperature of cross-strait relations. Malaysia's decision to delay the implementation of the ASEAN Free Trade Area for its motor industry, announced in May, also complicated regional ties as it sent the wrong message on ASEAN liberalization to the international market, and impacted particularly on Thailand which has a growing vehicle industry of its own.

The Anwar issue affected relations with almost all countries. A resolution highly critical of the judicial process in relation to Anwar was adopted by the Inter-Parliamentary Union at a meeting in Jakarta on 21 October. This reiterated concern that the motives for prosecuting Anwar for corruption and sodomy were not of a legal nature, and that the case was built on a presumption of guilt. The United Nations was out of favour throughout the year, initially because the Secretary General, Kofi Annan, met briefly with keADILan leader Wan Azizah, and compounded when a critical Malaysian lawyer, Param Cumaraswamy, was reappointed for a second time as a U.N. Special Rapporteur on the Independence of Judges and Lawyers. Dr Mahathir declined to attend the U.N. Millennium Conference in September, although he was in New York at the time.

Malaysia found itself isolated from a large part of the world after the sentencing of Anwar in August. The United States, Canada, Australia, New Zealand, and the European Union questioned whether due process had in fact been observed. Malaysia's foreign ministry sent strong protest notes to all, and Dr Mahathir took it as a personal affront: "We know these people ... we know who are our friends and who are our enemies".[27] Malaysia took some pleasure in the fact that Southeast Asian nations did not join public criticisms of the Anwar trial. However, their media and human rights groups were all critical. And the willingness of neighbouring governments to provide sympathetic hearings to visiting opposition leaders ensured that the Anwar issue remained a complicating factor in the region.

The Anwar factor was perhaps most keenly felt in Malaysia's relations with the United States. In its annual human rights report released in February, the State Department criticized Anwar's corruption trial. "For political reasons, Anwar was charged with obstruction of justice in 1998 and convicted in April (1999). Improper conduct by the police and prosecutors, along with many questionable rulings by the judge, denied Anwar a fair opportunity to defend himself."[28] Seven congressmen tabled a resolution in the House of Representatives on 27 October calling on the Malaysian Government to give Anwar a new, fair trial, or dismiss all charges against him. They were, Dr Mahathir declared, "stupid" and unfit for congressional office. The congressional moves came at a time when government hostility towards the United States had been heightened by reports of opposition groups lobbying in the United States and employing a commercial lobby group for this purpose. (Opposition groups denied that they had paid any lobby group.) Dr Mahathir and others also harshly criticized what they said was an *Asian Wall Street Journal* listing of Malaysia as "the least free country in the world".[29] (In fact, the 2001 Index of Economic Freedom issued by the *Wall Street Journal* and the Heritage Foundation did not say this; it simply shifted Malaysia from "mostly free" to "mostly unfree".) These disparate events were, according to the mainstream media and Dr Mahathir, a concerted conspiracy.

Dr Mahathir maintained his usual hectic international travel, departing every few weeks for destinations such as the United Kingdom (twice), Japan, the United States, Agentina, the West Indies, France, Italy, Bosnia, Hong Kong, and summit meetings in Cairo (G-15), Qatar (the OIC), Brunei (APEC), and Singapore (ASEAN). Visits to the United States and the United Kingdom, however, took on a new dimension after a Free Anwar Campaign (FAC) was set up in August. The FAC set up overseas chapters, and arranged small protest demonstrations against Dr Mahathir's visits. They also secured the co-operation of supporters in the Islamic Society of North America (ISNA), the main U.S. Islamic organization, persuading ISNA to withdraw an invitation to Dr Mahathir as a keynote speaker, over his handling of the Anwar case. The FAC also embarrassed Trade Minister Dato' Rafidah Aziz during a trade mission to the United States, when it inserted material on Anwar in hand-outs that the mission passed to potential investors.

By the end of 2000, Malaysian leaders were still describing Malaysia as a model for the Third World. In November, Malaysia hosted its annual Langkawi International Dialogue, at which it again offered expertise on implementing the Malaysian way to developing countries (particularly from Africa). Some Asians remained impressed by what they saw as a leader who had achieved economic success while standing up against the West. An address by Dr Mahathir to an Asia Society meeting in Hong Kong in October was a sell-out. Opposition groups in Thailand, including current Prime Minister Thaksin Shinawatra, saw Malaysia as an example that could be emulated in their own country. For the most part, however, Malaysia's international position has deteriorated since the Anwar ouster. By year's end, Dr Mahathir even accused unnamed Muslim countries of helping the opposition to bring down the government: "They do this so that there will be no Muslim country in the world that is as successful as Malaysia, and they will look like the good guys".[30]

Outlook

After UMNO's severe setback in the 1999 general election, the Malay ground moved further against the party and its leadership in 2000. This was particularly marked in the final two months, which saw a major opposition rally on 5 November, disappointing UMNO constitutional reforms, an upset victory by the BA in the Lunas by-election, controversial political-corporate manoeuvres and bail-outs centred on Renong and MAS, a resumption of emotional calls to defend Malay rights and oppose Suqiu, and open criticism within UMNO of Dr Mahathir's leadership. The path of restoration without UMNO or governmental reform, and without changing the manner of dealing with the Anwar issue, appeared increasingly untenable. It did not help that non-Malay coalition partners had problems of their own, which mirrored and seemed just as intractable as those of UMNO.

With Dr Mahathir's leadership coming under increasingly critical attention UMNO must now move to clarify the succession issue. The international media accepts that this will be Dr Mahathir's last parliamentary term, but his own signals have been equivocal. In June, he spoke of needing another ten years to achieve his objectives, and in recent interviews he has declined to rule out leading the BN into the 2004 elections. At the least, it seems, he wishes to remain influential within UMNO, which would leave him with a continuing important role for some time.[31] By year's end, the possibility of his being forced out of office did not seem an immediate prospect, though with open public criticism from within UMNO this has become a possibility in the longer term.

Opposition parties made some notable gains throughout the year. The PAS-led opposition livened up parliamentary meetings, the BA performed strongly in by-elections, PAS governments in Kelantan and Terengganu were generally well-received, and continuing public enthusiasm for *reformasi* was apparent in the 5 November rally. However, the BA was not short of its own problems. It failed to select candidates for two by-elections without a debilitating fight, and did not consult on a wide range of issues despite agreement to do so. PAS and the DAP clashed publicly over Islamic matters, and conflicts within keADILan continually made the headlines. Much needs to be done before the BA emerges as a real alternative to the governing coalition.

NOTES

1. S.G. Securities, quoted in *Asian Wall Street Journal,* 4 January.
2. See, for instance, the views of Minister for Rural Development, Datuk Azmi Khalid, in *Berita Harian,* 13 March 2000.
3. John Funston, "Malaysia's Tenth Election: Status Quo, *Reformasi* or Islamisation?" *Contemporary Southeast Asia* 22, no.1 (April 2000): 23–59. See also "Election Fervour: Political Contest in Thailand and Malaysia", Trends in Southeast Asia series 9[2000], (Singapore: ISEAS, September 2000), pp.1–23.
4. *New Straits Times,* 16 February 2000.
5. Fathi Aris Omar, "Dicari polis: Demonstran usia 2 tahun!" *Malaysiakini,* 20 November 2000.
6. *Utusan Express, 24* November 2000
7. For further details, see John Funston, *Election Fervour: Political Contest in Thailand and Malaysia,* pp.17–21.
8. "Islamising Malaysia", *Straits Times,* 17 October 2000.
9. *Star,* 22 June 2000
10. *Utusan Malaysia,* 27 November 2000.

11. 4 December 2000.
12. "Thinking Allowed", *Aliran Monthly*, 20, no. 5 (2000): 21–23.
13. *Business Times* (Singapore), 25 August 2000.
14. Zakiah Koya, "Dr M to blame for Lunas defeat: Umno veteran", *Malaysiakini*, 30 November 2000.
15. *Mingguan Malaysia*, 10 December 2000.
16. M.G. G. Pillai, "Tan Sri Mohamed Taib A Senator and Minister?" Written on 9 December and posted on 28 December on *sangkancil@lists.malaysia.net*; and *Straits Times*, 29 December 2000.
17. "Justice in Jeopardy: Malaysia 2000" (Report of a mission on behalf of the International Bar Association, the ICJ Centre for the Independence of Judges and Lawyers, the Commonwealth Lawyers Association, and the Union Internationale, released on 5 April 2000).
18. S. Jayasankaran, "Malaysia: Fifteen Years", *Far Eastern Economic Review*, 17 August 2000.
19. John Funston, *Election Fervour: Political Contest in Thailand and Malaysia*, pp.14–17.
20. *Business Times* (Singapore), 28 October 2000.
21. Lim Say Boon, "It's a Catch-22 situation for Malaysia", *Straits Times*, 4 December 2000.
22. *Business Times* (Singapore), 23 December 2000.
23. S. Jayasankaran, "Malaysia: Fifteen Years", *Far Eastern Economic Review*, 17 August 2000.
24. Sheila McNulty, "Losing his grip", *Financial Times*, 27 February 2001. Citing Kostas Panagiotou, senior economist at Kim Eng Securities.
25. *Utusan Malaysia*, 16 August 2000.
26. *UMNO-online*, 10 November 2000.
27. *New Straits Times*, 14 August 2000.
28. <*http://www.state.gov/www/global/human_rights/1999_hrp_report/malaysia.html*>
29. *Asia Wall Street Journal*, 1 November 2000.
30. *Straits Times*, 6 December 2000.
31. *Mingguan Malaysia*, 4 June 2000; *Asiaweek*, 26 January 2001 (web-only exclusive); and *The Hindu*, 8 February 2001.

THE UNRAVELLING OF A "MALAY CONSENSUS"

Maznah Mohamad

While the Asian financial crisis had ebbed by late 1999, Malaysia was still raging with its own political turmoil. Long after former Deputy Prime Minister Anwar Ibrahim had been sacked and imprisoned, opposition towards the Mahathir government appeared strident. The United Malays National Organization (UMNO) — hitherto seen as pivotal for political stability in the country — continued to grapple for a "blueprint" to sustain its dominance of the Malay polity. Although Prime Minister Mahathir Mohamad rode through both the financial and the Anwar crises relatively unscathed, albeit through heavy-handed measures, his political survival did not seem guaranteed.

The position UMNO finds itself in today is not comparable to the many rounds of crises that the party had been through in recent decades. Previous crises were resolved quickly, but the Anwar episode has deprived UMNO of a continuing ideological rationale for its self-perpetuation. UMNO and Dr Mahathir found themselves entangled in events which were reduced to a series of political responses, defences, and vendettas that contributed little to the party's consolidation.

This chapter analyses how and why UMNO successfully overcame earlier crises in contrast to its latest experience. Recent events show a beleaguered party attempting to rebound from the Anwar crisis. However, although faced by one of the worst challenges to its political dominance, the party may still maintain a prolonged national presence. This is because the general viability of other Malay-based parties in garnering wider, sustainable multiracial support as well as providing a course for a "new politics" is still in question. In this regard, the final section of this chapter discusses the problems and prospects of the two main Malay-based opposition parties, the Parti Islam SeMalaysia (Islamic Party of Malaysia, or PAS) and the Parti KeADILan Nasional (National Justice Party, or keADILan). These two parties came together with the Democratic Action Party (DAP) and the Parti Rakyat Malaysia (People's Party of Malaysia, or PRM) in 1999 to form the Alternative Front (Barisan Alternatif), constituting a much strengthened opposition force against the ruling National Front (Barisan Nasional) during the last general election.

MAZNAH MOHAMAD is an Associate Professor in the School of Social Sciences, Universiti Sains Malaysia.

Post-independence UMNO Crises

UMNO has experienced three post-1969 crises, the first between 1975 and 1978, the second from 1984 to 1990, and the third, from 1993 till the present time. Some of the elements of the present conflict over the Anwar issue are quite similar to those which ushered the earlier crises. As with most UMNO crises, rumblings within the party would initially revolve around competition for economic largesse and, later, over leadership control and influence on national policies. In the contest for party leadership, enemies and unsuccessful rivals were frequently purged through the use of judicial and even parliamentary instruments. The difference this time is that UMNO's latest crisis, sparked by the Anwar affair, has spilled over to affect broader trends, notably the heightened politicization of the wider Malay masses and consolidation of the Malay opposition.

The first crisis, which unfolded in 1975 during Tun Abdul Razak's term as Prime Minister, was probably the last time in which UMNO's democratic machinery (through party elections) was ostensibly used to end a bitter battle between several interest groups. Even so, the communist bogey was employed by some to persecute and coerce rivals in the party.[1] This early period pitted a group of "young Turks" (of which Mahathir was one of its representatives) wanting to engineer rapid social change against an "old guard" of disparate forces of feudal nationalists and individuals whose fortunes were tied to the institutional vestiges of the "old system". UMNO survived this crisis because the winning faction created a new role for itself — as purveyor of Malay advancement through new social and economic affirmative action policies. Then, Malays had little justification for not throwing their unflinching support behind UMNO, and this was followed by the party's resounding performance in the 1978 election.

From 1987 till 1990 the struggle for party control was waged between Mahathir and his former ally, Tengku Razaleigh Hamzah. Mahathir's agenda for change was deemed too rapid, too radical and too unorthodox by contending groups. Adding fuel to this intra-party difference was the revelation of large-scale government scandals, notably the Bumiputra Malaysia Finance (BMF) debacle. By then, the price for vote-buying in the UMNO polls had become extraordinarily high, a phenomenon that was not widely seen until then.[2] However, amidst the rapid slide towards corruption and authoritarianism, Mahathir's faction introduced elements of renewal within the party. A constitutional crisis during this period contributed to UMNO's sense of relevance. As the powers of the royal rulers were being reduced, this campaign was popularly perceived as a "reformation" to phase out elements of parasitical feudalism in Malay political culture[3] — hence, providing the *raison d'être* for UMNO in the modernization of Malay society.

1993–2000: The Most Serious Split?

Before the eruption of the Anwar crisis, UMNO's holding power over the Malay community was sustained by several factors. UMNO was not only the purveyor of the New Economic Policy (NEP), which granted special rights and privileges to Malays for their economic advancement, but it was also the institution which protected and promoted Islam. The party's engagement with Islam was a strategy that was carefully planned because Islam was essentially a two-edged sword. It was a force to be used (hence the beginning of a process of official Islamization for the state's populist legitimacy), and also a force to be contained (UMNO's traditional adversary, PAS, and other "extremist" movements, were continually kept at bay by both coercive and co-optive measures). As soon as Mahathir came to power in 1981, he was circumspect about dealing with the Islamic resurgence among Malay youths and young professionals. His strategy of bringing Anwar into UMNO was viewed as being part of a strategy to co-opt the movement while containing it. The move was expediently successful since it had the effect of depriving PAS of a potential charismatic leader, and the movement behind him. Anwar also represented the then collective voice of a new generation of Malay youth seeking to widen the influence of Islam in governance.

Instead of going against this tide, Mahathir saw the necessity of absorbing this movement for the enhancement of UMNO, and eventually even earning for himself the reputation of an Islamic modernizer.[4] UMNO's Islamization agenda remained uncontested right up to the early 1990s, so much so that by 1994 Mahathir was confident enough to persecute Islamic movements that did not fit squarely into his development framework. During that year, *Darul Arqam* sect leaders were arrested under the Internal Security Act (ISA) on charges of practising a "deviationist" faith. This movement, which preached an Islam not condoned by the establishment, was also economically self-reliant, having prospered outside the ambit of state patronage and was purported to have a membership of some 300,000. In actual fact, the profile of such a movement was potentially threatening to UMNO although the *Darul Arqam* leadership did not openly show any ambition to contest the elections. However, back then the *Darul Arqam's* ban under the Mahathir-Anwar government failed to elicit even a meek outcry among the Malays, denoting that UMNO's Islamic credentials were still very much intact.

Right up to late 1998, there was no alternative to UMNO, even though PAS was an active party. UMNO was not only perceived to be committed to the goals of Islamization, but it also evinced a performance-legitimacy by delivering the material goods. By September 1998 onwards, however, Mahathir's successful engagement with Islam seemed to have come to an end. If his victory began with the co-optation of Anwar Ibrahim in 1982, the unravelling of his Islamic agenda began to take its course with the latter's ouster.

The ability to co-opt the different strategic Malay constituencies at various phases of its evolution was one of UMNO's greatest successes. Early in its history, it depended on Malay teachers and religious leaders, then it cultivated the active involvement of pioneering Malay professionals, followed by the move to integrate radical Islamists, and later the incorporation of the Malay business-class whose interests were being made to lock in with those of the party. Malay businessmen now serve as the party's newest patrons and as its moneyed backbone, which is also the source of the party's social liability. To be sure, Anwar's source of conflict with Mahathir and his faction was not purely based on the issue of differences over Islam and Islamization. In fact, this played a minor part in the split. The rift possibly began in 1993 when Anwar contested Ghafar Baba's position, the then Deputy Prime Minister, as UMNO's Vice-President. His victory brought about a stark realization that within only ten years after joining the party he had mobilized a sizeable mass following, built up and patronized a coterie of wealthy business interests, and gained control over several major newspapers and a television station to boost his political career.[5] Anwar's impending political rise amidst a climate of Islamization, that showed no signs of letting up, was the writing on the wall which eventually decided Mahathir's subsequent course of actions.

By opting for the strategy of sexual vilification against Anwar, Mahathir appeared to be prepared to take on one of his biggest gambles. The gamble was that if he were to succeed in sticking the sexual misconduct charges on Anwar, the result would be a discredited opposition Islam which, although politically contained, was still potentially threatening to an overall secular, developmentalist agenda which Mahathir was determined to foster. There would be confusion and disillusionment among some sectors of the Malay population, causing them to avoid strident movements and seek the safety of establishment Islam. So far the gamble has not paid off. Instead, unintended consequences as in the further reinforcement of PAS and the emergence of the multi-ethnic but Malay-majority party, the keADILan, only hastened the erosion of a Malay consensus for UMNO.

Loosening Monopoly and Malay Identity Crisis

The Anwar crisis, which began as a contest over leadership in the party, culminated in the manifestation of a dislocation in Malay identity politics. Before this, UMNO had employed various flexible strategies to capture as much as possible of the Malay "voice", even to the point of being syncretic in its ideological thrusts.[6] When Tun Razak was Prime Minister (1970–75) UMNO went as far as to consult with left-leaning intellectuals and technocrats who were influential in introducing the idea that extensive control of public institutions was important for restructuring society.[7] In the 1980s, UMNO further acceded to the growing demands for widespread Islamization among Malay youths by instituting a concerted and planned Islamization programme. Later on, the party was seen as departing from Malay cultural conventions by challenging and eventually weakening the powers of the Malay rulers during the "Constitutional Crisis" of the early 1990s. But the Islamically-modern, market-friendly state which Mahathir was anxious to establish soon became a victim of his own design. Islam was gradually perceived by some of his backers to be in the way of an unfettered capitalist expansion and an entrenched secular system. At the other end, material austerity and social justice promoted by Islam converged with the ideologies of rights-based social activism, which opposed economic mega-projects and excessive public spending. As the Malay consensus ceases to become the monopoly of UMNO with the ouster of Anwar, the government is shown to be not simply unjust to one person but to an icon of Islam. The resurgent Islam, which Mahathir had captured at one time to consolidate his rule as well as UMNO's, now conflicts with his present goals of liberalizing the economy to accommodate meritocratic aspirations, and conceding to liberals and non-Muslims to preserve secularism. UMNO is becoming less effective at moderating the stepped-up calls for Islamization to spread into every terrain of public and private lives. The non-Muslim constituency, which fears the prospect of an Islamic state, is assuaged by the portrayal of the Islamic opposition as extremists and therefore having no credibility to rule. At the same time, to entice Malay support, the party's own brand of Malay chauvinism is brandished. However, this inability to re-emphasize its relevancy for the Malay constituency while sustaining non-Malay support, which it won during the last general election, has become UMNO's greatest bane.

As UMNO grappled with a much broader spread of Malay dissent, the party's performance in the 1999 elections failed to reaffirm its record of Malay allegiance and loyalty. Although the National Front was returned with a two-thirds majority in Parliament, the manifestation of popular disaffection was evidenced by several new developments: the capture of two Malay states (Kelantan and Terengganu) by PAS; the narrowed margins of wins garnered by the National Front compared with the 1995 elections; the reduced votes in Malay-majority areas for UMNO candidates; and the appearance for the first time in Malaysia's history of a Malay-based party as the main opposition in Parliament. Never before in the country's electoral history had UMNO faced such a major challenge against its stature as the Malay dominant party nonpareil.

UMNO now has to face several challenges. The financial crisis has only just abated and the *reformasi* movement is still being stoked among the public by an eclectic and fragile coalition of liberals, democrats, and Islamists. PAS is stronger than it has ever been and there is an Internet media which is belligerent, accessible, and a popular alternative to government propaganda. Still, UMNO's position as a large, well-financed political institution is a force to be reckoned with, in spite of its acrimonious internal battles. Many backers are not persuaded that the party and Dr Mahathir can be easily unseated.[8] However, it cannot be doubted that the latest crisis may have led to one of the most critical splits within the Malay polity since independence.

Ruling Dangerously

What happened in 2000 is a window to some of the above postulations about a weakening UMNO. Some of the major events were as follows:

The Umno General Assembly

Soon after its poor performance in the national elections, UMNO held its own Annual General Assembly to elect new party officials. The elections were postponed from June 1999 to May 2000, because of the tense political atmosphere generated by the Anwar crisis. However, in the run-up to the May 2000 elections, controversy began to brew as soon as the party's Supreme Council's decision of no-contest for the posts of party President and Vice-President was made. The uncontested position for party President was accepted as a *fait accompli* but the post of Deputy President was still left ambiguously open to allow for some degree of challenge. This invited speculation as well as calls for a contender to challenge the post held by the Deputy Prime Minister, Abdullah Badawi. The most likely contender then was Tengku Razaleigh, former head of Semangat 46 (an opposition party now defunct and whose members have since rejoined UMNO). Nevertheless, as widely expected, he failed to get the minimum number of required nominations from the party's divisional committees, since most members were not prepared to go against the Supreme Council's will. As this episode illustrates, instead of heeding the majority voice, the reverse trend prevailed, with all layers of the party strata complying with central orders without much uproar.

At the opening of the meeting, the party President's main theme in his speech was the rebuke of Anwar Ibrahim for his alleged misconduct, even though the sodomy trial was still in process. He also condemned the use of "money politics" by delegates in their contest to garner votes — an odd allegation, given that the same accusation was levelled upon the National Front in its aggressive and massively-funded campaign during the general election a few months back. Furthermore, earlier allegations of corruption against several UMNO officials made by the opposition were overlooked as "non-issues" at the Assembly. However, the outcome of the UMNO elections evoked much questioning, especially when the posts for the three Vice-Presidents were won by candidates who previously (under Anwar Ibrahim's endorsement in the 1993 Annual Assembly) had called themselves the *Kumpulan Wawasan*, or Vision Team. It is unclear whether this meant that support for Anwar within the party was still inherent or that the candidates won through the alleged use of "vote-buying". The other victors for the Supreme Council seats consisted of a mixed-bag of so-called Mahathir-supporters, as well as more critical and outspoken personalities, such as Shahrir Samad, a former Deputy Minister and Semangat 46 member. Furthermore, despite UMNO's projection of itself as a party concerned about women's advancement in the last elections, not a single woman was elected into the Supreme Council.

Allegations of Impropriety Against the Chief Justice

In June, a controversy over the credibility of the Chief Justice became the main news item in the country. Although allegations of corruption against him had already surfaced years earlier and pictures of him holidaying together with a prominent lawyer had appeared on Internet websites for months, it was Minister Rais Yatim's criticism of the Chief Justice to an Australian radio station that sparked the furore.[9] The Malaysian Bar Council called for an emergency meeting to discuss the possibility of setting up a tribunal to investigate the conduct of the Chief Justice, as well as to prevent the anticipated six-month extension of his tenure. UMNO Youth, and Finance Minister Daim Zainuddin, also came out to support Rais' action in questioning the Chief Justice's alleged impropriety. Their views were carried by the UMNO-controlled newspaper, *Utusan Malaysia*.[10] All this happened while Mahathir was away for an overseas meeting. When he returned, he declared that there was no need for a tribunal to be set up, and announced that the Chief Justice's term would be extended for another six months as there were matters that needed to be settled. This remark was widely interpreted to mean, *inter alia*, matters involving the "Anwar trial". The Bar Council's call for an emergency meeting to discuss the tribunal was ultimately halted by a court injunction, which ruled that the Bar Council would be committing contempt of court if the meeting were held. In November, the Attorney-General announced that the case against the Chief Justice was closed because of insufficient evidence to proceed with any charges.

The Selangor Religious Department Arrests of Malay Entertainers

Public interest in the Chief Justice's alleged impropriety was still at its peak when an issue involving the jurisdiction of the Selangor Islamic Religious Department (JAIS) occupied centre stage in the media. A nightclub was raided in Petaling Jaya (an urban, middle-class suburb), resulting in the arrests of a female singer, musicians, and entertainers (all Muslims) working at the outlet. The Deputy Prime Minister was one of the first officials to insinuate that the arrests were unfair as they deprived Muslims of seeking lawful employment. Those arrested claimed that they did not take alcohol but were merely serving drinks to customers or were entertaining them. The government-controlled media initially tried to link the arrests to a religious bureaucracy which was purportedly influenced by PAS. However, the employees of the club were arrested by state religious officials, on charges of "causing disrepute to Islam", under legislation which was passed by an UMNO-dominated State Assembly in 1995 and had no links to PAS.[11] Then, the Islamic lobby within the government was anxious to enforce its Islamization agenda by widening the jurisdiction of the Syariah courts to include legal provisions outside family laws. Among the laws passed was the seemingly arbitrary and open-ended ruling which deemed any action construed as "demeaning Islam" to be a criminal offence. The issue was quickly resolved, however, partly because the Deputy Prime Minister had already spoken out against the actions of JAIS officials and because of protests from women's groups headed by the Sisters in Islam.[12] Nevertheless, the "agreement" to drop the charges seemed to have been exercised by the executive arm of government, namely, the Chief Minister of Selangor, who took it upon himself to pronounce that the law was "ambiguous" and that the arresting officers had erred in "misinterpreting" the law.[13] This episode did not help the UMNO government in repairing its battered credibility since the opposition clamoured on the point that there was stark executive intervention in the judicial process. Two months later, the Chief Minister, who had played a part in getting the Islamic Department to drop the charges against the nightclub entertainers, was himself the subject of an embarrassing sex scandal which ultimately led to his resignation.

The Apostasy Bill

Much as the UMNO government was keen to attribute the over-zealousness of Islamization to PAS's so-called extremism, it was not able to prevent contests over what should constitute legitimate Islam, even within the milieu of the party itself. In April, the state government of Johor was already instituting punishment for "crimes" recognized by Islam but not contained in the penal code under the civil courts' jurisdiction, such as caning and jailing for offences like pimping, lesbianism, prostitution, sodomy, and the teaching or organizing of events contrary to Syariah laws. A further example of controversy on the issue of Islamic contestation was over a proposed law on apostasy. The Perlis State Assembly had passed such a legislation early in 2000 without much hue and cry. However, in September, when it was proposed that a federal bill be drawn up to address the "offence" of apostasy, much concern and debate ensued over it.[14] Public debate prompted by the proposal revealed that Malays, whether in support of UMNO or PAS, were split over this issue.[15] Although an apostasy bill had constantly been pushed by PAS in Parliament without success, this time the initiative was taken by some in UMNO itself.

The controversial bills sought to deal with the issue of apostasy among Muslims by detaining them for rehabilitation if they were found to have "strayed" from the faith. The bill was drawn up by religious functionaries under the UMNO government, revealing that some UMNO members themselves were keen to promote further Islamization. However, the Prime Minister indicated he was not supportive of the bill. The bill was eventually forced to be withdrawn back to the drawing board, seemingly because of "public protests".[16]

Some analysts have read the proposed bill as UMNO's attempt to out-Islamize PAS in order to win back its lost Malay ground. This may not necessarily be so, since the initiative for the bill did not emanate from the central leadership but was proposed independently by Islamic factions within UMNO. It was not endorsed by UMNO's top leaders. Thus, contestations around issues of Islamization within UMNO itself would not make it easy for Mahathir to continually manage, contain, and suppress the challenge of political Islam.

Allegations of Corruption Against Mahathir

Mahathir's credibility took one of its greatest beatings when in June a former Anti-Corruption Agency (ACA) Director testified at the Anwar trial that the

Prime Minister had interfered with the work of the agency. He claimed that the Prime Minister had directed the agency to cease investigations on the alleged discovery of large sums of money in the office of Ali Abul Hassan, a former Director-General at the Prime Minister's Department, who later became Malaysia's Central Bank Governor. KeADILan organized a nation-wide campaign to lodge police reports against Mahathir's alleged interference with the due process of law. There was no follow-up on this complaint by law enforcers and instead, in October, the case against Ali Abul Hassan was declared closed in Parliament because of insufficient evidence to proceed with the charges.

Mahathir Refuses To Appear As Witness in Anwar Trial
Within the month of June also, Anwar's defence lawyers' effort to subpoena Mahathir to appear as a witness in the trial failed. The judge ruled that Mahathir was not a material witness in the trial. This was yet another example used by critics to suggest Mahathir's devastating control over the judiciary. When Anwar was first arrested, Mahathir had announced freely to a worldwide media that he had enough evidence to prove Anwar's guilt and was prepared to divulge it all in court ("I am willing to testify").[17] During the months of June and July, political tensions ran high in anticipation of the Anwar verdict, which was delivered in early August. The trial was controversial on many grounds, including two amendments for the dates of the alleged sodomy, evidence solely based upon the testimony of one witness whom the defence lawyers had tried to prove impeachable, and claims that confessions by Anwar's adopted brother (charged together for the offence) were extracted through torture and coercion while under detention.

The Al Ma'unah Arms Heist
As if providing diversion from the much anticipated Anwar verdict, two army camps were looted of a large amount of weapons and ammunitions in July. The alleged bandits were then holed up on a hill, and in a stand-off with security forces, two hostages and one group member were killed. Identified as responsible for the heist was the Al Ma'unah movement, whose existence had hitherto not been heard of by the general public. Internet postings and opposition websites claimed that daily news reports on the event were giving contradictory and questionable accounts on the veracity of the alleged heist. A suggestion that the incident was staged-managed by UMNO in order to detract public attention from court allegations against Mahathir by the former ACA head and from Anwar's expected "guilty" verdict, circulated wildly among the public. Opposition groups also expressed their suspicions about the incident as Mahathir and the media sought to link the Al Ma'unah and PAS.[18] The Prime Minister also took the opportunity to warn non-Muslims about the dangers of supporting opposition political parties, especially PAS, claiming that only the National Front was capable of providing the moderating influence

against extremist forces. This was not a successful ploy, judging by the enormous scepticism generated, especially among a large cross-section of Malays. UMNO politicians had to go on a nation-wide campaign to counter the mockery.[19] In response to public scepticism, the Ministry of Defence even went as far as to re-enact the alleged heist to prove that it was possible to load three vehicles with the amount of weapons claimed to have been stolen. Finally, instead of charging the "militant" group under the penal offences of robbery, kidnap, and murder, the law used to prosecute the group was for treason and for "waging war" against His Majesty's Government.[20] This was a law that had never been used before. By the time the group was formally charged and their trial commenced, the public had all but lost interest in the case, with newspapers devoting only small columns to trial proceedings.

The Anwar Verdict

August was another explosive period because of the judgment on the Anwar trial for sodomy on 8 August. This also happened to be the day in 1988 that Tun Salleh Abbas, the then Lord President, was sacked from office. Although there was no massive demonstration on the day of the judgment, compared with the verdict at his first trial for corruption on 14 April 1999, the additional nine-year sentence aroused widespread national and international condemnation, against the judgment specifically and the Malaysian judicial system as a whole.[21]

A Chief Minister's Sex Scandal

Just a day after the Anwar verdict, the country was abuzz with revelations of a sex scandal involving the Chief Minister of Selangor. Allegations about him fathering a child with his sister-in-law had come out in the open and provoked opposition State Assemblymen to call for the matter to be investigated. At this, the Chief Minister swiftly conceded to resign, purportedly on health grounds. Although there was no open contest for the vacant post, UMNO stalwarts in Selangor keenly eyed the position. The Prime Minister's announcement of a 37-year old dentist and first-time State Assemblyman to the post came as a surprise to the nation. Such a turn of events naturally invited speculation about why the other senior politicians were overlooked for the coveted job. One hypothesis was that none of the senior politicians had a clean record from either corruption or sex-related scandals. The other speculation was that the Prime Minister was anxious to concede to a more youthful leadership in his government, given the indifference, if not abhorrence, of youth towards UMNO, which had become the party's major concern after its dismal performance at the general election.

Malay Rights, Suqiu, Communist Bogey, and UMNO Youth

Even before the issue of the Selangor Chief Minister's scandal could be settled, the pro-government Malay paper *Utusan Malaysia* started running headlines on a purported emerging threat to Malays over the provision of their "special rights".[22] This issue was blown up based on an interview given by David Chua, deputy chairman of the National Economic Consultative Council (NECC), who had earlier appeared in a story in the *Far Eastern Economic Review*.[23] It was reported that he had proposed that certain Malay special rights be done away with in order to stimulate growth in certain industries. A few days later, a group calling itself the Suqiu (Election Appeals Group) celebrated the first anniversary of its "17-Point Appeals" memorandum, endorsed by some two thousand Chinese organizations calling for various reforms just before the 29 November elections. *Utusan Malaysia* highlighted this event to feed the "Malay rights" controversy further, claiming that among the appeals was a demand that *bumiputra* (indigenous) special rights be revised. UMNO Youth acted immediately upon this "revelation" and organized two vociferous demonstrations — one in front of the Prime Minister's office in Putrajaya to demand his action, and another at the Selangor Chinese Assembly Hall in Kuala Lumpur to harangue Suqiu officials. Threats to burn down the hall were hurled against the Suqiu if it did not back down on its demands, and apologize to the *bumiputra* community.[24]

In his National Day speech on 31 August, the Prime Minister further fanned the controversy surrounding the above issue. He chided the Suqiu by equating it to communists and left-leaning groups, as well as to the extremist Al Ma'unah. He seemed to have forgotten that Suqiu's "17-point Appeals" had already been accepted in principle by his own Cabinet prior to the November 1999 general election. The use of the communist bogey by the Prime Minister was confounding. A few days later, he was photographed hugging Fidel Castro, the world's longest ruling communist leader, in New York. The mainstream media, nonetheless, glossed over the discrepancy in the Prime Minister's stance on communism.

Revocation of Oil Royalty Agreement
UMNO's most striking vendetta against PAS was waged when the Petronas oil royalty payment of 5 per cent to the state of Terengganu was revoked by the federal government in September — to deprive the PAS-led state government of lucrative revenue, and to "admonish" the people of Terengganu for voting PAS into office. In this scheme, an equivalent sum would be used as development allocations for specific projects such as housing and infrastructure in place of direct royalty payment to the state government. The management of such funds would come under the control of the federal authorities. The widespread anger provoked by the plan was probably underestimated by Mahathir. A large protest against the revocation of royalties was staged on 25 November 2000 in front of the Finance Ministry in Kuala Lumpur, although not one local newspaper reported the event.[25]

Foreign Snub
In September, Mahathir experienced his first international snub when the Islamic Society of North America (ISNA) withdrew its invitation to the Prime

Minister to be a keynote speaker at one of its meetings. Mahathir's invitation by a group of pro-government students based at Cambridge University to a workshop in October also sparked a controversy when a rival group calling itself the Cambridge Coalition for a Free Malaysia reacted to the invitation by calling for a boycott of the planned event.[26] The event was not cancelled, but Mahathir was met by protestors, mainly Malaysian students and members of the Cambridge University Amnesty International group.[27]

Putrajaya as Federal Territory

In October, an official announcement was made that Putrajaya, the site of the new administrative centre, would be converted into Federal Territory. This was the second parcel of land within the state of Selangor, after Kuala Lumpur, to come under federal government jurisdiction. There was dissatisfaction, even among UMNO members in Selangor, about this new decree, since the terms and amount of compensation of RM200 million and cash of RM7.5 million per year had been predetermined without prior negotiations with state legislators. The Memorandum of Understanding (MOU) specifying the transfer was signed in November, ahead of the passing of the necessary bills at both the Selangor State Assembly and Parliament. While the MOU was being signed, the motion to debate this issue in Parliament by the opposition was denied by the Speaker on grounds that it was not an urgent matter. Accession of the territory to the federal government formally took place in early 2001.

Traitors' Charge, and Kesas Demonstration

The whipping up of nationalist and anti-foreign sentiments is one of Mahathir's favourite tactics to shore up his credentials. The mainstream media contributed to this in October by railing against keADILan members meeting with foreign leaders, depicting this as an act of disloyalty to the country. Mahathir and UMNO Youth called Ezam Mohamad Noor, leader of keADILan's Youth wing, a traitor because he berated the Malaysian Government during his meeting with an American congressman. UMNO Youth went so far as to ask that his citizenship be revoked — an unprecedented call for banishment by Malays against another Malay.[28] Here again, Mahathir may have misjudged the reaction of Malays towards Ezam. It was not resentment that was evoked. Instead, Mahathir's and UMNO Youth's censure against Ezam may have had the opposite effect of increasing his popularity and resuscitating the seemingly flagging *reformasi* movement.

In late October and early November, two demonstrations showed that the spirit of *reformasi* had not been extinguished. On 29 October, thousands of people gathered in Kamunting, the site of the detention prison for Internal Security Act (ISA) detainees, to protest against the ISA legislation on its fortieth anniversary. A week later, on 5 November, a massive convergence of demonstrators occurred in Shah Alam, Selangor. The actual gathering was thwarted by police who were alleged to have exerted violent means and caused a massive traffic jam along the Kesas highway to stop some several thousand motorists from reaching the destination of the planned gathering, dubbed the "*Himpunan 100,000 Rakyat*" (Gathering of 100,000 People) with the slogan of "*Kembalikan Hak Rakyat*" (Restore the People's Rights). More than 100 people were arrested, and charges of police brutality subsequently prodded the National Human Rights Commission to conduct an inquiry.

Lunas By-Election

On 29 November, a by-election was held in the State Assembly constituency of Lunas, Kedah, following the death of its National Front representative. This was a mixed constituency with 43 per cent of the voters being Malays, 37 per cent Chinese, and 19 per cent Indians. The victory of keADILan over the National Front at this by-election, on the first anniversary of the country's tenth general election, showed that after one year UMNO was still unable to recover lost ground, and that the dependence of the National Front coalition partners on a no longer strong UMNO would have to be reconsidered. The National Front even lost its previously assured support from non-Malay voters. Although keADILan won with a majority of 530 votes, it managed to swing a large number of votes which had previously gone to the National Front. The Alternative Front started at a disadvantage following a squabble over which of the component parties' candidates should contest in the election. It was a traditional DAP seat, but after a tussle and wrangling by members of keADILan's Youth wing, the Alternative Front decided on a keADILan Malay candidate over the DAP's Indian choice. This split in opposition ranks was fully exploited by the media as a case of racism within the Alternative Front, particularly against Indian minorities.[29] However, the National Front had alienated Chinese voters by attempts to force the "Vision School" issue, and Dr Mahathir's and UMNO Youth's derisive treatment of the Suqiu episode. The Chinese community had been suspicious of the benefit of the "Vision School" project, in which primary schools of the three language mediums (Malay, Chinese and Tamil) would be housed in one premises to share certain common facilities as a way of fostering unity. This project was read as a government ploy to dilute the autonomy and strength of Chinese-medium schools. The National Front's loss in this election even invited scathing and forthright criticisms from an UMNO Supreme Council member, Shahrir Samad, who attributed the defeat to "the character of our leader, Dr Mahathir".[30]

Amendments to UMNO's Constitution

After its General Assembly in May, UMNO prepared to amend its Constitution. Initially, there was a proposal to reduce the term of its office-bearers within the Supreme Council and allow some 30,000 members to participate in party elections instead of the 2,000 or so delegates to the assemblies. Later, there emerged an alternative proposal to prolong the term of office from three to five years. Rafidah Aziz, head of Wanita UMNO (Women's Wing), also suggested that the post of the three Vice-Presidents be scrapped. None of these ideas were accepted. A proposal for the setting-up of a Women's Youth wing, the Puteri UMNO, hit a snag, with women leaders expressing their differences over its terms of reference, particularly the age requirements for membership into the new wing. UMNO also moved to set up service centres, perhaps modelled on a successful Malaysian Chinese Association project, with the opening of a Civil Action Bureau in Sungai Way in October 2000. There is no evidence that UMNO is succeeding in getting more youth to join the movement. As of now, the image of UMNO Youth does not appear to have gone through any "reinvention". It was still playing out its role as the vociferous, aggressive, agitator arm of the party, as witnessed during the Suqiu Appeals controversy.

On 18 November, a special UMNO meeting of the General Assembly was held to debate and pass some fifty amendments to the party's Constitution. News reports depicted a sombre mood during the meeting, with little contentious debate over the amendments.[31] The membership did not seem to have taken the amendments seriously, to constitute a substantive basis for far-reaching party reforms. The President's plea for corruption to be wiped out was emotional and tearful, but if amendments to party rules were all passed within a day's work, could this conceivably lead to a restructuring of the party? Actually, some of UMNO's weaknesses are entrenched in a culture which found its historical roots in the struggle for establishing Malay political hegemony. As part of this, the cultivation of UMNO into becoming the wealthiest party seemed to be a prerequisite for the deliverance of Malay supremacy. However, such a trajectory was inevitably infused with the likelihood of ill-gotten accumulation and underhand politicking, from which the party is now finding it difficult to disengage.

Alternative Malay Parties

There are at present two Malay-based parties that will pose a considerable challenge to UMNO. The traditional adversary, PAS, is enjoying its strongest support since it was formed in 1951. In the November 1999 general election, PAS emerged as the largest opposition party with 27 parliamentary seats. For the first time in Malaysia's history, the leadership of the opposition in Parliament is held by a Malay representative, Fadzil Noor, who is the President of PAS. However, given PAS' "theocratic" bias in leadership and policy and the "fundamentalist-extremist" card that the National Front can conveniently use to counter the Islamic party's influence, PAS may face future difficulties in achieving wider national support.

Another Malay-majority party, keADILan, which is nominally multiracial, has a very recent existence but has attracted the support of many urban Malays. It was formally launched in April 1999, eight months after Anwar was arrested. Although keADILan won only five seats in the general election, many of its more prominent leaders were narrowly defeated. In terms of popular votes, the party made a big impact in Selangor, the Federal Territory (Kuala Lumpur),

Negri Sembilan, and Penang (Anwar's home state). KeADILan does not yet pose a threat to the ruling UMNO, but its future relevance would depend on the extent to which PAS is able to win over the non-Muslim and liberal Malay constituencies.

If UMNO is not able to sustain its monopoly over the Malay constituency, then keADILan may be able to play a role in capturing "middle Malaysia". A weakened UMNO will also debilitate the National Front coalition, persuading more Malay voters, who are not drawn to PAS's Islamic politics, to keADILan. The more democratic, plural, middle-class voters who do not identify political preference with race may also switch to this party. At the moment, large sections of this constituency are still in doubt about keADILan's ability to deliver, especially its ability to temper the intrusion of fundamentalist Islam into secular as well as private domains. In fact, keADILan has largely remained on the sidelines when it comes to controversial issues involving some of the rulings made by the newly-elected Terengganu PAS government. The state government had tried to enforce compulsory veiling of women in the workplace, banned unisex hairdressing salons, and enforced separate check-in counters at supermarkets for men and women — measures which had impinged on the rights of non-Muslims and women. It was the DAP which provided PAS with the strongest challenge on those issues, to the extent of a near break-up of the Alternative Front coalition in August. The DAP and the keADILan also fell out over the latter's insistence on fielding its own Malay candidate in the Lunas by-election.

KeADILan's political platform has remained ambivalent since it is still very much focused on campaigns to free Anwar from his imprisonment. Nevertheless, the drawing power of keADILan is its association with the elements of youth and renewal. Some of the party's more popular personalities, such as Ezam Mohd. Noor, leader of its Youth Wing, have succeeded in drawing large crowds at political rallies and events. Anwar's eighteen-year old daughter, Nurul Izzah, has also become a popular icon among Malay youths. Another keADILan leader, Tian Chua, has grabbed the national limelight with his bouts of imprisonment, beatings, and assault at the hands of riot police, and provides a likely role-model for youth as a fearless, if not impulsive, fighter.

However, because of the constraints of its association with the "Anwar" factor, keADILan has yet to succeed in building itself up as a populist party that is widely multiracial and committed to specific ideals of governance appealing to a larger cross-section of the Malaysian population. At the back of critics' minds is the durability of keADILan, especially if and when Anwar is freed from his imprisonment. The future scenario could include the return of Anwar into UMNO's fold and his completing the party's reforms, in which case, the accusation that keADILan is a party created solely for securing the release of Anwar Ibrahim and charting the fall of Mahathir Mohamad would then be proved correct. Would the party go the way of Semangat 46, which found itself reduced to redundancy as soon as the relevancy of UMNO was re-embraced by Malays?

Given the change in Malay political culture, and the strengthening of PAS as a popular antithesis to UMNO, what lies in store may be much more complex, and disprove common presumptions hitherto about the "predictability" of Malay political behaviour.

Looking Forward

Sorting out the options for a new Malaysia will be a difficult, even bewildering process, which is greatly complicated by the unravelling of "Malay unity" in the wake of *reformasi*. The transformation of Malay political culture during Malaysia's post-independence era from one which used to be characterized by unqualified allegiance to the state, treated as indistinguishable from UMNO, to a phenomenon of dissent against traditional authoritative structures and concentration of power, is a notable watershed in Malaysian politics. However, whether this feature will be sustained and lead to a bigger overhaul of the Malaysian political system is a question that will vex many observers.

If the spread of Malay dissent against UMNO widens, then UMNO can only continue to survive (at least in elections) by conceding more to the once "politically disenfranchised" non-Malay constituency through dismantling the notion of Malay hegemony in politics and control over public resources. This was what had happened during the last general election when the National Front won because of strong support from non-Malay voters, having made several concessions to the community on issues of education, the economy, and culture. However, to what extent can UMNO uphold this pact without further alienating itself from its Malay base? In a sense, this inevitable drift towards blurring communal interests converges with the ultimate goal of Mahathir's *Bangsa Malaysia* (Malaysian Race). To achieve this, he had envisaged the removal of all social and economic props for Malays so as to enhance their resiliency to compete equally with the other communities. For this reality to match his rhetoric, however, even UMNO could be dispensable as a vehicle to reach such an end. The fact that more Malays are not counting on UMNO's relevance anymore may mean that they are prepared to let go of "crutches" such as special privileges and the continuance of affirmative action policies to assert themselves, which can now, for example, find expression in the reaffirmation of an Islamic identity. Either that or the Malays cannot yet foresee the possibility of any alternative governance forsaking policies which would still place them in a "special" position (however that may be defined), simply because such an ideology is embedded within the political system. Still unprepared to see the Malays cut their umbilical cord with UMNO, Mahathir unsuccessfully tried to invoke the notion of Malay ungratefulness among his detractors, using lines such as: "They have forgotten Allah's promise that the ungrateful will not receive blessings and the punishment of God will be very painful".[32] Generations of Malays who had thrived under the aegis of the New Economic Policy may still be grateful to UMNO for enabling their upward mobility, but as they become more self-assured in their role as the new middle-class, not just in the socio-economic sense but also in a more politically astute context, the patron–client contract which UMNO had for so long thrived upon may no longer resonate with their aspirations.

NOTES

1. Harold Crouch, "The UMNO Crisis: 1975–77", in *Malaysian Politics and the 1978 Election*, edited by Harold Crouch, Lee Kam Hing and Michael Ong (Kuala Lumpur: Oxford University Press, 1980), pp. 20–27.
2. Terrence Gomez, "Anwar Vs. Mahathir?" *Aliran Monthly* 15, no 9 (1995).
3. The rising Malay "New Rich" saw the feudal class, with political connections, as having an unfair advantage over them in business. The other more apt reason for curtailing the powers of the Malay rulers was to "establish once and for all that the governmental powers lie with the executive arm of government and not with the hereditary Rulers." See H.P. Lee, *Constitutional Conflict in Contemporary Malaysia* (Singapore: Oxford University Press, 1995), p. 96.
4. Kikue Hamayotsu, "Reformist Islam, Mahathir and the Making of Malaysian Nationalism" (Paper presented at the Second International Malaysian Studies Conference, Kuala Lumpur, Malaysia, 2–4 August 1999).
5. Terrence Gomez, op. cit., 1995.
6. See Jesudason for a fuller use of the concept of "syncretism", as practised by the National Front to protract its political legitimacy. James Jesudason, "The Syncretic State and the Structuring Oppositional Politics in Malaysia", in *Political Opposition in Industrialising Asia*, edited by Garry Rodan (London: Routledge, 1996).
7. Tun Abdul Razak, the former Prime Minister, had drawn many socialist-leaning intellectuals into his inner circle of advisers. The influence of such intellectuals upon policies contained in the Second Malaysian Plan, and later the New Economic Policy, was quite considerable. For an account of this, see Dominic Puthucheary, "James Puthucheary: His Friends and His Times", in *James Puthucheary, No Cowardly Past: Writings, Poems and Commentaries*, edited by Dominic J. Puthucheary and K.S. Jomo (Kuala Lumpur: INSAN, 1998), pp. 30–37.
8. One of the most popular, if not flattering, arguments about Mahathir's resiliency is his personal charisma and shrewd political and economic manoeuvring, which appeals to the "security and consumer-oriented" middle-class. See Abdul Rahman Embong, "Political Dimensions of the Economic Crisis in Malaysia", in *Southeast Asia into the Twenty First Century: Crisis and Beyond*, edited by Abdul Rahman Embong and Jurgen Rudolph (Bangi: Penerbit UKM, 2000), pp. 139–46.
9. For a full text of the interview, see *Harakah*, 16–30 June 2000.
10. "Pemuda UMNO Sokong Teguran Rais [UMNO Youth Supports Rais' Rebuke]", *Utusan Malaysia*, 8 June 2000; and "Rakyat Berhak Tegur Badan Kehakiman [The People Have the Right to Question the Judiciary]", *Utusan Malaysia*, 9 June 2000.
11. Section 10 of the Selangor Syariah Criminal Enforcement (1995). This law deems any action which brings "disrepute to Islam" an offence.
12. Sisters in Islam issued several "Joint Press Statements" on behalf of women's groups, including on 24 and 29 June 2000. The endorsers consisted of a wide range of NGOs and prominent individuals, including the wives and daughters of the Prime Minister and Deputy Prime Minister. Among the issues raised was the growing intolerance of religious forces, selective prosecution involving women, and violation of fundamental employment rights.
13. "Charges Dropped: JAIS Officers Misconstrued the Law", *Star*, 29 June 2000.
14. A protest letter by Sisters in Islam, "It's Not Right To legislate On Faith" was published in almost all major newspapers. See the *Star*, 30 September 2000. Another piece by Salbiah Ahmad, "Keeping Faith in a Freedom of Religion Bill", which

appeared in the Internet newspaper *Malaysiakini.com,* 26 September 2000, proposed a counter-legislation, the Freedom of Religion Bill, to deal with the issue.

15. In a workshop organized for UMNO activists in Johor, many of the participants were concerned why Islamic laws could not be readily implemented by the government. See Shahanaz Sher Habib, "Lifting the Veil On A Burning Issue", *Sunday Star,* 22 October 2000.

16. Twenty-nine Muslim individuals protested against the bill to the National Human Rights Commission. See, "Rais: Proposed Apostasy Bill To Be Thoroughly Studied", *Star,* 29 September 2000.

17. Martin Jalleh, "Justice Mahathir is Court Shy!" *Aliran Monthly* 20, no. 5 (2000).

18. Minister in the Prime Minister's Department Rais Yatim claimed that he would provide proof of the Al-Ma'unah-PAS connection in its White Paper. See "Rais: Various Acts Can Be Used Against PAS", *Star,* 23 July 2000. There has been no White Paper since.

19. "Lack Of Information Can Spell Danger", Editorial in the *Star,* 19 July 2000.

20. The group was charged on 8 August 2000 (the same day that Anwar's verdict was handed down), under Section 121 of the Penal Code.

21. See *Aliran Monthly* 20, no. 6 (2000), for a collection of statements issued nationally and internationally.

22. "Hapus Hak Istimewa Melayu" [Do Away With Special Malay Rights], *Utusan Malaysia,* 14 August 2000.

23. *Far Eastern Economic Review,* 10 August 2000.

24. For an account of the controversy, see Francis Loh, "A Crisis of Malay Rights Or An UMNO Crisis?" *Aliran Monthly* 20, no. 7 (2000).

25. "Thousands Protest Malaysian Takeover of Opposition Oil Revenues", AFP News Service, 25 November 2000.

26. See the *freeeanwar.com* website for details.

27. "Demonstrasi Di Luar Negeri Derhaka" [Demonstrations Outside Country is Traitorous], *Berita Harian,* 9 October 2000.

28. *Star,* 3 November 2000.

29. K. Parkaran, "Impassioned Plea to Lunas Voters", *Star,* 24 November 2000.

30. Zakiah Koya, citing Shahrir Samad, in "Dr M To Blame For Lunas Defeat", *malaysiakini.com,* 30 November 2000.

31. See, for example, Mergawati Zulfakar, "Graft Talk Fails To Ring The Bell", *Star,* 20 November 2000.

32. *New Straits Times,* 31 August 2000.

MYANMAR

MYANMAR
Beyond the Reach of International Relief?

Bruce Matthews

"Like my own people in neighbouring Tibet, you suffer under an oppressive regime beyond the reach of international relief." These words addressed to Daw Aung San Suu Kyi by the Dalai Lama on her 55th birthday provide a focus to the myriad challenges that confronted Myanmar in 2000.[1] They point to the sombre life-style of a people who, though not starved or enslaved, survive in what is largely a subsistence economy, for the most part in an atmosphere of political resignation and uncertainty.[2] The lack of a rule of law means that anyone can face arbitrary and capricious treatment. There is no press freedom and no right of assembly. Isolated for decades from the outside world, it can rightly be claimed that many in Myanmar are "psychologically paralyzed ... living without even realizing that their thinking is being damaged by the military government".[3] Except for the efforts of a few international relief organizations and non-governmental organizations (NGOs) (such as the UNDP, World Vision, Médecins sans Frontières), no external aid of consequence is available to make the lot of the average citizen easier. Loans and grants for some grass-roots projects and technical assistance have been extended by Japan, India, Malaysia, Thailand, and Singapore. However, it has been thirteen years since any leading funded programmes from multilateral institutions (like the International Monetary Fund, the World Bank, or the Asian Development Bank) have been forthcoming, nor are they a likely prospect in the near future.

It could be argued that "international relief" is more than just a monetary phenomenon. There is also the matter of moral and political support that comes from the world beyond. In this case, Myanmar, like Tibet, is a *cause célèbre*. Its situation also presents a dilemma to those in the international community who would like to see a new Myanmar take its rightful place as a modern nation in the region, and the world at large. So-called "soft" and "hard" options based on strategies such as constructive engagement and economic sanctions continue to bedevil any consensus. An agile military government prolongs its power by careful exploitation of this lack of

---

Bruce Matthews is the C.B.Lumsden Professor of Comparative Religion at Acadia University in Nova Scotia, Canada. He has published widely on contemporary issues in Myanmar and Sri Lanka.

international agreement, as well as balancing its vital relationships with China, India, Pakistan, Thailand, and ASEAN. Indeed, no longer is Myanmar the "hermit kingdom". The controlling junta plays a few of its diplomatic options with consummate skill, and can count on sufficient external support (particularly from China, and increasingly from India) to survive indefinitely, albeit in reduced circumstances.

There are other forces at work, however — democratic, economic, internal and external — that suggest a future identified by military rule is by no means a surety. This chapter reviews selected events and themes in the year 2000 that mark Myanmar's continuing struggle to bring to birth a new polity, economy, and society. It assumes that internal change is taking place, slowly but unpredictably. Although statistics from various recognized sources are appealed to when appropriate, many observations in this chapter are of necessity anecdotal, what is gained through conversations and observation both within and beyond Myanmar. For example, *Selected Monthly Economic Indicators* are available from Yangon's Central Statistical Organization, but they do not provide a reliable day-to-day cost of living analysis. Yangon has not published an annual economic review for over three years. Evidence for microeconomic conditions and the general temper of the times best comes from travelling widely and frequently within Myanmar. By way of method, this chapter first reflects on the current structure of the military government and the *Tatmadaw* (an honorific for *Sit Tat*, or armed forces), its ambition to provide what it assumes to be good governance, and the response of the opposition National League for Democracy (*Amyotha Democracy Aphwe*). Secondly, the chapter considers Myanmar's human resources and the economic, educational and religious dimensions of civil life. If it concludes with an appeal to an astrologer for a glimpse into the future, it is only because Myanmar's enigmatic situation defies the hubris of those who would dare predict its destiny.

The Polity and Its Sibling, the *Tatmadaw*

In 2000, Myanmar's military government continued to depend on the loyal acceptance of an unbending hierarchical chain of command. Absolute power resides at the top, with various degrees of political authority and influence dispersed through three so-called Secretaries, the chiefs of the small naval and air forces, and, more importantly, the twelve *taing hmus*, or regional commanders. This entire apparatus is termed the State Peace and Development Council (SPDC, *Naing gan daw aye chan thaya yae hnint phwinp phyoe yae kounsi*), structurally in place since 1997. There is also a thirty-nine member Cabinet (thirty-two actual ministries, only twelve of which have civilian ministers), but its function is administrative and is rarely called upon for policy initiative. Senior General Than Shwe, who is 68 and reported to be somewhat ailing, remains at the top as SPDC Chairman. The Vice-Chairman is still General Maung Aye, who is 63 and a reputed hardliner, suspicious of international *rapprochement* and disdainful of the celebrated opposition leader, Daw Aung

San Suu Kyi. A regimental soldier with all the lustre of battle-hardened field command that image might convey, Maung Aye appears to remain comfortably popular as commander-in-chief of the army. Three lieutenant generals or Secretaries stand directly below in the chain of command. Arguably the most important of these (and visible in the public eye) is Khin Nyunt (61), putative friend of China and ASEAN and architect of most of the ceasefire arrangements with anxious ethnic groups (for example, the 1994 Kachin agreement).[4] Quite apart from these senior generals, there are also the regional commanders that need to be taken into consideration. All of them are either major generals or brigadiers with considerable autonomy and extensive authority, and many of them are relatively young men. Some changes were made in their command placements in 2000.

The five top generals continue to govern secretively and by fiat. Their aims, like those of the *Tatmadaw* in general, are theoretically couched in terms of development. (They also would like to be rid of Daw Suu Kyi.) But 2000 showed no advance in their understanding of market forces, no acknowledgement of the damage inflicted by arbitrary regulations, or of the unfavourable consequences of state monopolization of key export industries like rice and teak. Vital economic decisions continued to be made largely by Maung Aye as chairman of the Industrial Development Central Committee, and overseer of foreign investment. His decisions are seen by most analysts and economists to be spontaneous and fickle, rather than carefully considered ones based on a sound long-term macroeconomic scheme. Despite its ineptitude in matters of finance and economy, the *Tatmadaw's* grip on joint venture projects allows it to achieve monopoly profits (economic rent), supporting a wealthy enclave of military personnel and associated civilian entrepreneurs. The two conglomerates used in this task are the Union of Myanmar Economic Holdings (UMEH or MEHL), and the Myanmar Economic Corporation (MEC).[5]

Martin Smith is certainly correct when he avers that despite the ambition of having a half-million personnel under arms by 2000, the *Tatmadaw* (currently about 450,000 strong) is not a monolith.[6] There are schisms to be sure, but collective self-preservation comes first, with stability entirely dependent on the hierarchical chain of command. To quarrel openly would invite chaos for both the generals and the people subservient to them (conscious indeed of the old Burmese saying, "when the water buffalo fight, the rice dies"). Perceived factions (including personalities, different intelligence networks, and even officer training programmes) are no secret, but their capacity to introduce change should not be overestimated.[7] Periodic incidents suggest that the officer corps is not without maverick figures. For example, in a widely publicized incident in July 2000, Deputy National Planning and Economic Development Minister Brigadier General Zaw Tun was dismissed for a speech openly critical of government failure to introduce promised economic reforms. Certainly, there are reform-minded officers — indeed, the results of the 1990 national elections indicated much support for Daw Suu Kyi in constituencies near army bases.

However, it remains too dangerous for them to challenge the system. Interestingly, the younger officers are not necessarily more sensitive to alternative policies or democracy. Mary Callaghan has rightly argued that although junior officers today may not share with senior command "the same sense of siege and threat ... that doesn't mean they'll be more open to progressive reform". Indeed, Daw Suu Kyi has averred that "senior military leaders ... are more open to her ideas than the more rigid, less tolerant junior officers".[8]

In 2000, the *Tatmadaw* continued to re-arm itself and enlarge its size, progressively and successfully building up a programme that began after the uprising of 1988. A precise order of battle is not in the public domain, but it can be safely assumed that well over four hundred infantry battalions comprise the spine of the army. These units, together with artillery and armoured regiments, are ubiquitous throughout the country. In some places, an army camp of company or regimental size can be found every five or ten miles, something clearly evident when travelling on major connecting roads, for example, in Kachin or Kayin States, where there is a history of ethnic struggle against the state. An estimated US$2 billion expenditure on arms (largely of Chinese manufacture) in the last few years has supplied the *Tatmadaw* with sophisticated weapons, including combat aircraft and navy vessels.

Official statistics from the government's annual budget show current and capital spending on defence of 38.1 billion kyat (26 per cent out of a total expenditure budget of K145.6 billion). This does not include costs associated with such paramilitary units as the police or NaSaKa (Border Administration Force).[9] However, foreign analysts usually assume that defence expenditures are between 30 and 40 per cent of the total budget.[10] Importantly, military salaries were significantly raised in April 2000, more than matching those accorded to the civil service.[11] Some perquisites made available to service personnel continue, but apart from rice (6 *pyi* per month, about 12.6 kgs), all other food rations have been cut in half. Given the general rate of inflation and cost of living, salaries are still not high enough to meet the minimal needs of most families — estimated to be K30,000 per month for an urban family of five.[12] This has led to moonlighting and other additional ways of supplementing income, including the sale of personal supplies to civilians. It cannot be said that army life in the ranks is much sought after as a career. Harsh conditions and unsatisfactory management have diminished whatever attraction the armed forces traditionally claim. Manpower needs for the expanded *Tatmadaw* are barely met through voluntary means (there is some coercion in certain village areas for recruits that approximate what might be called unofficial conscription). Notwithstanding this, the *Tatmadaw* continues to represent a virtual controlling caste in Myanmar society. If it can be assumed that each member of the forces is in turn supporting three to five family members, the sum of those directly dependent on the *Tatmadaw* is over two million, a formidable number indeed.

In 2000, military rule continued to exhibit all the signs of hubris and self-righteousness that began nearly forty years ago in the Ne Win *khit* (era). Citizens are still subject to rigorous checks on their identity and place of residence. This is done through such devices as strictly maintained household registration lists at the village or city block level (*ein daungsu sa yin*) and co-operative stores (*tha ma wa ya ma*). Myanmar is totally bereft of any public institutions aimed at giving constructive direction to the progress of the country apart from certain technological and scientific departments attached to defence colleges. Information technology is far from satisfactory in every sector of society not associated with the military or the banking sector. More importantly, nation-building continues to be largely conceived in terms of bridge and road construction, and of agricultural production. Like the last Konbaung kings of the nineteenth century, the present junta appeals in one way or another to the mannerisms and old tradition of despotism (*padaithayit*) as the authentic expression of legitimate Burmese polity. If the country is basically there to grow rice, then who needs advancement in computers and modern educational and industrial aims? Furthermore, the junta appears to have persuaded itself of widespread support through its "political wing", the much-overrated Union Solidarity Development Association (USDA or *Pyidaungsu Kyan Khaing Yei Hnin Hpyint Hpyo Yei*), with its vigilante squads and orchestrated mass demonstrations. With membership anywhere between 8 and 15 million (numbers fluctuate wildly according to sources), the USDA sounds more formidable than it really is. There are perquisites, to be sure (for example, possible access at an elementary level to what few state computer programmes may be available outside of the armed forces). A membership card (with photo) can help in certain circumstances when one is travelling about — but then so too can membership in the Women's Maternal Child Welfare Organization (*Mi Khin Hnint Kaley Saunk Shauk Yei*, to which many men belong as well).

The Junta, Ethnic Minorities, and Regional Relationships

In 2000 the junta did not encounter serious challenges from activists or dissidents within Myanmar. The military continued to successfully spread its forces into all border zones except those designated by agreement as being under Wa and Kokang control. Ceasefire arrangements with various ethnic groups dating back to the late 1980s have continued to help keep the peace in areas at one time associated with strong local militias bent on secession from the state. Bertil Lintner provides a concise account of the "alliances of convenience" that mark the period of agreements between several large and powerful ethnic forces (for example, the Kachin Independence Army, October 1994) and Yangon.[13] Currently, only the "badly fractured Karen National Union (KNU)" and a few "scattered units" of pro-democracy students are still in official resistance. Among these in 2000 were "God's Army" (*Kaser Doh*), a marginalized group of Karens trapped by the Yadana pipeline project (which cut right through their traditional territory) led by the twelve-year-old Htoo brothers, Johnny and Luther. They came into prominence in January with a bizarre attack on a Thai provincial hospital. A similarly arcane incident involved the so-called Vigorous Burmese Student Warriors at the Myanmar embassy in Bangkok in October 1999. Although not directly related to God's Army, they nonetheless took refuge with the latter in the hills after the incident. Both of these events represented movements of disgruntled KNU soldiers with nothing to lose by their actions. Furthermore, Lintner rightly argues that although the "threat from the border areas" may be thwarted, because of the direct connection this provides to the narcotics industry, the "consequences for the country are disastrous".[14]

This is clearly the case with the United Wa State Army (UWSA). It has enjoyed almost complete autonomy under the terms of its 1989 ceasefire. The estimated 20,000 strong UWSA army has since expanded its control over large Myanmar sectors of the China and Thai borders. It has forced the relocation of thousands of Wa and ethnic Kokang from village areas across the border from China. The UWSA has even built a new "capital" at Mong Yawn, adjacent to Thailand's Mae Ai district and far from its former stronghold at Panghsang. With the surrender of Shan drug baron Khun Sa in 1996, the Wa began a penetration of Shan areas, where they periodically confronted Col. Yawd Serk's less muscular but still formidable 2,000-strong Shan United Revolutionary Army, or Shan State Army (SSA), in an intense struggle to control territory. The Myanmar government may want the UWSA as a buffer against the Thais, although current Wa autonomy is probably more than Yangon initially bargained for (it is inconceivable that the Wa will surrender any of their de facto independence should relations with Yangon sour). It is even claimed that Wa expansion is part of a government of Myanmar opium eradication strategy. However, in 2000, the Thai Government of Chuan Leekpai rejected this claim and declared the Wa a security threat because of their control of the vast importation of methamphetamine tablets (*yaa baa*) and heroin into Thailand.[15] It should be noted that the newly elected government of Thailand under Prime Minister Thaksin Shinawatra (confirmed on 10 February 2001) was immediately confronted with the challenge of Myanmar troops carrying out an assault against displaced Shans fleeing into Thai territory. Despite this serious crisis, Thaksin has indicated that his Myanmar policy will be one of "forward engagement", focused on improving economic ties with Myanmar. This also appears to be the position of ASEAN, which Myanmar joined in July 1997. Indeed, in May 2000, Myanmar hosted its first ministerial-level ASEAN talks in Yangon, which happened to be on economics, and which contained no overt ASEAN challenge to Myanmar's continuing image and reputation as a police state.[16]

Relationships with Myanmar's five border neighbours are not infrequently sensitive and problematic, as the case of Thailand indicates. Over 120,000 Myanmar refugees crowd border camps in Thailand. At times, up to 1,000 new refugees streamed into these camps each month during the past two years.[17]

An unknown number of illegal Myanmar migrants, possibly several hundred thousand, work or hide out elsewhere in Thailand, often as underpaid labourers, or sadly, involved in the sex trade. In Bangladesh, a similar aggrieved refugee community of about 25,000 Muslim Rohingya from Myanmar's western Rakhine state seek sanctuary.[18] India, too, is home to more than 100,000 Myanmar refugees or illegal migrants. But Indo-Myanmar relationships are not troubled by what this must represent in terms of an escape from oppression and poverty. Beginning in 1994, as part of its new "Look East" policy, India began to abandon its support for pro-democracy forces in Myanmar. Indeed, a landmark diplomatic exchange with India, including a visit by India's top general, V. Prakesh Malik in January 2000 (a return visit to India was made by Myanmar's army commander-in-chief Maung Aye in November), continued to help insulate the junta from international condemnation for its lack of political and economic transparency and unfortunate human rights record. Apart from General Malik, a wave of top-ranking emissaries from India continued to visit Myanmar. External Affairs Minister Jawant Singh's official opening of a road that links Imphal in India with Kalewa in Myanmar on 15 February 2001 was a particularly important sign that the two countries increasingly need each other for commercial and security reasons. In this regard, Myanmar's cordial economic and military relationship with China has taken on greater geopolitical significance. India remains concerned about China's long-term aims if it gains access through Myanmar to the Bay of Bengal. Hence, the flurry of diplomatic and other initiatives on the part of India to keep Myanmar from becoming in effect a client state of China. Of the several ways in which India has made overtures to Myanmar, a relatively new one is, ironically, through religion. Under India's Bharatiya Janatha Party government, there is increasing acknowledgement of shared religio-cultural features with Myanmar. Hinduism and Buddhism are referred to as "branches of the same tree". In August 2000, India's Hindu extremist movement, Rashtriya Swayamsevek Sangh (RSS), noted for its intolerance towards Muslims and Christians, was reported to have opened a branch (*shaka*) in Yangon under Myanmar government patronage (although the author has had difficulty verifying this).[19] There is a Sanatan Dharma Swayamsevak Sangh in Myanmar, to be sure, with centres in sixteen locations. It is not new to the country and claims to have a strictly religious educational focus only (for example, teaching Sanskrit, yoga techniques, etc.), aimed at Myanmar's estimated 1.2 million Hindu devotees.

Notwithstanding a status quo that is clearly in its favour, the junta is visibly uncertain about its long-term prospects. It constantly struggles to justify its rule through cultural and religious activities, as if to reinforce its collective *karma*, its representation as a *dharmishta,* or "righteous", polity. For example, the effects of the April 1999 three-day ceremony at the Shwedagon Zeidi (Myanmar Buddhism's *axis mundi*), where a new jewelled top (*hti*) was placed with due ceremony on the pagoda by Secretary 1 Khin Nyunt and other junta dignitaries, were still felt in 2000.[20] The names of these generals are said to be inscribed somewhere on the *hti*, a virtual time capsule to honour their rule. In addition, in the south entrance to the Shwedagon, a new panel painted in the traditional style depicting the four senior generals in their usual battle fatigues — but smiling graciously on a model of the great *zeidi* — can be found alongside pictures from the Jataka tales and from Myanmar Buddhist history and folklore. New initiatives to gain merit and possible public adulation through junta religious activities marked virtually every edition of the daily newspapers, *Kyemon* (*The Mirror*) and *The New Light of Myanmar*. Much was made of a new colossal image of Gautama Buddha, the Mindhamma Loka Chantha Abhaya Labha Muni, sent down as a partially carved slab of marble from near Mandalay to the Yangon suburb of Insein, where it was finished and erected at an *aung myay* ('winning ground' or 'victory spot') identified by astrologers. These and associated rituals that might help circumvent the effects of bad *karma* (*yadaya chay*) are a prominent feature of military rule. Gustaaf Houtmann is certainly correct when he observes "the current battlefield is now over the spiritual and psychological culture, something the regime wants to control, but unlike the material culture, it can't."[21]

Daw Aung San Suu Kyi and the National League for Democracy

In this regard, Daw Aung San Suu Kyi remained the vital figure she has been for over a decade in the political life of Myanmar. For many in the country, Daw Suu Kyi is perceived as possessing the characteristics of respectability, wisdom, and personal appeal (*awza*) that mark a good ruler. By her self-sacrifice and steadfastness, she also shows key restraining qualities (*ein-da-yay*) of virtue and gentleness, in contrast to SPDC leadership. For most of 2000, the junta made every effort to portray Daw Suu Kyi "as some sort of Western-imposed saviour, irrelevant to Myanmar's harsh realities."[22] Yet it is her reputation as an educated, internationally respected figure that has gained her loyalty within Myanmar, and prevents the junta from casually eliminating her from public life.

In 2000, Daw Suu Kyi made two attempts to leave Yangon to visit supporters, which were both quickly thwarted by the government. Halted on 24 August on her way to Kungyangon, she and a dozen companions spent nine days by the roadside before being forced to return to the city. Again, on 6 October, Daw Suu Kyi attempted to leave by train for Mandalay, only to be turned back. Yet, despite these incidents and other signs of the deliberate destruction of the National League for Democracy (virtually the only NLD office left standing in the country is the main headquarters on Yangon's Shwegonedine Road), Daw Suu Kyi's political importance is in some ways greater than ever. Criticism of her obduracy in meeting junta demands and reluctance to engage in *realpolitik* (for example, to give up claims to the legitimacy of the 1990 elections) is not uncommon outside Myanmar (one major publication even suggested it was time for her to leave the country).[23] Some argue that after thirteen years, her campaign is only a moral one, without a "pragmatic strategy for change."[24] Yet, like Mohandas Gandhi or Martin Luther King — both of whom said and did things that transcended the usual way, or were thought at the time to be too inflexible — Daw Suu Kyi appears anchored to the notion that if she surrenders one of her major principles, the rest become meaningless. It is true that she has to "make news", that she and the forces of democracy have very much to depend on the BBC, Voice of America, and other Western media sources to keep the world, including Myanmar, alert to what she continues to represent. As someone who has the potential to help bring Myanmar back from the brink of economic insolvency and pariah state status, Daw Aung San Suu Kyi cannot be ignored or idly disposed of like many ordinary politicians. Towards the end of 2000, her political importance again became evident when the local press suddenly stopped vilifying her. It even referred to her not as "this woman" (*mainma*), but by her proper Myanmar name (Aung San is still the most heroic name in modern Myanmar history because of its association with Daw Suu Kyi's father, the Bogyoke or leader who negotiated the country's independence). Secret talks between Daw Suu Kyi and the junta commenced in October, reinforced by the several apparently fruitful visits of the United Nations envoy Tan Sri Razali Ismail. There is evidence that in the autumn of 2000, an unusual sequence of pressures coalesced to oblige the Myanmar authorities to engage in some "sunshine politics", to give the international community the impression that dialogue with the NLD and possible reforms were still a possibility. These pressures included a deteriorating economic situation (the value of the kyat has depreciated 92 per cent in three years), the potential economic impact of a disastrous report in November by the International Labour Organization on Myanmar's notorious reputation for press gangs, porterage, and other forms of forced or unpaid labour, and the spectre of a visit to Myanmar of a European Union (EU) mission in January 2001. For whatever reasons, the year ended with Daw Suu Kyi firmly back in the process of political dialogue. She may not have had the strength to unseat the military government, but she had the power to prevent it from feeling secure.

Economic Conditions and Civil Life

Turning now to economic conditions within Myanmar in 2000, and how these affected civil life, both urban and rural, the country's economic position relative to its neighbours continued to weaken. Any economic gains achieved from so-called market reforms were not widely shared, tax revenue remained extremely low (only 3.5 per cent of gross domestic product [GDP] compared with a regional average of 15 per cent), and crony capitalism continued to make its mark. Ostentatious displays of wealth, marked in particular by luxury vehicles and grand new houses (such as in Shwe Taung Gyar and other wealthy enclaves of Yangon) have somehow become acceptable to a regime that should be fearful of the consequences of a shrinking middle class and increasing polarity between rich and poor. Although there is no visible grinding poverty, impoverishment is widespread, with at least one quarter of the population estimated to be living below minimum subsistence levels.[25] The government claimed a high GDP growth for mid-2000 at 10.5 per cent year-on-year, but this figure cannot be verified.[26] It is more likely to be around 4.5 per cent.[27] The GDP for the fiscal year 1 April 1999 to 31 March 2000 is estimated to be US$6.2 billion, with per capita GDP at $124.00 (at the free market rate of K440 to the U.S. dollar — a major difficulty here, discussed below in detail, is converting government figures in kyats to U.S. dollar equivalents, given the volatility of the kyat and the existence of more than one exchange rate.)[28] However, an April 2000 substantial raise in civil service salaries (including those of school teachers) in the range of 350 – 400 per cent may affect the per capita indicator for the latter part of 2000, particularly when combined with the massive raises given to the *Tatmadaw* at the same time. The revised monthly salary scales of government employees range from K15,000 at the highest level (Grade 12) to K 3,000 (Grade 1).[29] For the time being, this will help alleviate the impact of inflation, which the latest available Yangon consumer price index suggests is 18.4 per cent (1999 figure).[30] Late 2000 also saw food prices for some staples (especially rice) come down, easing consumer costs considerably. On the other hand, those working for the private sector (especially foreign enterprises) usually have higher wages. For example, the public sector unskilled labour wage in 2000 was a maximum of K100 per day, but five times that in the private sector construction industry. There, skilled labour earned K1000 per day, the same wage that a senior Grade 12 civil servant would receive.

Despite some attempts to introduce free-enterprise economic opportunities, Myanmar's controlled economy continues to favour state economic enterprises (SEEs or SOEs). Some of these are industrial (1,600 factories employ about 2 per cent of the work-force). More significant is the government monopoly on all exports of rice, rubber, sugar, minerals, gems, marine, and forest products. This leaves only garments, pulses and beans available for private export contracts.[31] Despite economic sanctions prohibiting new investment (but, ironically, not new trade) by the United States, Canada and the EU, Myanmar still managed to attract a cumulative total of 329 approved foreign direct investment (FDI) projects at a combined value of US$7.186 billion in the decade leading up to 2000. These ventures ranged from oil and gas (32 per cent of the approved projects), to hotels and tourism (14.7 per cent), mining (7.3 per cent), and transport and communications (3.8 per cent).[32] Not all of these projects are working at anywhere near capacity, however. As any visitor to Yangon will testify, foreign tourists are few and the construction of hotels has come to a halt (throwing half a million construction labourers out of work). American and Franco-Belgium investment in the Yadana and Yetagun natural gas projects remains open to very serious criticism in the West, as does the Canadian-based Ivanhoe copper mining project. Any future Western investments in Myanmar are likely to face legal obstacles and public opprobrium at home, throwing into doubt their long-term viability.[33]

Myanmar continued to experience a considerable trade imbalance between exports and imports. The government estimated that total exports in 2000 were K7 billion in rounded figures (US$15.9 million at the free market rate, US$1.25 billion at the official exchange rate). This included border trade with Myanmar's four immediate neighbours, accounting for 30 per cent of exports by some estimates. Imports, on the other hand, were valued at K16.25 billion (US$36.9 million at the free market rate, US$2.6 billion at the official rate).[34]

The U.S. Dollar and the Foreign Exchange Certificate

Perhaps the foremost harbinger of Myanmar's precarious economic situation is the falling value of the kyat compared to the U.S. dollar and its impact on the Foreign Exchange Certificate (FEC). Although introduced in 1993 against six major convertible currencies, the FEC is usually pegged to the U.S. dollar, and is radically higher than the official exchange. The completely unrealistic official K6.4 rate has remained unchanged since 1977, and continues to benefit state-controlled SEEs. For example, these enterprises can import machinery and other items at a fraction of the price available to the private sector. SEE financial statements often show profits because they import at the skewed K6.4 rate, but sell their products at market rates. A situation has now emerged where there are three other exchange rates for the kyat beyond the official one. Thus, secondly, at the end of 2000, the "greenback" (as U.S. banknotes are referred to on the street) was K440 for one dollar (though in a free-fall it headed towards K500 to US$1 by February 2001). This was what one received when exchanging U.S. funds at any money-changer (a completely legal transaction — there is no black market in this commodity). Thirdly, a "customs rate" of K180 – K250 to the dollar appears to be applicable as duty on imports, or on profitable exports as tax. Fourthly, the Myanmar Government obliges its own citizens who earn U.S. dollars to convert them into FECs when these are brought into the country (including salaries paid in U.S. dollars to those employed by foreign companies or institutions, and pensions). For most of 2000, there was not much difference between the "greenback" and the official FEC rate, but by the end of the year, the FEC rate began to slide (by January 2001 it was K350 per dollar). An estimated 400 million FECs are in circulation. Rumours of devaluation to K250 before possible closure and elimination of the FEC indicate little public confidence in this specie. Such an eventuality would lead to widespread bankruptcy, and memories of the 1987 sudden elimination of big banknotes are a reminder that fickle policy leading to devastating economic conditions can be introduced without warning.

Availability of Rice and Its Place in the Economy

Myanmar's agro-forest output accounts for 50 per cent of its GDP and 65 per cent of its work-force.[35] Three quarters of the population are farmers, or farm family members. This includes hill people considered *taungya*, or practitioners of swidden or slash-and-burn (*chena*) cultivation. Most farmers grow rice as their major crop, but if possible, they grow a second crop of beans or pulses, which they can sell privately for more profit. Rice grows on approximately 16 million acres (6.4 million hectares). Plans to have private entrepreneurs develop over 1.7 million more acres on reclaimed wetlands over the last three years have only yielded an additional 14,970 acres. All agricultural land is state-owned, and farmers have tilling rights only. Though their lease can be transferred to other family members, land tenancy rather than outright ownership has reduced the initiative for investment and improvement. Rice is sold in various volumes, from the empty condensed milk tin (*nosibu*, usually a Dawn condensed milk tin from Malaysia) to the metric ton. In this regard, street-level measurements and prices are important. A farmer or labourer will generally need to consume two *nosibu* of milled rice a day (each with 7 ounces, or 390 grams). Eight *nosibu* = 1 *pyi* or 2.13 kg; 16 *pyi* = 1 basket (34.01 kg); 24 *pyi* = 1 bag containing 50 kg.[36] Most rice is grown in the wet season (*Moe saba*, planted in July, gathered in December), and much less in the dry season (*Natay saba*).

The question of a ready supply of rice at affordable prices is always of utmost political importance. The domestic price of rice is therefore insulated from international price fluctuations. A procurement agency, the Myanmar Agricultural Produce Trading (MAPT), buys and distributes about 20 per cent of the total rice harvest at set prices, paying farmers about one-third to one-half the market rate. Farmers are obligated to sell at these procurement prices according to the fecundity of the area (from 30 to 12 baskets per hectare). In 1999, MAPT procured 1,099,000 metric tons (mt) of milled rice at prices between K14,000 and K19,000 per metric ton (depending on quality, or K400 per basket), with a distribution of 600,000 metric tons to special target groups (such as the civil service, and armed forces, at a cost to the state of K10 billion). In 2000, the final paddy crop was expected to yield a total of 19.8 million metric tons, three million metric tons more than the year before.[37] MAPT procurement prices were therefore unusually depressed when obligated purchases of paddy began in October, because of a large surplus of rice already in storage and weak international sales. In 2000, Myanmar exported 148,000 metric tons of milled rice and 17,207 metric tons of paddy. Border trade, especially with storm-ravished Bangladesh, was the saving grace in an otherwise dismal export market. However, a crucial problem will emerge in 2001 if the surplus rises to 1 million metric tons, far too much for the MAPT to profitably dispose of.

The quality of Myanmar rice has not kept pace with that of neighbouring Thailand, which dominates the lucrative export market. Myanmar has arguably placed too much emphasis on high-yield but non-tasty varieties and has done little to rectify sub-standard technology for drying, milling and storage (rice must be dry to consume, a process that takes four months, but cannot be stored thereafter for more than one year in Myanmar without exposure to rot). Furthermore, the high price of fertilizer in 2000 increased the expenditure per acre for the farmer, such that, with reduced government quotas and lower domestic market prices, many farmers have been unable to recover costs. Those that could turned to cash crops during the dry season, particularly pulses, sunflower, sesame, and groundnuts. Farmers keep for their families sufficient rice of good quality for their own use (*wunza*) and, with access to fish paste (*ngapi*), fruits and vegetables, are generally able to sustain themselves beyond a money economy. It could be argued, however, that the state procurement system is a disadvantage for the farmer, subsidizing the cities with their potentially more inflation-prone and therefore volatile population. In this regard, rice is a key economic indicator, and 2000 saw price stability or even some price reduction in most grades. In Yangon, prices for milled rice in December 2000 were K180-200 per *pyi* of best grade *Paw san hmwe* (a decline from K224 in1999), K90-125 for mid-grade *Ehmata* (a decline from K137), and K80 for low grade *Nga sein* (a decline from K120). Cooking oil is the other vital item, with *Pae see* (peanut or groundnut) at K570-600 per *viss* (1.54 kg), edible or palm oil (*Sar ohn see*) at K370-450 per *viss*, both prices decreasing by one-fifth from 1999. Fish paste, possibly the most essential ingredient besides oil for a rice diet, was K267 per *viss*.[38] By way of summary, rice and other staple prices stabilized in 2000. There was no agricultural crisis resulting from drought or bad weather. Such a phenomenon is what the government fears most, for, although it may be true that most citizens are scrambling to just get by, and do not particularly care who is in power, a serious food shortage would bring them out into the streets.

Human Resources

Myanmar's farmers, forestry workers, and fishermen and women have a much more crucial role to play in bringing quality of life to society than those in the armed forces or the inefficient bureaucracy of the once-proud institution of the civil service. However, perhaps more important for the future of the country are the youth, in many ways a tragically by-passed constituency that has received little chance for educational advancement. It should be noted that by one estimate, 37 per cent of the population is fifteen years or younger.[39] Together with older teenagers, this generation has the most to lose from the near-catastrophic difficulties confronting education. These include such commonplace features as poor teacher training, insufficient number of textbooks and, above all, the closure of Myanmar's post-secondary institutions for some twenty months between 1988 and 2000. There are an estimated 37,627 primary schools, 3,695 junior high schools, 1,572 high schools, and 225,403 teachers, but education in total receives only 0.4 per cent of the GDP (compared to the ASEAN average of 2.7 per cent).[40] Most children aged five to ten obtain some form of schooling. Primary and secondary education is theoretically free, but there are many supplementary "donations" required of parents to keep the schools operating. Only an estimated 22 per cent of rural children and 37 per cent in urban areas complete Grade 4 (about eleven years of age). According to one estimate,

Buddhist monastic educational outreach could be taking care of as many as 39 per cent of children whose families cannot afford state schools.[41] At least one million young people have suffered a truncated educational experience in the last twelve years, and 400,000 have yet to try their chance at university education, which has been put on hold since 1996, when all post-secondary institutions were completely shut down (though not medical schools or military academies). In most instances, universities and institutes have now been relocated in distant locations (three centrally-located campuses at Yangon, Hlaing, and Botahtaung only received graduate students, about 7,000 in number). Undergraduate campuses were shifted to sites near army and police bases, often at the end of bridges, and devoid of hostels. Most are in Yangon's dreary satellite towns, such as Dagon, Thanlyan, and Ywar Thargyi, where, for example, the Institute of Economics is now situated, far away from the city centre. Some third and fourth-year undergraduates were allowed to resume studies as a trial "soft opening" in September 1999. All universities suddenly re-opened in June 2000 for 20,000 fourth-year undergraduate students, but only after extraordinary precautions. One month later, 60,000 first, second and third-year students returned. During the long hiatus of university closure, distance education programmes were one of only two options available for post-secondary education. The other was an increasing influx of expensive private foreign programmes (for example, from Malaysia, New Zealand, Singapore, some requiring payment in FECs), most offering courses in information technology (although there are few jobs for graduates because of Myanmar's virtual absence of basic IT services like e-mail and Internet access).

These reflect the paucity of state educational facilities. They cannot do much more than supplement what should be a first priority: to re-engage Myanmar's youth with programmes that prepare them to take their rightful place amidst Southeast Asia's economic, political, and social development. University education in particular needs intellectual freedom, something the state has not permitted anywhere. Perhaps for this reason, critics have claimed that the whole "re-opening" procedure is a sham. Universities have in effect become cram schools for brief interludes when students are permitted a few weeks of access to the academy. University professors have also been seriously affected by years of closure. All are still obliged to take some form of military-style training in order to control students and to situate themselves in the state ideological model. Merit and academic professionalism do not matter as much as loyalty to the system. Furthermore, graduate schools have not been able to provide sufficient qualified replacements for those retiring. Some professors whose qualifications are at the master's degree level have been forced to accept state-imposed and humiliating "honorary" doctorates to bring them up to supposed international standards. Graduating standards at every level have likely been compromised.

Another resource in any society is religion and culture. As noted above, the Myanmar regime has not been timid in using these crucial features to justify years of political domination. In 2000, Buddhism was also used as part of an ongoing government "Myanmarization" strategy. This includes reinforcing the dominance of the *Ba ma lo,* or Myanmar language, and the visible penetration of Buddhism into remote areas traditionally populated by people of other religions (the state-organized Buddhist mission programme has not proved successful). More problematic is the potential of the Myanmar *sangha* (clerical order) to become politically restless under the junta's heavy hand. There are 250,000 to 300,000 monks (conservative estimates are 190,000 novices or *thamanay,* 130,000 fully ordained *pongyi* and *sayadaw*) and 20,000 nuns (*silashin,* by Theravada custom not fully ordained). They have a long history of political activism and civil disobedience, notably through such organizations (now outlawed) as the Yahanpyo Aphwe (Younger Monks Association). Although the last major demonstration by monks occurred in March 1997, memories of their participation in the 1988 uprising and their "over-turning of the begging bowl" (*patta ni kauz za kan,* or refusal to accept spiritual merit-making from the military) are still vivid. In July, Ministry of Religious Affairs official U Aung Khin warned the *sangha* that "undisciplined monks" were still "tarnishing the dignity of the clergy".[42] Despite efforts to control the *sangha* through the Ministry of Religious Affairs' administrative directorate (*Tharthanar-ye Oo-zi Htar-na*), and crackdowns on suspect monasteries (including summary disrobing or incarceration of radical monks), there are some outspoken critical *sayadaws* who are too prominent for jail. These include Venerable (*Ashin*) Kundalabiwuntha of the strict Shwegyin sect's huge teaching monastery Mahagandhayon Sarthintaik in Amarapura, Ven. Pegu Kyakhatwaing and the Ven. Thamanya of Hpa-an. They have done nothing more than petition for dialogue between the junta and the NLD, but in Myanmar, even that is a bold step. Furthermore, although some members of the *sangha* have been compromised by the state (accepting emoluments, promotions, and awards), there is no evidence of an ideological generation gap. In general, monks are well-informed about Myanmar's political impasse. The country's stagnant economic condition is too visible for them to ignore. This key element of society awaits its destiny to actively participate once again in the welfare of the people.

In sum, education in Myanmar is the most serious issue confronting the nation in the near future. Much latent talent lies unused and ignored, at a juncture when the region in general is emphasizing the need for educated young people to sustain the economic vigour of their societies. At the same time, the vast Buddhist clerical order, which has the potential to be a catalyst for change, is kept under strict political control. These crucial elements of society, students and monks, will continue to be sources of pressure beyond complete government control.

Conclusion

Two final observations should be made. First, the military government faces economic uncertainty on a scale more ominous than anything encountered before. An informal, essentially illegal economy based on narcotics revenue and corruption, and possibly as large as the legal economy, wreaks its own havoc and disorder. When a government has a system that is so distorted, any time there is change in the air, it could lose control. This is so in Myanmar, where national news of consequence, good or bad, is rarely reported. A natural disaster, to say nothing of current military campaigns or ethnic communal distress, is virtually absent from the local press. Even good news, like the dialogue between Daw Suu Kyi and the junta, or Razali Ismail's possibly successful mission, is never mentioned in the media.

Secondly, although the military government shows no sign of losing or loosening its long-term aim of dominating Myanmar's polity, a random event out of the blue may cause a political implosion and junta collapse. Many previous Asian regimes have seemed rock solid until they crumbled, as Soeharto's Indonesia did in 1998 (or Ferdinand Marcos in 1986). There are too many unknown factors confronting Myanmar at present to permit the regime much room for liberalization or power-sharing lest this occur. Their present effort to show a kinder, more conciliatory face by conducting secret talks since October 2000 with the opposition is not new. The junta did the same thing in 1994, only to return to the usual uncompromising stance once international attention was diverted elsewhere. Hence, any major change to the political status quo in the near future appears unlikely. Indeed, in 2000 there were signs of turning increasingly inward — for example, import substitution efforts, an even more secure relationship with China, and other means of self-reliance. At the same time, the army is used to parade ground drill, to 180-degree turns on the march, so to speak. When the opportunity is appropriate, an honourable place in history bargained for perhaps, and exit strategies secure, the *Tatmadaw* may find it can take on another role in society and polity without loss of face. The alternative is to await new, unpredictable events which sooner or later are bound to embroil the nation in fearful struggle.

NOTES

1. Toronto Burma Roundtable, 6 June 2000. Daw Suu Kyi was born on 19 June 1945. Important differences between Myanmar and Tibet are acknowledged. Myanmar is a sovereign state, while Tibet forms an autonomous region of China. Unlike in Tibet, the problem of limited international relief encountered in Myanmar is self-inflicted.
2. Although most sources cite a population of approximately 45 million (such as *EIU Country Profile 2000 Myanmar* [London: The Economist Intelligence Unit, 2000], the government of Myanmar cites 50.1 million. See *Country Commercial Guide, Burma/ Myanmar*, Fiscal year 2000 (Yangon: U.S. Embassy, U.S. Department of State, September 2000), p.1. It should be noted that no reliable official census of Myanmar's ethnic constituencies has been made since 1931. There was a country-wide census in 1983, but minorities generally claim a much larger size than those figures given in official estimates. The same can be said for adherents of minority religions.

3. *Burma Debate,* Fall 2000, p. 31.
4. The other Secretaries were Chief of Staff Lieutenant General Tin Oo and Lieut. Gen. Win Myint. Tin Oo was killed on 19 February 2001 in an air crash, together with the Southeast Region commander, Brigadier General Sit Maung. Both individuals were considered hardliners and strong allies of General Maung Aye.
5. UMEH has a registered capital of US$1.4 billion (at the official exchange rate of K6.4 to US$1), but does not issue any reports. It is 60 per cent "owned" by active and retired officers. The Directorate of Defence Procurement owns 40 per cent.
6. Martin Smith, *Burma: Insurgency and the Politics of Ethnicity* (New Jersey: Zed Books, 1991), p. 423.
7. The paramount intelligence agency is the Directorate of Services Intelligence (DSI), which was greatly expanded in the 1990 reorganization of the Ministry of Defence. In 1994, the Office of Strategic Studies (OSS) was established as a "semi-academic" think-tank. It played an important role in Myanmar's 1997 political restructuring as the State Peace and Development Council. Andrew Selth indicates how these units, together with a much improved military communications system, "help the Rangoon regime predict and counter any signs of renewed internal unrest". Andrew Selth, "The Future of the Burmese Armed Forces", in *Burma/ Myanmar: Strong Regime, Weak State?* edited by Morten Pedersen, Emily Rudland, and R.J.May (Adelaide: Crawford House, 2000), p.58. The Defence Services Academy at Pyin Oo Lwin (Gen. Maung Aye's *alma mater*) has provided ten of the current twelve regional commanders. Officer Training Schools (OTS) at Ba Htoo, Kalaw, and Mingaladon are less prestigious. Lieut. Gen. Khin Nyunt is an OTS graduate.
8. Mary Callahan, "Cracks in the Edifice? Changes in Military-Society Relations in Burma since 1988", in *Burman/Myanmar: Strong Regime, Weak State?* edited by Morton Pedersen, Emily Rudland and R.J. May (Adelaide: Crawford House, 2000), p.43.
9. *IMF Staff Country Report 01/16, Myanmar: Statistical Appendix* (Washington: January 2001), Table 21, p.23. Sources cited in this report are from the Budget Department, the Myanmar Ministry of Finance and Revenue, and from IMF Fund staff estimates.
10. Selth, op cit., p. 62. Tin Maung Maung Than cites a defence budget of 34 per cent in "Myanmar: The Dilemma of Stalled Reforms", Trends in Southeast Asia No.10 (Singapore: Institute of Southeast Asian Studies, 2000), p.19.
11. Military salaries increased by 500 per cent in April 2000 (compared with a 400 per cent rise for civil servants). These salaries are not published, but anecdotal evidence suggests that a full general holding ministerial status can earn as much as K150,000 per month. The basic salary of a brigadier is now K20,000, but depending on his command, he will have access to many perquisites above and beyond the usual subsidized items, such as housing, transport, petrol, etc. A colonel earns K16,000 per month, a major K13,000, a captain K11,000, a lieutenant K10,000, a warrant officer K7600, a sergeant K5,300 and a private K3,500. Regimental co-operatives can provide additional unit-shared profits and access to cheap supplies. All ranks can have shares in the military's Myanmar Economic Holding Corporation, a major source of largesse. There may also be a corruption factor that significantly increases take-home pay. Furthermore, commonly heard (but unverified) reports claim that officers receive half of their salaries in Foreign Exchange Certificates.
12. *Country Commercial Guide Burma (Myanmar),* Fiscal Year 2000 (Yangon: U.S. Embassy, September 2000), p.9.
13. Bertil Lintner, "Drugs and Economic Growth in Burma", in *Burma/Myanmar: Strong Regime, Weak State?*, edited by Morton Pedersen, Emily Rudland, and R.J. May (Adelaide: Crawford House, 2000), p. 172.
14. Ibid., p. 187.

15. *Nation* (Bangkok), 19 February 2001.
16. A retired Myanmar diplomat indicated that ASEAN participation can demand up to 300 meetings a year by a participating country, which will continue to be financially very taxing on Myanmar's already stretched foreign reserves. Interview, Yangon, 10 January 2001.
17. The February report of the Burma Border Consortium indicates a case-load of 127,914 Myanmar refugees in December 2000. Challenges associated with the Myanmar refugee problem are outlined in the *Burma Border Consortium Relief Programme* (Bangkok: 12/5 Convent Road), August 2000, p.1.
18. The Rohingya refugees, still encamped near Cox's Bazaar in Bangladesh, are remnants of an estimated 250,000 Rohingyas who fled Myanmar in 1991-92. They escaped an outburst of genocide perpetrated by anti-Muslim forces in the Arakan or Rakhine state. The vast majority of Rohingyas are not recognized under Myanmar's 1982 Citizenship Law as being citizens. There may be as many as two million Rohingya in Myanmar. In addition, up to 200,000 Rohingya may have entered Pakistan as illegal migrants in the last few years (BBC report, 8 February 2000). In February 2001, a sudden attack on the Rohingya community in Sittwe and environs caused widespread destruction and reports of atrocities. Given the anti-Islamic nature of the pogroms that periodically sweep across the Arakan, and the likely involvement of at least some elements of the Myanmar armed forces in these tragedies, it is a mystery why there is not more criticism of Myanmar by Malaysia and Indonesia, two largely Muslim regional neighbours, and ASEAN fellow-members.
19. *Times of India*, 1 August 2000
20. See *Ant Chi ma Kon Mya Shwe Dagon* [Limitless Wonders of the Grace of the Shwedagon] (Shwedagon Zeidi Multifaceted Renovation Committee, Yangon, 1999), for a graphic representation of this event. Glossy pages show more junta officials in uniform and devotional sash (*debet*) than Buddhist clergy. It includes some revisionist rewriting of Myanmar Buddhist history, such as the placement of the original "Okkalapa" at Yangon, rather than in India (ibid., p.4). Khin Nyunt claimed that "the happiness I feel for this occasion is incomparable to anything, anything at all in my life. It is the height of my joy. I feel I can die contented." *Myanmar Times*, 15 January 2001. *The New Light of Myanmar* (7 April 1999) noted "the brilliance of that bud is ... as if it was anointing and blessing the close camaderie that exists between the rulers and their subjects".
21. Gustaaf Houtmann, *Mental Culture in Burmese Crisis Politics: Aung San Suu Kyi and the National League for Democracy* (Tokyo: Tokyo University of Foreign Studies, 1998), p.182.
22. *The Economist*, 27 May 2000.
23. *Asiaweek*, 15 December 2000.
24. *Far Eastern Economic Review*, 3 August, 2000.
25. *Country Commercial Guide Burma Myanmar*, Fiscal Year 2000, p.4. There is no official "poverty line". Incidents of poverty vary by region (for example, Chin State poverty is estimated at 42 per cent) and by such factors as households headed by women (31 per cent). *IMF Staff Country Report 99/134, Myanmar: Recent Economic Developments* (Washington: International Monetary Fund, November 1999), p.30.
26. Ministry of National Planning and Economic Development, as cited from Tin Maung Maung Than (2000), op. cit., p. 15.
27. *Asia Yearbook 2001* (Hong Kong: Far Eastern Economic Review, 2001), p.93.
28. *EIU Country Report Myanmar (Burma)* (London: The Economist Intelligence Unit, November 2000), p.5.
29. *Upward Revision of Monthly Salaries, Pension Entitlements and Daily Wages of Government Employees* (Yangon: Ministry of Finance and Revenue, 26 March 2000), Administrative Order 57/2000. The civil service likely employs about half a million

(including school-teachers). This, combined with 450,000 in the armed forces, gives an indication of how many out of Myanmar's 19.7 million work-force are in government service. See *Asia Development Outlook 2000* (Hong Kong: Oxford University Press, 2000), p.1.

30. *EIU Country Profile 2000 Myanmar*, p.27. On the other hand, the *Asia Development Outlook 2000*, p.99, cites a Yangon inflation rate of 49 per cent in late 1999. Inflation is seen not so much in foodstuffs as in items like electricity costs (for example, K20 for one fluorescent light between 6 pm and 10 pm in Mawlamyine, typical of urban areas outside the downtown core of Yangon where electricity is available only for a few hours each day). Automobiles are another inflation-prone item (with few new vehicle imports allowed — an import licence costs US$25,000 and there is at least a 30 per cent profit on used cars). Yangon is crowded with cars and trucks, and experiences previously unheard of traffic jams. Elsewhere, traffic remains light.

31. These can be very profitable. An unofficial figure of garment export values of about US$185 million for 1999 was cited by a leading private entrepreneur, with final expectations for 2000 being three times that number. Myanmar citizens of Indian extraction control beans, pulses (peas), plastics and scrap metal industries, exporting largely to India, sometimes with excellent profits. A hidden economic factor is narcotics, the profits from which likely infiltrate into state-run enterprises and private banks.

32. *Country Commercial Guide Burma (Myanmar)*, Fiscal Year 2000, p.89.

33. The 416-mile, US$1.2 billion Yadana joint venture with Myanmar Oil and Gas Enterprise, the Petroleum Authority of Thailand (PTT), Unocal and Total survived delays and delivered 65 million cubic feet of gas per day in 2000. Unable to fully complete the Ratchaburi generating plant in Thailand in time for receipt of this delivery, Thailand had to pay US$280 million in compensation according to the contract. It honoured the commitment in late 2000, a windfall for Myanmar's strapped foreign exchange reserves.

34. *Selected Monthly Economic Indicators, October 2000* (Yangon: Central Statistical Organization), Table 1. Imports comprised 50 per cent capital goods, 12 per cent intermediate goods, and 38 per cent consumer goods. Priority lists were introduced in 1998 to control imports, with limited success.

35. *IMF Staff Country Report No.99/134*, p.10. R.B.Young, and Gail Kramer, *An Economic Assessment of the Myanmar Rice Sector* (Little Rock: University of Arkansas, 1998), p.14, estimates that there are 4,442,000 farms in Myanmar, supporting 75 per cent of the population. The minimum size for a sustainable farm is three acres.

36. The "basket" is the common volume of mass. One basket of unmilled paddy = .02086625 metric tons (20.8 kgs). On the other hand, one basket of milled rice is 34.01 kgs. Paddy refers to the unmilled product, rice to the milled (husked).

37. *EIU Country Report, Myanmar (Burma)*, November 2000, p.23.

38. Other consumer prices for 2000 were: poultry (*be hlat kyet*) at K600 per *viss*, free-range chicken (*bemar kyet*) at K800 per *viss*, ten pieces of bread (good quality) at K150, beans (*pae ni*) at K700 per *viss*, dry chilly at K1600 per *viss*, salt at K40 per *viss*, and ghee at K1500 per *viss*. Prices for sugar, dahl, potato, onion, garlic, and ginger were within the range of the year before. Condensed milk (390 grams) was priced at K190. Tamarind climbed from K300 to K800 (soft drink manufacturers cornered the market). Farmer's markets (so-called "pre-tax" because they operate as independent free-enterprise initiatives) have helped to keep the price of vegetables stable. On the other hand, petrol costs vary greatly by region. In Yangon in 2000, to help curb urban discontent, petrol was available at the subsidized price of K180 per gallon (3 gallons per day); the private market price was K350. In the more remote locations, no subsidized petrol was available. In Myitkyina, for example, petrol cost K800 per gallon (diesel K850).

39. *Report to the Pyithu Hluttaw on the Financial, Economic and Social Situation* (Rangoon: Ministry of Planning and Finance, 1985), p.19, Table 3. By extrapolation, this figure can still be considered viable.

40. *Xinhua News Service,* 30 April 2000; and *IMF Staff Country Report 99/134,* p.33. Notwithstanding these negative observations, in a recent country-wide visit, I noted that regional schools were generally well taken care of, students neatly turned out in uniform (green skirt or *longyi*), with homework an everyday responsibility. Myanmar is one of the few countries in the region which teaches English as a compulsory second language at grade school level (though with somewhat haphazard standards according to location). One reliable source argues that "even now the extent of general education in the country is not far behind more developed countries in Southeast Asia". Khin Maung Kyi et al., *Economic Development of Burma: A Vision and a Strategy* (Stockholm: The Olaf Palme International Center, 2000), p. 24.

41. Ibid., p.147.

42. Reuters, 9 July 2000.

THE PHILIPPINES

Southeast Asian Affairs 2001

PHILIPPINES
Trauma of a Failed Presidency

Alexander R. Magno

The year 2000 ended violently in the Philippines, signalling a period of turbulence that puts the country's democratic institutions to the severest test.

On 30 December, as Filipinos prepared to celebrate the start of a new year, five powerful bombs ripped through the Manila area. The bombs were set off on a crowded commuter train, a packed bus, near a hotel in the business district, a public park across from the American embassy, and in a restricted area close to the fuel depot of the airport. The bomb attacks, still unsolved at the time of writing, killed twenty-two and injured over a hundred.

The sophistication of the explosives, the methodical execution of the terrorist operation, and the timing of the attacks raised many questions among a stunned public. The police went through the usual suspects: the armed communist factions, the Islamic separatist movements, and the military groups responsible for the coup attempts of the late eighties. Somehow, none of the usual suspects were acceptable explanations for the senseless bombing.

The bombings, after all, occurred during a period of high political tension. President Joseph Estrada has become the first Asian chief executive to be formally impeached. On the last day of trial before the holiday break, a senior bank executive gave explosive testimony before the Senate sitting as an impeachment trial court. Clarissa Ocampo, senior vice-president of one of the Philippines' largest banks, told the court that Estrada, under a false identity, was the true owner of several bank accounts holding hundred of millions of pesos.

Recalling the incidents of 1972, when Ferdinand Marcos ordered bombing attacks on the metropolis to justify his imposition of martial rule, many Filipinos feared that the 30 December bombings were a prelude to an adventurous scheme to retain Estrada in power in the face of mounting evidence of misdeed. The year ended with even more pessimism than it began.

The bomb blasts and the explosive evidence being introduced in the Senate were not the only pieces of bad news troubling a confused population. The Finance Secretary announced at year-end that the national budget deficit could

---

Alexander R. Magno is Professor of Political Science at the University of the Philippines.

rise to P130 billion — or more than double the target of P62 billion set at the start of the year. The mammoth deficit, owing largely to poor revenue performance, will have devastating effects on the national economy.

Combined with substantial capital flight during the year, the collapse of confidence in the stock market, a sharp decline in investments, and a drop in export growth, the Philippines seems to be on a path towards economic failure, growing misery, rising social stress, and sharp political confrontations. At the centre of this traumatic episode is what is now clearly the failed presidency of movie actor Joseph Estrada.

The Road to Crisis

The road to the paralysing economic and political crisis in the last quarter of 2000 has been a long and complex one — although on hindsight, probably inevitable.

Filipino politics has long been burdened by weak political party systems, strong personal affiliations and, after many years of dictatorship, a stagnant political class. Political identification shifted according to which leader wielded power at the moment. So it was that when Ferdinand Marcos ruled, nearly all elected officials identified with his Kilusang Bagong Lipunan (KBL) party. When Corazon Aquino was President, the Laban ng Demokratikong Pilipino (LDP) enjoyed vast majorities in Congress and among local governments. Fidel Ramos, when he rose to the presidency, reassembled political allegiances around the Lakas-NUCD party. Political parties were inconstant; charisma defined constituencies more effectively.

In the wake of the 1986 uprising, however, some semblance of a political consensus predominated Filipino politics. It was a consensus woven around the ideal of a responsive democracy, effective and honest government, professional management of the public sector, and strong mechanisms of accountability. This may be described, for want of a better term, as the "middle-class consensus" emerging from an uprising led and participated by the urban middle class in the Philippines.

The "middle-class consensus" was expressed in the 1992 elections in the rejection of candidates identified as "traditional politicians", such as Ramon Mitra and Eduardo Cojuangco. It translated into strong support for two candidates with backgrounds in the civil service and perceived to be non-politicians: Fidel Ramos and Miriam Defensor-Santiago, who were placed first and second respectively.

In the 1998 elections, however, the post-EDSA political consensus was shaken by a convergence of factors. The 1997 Asian financial crisis had weakened public faith in the paradigm of liberalization and deregulation. The multi-party system had divided and dispersed the middle class vote such that Joseph Estrada, pitted against eight other candidates more or less representing the post-EDSA middle-class consensus, won the elections with 39 per cent of the vote. The weakening of public confidence in the viability of the liberalization model reawakened strong populist sentiments among Filipino voters. Greater access to information and the almost complete erosion of the system of "command votes" centred on major land-owning families encouraged lower-class voters to make independent electoral choices — with a great number casting their votes to favour a movie idol who had played memorable roles as a defender of the poor and the powerless.

Estrada's campaign handlers smartly exploited the screen popularity of their candidate, his attractiveness among the newly independent lower class voters, and growing disenchantment with the liberalization paradigm advanced by the technocracies of the two previous presidencies. They packaged Estrada as the champion of the masses and promised a government that would finally bring relief to the poor.

Their concentration on the lower income constituencies proved accurate. Only a few from the A, B and C income sectors voted for Estrada. The candidate won overwhelmingly among the more numerous D and E income brackets, paving the way to the presidency whose main constituencies were among the poorest, most backward, and marginalized sectors of Philippine society. Those who long felt excluded from the decision-making process in a society of gross inequities thought they had found the leader who would speak for them.

The 1998 elections thus produced a presidency whose political base was sharply skewed towards the poor and the powerless. Estrada was a President elected to office by those with the most pompous populist expectations about what a "pro-masses" leader could do. These were expectations that ran against the grain of what business leaders, economists, and most of the educated sectors of society thought was the way to sustainable progress: a competitive and open economy directed by effective, accountable, and far-sighted institutions of governance.

After Estrada assumed office, the poor voters who elevated him to the post wanted instant dividends. In order to attend to his electoral promises, Estrada immediately opened a "Presidential Assistance Office" at the palace. The office dispensed letters of recommendation to various public offices — a largely meaningless gesture. Nevertheless, the office was deluged by thousands every day. People hoped the new President would give them jobs, provide them housing, get them visas to foreign places of work, or remove injustices done them. Many of the petitioners stayed through the night to get ahead of the queue. The office was closed down shortly after it was opened, after two died in a stampede.

The episode, nevertheless, illustrated the intensity of expectation invested in the Estrada presidency by the most desperate in society. As subsequent events proved, the poor and powerless supporters of Estrada were tenacious in their hope that the movie idol would deliver as he always did in his screen roles. It is a tenacity that baffles those with a more modern sensibility. Like movie fans and groupies, they stood by Estrada against the odds and against the evidence.

It is noteworthy, considering all that has happened so far, that during the 1998 electoral campaign the Catholic bishops and leaders of other religious groups had campaigned hard against Estrada. They had warned voters about Estrada's unusual lifestyle: his alcoholism, his obsessive gambling, his many mistresses, and the shady characters that kept the insomniac company late into the night.

After Estrada assumed office, business leaders were concerned that the new President would drift into populism and undermine economic growth and competitiveness. They were likewise concerned about the resurgence of cronyism, involving both Marcos period personalities and hustler businessmen who invested heavily in the Estrada campaign and would almost certainly expect a payback. In order to minimize these dangers, mainstream business groups closely engaged with the new presidency, volunteering in government–private sector councils, and providing business advice to Estrada's officials. The continuing avalanche of scandals and rumours of wrongdoing on a massive scale disheartened the business community, making the political honeymoon turbulent and brief.

Eccentric Leadership

Two years after he became President, Joseph Estrada showed little convincing proof that he understood the demands of his job and the dimensions within which policy-making should be done. His most avid supporters pleaded that the new President needed a "learning curve" before becoming fully functional in his role.

After a year in office, Estrada had not passed a single one of the long list of economic reform measures he promised businessmen at the onset of his term in order to reassure them. That failure led to a relatively weak economic performance. Although the Philippine economy was acknowledged to be among the least damaged by the 1997 Asian financial contagion, by the end of 1999 it was growing at a rate only slightly better than regional tail-ender Indonesia.

The business community continued to be disturbed by preferential treatment given to presidential friends. A number of executive orders (quasi-legislative policy enactments signed by the President) had to be recalled because of strong opposition from the mainstream business groups. These executive orders departed from standing policies and favoured individuals close to Estrada.

The business community was likewise disturbed by rumours of politically-brokered mergers and acquisitions that were said to have been put together by close Estrada allies in exchange for large commissions. The giant Philippine Long Distance Company, for instance, was acquired by the Salim group's First Pacific Corporation despite resistance from its original owners. A commission amounting to billions of pesos was reportedly paid Estrada associate Mark Jimenez.

The same Mark Jimenez was said to have engineered the acquisition of the Philippine Commercial and Industrial Bank by the smaller Equitable Bank, owned by the family of Estrada ally George Go. This acquisition was made possible through large investments made by the two government-controlled pension funds. Rumours have it that Estrada himself made large commissions from this deal. The Go-owned bank was to play a central role in the impeachment hearings later.

An air agreement with Taiwan was likewise abrogated unilaterally by the Estrada government. The controversial move was said to be at the behest of tycoon Lucio Tan, who controls the beleaguered Philippine Airlines (PAL). Tan, most often mentioned as the example of resurgent cronyism, likewise won control of the Philippine National Bank, the main creditor of PAL. The same bank extended a large loan to the controversial BW Resources Corporation without collateral, and as subsequently established, at the behest of Estrada himself.

In addition to mounting evidence of cronyism, the Estrada administration was besieged by a nearly incessant stream of scandals involving the President's friends and relatives. Government contracts, smuggling operations, and even commissions collected from foreign investors were often linked to one or another of Estrada mistresses, all of whom began building large mansions that became the subject of public scrutiny.

The situation was not helped by Estrada's eccentric leadership and management style. He convened his Cabinet irregularly, preferring to deal with his department secretaries individually — usually by phone, and late at night. It seemed to many that Estrada spent much more time with his friends — drinking, gambling, and carousing at night — than with his officials. Often, Estrada's buddies would draft orders and have him sign these without the knowledge of the Cabinet secretary concerned. The group of Estrada buddies who convened at the presidential residence late at night was eventually referred to as the "Midnight Cabinet" — believed to be more powerful than the officially-designated and regularly accountable Cabinet. All these led to inaction by many departments and incoherent policy approaches by the entire executive branch.

A vital council, the Legislative-Executive Development Advisory Council (LEDAC), was convened only twice during the Estrada administration — both after Senate resolutions were passed asking that the body be convened. The LEDAC is required by law to be convened at least twice a month. The Council, composed of committee chairmen from both the Senate and the House of Representatives and the secretaries of the executive departments involved in economic policy-making, was legislated into existence during the Ramos presidency. It was designed as a forum for establishing consensus on priority policies and for avoiding the gridlock often associated with the presidential form of government.

In addition, Estrada seemed indisposed towards attending to the other demands of statesmanship. Rather than reach out and establish lines of dialogue with strategic sectors suspicious of his presidency — such as church leaders, business associations, and civil society groups — Estrada seemed content in the stability of his lower-class political base. He blamed previous administrations for every problem that arose and attributed scandals to demolition jobs performed by his political opponents. Unlike his predecessor, Fidel Ramos, who seemed obsessed with constantly broadening his base of support and maintaining dialogue with all social groups, Estrada's presidential style was exclusionary and confrontational.

This characteristic alienated many important social sectors. The presidency, in a rapidly evolving and increasingly more complex Philippine society, is the central point for maintaining a high degree of consensus. Estrada seemed to have missed that important point.

It is fascinating to note than in his two years in the presidency, Estrada fathered several children by a number of mistresses and paramours. He has explained the sudden appearance of his vast property holdings as the fruits of gambling wins. All the while, a political volcano was gathering steam.

Wagging the Dog

In the last two quarters of 1999, Joseph Estrada began paying the price for lackadaisical presidential leadership. Public opinion surveys began showing a dramatic drop in his approval ratings. The erosion of support was alarming.

Estrada began the year 2000 announcing a "reformed" presidency. The resignation of Finance Secretary Edgardo Espiritu, whose department was responsible for the declining revenues and a budget deficit almost twice the original target, was accepted. Espiritu would later blame the miserable revenue performance on presidential friends evading taxes and protecting smuggling operations on a large scale.

The Estrada Cabinet was reshuffled to underscore the administration's determination to manage the economy more effectively. Trade Secretary Jose Pardo, respected in the business community, was moved to the post vacated by Espiritu. Manuel Roxas, a young congressman from a well-established political clan, was named Pardo's replacement at the Trade and Industry department.

In addition, an Economic Coordinating Council (ECC), composed of the administration's economic managers, was organized. Chaired by Estrada himself, the ECC was intended as a clearing house for all economic policy initiatives. The move was intended to reassure the business community that the erratic policy-making brought about by the undue influence of the "Midnight Cabinet" would be corrected. Estrada, in announcing the formation of the ECC, also pledged that the practice of inviting presidential friends to the palace for late-night drinking and gambling sessions would be ended. Later in the year, as additional reassurance to the business community, Estrada yielded the chair of the ECC to Pardo.

The ECC was supplemented by a Council of Senior Economic Advisers composed of some of the most respected personalities in the Filipino business community. Estrada never formally convened this council, however. When the gambling scandal broke out in the fourth quarter of the year, the members of this Council resigned *en masse*.

In order to reinforce the message that a tighter, better-run executive department was achievable despite Estrada's personal eccentricities, a Filipino-

Canadian academic — Aprodicio Laquian — was named presidential chief of staff. Laquian resigned after a few weeks, however. He enraged Estrada by publicly admitting that the "Midnight Cabinet" was still in session and that Estrada's drinking habits remained despite the President's public promise to stay away from liquor. No one was appointed to the post after Laquian's sudden exit.

Whatever positive impact on the country's economic performance the organizational changes in Estrada's staff might have had was quickly negated by the stock market scandal involving the BW Resources Corporation (BWRC). The stock had risen from less than P2 to a high of P107 before collapsing late in 1999. BWRC is controlled by close Estrada associate Dante Tan. An internal investigation conducted by the Philippine Stock Exchange concluded that manipulation on an unprecedented scale had happened. Foreign institutional investors, alarmed at the brazenness of the manipulation, withdrew from the Philippine market, causing a dramatic fall of the index.

The loss of credibility of the stock market had great economic ripple effects. Domestic firms cut down on expansion plans and investments were shelved. Foreign investors withdrew direct investments. Business confidence weakened. By April, unemployment was reported at 14 per cent, double the low of 7 per cent reported during the Ramos years. Between January and July 2000, portfolio investments decreased by 80 per cent while foreign direct investments decreased 61 per cent compared with the same period in the preceding year.

To compound things, international credit rating agencies downgraded the Philippines. Standard and Poor's downgraded the Philippines from "stable" to "negative." The International Monetary Fund (IMF) and the World Bank withheld US$510 million in concessional loans as a consequence of poor fiscal management by the Estrada government. At the beginning of the year, the Philippine Government had committed to a deficit ceiling of P62.5 billion. At the end of the year, the deficit was estimated at a record P139 billion.

Buffeted by political turbulence, the peso's exchange value became unsteady in October and November, dropping from about P46 to P52 to the U.S. dollar. The currency's depreciation magnified the impact of politically sensitive oil prices. The two combined helped fuel political tensions further.

A slowdown in import growth in the latter half of the year indicated weakening consumer confidence, expectations of slower growth, and a less vigorous export performance in the coming period. The problematic macroeconomic indicators signalled further declines in political support. Given the prospects, the Estrada administration shifted to full-throttle the public relations mode.

In the face of a stubborn insurgency in the Muslim south, Estrada in February rattled sabres at the Moro Islamic Liberation Front (MILF). The rebels reacted by rolling over a small town in western Mindanao in March. Estrada ordered a full-scale military offensive to clear the rebel camps. After three months of intense fighting, government forces cleared a total of forty-two rebel encampments. However, the secessionist movement appeared to have conserved the bulk of its fighting forces by withdrawing in the face of superior forces.

Pollsters have discovered that any act of decisiveness by a Filipino President produces an increase of public support. The war in Mindanao did, indeed, rally public support for Estrada. By mid-year, his approval ratings began showing signs of a rally.

The military victories against the MILF were, however, undermined by kidnappings in the distant southern islands of Basilan and Jolo carried out by the radical Islamic guerrilla group Abu Sayyaf. In March, the guerrillas took a group of schoolchildren and teachers in Basilan island. After negotiations proved futile, the Army stormed the rebel stronghold to rescue the victims.

The Basilan incident was quickly overshadowed by another kidnapping operation pulled by the Abu Sayyaf. About two dozen tourists were taken from the Malaysian resort island of Sipadan. The hostages were brought to the island of Jolo, seat of the old Sultanate of Sulu. Additional hostages were taken in the course of the long negotiations that involved European governments and Libya. Large ransoms were eventually paid by Malaysian tycoons, the Ghaddafy Foundation, and European media organizations whose journalists were also taken hostage. Numerous stories about government negotiators taking "commissions" from the bandits circulated, further discrediting the Estrada leadership.

The prolonged and murky handling of the hostage incidents conveyed the picture of a bungling Estrada leadership. To be sure, these incidents killed whatever prospects there were for the revival of the Philippines' tourism industry. More importantly, the incidents reinforced the impression among business decision-makers that the Estrada leadership was losing control of the situation.

In September, a few days before the quarterly surveys on his popularity were due to be released, Estrada ordered a full-scale military assault on the island of Jolo to free the remaining hostages and crush the radical rebel group. This reinforced the theory that Estrada was increasingly relying on the application of military force to distract public attention from failure in other areas of governance. It was a strategy described as "wagging the dog" after a popular American movie on the same theme.

If this was indeed the motivation, it was not entirely without some basis. The third quarter surveys showed Estrada continuing his recovery in popularity. However, by the time the results of the survey were released, a worse crisis had broken out, casting a large cloud of doubt on Estrada's ability to remain in office for long.

Explosive Scandal
Late in the night of 3 October, Luis "Chavit" Singson's bullet-proofed vehicle was stopped by heavily-armed policemen on a dark street in Manila. Sensing

something was amiss, Singson refused to step down from his vehicle and instead made an urgent call to mayors from his Northern Luzon region assembled in a nearby hotel. The mayors rushed to the scene and averted what Singson subsequently described as an attempt to assassinate him.

Singson has always been a controversial figure in Philippine politics. The governor of the tobacco-producing northern Luzon province of Ilocos Sur for nearly three decades, he has been described as a "warlord". He has maintained a lifestyle that cannot be explained by his official income — regularly gambling for high stakes in the casinos of Manila and Las Vegas, maintaining a number of yachts and a fleet of private planes, making large campaign contributions to politicians, and moving about with a large retinue of bodyguards.

Singson has also been a close associate of President Estrada. He was a regular attendee of the so-called "Midnight Cabinet" and accompanied Estrada on most of his foreign trips. He was widely perceived to be controlling illegal gambling as well as smuggling operations.

A few days after the incident with the policemen, Singson issued an affidavit alleging that the attempt to kill him was motivated by others similarly allied with Estrada. A struggle over gambling turf and efforts to cover up diversions of public funds were the immediate reasons, he claimed. The beleaguered provincial governor went on to detail how protection money for an illegal numbers game called *jueteng* was channelled, through him, to Estrada. Large kickbacks were also involved, with Singson's participation. The money was ploughed back to Estrada himself, his wife and son, as well as his mistresses.

Singson's revelations triggered a major political earthquake. Earlier in the year, several middle-class groups had banded together to demand Estrada's resignation for corruption and incompetence. The initiative, calling itself the "Silent Protest", was denoted by an exclamation mark, indicating the outrage felt by those who felt they were not getting the government they deserved. After a few weeks, the initiative seemed to fizzle out.

After the Singson revelations, however, a clear rallying point for the building discontent was established. Manila archbishop Jaime Cardinal Sin, remembered for the pivotal role he played in the 1986 uprising that ended the Marcos dictatorship, declared that Estrada had lost the moral ascendancy to lead, and demanded his resignation.

Sin's call was echoed by former presidents Corazon Aquino and Fidel Ramos. It was affirmed by the powerful Catholic Bishops Conference of the Philippines, as well as by the Protestant churches through the National Council of Churches in the Philippines. The Council of Ulamas, representing the Islamic religious leaders, joined the call.

Estrada's elected Vice-President and constitutional successor Gloria Macapagal Arroyo resigned her Cabinet post as Social Welfare Secretary. This was followed by the resignation of Trade Secretary Manuel Roxas and Estrada's political adviser. Business leaders resigned in quick sequence from the Council of Senior Economic Advisers, the APEC Business Council and a number of other government–private sector commissions. Senate President Franklin Drilon and House Speaker Manuel Villar also resigned from the Estrada coalition. Both were immediately expelled from their posts by senators and congressmen loyal to Estrada.

With the moral reference points of Philippine society taking a strong political position, civil society groups quickly assembled to terminate the Estrada presidency. All the major business groups, together with all the trade unions across the ideological spectrum, joined in the call for Estrada to resign. Hundreds of non-governmental organizations, professional associations, academic communities, and political movements reconstituted the Kongreso ng Mamayang Pilipino (Congress of the Filipino People). This large coalition provided the central direction for the diverse groups that participated in the uprising of 1986.

Throughout October and November, extensive coalition-building and large protest rallies were conducted nationwide. From reliable accounts, Estrada did seriously consider resigning early in November. He was held back by allies who convinced him that the political storm could be weathered.

Shortly after Cardinal Sin issued the call for Estrada's resignation, a small group of congressmen, supported by non-governmental organizations, filed an impeachment motion at the House of Representatives. Few expected the motion to prosper, considering the large majority enjoyed by Estrada supporters in that chamber. However, with the defection of the Villar faction from the pro-Estrada coalition, enough congressional support was gathered to meet the required one-third of all members of the House to bring the impeachment complaint to the Senate.

The swift progression of events caught everyone by surprise. Estrada became the first Asian leader to be formally impeached. The Philippine Senate hastily convened itself into an impeachment court presided over by the Chief Justice. A remarkable impeachment trial began to unfold in the first week of December.

Ironically, the onset of the impeachment trial took the wind out of the street-based protest actions to force Estrada from office. The people wanted the institutional process to complete itself. Covered live by the major television and radio outlets, the trial broke all audience records. The trial has become the single most important educational event on civics and the rule of law in Philippine political history.

Estrada faced four articles of impeachment: bribery, with specific reference to the collection of hundreds of millions of pesos in protection money from illegal gambling; graft and corruption, with specific reference to the diversion of money from tobacco fund allocations; violation of public trust, with specific reference to Estrada's efforts to obstruct justice in the BW stock manipulation case and the amassing of unexplained wealth in connection with large bank accounts and over a dozen freshly-built mansions attributed to his mistresses; and, culpable violation of the Constitution for a number of specific acts.

Conviction on any of the four articles of impeachment would cause Estrada's removal from office. By the close of the year, with the trial less than halfway through, a critical mass of public opinion had deemed Estrada guilty. The question is: will an acquittal by the Senators be accepted by a public where the most strategic sectors — such as the business community, the churches, the unions, and sections of the military — have convicted him in the arena of public opinion?

Crisis and Consequences

Joseph Ejercito Estrada was elected to the Philippine presidency during a time of great change and immense challenge.

It was important to restore the momentum of growth diminished by the Asian contagion. In an increasingly competitive global economy, much had to be done to raise Philippine competitiveness. In order to lower the costs of doing business in the country, infrastructure needed to be modernized quickly, the economic policy architecture required urgent reforms, governance must be brought to world standards, and a unifying vision must be articulated to unite a complex and often confused society.

These did not seem to be the goals of the Estrada presidency.

On the contrary, Estrada's leadership style and the political forces he personified represented the resurgence of the past, militating against the demands of the future. Estrada was a man of great charisma but not of vision. In a world that demands policy-based leadership, Estrada was a throwback to the age of sultans: particularistic, inward-looking, dependent on patronage as the means for gathering political support. In a period and a political system where the presidency plays the most vital role in national consensus-building, Estrada was unable to rise above his own vices and his own pettiness. He did not reach out to the broad constituencies and offer them a view of the future a whole nation could unite on. Instead, he pampered his extended family with the spoils of corrupt politics, he looked after the interest of his friends above the interest of the nation, and he tolerated wrong-doing, presuming this to be the norm.

In a perverse way, Estrada was a gift to the Filipino nation. His faults stood large and his virtues scarce. His rise to the presidency alerted Filipinos to the neglected imperfections of this political culture: the reliance of electoral players on money generated in the gray economy; the extent to which patronage politics undermined public morals; the poverty of political discourse; and the vulnerability of those who are desperately poor to those who promise to use state power in order to commandeer wealth and distribute it on the basis of political loyalties.

When Filipinos rose in revolt in 1986, the choices were stark, the atmosphere emotional, and the transition euphoric. There were martyrs and saints to guide partisanships. It was a process once described, quite correctly, as a morality play.

On hindsight, there was very little disciplined public discussion about the quality of governance needed to progress, the mechanisms of accountability that needed to be enforced to break the cycle of corruption that plagued the political system, and the civic virtues that must be enhanced in order to make democracy work. In the long impeachment trial that engrossed the Filipino nation, these were precisely the issues every citizen had to deal with in his mind.

The impeachment trial has been described as a telenovela that outclassed all the others simply because it was real. The characters were not contrived. They were real people, inhabiting the present, personifying the ills that made the Philippine political community problematic and prone to turbulence.

More than just being yet another form of public entertainment, the trial was a large classroom where the weaknesses of institutions were exposed and the innermost secrets of political corruption revealed. It was a crash course on the values and the principles on which modern nationhood may be sustained. It was a vivid seminar on the requirements of leadership in a world that demanded transparency, competence, and adeptness.

More than ever before, Filipinos realize the unbreakable bond between good governance and a dynamic economy. Unless regulatory capacities are improved, the rule of law strengthened, and responsible governance ensured, the entire country will fail. In a highly integrated global order, the margin for error is ruthlessly slim. The costs to the national economy of failed leadership are both severe and immediate.

However the trial turns and regardless of its immediate political aftermath, this traumatic episode teaches all Filipinos to treat the responsibilities of democracy more seriously.

It has not only put a President on trial and put institutions to their severest test. It has also put on trial a political culture that failed to adapt rapidly to the changing circumstances of modernity.

MUSLIM MINDANAO
Four Years After the Peace Agreement

R.J. May

In September 1996, the Government of the Philippines and the Moro National Liberation Front (MNLF) signed a Peace Agreement. At the time there were many who hailed the agreement as bringing to an end a conflict between Muslim and Christian Filipinos which had begun with Spanish settlement in the Philippine islands in the sixteenth century but had entered a new, violent phase in the early 1970s.

Such optimism, however, was poorly founded. For one thing, the Agreement, which was subtitled "The Final Agreement on the Implementation of the 1976 Tripoli Agreement" [between the Government of the Philippines and the MNLF], covered the thirteen provinces which constituted the MNLF's minimum territorial demand for an autonomous "Bangsa Moro" (or Moro Nation). Already by 1976, only five of these provinces contained a Muslim majority population and in 1977, and again in 1987, attempts to promote a peaceful settlement through the establishment of an autonomous region had failed when autonomy was rejected, in mandated plebiscites, by the non-Muslim majority in most of the thirteen provinces. In 1996, the holding of a plebiscite was postponed, but the requirement that a plebiscite eventually be held hung over the newly established Special Zone of Peace and Development (SZOPAD) and its Southern Philippines Council for Peace and Development (SPCPD). Secondly, the 1996 Peace Agreement was specifically between the Government of the Philippines and the MNLF. It did not include the other major Moro faction, the Moro Islamic Liberation Front (MILF), which vowed to maintain the armed struggle for an independent Bangsa Moro. Thirdly, it was clear, even in 1996, that the Philippine Government and the SPCPD were not going to be able to meet the exaggerated developmental expectations of the Philippine Muslims, and that the promised integration of former Bangsa Moro Army guerrillas into the Armed Forces of the Philippines was unlikely to proceed smoothly.

In the event, even the sceptics might have been disappointed at the way things have developed since 1996. First, more than four years after the Peace

---

RONALD J. MAY is a Senior Fellow in the Department of Political and Social Change, Research School of Pacific and Asian Studies, Australian National University.

Agreement was signed no plebiscite has been held and the spectre of a plebiscite thus still hangs over the SZOPAD/SPCPD. (Elections for the exiting four-province Autonomous Region of Muslim Mindanao [ARMM], created in 1987, have also been put off, twice.) Meanwhile, claims that the ARMM has not been adequately funded, allegations that funds have been misused, and unfulfilled expectations have created tensions in relations between MNLF leaders and the Philippine Government and have tended to undermine the position of MNLF chairman and ARMM governor/SPCPD chair, Nur Misuari. Secondly, repeated attempts to negotiate a peace agreement with the MILF have had little success, and in 2000 growing frustration on the part of the government culminated in a major military offensive against the MILF. Thirdly, another Muslim faction, Abu Sayyaf, a group which in 1996 was regarded as a small and poorly organized band engaged mostly in local brigandry, emerged in 2000, through a series of kidnappings, as a significant source of political disturbance, locally and with international implications. Around mid-year President Estrada's hardline stance towards both the MILF and the hostage-takers appeared to raise his popularity ratings; by October, however, the government's continued inability to resolve the problems in the south was a contributing factor to calls for the President to resign.

This chapter reviews developments during 2000 in three areas — the MNLF/SPCPD/ARMM, the Philippine Government–MILF confrontation, and the Abu Sayyaf hostage-taking — and examines their longer-term implications for the Philippines' domestic politics and international relations.

The Politics of the ARMM and the SPCPD

Following the "People Power" Revolution in the Philippines, a new constitution was ratified in 1987. The new constitution made specific provision for the creation of an Autonomous Region of Muslim Mindanao (and for a Cordillera Autonomous Region), and a Regional Consultative Commission (RCC) was set up to draft the legislation for an ARMM. The RCC process, however, was deeply flawed,[1] the MNLF did not take part in the negotiations, and when the required plebiscite was held in 1989 only four of the thirteen provinces and none of the nine cities within the proposed ARMM voted to join it. The ARMM was thus established, but it lacked public support and with limited powers and modest funding it achieved little. Indeed, under the administrations of governors Zacaria Candao and Lininding Pangandaman, the ARMM was marked by inefficiency, political patronage, corruption, and squabbling between factions.[2]

In 1992 Fidel Ramos succeeded Corazon Aquino as President of the Philippines, and soon after taking up office he revived negotiations with the MNLF. In October 1992 a statement of understanding was signed by the MNLF and the Philippine Government in Libya. A series of peace talks followed, with the participation of the Organization of Islamic Conference (OIC) and its Ministerial Committee of Six, chaired by Indonesia. The eventual outcome of these negotiations was the agreement signed in Jakarta in 1996 by Misuari and Ambassador Yan (as chair of the Government of the Philippines Peace Panel).[3] The agreement provided for the creation of the SZOPAD, comprising the (now) fourteen provinces and nine cities specified in the Tripoli Agreement, to "be the focus of intense peace and development efforts" over the next three years, and the SPCPD.[4]

The SPCPD was to comprise a chairman, vice-chairman, and three deputies to represent the Muslims, the Christians, and the Cultural Communities. It was mandated to "control and/or supervise" "appropriate agencies of the government that are engaged in peace and development activities in the area [of the SZOPAD]"; such agencies included the Southern Philippines Development Authority, set up by the Marcos administration to promote development in Mindanao (but which in practice almost certainly did more for the Christian areas of Mindanao than for Muslim Mindanao), regional offices of the Office of Muslim Affairs (OMA) and the Office of the Southern Cultural Communities, and the Special Development Planning Group, an *ad hoc* body of government officials from the Department of Trade and Industry, the National Economic and Development Authority, the Department of Public Works and Housing, and other agencies. Local government units in the area, including the ARMM, were to remain subject to the existing (national) legislation.

The functions and powers of the SPCPD were described as "derivative and extension of the powers of the President", and the operating funds of the SPCPD and its subsidiary bodies were to be initially sourced from the Office of the President.

The Agreement also provided for a Consultative Assembly of 81 members, comprising the chair of the SPCPD as head, the governor and vice-governor of the ARMM, the 14 provincial governors, and 9 city mayors of the SZOPAD, 44 members of the MNLF, and 11 sectoral representatives nominated by non-governmental organizations (NGOs) and people's organizations (POs). The Consultative Assembly's functions were listed as:

- To serve as a forum for consultation and ventilation of issues and concerns;
- To conduct public hearings as may be necessary and to provide appropriate advice to the SPCPD; and
- To formulate and recommend policies to the President through the chairman of the SPCPD and make rules and regulations to the extent necessary for the effective and efficient administration of the affairs of the area.

The SPCPD was to be assisted by a Darul Iftah (religious advisory council) appointed by the chair of the SPCPD.

The OIC was specifically requested to support the implementation of the agreement and, together with the Government of the Philippines and the MNLF, was represented on a Joint Monitoring Committee created to oversee the ceasefire and peace process.

A particular feature of the 1996 Peace Agreement was the provision for the integration of 7,500 former MNLF (Bangsa Moro Army) fighters into the Armed Forces of the Philippines (AFP) and the Philippine National Police (PNP): 5,500 into the AFP and 250 as AFP auxiliaries, and 1,500 into the PNP with a further 250 as PNP auxiliaries. In addition, a special socio-economic, cultural and educational programme was to be developed for MNLF forces not absorbed into the AFP/PNP to help them and their families acquire education, technical skills, and livelihood training.

The 1996 Peace Agreement was to be implemented in two phases. Phase 1 was to cover three years, beginning with the signing of the Agreement and issuance of an executive order establishing the SZOPAD, SPCPD, and Consultative Assembly. Within this period, legislation was to be drawn up to repeal or amend the organic act (RA 6734) under which the ARMM had been set up in 1987, to "include the pertinent provisions of the Final Peace Agreement and the Expansion of the present ARMM area of autonomy". Such new legislation, having been passed by Congress and approved by the President, was to be submitted to a plebiscite in the SZOPAD within two years from the establishment of the SPCPD (that is, by September 1998): "The new area of autonomy shall then be determined by the provinces and cities that will vote/choose to join the said autonomy (1998)".

The provisions for a new ARMM were anticipated in the Agreement. They included the creation of an executive council, legislative assembly, and administrative system. The proposed regional legislative assembly was to have legislative power "in the area of autonomy"; thirteen specific areas were noted for exclusion (foreign affairs, national defence and security, post, coinage and fiscal and monetary policy, administration of justice except on matters of Syari'ah [Islamic Law], quarantine, customs and tariffs, citizenship, immigration and deportation, general auditing, civil service and elections, foreign trade, transportation beyond the autonomous region, and patents and copyright).

Residents of the Autonomous Region were also assured of "representation and participation" in the national government and "all organs of the state", including at least one member of Cabinet, recommended by the head of the autonomous region, and one representative in Congress as a sectoral representative. The head of the autonomous region was to be an *ex officio* member of the National Security Council on all matters affecting the autonomous region. Phase 2 was also to see to the establishment of Special Regional Security Forces (SRSF) — in practice, a PNP regional command — in the Autonomous Region. (Provision for SRSF had been a significant point in the Tripoli Agreement.)

Potential problems concerning the respective roles of the SPCPD and the existing ARMM were avoided when Misuari, having returned to the Philippines and been appointed chairman of the SPCPD, was elected unopposed as governor of the ARMM in September 1996.

Regional Autonomy in Practice

The negotiation of the 1996 Peace Agreement was undoubtedly a major achievement, but in the euphoria which surrounded its conclusion, many commentators failed to acknowledge its limitations.[5]

For one, the 1996 Peace Agreement generated considerable anxiety among non-Muslim communities in Mindanao, who expressed exaggerated fears that they would be subjected to Muslim dominance. Christian community leaders, led by Congresswoman (and later mayor of Zamboanga) Maria Clara Lobregat, organized demonstrations against the agreement, and there were threats that the Christian vigilante groups, which had been active during the conflicts of the early 1970s, would be revived. In Congress, where public hearings on the Peace Agreement were held in the latter part of 1996, there was opposition to the granting of autonomy, complaints that civil society organizations had not been party to the negotiations, and accusations that President Ramos had "sold out" to the militant Muslims. In the Senate, there were demands for the withdrawal of powers from the SPCPD and Consultative Assembly and for the exclusion of local government units from SPCPD control; six of the twenty-four senators (including the Senate president) voted against a resolution supporting the peace agreement. In the House of Representatives, the House Appropriations Committee threatened to block funding for the SPCPD and Consultative Assembly. Just prior to the signing of the final agreement, a group of congressional representatives and a provincial governor filed a petition in the Supreme Court seeking the invalidation of the agreement.

Against this background, a number of amendments were made to the agreement before it was signed in September 1996, and when the implementing executive order (EO 371) was signed in October 1996, it was a significantly weakened version of the agreement. As one commentator wrote in 1999:

> ... the transitional structures [the SPCPD and Consultative Assembly] ... were too powerless to make an impact. They had very limited funding, no police powers, no control over national projects and programmes that were supposed to be within their remit, and no jurisdiction over significant sections of the bureaucracy in the region.[6]

Among other things, the provision in the Agreement for forty-four MNLF members in the Consultative Assembly was dropped, and the provisions of the Agreement which placed specified government agencies under the control and/or supervision of the SPCPD were deleted. In fact, the SPCPD was given little scope for policy action except through the Office of the President. The Darul Iftah was not mentioned.

In the 1998 elections, a number of local politicians who had supported the Peace Agreement were voted out, and MNLF candidates (who had supported the Ramos administration's Lakas-NUCD party, whose presidential candidate lost to Joseph Estrada) polled poorly at the national level.

Secondly, there seems to be a widespread and growing feeling among the Muslim population that the creation of the SZOPAD and SPCPD has not brought the expected benefits. In the early months after the SPCPD's establishment, Governor Misuari and his administration actively sought foreign investment (especially from OIC countries), and development assistance. Despite some success in these efforts (notably through a United Nations Multi-Donor Assistance Program which provided emergency relief and livelihood projects and skills training for targetted groups), ARMM officials have continually complained of inadequate resourcing from the national government, and Misuari, as early as March 1999, had warned that unless conditions improve, former MNLF fighters would return to the hills. Already in 1997 there had been reports of former MNLF fighters leaving the MNLF to join the more militant MILF. Moreover, Misuari himself has been criticized by elements within the MNLF, and *lumad* ("tribal" or cultural minority community) spokesmen have complained of undemocratic practices in the selection of *lumad* representatives in the SPCPD and Consultative Assembly. Reviewing the situation in 1999, Gutierrez commented:

> The MNLF must review its goals and re-create itself. Based on their performance so far, some MNLF leaders are beginning to look like traditional politicians using patronage and political office to increase their wealth and status.[7]

Challenges to Misuari's leadership came in 1999 from the National Islamic Command Council (NICC), a splinter group formed in 1991 by former MNLF chief of staff Melham Alam and initially based on the Zamboanga peninsula. Misuari, however, retained his position.

The integration of former MNLF fighters into the AFP has been a particular source of friction. By August 1998, some 3,800 former MNLF personnel were being integrated into the armed forces, but on more than one occasion, groups of MNLF inductees have quit, complaining of discrimination and ethnic bias. Some AFP members, on the other hand, have clearly resented the entry of the former MNLF fighters, who, apart from being "the enemy", have, in order to achieve the numbers, been exempted from normal AFP requirements regarding education, aptitude, age, and height.

The creation in July 2000 of a Mindanao Coordinating Council (MCC) to regulate infrastructure projects in the ARMM further alienated Misuari, who denounced it as a violation of the 1996 Agreement. The MCC, chaired by President Estrada, virtually ignores the SPCPD/ARMM structure. More significantly, hanging over the entire SZOPAD/SPCPD exercise has been the prospect of the mandated plebiscite. In the terms of the 1996 Agreement, RA 6734 should have been repealed or amended, and new legislation put to a plebiscite by September 1998. The plebiscite was subsequently rescheduled to 1999, and then rescheduled again to September 2000. The necessary legislation, first drafted in 1998 and put before Congress early in 2000 has still not been passed, and the plebiscite was rescheduled for February 2001, but in January 2001, under Senator Bill 2129, it was rescheduled yet again to May 2001 . It seems inevitable that when the legislation is put to a plebiscite, the pattern of the earlier polls will be repeated; of the now fourteen provinces and nine cities covered by the proposed autonomous region, only five provinces (Lanao del Sur, Maguindanao, Sulu, Tawi Tawi — the four provinces comprising the present ARMM — and Basilan) now have a Muslim majority, and only one city (Marawi). If, once again, a plebiscite yields a vote for autonomy in only four provinces, the Muslim population is likely to feel that it has again been betrayed and may pursue what it sees as its legitimate claim to a Moro homeland through other means.

A further, critical limitation on the Agreement of 1996 is that the MILF was not a party to the agreement.

The MILF

The Moro Islamic Liberation Front was one of the two major factions which split from the MNLF in 1977 in the aftermath of the Tripoli Agreement.[8] Initially, it was a junior element in the Moro movement and more religiously orientated than militant. Its support came predominantly from the Maguindanao ethnic group, though its leader, Hashim Salamat, is Iranun, one of the smaller ethnic groups in Muslim Mindanao, with links to both the Maguindanao and the Maranao of Lanao.

In 1987, the Aquino government attempted to initiate talks with the MILF, but as the government became preoccupied with its negotiations with the MNLF, these talks petered out. Three years later, the MILF sent a delegation to a summit organized by the OIC but again nothing materialized.

During the early 1990s, the MILF appeared to have grown significantly in strength and militancy, augmented by defections from the MNLF. Permanent camps were established, first at Camp Abubakar in the province of Maguindanao, and then at Camp Bushra in Lanao del Sur, and the MILF were said to be undergoing a transition from a guerilla force to a "semi-conventional army". Camp Abubakar, and to a lesser extent Camp Bushra, were, in effect, small municipalities under MILF administration rather than military camps.[9] During the Ramos presidency, there was a tacit agreement that the AFP would not attack the two camps. At the time of the 1992–96 peace negotiations, however, the MILF was not a party to the peace process. Not only was the MNLF the major faction of the Moro movement, and hence the principal target for a peace settlement, but it was Misuari and the MNLF who were recognized by the OIC. Consequently, in 1996 the MILF dissociated itself from the Agreement and vowed to continue the armed struggle for a Bangsa Moro.

In 1992, there had been talks between the MILF vice-chairman for military affairs, Al-Haj Murad, and Haydee Yorac, the chair of the National Unification Commission established by incoming President Fidel Ramos, but proposed peace talks between the government and Hashim Salamat did not eventuate. Soon after this, clashes occurred between the MILF and the AFP, principally over a controversial irrigation project in Carmen, Cotabato. Peace talks were revived in 1996, and a ceasefire was negotiated early the following year. In July 1997, a "general cessation of hostilities" was signed, and the following year the two parties finalized a General Framework of Agreement of Intent. A NGO-private sector fact-finding committee, headed by Fr Eliseo Mercado, was appointed to monitor the ceasefire, and the Philippine Government agreed to recognize some 44 MILF camps as "zones of peace and development", and to provide livelihood and economic programmes for MILF supporters in Mindanao. There were frequent ceasefire violations on both sides, however, and the AFP pursued an aggressive policy of resisting the expansion of MILF areas of control.

A Bishops-Ulama Forum was created around 1996 to assist the peace process, and received support through the Office of the Presidential Adviser on the Peace Process. After President Estrada came to office in 1998, negotiations with the MILF were continued, principally (but not exclusively) through Estrada's political adviser Robert Aventajado. However, little progress was made towards peace and in early 1999, following further AFP-MILF clashes and MILF demands for an Islamic state, proposed peace talks were called off.

Formal peace talks eventually resumed in October 1999, and President Estrada set December as a deadline for a substantive agreement. December passed without a settlement, however, and early in 2000 the MILF attacked and occupied two municipalities in Cotabato. In February, it was reported that the AFP had initiated a new offensive against the MILF in North Cotabato, resulting in 70 MILF fighters being killed and some 16,000 villages evacuated. This marked the beginning of an escalation of MILF-AFP fighting, which culminated in the overrunning of about fifty MILF camps in Mindanao, including Camps Bushra and Abubakar, which fell in July 2000. It was reported that Hashim Salamat took refuge in Malaysia, from where he called on the Moro people to rise in a *jihad*.

The military campaign of 2000 undoubtedly represents a major setback to the MILF, and there have been reports of large numbers of MILF fighters surrendering to the Philippine Government. Nevertheless, it is clear that the majority of the MILF simply abandoned camps and retreated elsewhere to continue the struggle. Fighting has since continued, spasmodically, although in October 2000 the Philippine Government announced that it had withdrawn criminal charges against the MILF leadership and, with offers of amnesty and safe passage, was yet again attempting to revive peace talks with the MILF.

Abu Sayyaf

While the offensive against the MILF was in progress, another Muslim group, the Abu Sayyaf, attracted publicity following hostage-taking incidents in March-April 2000.

The Abu Sayyaf first attracted notice in 1991 following several bombings, kidnappings, and other incidents around Zamboanga City. Its leader, Abdurajak

Janjalani, had been a member of the MNLF but was an outspoken critic of Misuari's leadership. In 1986, Janjalani was sent to Libya to undertake religious training. Returning five years later, to Basilan, he became a charismatic preacher and an advocate of an Islamic state in Mindanao, with a small but committed following including young MNLF supporters, some of whom were said to have fought in Afghanistan. He also became involved in kidnapping and extortion. Writing about the Abu Sayyaf in 1999, Vitug and Gloria summarized the general impression of Abu Sayyaf:

> ...how and why exactly the Abu Sayyaf was founded is a question for which neither the military nor Janjalani had a solid answer. The group remains as nebulous as its beginning, and as shadowy as its charismatic founder.[10]

The group appears to have had links to radical Muslims in the Arab world (through Saudi Arabian Mohammad Jamal Khalifa) and also to have been infiltrated by the AFP. In 1998 Janjalani was killed in a confrontation with police on Basilan, but Abu Sayyaf elements continued to operate, principally through kidnappings and other acts of "commercial insurgency".

Developments in 2000 marked a new phase of Abu Sayyaf activity. In March 2000, fifty-three people, including a priest, several teachers, and students returning from an excursion, were taken hostage as an Abu Sayyaf group was retreating from an encounter with the AFP. The Abu Sayyaf immediately announced ransom demands, and when these were not met two of the hostages were reportedly beheaded. Negotiations with the group commenced, but before these had reached any conclusion, it was reported that apparently another Abu Sayyaf group had kidnapped twenty-one people — including nine Malaysians, three Germans, two French, two South Africans, two Finns, a Lebanese woman, and two Filipinos — from the Malaysian island of Sipadan. The hostages were taken to an Abu Sayyaf camp on Tawi Tawi and then on to Jolo.

Following an unsuccessful military raid against the Abu Sayyaf, European, Malaysian, and Libyan envoys joined Filipino negotiators in seeking the release of the hostages. While no one underestimated the seriousness of the situation, the following events took on a somewhat farcical quality. The Abu Sayyaf issued a series of demands, which included an independent Moro state, the release of international terrorists held overseas, the banning of foreign fishing boats from the Sulu Sea, protection for Filipinos in Sabah, and ransom payments of up to US$1 million per hostage. It also dictated who it would accept as government negotiators, rejecting, amongst others, Governor Misuari, who subsequently dismissed the group as "a bunch of kidnappers". A German reporter from *Der Spiegel*, visiting the hostages in July, was kidnapped, released on payment of ransom, returned, and was kidnapped again, as was a three-member French TV crew, two Filipino TV journalists, and a group of thirteen Filipino evangelists from the charismatic Jesus Miracle Crusade who went to an Abu Sayyaf camp to pray for the hostages. In late August, a U.S. citizen was taken hostage after visiting an Abu Sayyaf camp, and a large ransom was demanded; it was later alleged that the American had been negotiating an arms sale. In the midst of all this, an inquiry was initiated into allegations that senior Philippine Government officials had been assisting the Abu Sayyaf to obtain weapons, and in September an article in *Der Spiegel* claimed that the Philippine Government's chief negotiator, Robert Aventajado, had taken a cut of the ransom payments for the release of the foreign hostages (a claim denied in Manila).

Between May and August, foreign ministers from Germany, France, and Finland flew to Manila to discuss the crisis, and Libyan envoy Rajab Azzarouq visited the rebels to negotiate on the hostages' behalf. In mid-August, it was reported that Azzarouq had secured the release of seventeen hostages from Sipadan, on payment of US$25 million, and a chartered plane arrived to take the hostages to Libya. However, it took another two weeks for the hostages to be flown out. Meanwhile, in September three Malaysians were abducted from another Malaysian resort, the Abu Sayyaf abductors reportedly outrunning a Malaysian naval vessel in a high-speed boat purchased from the proceeds of their earlier hostage-taking. In the same month, government emissaries were ambushed on their way to an Abu Sayyaf camp to negotiate the release of the hostages. The process was also hampered by faction fights amongst the Abu Sayyaf hostage-takers.

Increasingly frustrated, in September the AFP mounted a heavy assault on Abu Sayyaf strongholds on Basilan and Jolo, causing large-scale damage and civilian evacuation. It was subsequently reported that more than 100 Abu Sayyaf members had been killed, about 50,000 civilians had fled to Malaysia, and substantial numbers were surrendering or otherwise abandoning the Abu Sayyaf. Late in 2000, however, two hostages — the American and a Filipino — were still being held.

Impact of the Mindanao Crises

The conflict in Muslim Mindanao has been a thorn in the side of successive Philippine presidents. When he came into office in 1998, in the wake of the 1996 Peace Agreement with the MNLF, Mindanao was not high on President Estrada's agenda. However, developments during 1999-2000 changed that.

Faced with the increasing militancy of the MILF, including the demand in 2000 for a U.N.-supervised referendum on independence, and continued failure to achieve progress towards a peaceful settlement, President Estrada eventually opted for "all-out war". His bellicose response to the MILF, and partial military successes, initially raised Estrada's popularity rating, but by year-end other developments had reversed that. Meanwhile, the military campaign against the MILF has been costly in terms of both expenditure on the military and on post-conflict reconstruction, and the adverse impact on foreign investment. The further deferral of the ARMM plebiscite, and growing dissatisfaction over the modest outcomes from the 1996 Agreement with the MNLF, raise the additional prospect of a breakdown in relations between the MNLF and the government. The antics of the Abu Sayyaf in 2000 provided another unwelcome distraction.

In 1997, Nur Misuari, speaking to a meeting of the Mindanao Republican Movement, had advocated a federal-style election of senators by region, and called for a Mindanaon vice-president (perhaps with himself in mind as a prospective Lakas-NUCD candidate in the elections of 1998).[11] This "Mindanao Agenda" failed to win substantive support, however, and with the election of President Estrada, the issue faded. During 2000, the idea of a federal "solution" to the conflict in the south was revived. In May, prominent senators Francisco Tatad, John Osmena, and Aquilino Pimentel proposed that the Philippine Congress initiate a constitutional convention which could consider the creation of a federal system as "the ultimate solution to the peace process in Mindanao". They were supported by the chair of the Senate Committee on Constitutional Amendments and Revisions (Miriam Defensor Santiago), and also by Robert Aventajado, former congressman and Muslim scholar Michael Mastura, former University of the Philippines president Jose Abueva, and the Institute for Popular Democracy.[12] In the following month, Tawi-Tawi congressman Nur Jaafar filed a resolution calling for a constituent assembly to consider the amendment of the constitution to implement a federal system. At least two NGOs have emerged to press for federalism: the Federal Movement of the Philippines and Lihuk Pederal Mindanao, a coalition of pro-federal groups and individuals. It seems unlikely that the Philippines will opt for a federal system, but the subject is now under debate, and is seen by many as a means of dealing with the demands for Moro separatism.

Externally, developments in Mindanao in 2000 brought greater international awareness of the tenuous nature of state control in western Mindanao and Sulu. Malaysia, whose tourism industry suffered a setback from the foreign hostage-taking by the Abu Sayyaf, stepped up its naval patrolling of the Philippines–Malaysia border area, and following the kidnapping of the American, the U.S. Government offered to help the Philippines develop, train, and equip a military counter-terrorism unit. The European countries whose nationals were abducted from Sipadan were at first critical of the Philippine efforts to secure the release of hostages, but eventually thankful that their citizens were freed; however, their interest in the Philippines will probably quickly subside.

On the other hand, the prominent role played by Libya in negotiating on behalf of the hostages, most of whom were initially flown to Libya, indicated the continuing importance of the Philippines–Libya relationship in dealing with the Moro separatist issue, even though Libya's actions probably had more to do with gaining leverage over France, through securing the release of French hostages, to support Libya's efforts to re-establish diplomatic relations in Europe.

The other major external actor in the southern Philippines in 1999–2000 was the Organization of Islamic Conference, and specifically its Ministerial

Committee of Six. In 1996, President Ramos and Foreign Minister Siazon had sought OIC observer status, arguing that, following the Peace Agreement, it was appropriate that the Philippine Government, rather than the MNLF, be invited to OIC meetings, but that Misuari could be the Philippines' representative. The Philippine Government was invited to a meeting of the OIC in 1999, but observer status has yet to be granted. In mid-2000, an OIC meeting in Malaysia called on the Philippine Government to "immediately halt its military offensive against the [MILF] and the Bangsamoro people" and to postpone the ARMM plebiscite to 2003. Despite this setback, in October, an OIC delegation visited the Philippines to assess the situation in Mindanao-Sulu and evaluate progress on the implementation of the 1996 Agreement. There seems to be a possibility of the OIC playing some role in revived peace talks with the MILF, as it did in the 1992–96 negotiations between the Philippine Government and the MNLF. Compared to the situation in the 1970s and 1980s, the Philippine Government appears to have improved its working relationship with the OIC.

Conclusion

Despite the gains made in 1996, the situation in the southern Philippines remains unstable. The settlement with the MNLF, through the SZOPAD and ARMM, looks increasingly fragile. Whether through lack of competence or lack of resources, the SPCPD/ARMM administration has done little to address the developmental demands, or even the basic needs, of Muslim Filipinos, and the ARMM remains an area of widespead poverty. Misuari's leadership appears to be coming under increasing challenge, and relations between the SPCPD/ARMM administration and the central government have deteriorated over the past two years. Meanwhile, the mandated plebiscite for an extended ARMM still looms. Problems of lawlessness associated with the Abu Sayyaf, the MILF, and the MNLF "lost commands" grew in 2000. The kidnapping raids across the border with Malaysia once again demonstrate the fatuousness of the idea that separatist movements like the MNLF, MILF and Abu Sayyaf (or, one might add, the Free Papua Organization [OPM] in Papua or the Free Aceh Movement [GAM] in Aceh) are solely the concerns of individual states. With bomb explosions on New Year's day killing twenty-two people in Metro Manila, there were also suggestions (denied by the MILF leadership) that Muslim guerrillas had moved to the northern cities. Despite the apparent military successes of the AFP, the armed conflict with the MILF continues, alongside efforts to revive the long ongoing peace talks. Recent events in Manila have tended to overshadow the situation in Mindanao. Four years after the Peace Agreement, however, peace remains elusive.

NOTES

1. See, for example, M.S. Lalanto and N.T. Madale, *Autonomy for Muslim Mindanao: The RCC Untold Story* (Marawi City: B-lal Publishers, 1989).
2. See, for example, E. Gutierrez and M. Danguilan-Vitug, "RMM After the Peace Agreement. An Assessment of Local Capacity in the Autonomous Region of Muslim Mindanao", Occasional Paper no. 3 (Institute for Popular Democracy, 1997); and M. Danguilan Vitug and G.M. Gloria, *Under the Crescent Moon: Rebellion in Mindanao* (Quezon City: Ateneo Center for Social Policy and Public Affairs and Institute for Popular Democracy, 2000), pp. 77–94.
3. Former President Fidel Ramos has documented this process in *Break Not the Peace: The Story of the GRP-MNLF Peace Negotiations, 1992-1996* (Quezon City: Friends of Steady Eddie, 1996). See also Fr Eliseo R. Mercado, *Southern Philippines Question: The Challenge of Peace and Development* (Cotabato City: Notre Dame Press, 1999).
4. The 1996 agreement is reproduced in Mercado, op.cit. For a discussion of the circumstances surrounding the agreement, see M. Coronel Ferrer, ed., *The Southern Philippines Council for Peace and Development. A Response to the Controversy* (Quezon City: University of the Philippines Center for Integrative and Development Studies, Program on Peace, Conflict Resolution and Human Rights, and the Mindanao Studies Program, 1997); and F.V. Magdalena, "The peace process in Mindanao: Problems and prospects", in *Southeast Asian Affairs 1997* (Singapore: ISEAS, 1997).
5. A useful exception to this is "Compromising on Autonomy. Mindanao in Transition", *Accord*, Issue 6 (London: Conciliation Resources, 1999).
6. Eric Gutierrez, "The Politics of Transition", *Accord*, Issue 6 (1999), pp. 66–67.
7. Ibid., p. 73.
8. The other main faction, the MNLF-Reformist Group, broke away in 1982, but it seems to have faded out by the 1990s. See R.J. May, "The Moro Movement in Southern Philippines", in *Politics of the Future: The Role of Social Movements*, edited by C. Jennett and R.G. Stewart (Melbourne: Macmillan, 1989).
9. For descriptions of the camps, see, for example, N.G. Quimpo, "The Thorny Issue of the MILF Camps", *Philippine Daily Inquirer*, 31 May, and 2 June 2000; and R. Tiglao, "Special Report" [on the MILF], *Philippine Daily Inquirer*, 7, 8, 9 June 2000.
10. Marites Dañguilan Vitug and Glendam Gloria, *Under the Crescent Moon: Rebellion in Mindanao* (Quezon City: Ateneo Center for Social Policy and Public Affairs, Institute for Popular Democracy, 2000), p. 210.
11. See C.O. Arguillas, "Special Report" [on the "Mindanao Agenda"], *Philippine Daily Inquirer* 8, 10 October 1997.
12. See, for example, *Philippine Daily Inquirer*, 31 May, 1 June, and 15 June 2000; and *Far Eastern Economic Review*, 28 September 2000.

SINGAPORE

ISLAND IN THE WORLD
Globalization and Singapore's Transformation*

Simon S.C. Tay

Introduction: Singapore in Post-Crisis Asia

By the end of 2000, the worst of the economic crisis that had swept through the region from mid-1997 was over for most countries. Difficult challenges, however, still continue in a number of countries, most notably in Indonesia, but also in others, such as the Philippines, Thailand, and Malaysia. The crisis has been short but intense. What has happened is not simply a blip on the chart of growth; the Asian "miracle" will not resume as though nothing ever happened. The crisis has set in train the transformation of society and politics in the region that some have dubbed "creative destruction".[1]

Amidst these considerable changes, there are some who seem to suggest that Singapore has stood still, unchanging. It is true that the Singapore economy weathered the Asian crisis better than most others. It was drawn in late, and more by contagion and knock-on effects than by its own faults. The Singapore economy was also the first in the region to recover. In 2000, growth reached some 9.9 per cent, a figure not seen since 1994.[2] Foreign direct investment returned to pre-crisis levels, with some $9.2 billion for manufacturing, including knowledge-intensive industries like pharmaceuticals and high-end electronics, and a further $1.9 billion in total business spending committed for services.

It is also true that Singapore's politics have not witnessed the dramatic revolt against incumbents that was seen in Indonesia and Malaysia. The People's Action Party (PAP) that has ruled Singapore since 1959 holds 81 out of 83 elected seats in Parliament. It will call for elections in 2001–02 without any real challenge to its hegemony.

However, this chapter argues that the crisis has not left Singapore untouched. Many changes have occurred or are emergent in Singapore. The crisis, the new emerging order or disorder in the region, and the increased global competition in the post-crisis period have set the context for these changes. The changes are, moreover, not only economic, but also political and social. They are not only domestic but also concern Singapore's foreign policy,

SIMON S.C. TAY teaches international law at the National University of Singapore, with a focus on the environment and human rights, and is concurrently chairman of the Singapore Institute of International Affairs and a Nominated Member of Parliament.

with both internal and external dynamics at play. Indeed, real changes are occurring that go well beyond millennial hype or the previous ideas of Singapore being able to "manage" or "re-engineer" its current policies of success. While recognizing the imperatives of change, the ideas of management and re-engineering suggest a sense of calibration and incremental process, in contrast to sweeping and rapid change. In the view of this author, Singapore is being transformed, quite rapidly and fundamentally.

In making this argument, this chapter challenges three ideas. Two concern Singapore itself: first, that Singapore's PAP government is all powerful and unchallenged; and, secondly, that the island-city-state is unique. The third idea to be questioned is a major generalization about globalization. This is the idea that globalization, as Thomas Friedman argues, means that governments today are fitted into a "golden straightjacket", that is, a "one size fits all" policy choice in economic policy and social arrangements.[3]

It is undeniable that Singapore's geography is very different from the other countries of the region, and perhaps most in the world. Densities of space and population, limits of essential natural resources, a high per capita income, and racial mixture all make Singapore different. So does the continued predominance of the PAP. Emphasizing the ideas of PAP omnipotence and Singapore's uniqueness, however, tends to treat Singaporean politics and policies as *sui generis*, explicable only by local context and conditions. Such an approach fails to fully appreciate other factors that pressure and limit the government's policy-making and control of the political agenda. It also disables comparisons between Singapore and other countries.

In contrast, this chapter argues that Singapore's politics and policies can and should be increasingly seen in the context of globalization. It further argues that globalization limits and narrows the power of the PAP government and exposes certain common concerns between Singapore and its neighbours, and indeed, the world.

On the question of globalization, this chapter accepts that ideological differences have narrowed since the end of the Cold War, with far less tolerance in the USA-led international system for differences in economic and political systems. Most dictators are no longer tolerated; democracy is promoted.[4] Open economies are increasingly the norm. However, it is argued here that limited but critical differences can be negotiated by governments. There are trends and pressures but there are also policy choices that governments like Singapore's can take. There is no "straitjacket" as Friedman argues.

In making this argument, the chapter will consider recent initiatives in Singapore's domestic and foreign policies, in the spheres of economics and commerce as well as of society and politics. The mechanisms and processes by which Singapore mediates the impacts of globalization and, indeed, tries to have an influence on external factors will also be considered.[5]

The chapter will begin with a review of economic and political developments in Singapore. It will then set these changes in the context of the region and globalization. In looking at the Singapore economy, moves towards further liberalization and open markets, and calls to reduce the role of the state and government-linked companies will be considered. In politics, the rise of a civil society, and the ambivalent response of the government — at times supportive and, in other instances, constraining — will be emphasized.

Finally, Singapore's foreign policy will be addressed, especially as it relates to the region, but also as it connects to the wider international community. Aspects of traditional security will be examined, alongside new initiatives for freer trade and closer economic co-operation with non-ASEAN partners. In this, the chapter will consider the question whether Singapore is "driving or suffering" the region, as put by one noted commentator, or indeed, is it "leapfrogging" the region in favour of linking across the globe?[6]

The Transformation of Singapore's Economy: An Overview

Singapore's Prime Minister Goh Chok Tong entitled his National Day Rally Speech, "Transforming Singapore".[7] The Prime Minister's speech emphasized "major adjustments in our economy and society" that are required in response to "changes sweeping the world". He stressed that the changes are "discontinuous" and that Singapore cannot depend on "yesterday's experience". He called on Singapore to be "more versatile, and more ready to adapt than ever before" and for Singaporeans to "think and act like revolutionaries", and to "innovate, not merely imitate".[8]

Similar ideas were raised by other political leaders, both before and after the Prime Minister's speech. In some media, Senior Minister Lee Kuan Yew referred to Singapore as being in the process of "creative destruction".[9] The policies being transformed in Singapore were in many different areas: economics, immigration, employment, education, and politics.

In economics, the major trend was the move towards freer markets and less government involvement. In the financial sector, Singapore has further liberalized its banking policies to allow selected foreign banks to have more freedom to compete in the domestic market. (Four licences were awarded in 1999 as Qualifying Foreign Banks [QFBs], with other schemes to expand the privileges of offshore banks.) This was done not because Singapore banks were insolvent or vastly affected by the crisis. In comparison to other countries in the region, Singaporean banks remained strong and creditworthy. Rather, the liberalization of the banking sector was to increase competitiveness in order to be "world class". Regionalization, mergers, and the proliferation of new banking products were also encouraged. The general tenor has been for the Singapore Government, through the Monetary Authority of Singapore, to move towards a "lighter touch" in regulation. Similar changes have been fostered for rules in areas of economic activity, such as insurance, fund management, and the stock exchange.

Liberalization and competition were also keenly felt in the telecommunications sector. The government had earlier ended the state monopoly over both fixed and mobile telecommunications, by corporatizing and publicly listing its former government authority as Singtel. It had, however, proposed a duopoly, between Singtel and the new entrant Star Hub, for fixed telephone lines. In 2000, however, this duopoly was ended prematurely. The government accelerated the opening of the market to more competitors as it was convinced that greater competition would bring more benefits and efficiencies. To do so, it paid a high compensation package to the two incumbent companies.

Other state monopolies, such as electrical energy, were also privatized and opened to competition. In 2001, the energy sector was opened with the devolution of regulation to a new authority, the Energy Market Authority, and free competition allowed among different companies in power generation. These moves towards privatization and markets are not, of course, new policies in the international context. They were pioneered in Thatcherite Britain and have been tried in a number of developing countries in Latin America, Asia, and elsewhere. Where the state provision of these utilities was inadequate, privatization was seen as a critical way of bringing investment and improvement. The Singapore Government's efforts to privatize are aimed at maintaining the country's competitiveness *vis-á-vis* many other regional and global countries. Prime Minister Goh said in his National Day Rally Speech 2000 that, "They [companies in other Asian countries] are no longer sheltered, state-owned companies which we can easily compete against. To stay ahead of our competitors, we must take the leap to a higher level of performance."

Yet the exercise of privatization and moving to the market differs in Singapore in a number of ways. First, the state's provision of services in Singapore was perceived to be mostly efficient and at reasonable prices. Secondly, given Singapore's limited size, there are doubts whether the market in some sectors is large enough to attract sufficient players to bring true competition. Thirdly, privatization in Singapore has traditionally been associated with the devolution of activities to government-linked companies (GLCs), rather than the "real" private sector. In toto, concerns are that an oligarchy of large GLCs and some private foreign companies may come to dominate Singapore, exploiting market strength to set prices and extract unfair profit.

It is therefore notable that the Singapore Government has tried to address perceptions that GLCs overly dominate the economy and unfairly squeeze out private sector competition. In early 2001, the results of a government study were released to show that the contribution of GLCs to the domestic economy was only some 12.9 per cent in 1998. This amounted to more than a quarter of locally-controlled companies' estimated contribution of 46.0 per cent to gross domestic product (GDP), but was still less than what most had thought. Instead, the foreign multinationals, while far fewer than Singapore-controlled companies, were shown to account for the largest part of the economy, with close to 42 per cent of GDP.[10]

Furthermore, the government announced its intention to lower its stake in the GLCs. The move, announced in Parliament in March 2001 by Deputy Prime Minister BG Lee Hsien Loong, would see only controlling stakes in strategic companies vouchsafed, presumably in defence industries, high technology, and key infrastructure. This opens the way to the "privatization" of the Singapore economy in a second sense of the word. Not only would public entities be corporatized but government ownership and control of private economic actors would be diminished.

The manner in which the government will reduce its stake in GLCs, however, has yet to be decided. Government divestment could be through an array of methods, such as giving out shares to citizens, selling shares to the public through listing, selling shares to a single, large shareholder — whether Singaporean or foreign — or by watering down ownership through mergers and acquisitions between GLCs and other companies.

Creating markets and the methods of divestment will be more than mere mechanics. Looking ahead, it is likely that substantial economic, political, and social consequences will flow for Singaporeans.[11]

While the government may seek to reduce its role as a direct actor in the economy and to lighten its touch as regulator, Singapore in 2000–2001 witnessed new efforts at industrial policy to set key directions for investment. The government is promoting growth sectors and high value-added industries to move up the value chain in such areas as life sciences, Internet business, and research and development.[12] Assistance to small and medium-sized enterprises and entrepreneurs was also increased.[13]

Immigration policy and the role of foreigners in the Singapore economy has become a significant issue especially during the crisis years. The government has increasingly welcomed "foreign talent" to live, work, and reside in Singapore. This goes beyond entry level jobs, such as construction-site workers, and domestic helpers. Government leaders are convinced that in order for Singapore to succeed in its next phase of economic development and to compete in the global economy, a different type of work-force will be required. At various levels, and not just the top, workers should be able to acquire, apply, and create knowledge in flexible and innovative ways to generate greater value. Acquiring foreign talent, or "global talent", in this context, is seen as a long-term strategy to enable Singapore to sustain its competitiveness and prosperity.

Yet, while the rationale for welcoming "global talent" is economic, its social dimensions need to be managed. This became especially evident during the economic crisis in 1998 and 1999. As the government continued to allow foreigners to live, work, and settle in Singapore while Singaporeans were experiencing lay-offs, resistance from some Singaporeans grew against the influx of foreign talent. In 2000, Prime Minister Goh addressed the issue in his National Day Rally speech, calling on Singaporeans to change their mindset towards "global talent". He asked Singaporeans to welcome them, offer them the status of permanent residents, and "absorb them as Singaporean citizens, wherever possible". The government itself strongly signalled change in this area by appointing foreigners to head two GLCs, the Development Bank of

Singapore (DBS Bank), and Neptune Orient Lines, the national shipping line that Prime Minister Goh himself once headed before entering full-time politics.

The appointments caused some consternation as a sense of nationalism continues to suggest that a Singaporean should head these Singaporean institutions. At the DBS Bank, the appointment of the new Chief Executive Officer (CEO) was followed by a levy on small accounts previously held by the Post Office Savings Bank (POSB) that had been merged with DBS Bank. This led to public concern that the social mission of the POSB — to encourage all Singaporeans to save — had been lost. Given the ambitions of the foreigner-led corporate leadership to make the bank "world-class", the closure of many branches and a number of unprecedented service lapses attracted considerable attention. At the Neptune Orient Lines, staff changes with the hiring of more foreigners led to the joke that NOL now stood for "No Orientals Left".[14]

The government defended its stand by saying that a Singaporean would be CEO of NOL or any other GLC if he or she was suitable. Prime Minister Goh cautioned against excessive nationalism, however, arguing that the job was too important to be left for Singaporeans only. He rebutted the NOL joke with another: that if not run properly, regardless of nationality, NOL would be "No One Left".[15]

The happenings at these two GLCs echoed concerns in many other companies and sectors. However, the social friction created by the influx of foreign talent in Singapore was eased by the economic recovery. In 2000, more than 110,000 jobs were created, far surpassing the 40,000 in 1999. Retrenchments also tailed off, falling from 14,600 in 1999 to 11,500. As a result, unemployment fell to 2.8 per cent in December 2000.[16] Employed and reasonably paid, most Singaporeans did not complain too much. Another downturn such as the one in 1998 might, however, bring more tensions to the surface.

Two other areas of possible social stress relate to structural unemployment and to a widening income gap in Singapore's globalized economy. These by-products of globalization are common to most developed economies. It is widely accepted that globalization benefits an élite, while creating income gaps between them, the middle class, and the lowest earners in society.[17] The example of Singapore had in the past bucked this trend: growth and globalization in Singapore had raised the standards of living for the vast majority of its people, and provided nearly full employment. If further globalization accelerates income disparities and unemployment for some, such trends will require political attention and the crafting of appropriate policy responses.

In 1999 and 2000, it was notable that many of the new jobs created were different from the jobs lost during the crisis. The changing structure of the economy was forcing many of the more low-skill jobs to move to other countries. In large part, this is indeed consciously encouraged by the Singapore Government as it believes that Singapore cannot compete for lower value-added jobs with countries that have much larger populations, lower wages, and cheaper land. Hence, the Singapore work-force would necessarily have to change if structural unemployment is to be avoided. The government estimates that, in ten to fifteen years, the economy will require a work-force in which 65 per cent have at least post-secondary education. However, as of 1999, only 35 per cent of Singaporean workers have post-secondary, or higher education.[18] A widening income gap among Singaporeans has recently been noted. A newspaper report in 2000 headlined a study which found that among the bottom 10 per cent of society, including those who were unemployed or were retired, the average income was $133 per month. This received considerable attention among the public and in Parliament.

The government pointed out, however, that the income of those employed was considerably higher, and argued that the bottom 10 per cent on average enjoyed a "modest but reasonable standard of living".[19] Moreover, the government argued that redistribution and wage suppression of those who were doing well were not feasible in a globalized economy. Nor were measures to artificially bolster the wages of entry-level jobs, as "companies will simply relocate to lower-cost countries".[20]

The government's response to the widening income gap was, therefore, to reinforce the idea of meritocracy, a foundational idea in the imagining of modern Singapore, to emphasize that those who work hard can get ahead in life, regardless of their background. This emphasis has brought more focus on the education policy, not just for its own sake, but as a vital complement to the globalization process.

Education in Singapore has moved in the past few years away from rote learning for students, to increasingly emphasize new elements. Perhaps the most notable of these elements is creative and critical thinking. The government budgets of the crisis years and after have recognized the new importance of education with increased funding.

Beyond the formal education sector and schools, worker upgrading and the learning of new skills, including in the smaller and medium-sized enterprises, have received more emphasis. Schemes to help achieve this include the Manpower Development Assistance Scheme to help those in the work-force to upgrade their skills and knowledge continuously; and the Lifelong Learning Endowment Fund announced by Prime Minister Goh in August 2000, with a budget of $1 billion, to help equip workers with the skills to take on existing and new jobs, create new products and services, and capture new markets in this stage of economic development.

The government also moved to help businesses that were not doing well or facing diminishing prospects to cope with change. This was, however, not to be done by hand-outs or protective subsidies. Rather, the approach is to prod these businesses to either upgrade and modernize their operations, or shift to industries with better prospects. One sector to be targeted will be the retail sector, for which a ten-year strategic plan, titled Retail 21, will shortly be released. Within the retail sector, particular attention will be given to the neighbourhood shops, markets, and hawker centres in public housing developments, as these connect to the "grass-root" constituencies of smaller and often family-run businesses, and therefore potentially impact political support. In cases where small retailers and especially family-run shops decide to cease business, the government has in fact mooted the idea of a one-time *ex gratia* payment to them.

Singapore has moved away in these past decades from socialism and traditional forms of state welfare; indeed, political leaders have often warned against "welfarism" as a cancer that eats away at the motivation to work. This should not be mistaken, however, to mean that the Singapore Government does not give out subsidies and grants. Rather, where such payments are made, principles such as requiring co-payment from the citizen have been adopted and private charity groups are encouraged. Efforts are also made to specifically target those in the lower economic strata, and to give the benefits through long-term endowments, or through the citizen's Central Provident Fund (CPF) account, which creates savings for retirement. Also emphasized is the need for the government as a whole to generate budget surpluses to ensure that all Singaporeans benefit from the nation's success.

In January 2001, Singaporeans received a first payment of the CPF Top-up promised in August 2000. The CPF Top-up is a tangible way of sharing the nation's success with Singaporeans and, for the first time, was structured to give more to those in the lower income groups. Other rebates on taxation and government charges were also given, again targeting the poorer households and lower income taxpayers.[21] Efforts to help pensioners, to some degree, and for the medical care of the elderly and poor were also strengthened.[22]

The Minister for Finance, Dr Richard Hu, set the context in his Budget Speech 2001:

> While we make these adjustments to anticipate and embrace global trends and changes, we must continue to be mindful of our local context: those who can run faster should pave the way for the rest; however, those who may be unwittingly left behind must not be left with no help.
>
> The government realises that realignments of our economy have often meant displacement of jobs, or even disappearance of industries, but for every door closed, we have opened many others, leading to greater opportunities. We understand that it is not easy for workers to continually learn new skills and work in a new environment, or for enterprises to quickly change direction and pursue business prospects in new areas.
>
> It takes a great deal of courage to embrace changes, and take the steps to walk through new doors of opportunity. The transition often entails adjustments which are sometimes painful. But we want to help. We want to lessen the hardship for those who find it difficult to adapt to the changes. But change we must. And at the end of the day, we have to ensure that every Singaporean has a place in the Singapore of the new millennium.

There has been a growing realization in Singapore that the imperatives of trying to enter the new economy and to transform Singapore — with a more creative and critically aware work-force and citizenry, considerable socio-economic change and adjustment, and a widening income gap — have social and political implications. Immigration, education, and social assistance policies have therefore become imperatives, setting new directions, and receiving more funding. What about politics itself?

Singaporean Politics: No Transformation but Tentative Change?
Changes in Singapore politics are not as dramatic as those that have swept other countries in the region or as transformative as the economic changes surveyed. Indeed, in politics, there is a sense of tentative change, and of a government seeking to manage social change. There has been little progress in party politics, with the PAP continuing to hold 81 out of the 83 elected seats in Parliament. There has, however, been some development in the arena of civil society. This is arguably a precondition for a sustainable democratic ethos and further development of the political system, as well as a marker of the relative state of political openness in Singapore. It has been argued, in this regard, that Singapore since 1997 has been witnessing a government project to manage civil society. In this, the government has encouraged and shaped what it sees to be positive elements, and to constrain and contain what it deems to be negative ones.[23]

In endorsing civil society in 1997, Prime Minister Goh tied it to a wider ranging "new vision" for the nation, called Singapore 21. Civil society was one of five elements identified as supporting such a vision. The idea of Singapore 21 was explained by the Prime Minister:

> We need a new vision for Singapore, an ideal, a fresh mindset. We need to move beyond material progress, to a society which places people at its very centre. Singapore 21 is my team's vision for the future of Singapore, a Singapore where people make the difference, where each citizen is valued, a Singapore which is Our Best Home, an ideal home which we all help to build.
>
> ... The Government can provide the conditions for security and economic growth. But in the end, it is people who give feeling, a human touch, a sense of pride and achievement, the warmth. So beyond developing physical infrastructure and hardware, we need to develop our social infrastructure and software. ... We need to go beyond economic and material needs, and reorient society to meet the intellectual, emotional, spiritual, cultural and social needs of our people.

Similarly, in his much earlier speech, then Arts and Information Minister George Yeo also argued that civil society would have the function of enhancing the citizens' "emotional attachment" to Singapore, fostering a "soul" and thereby making the nation-state more attractive and competitive.[24] Functional reasons for civil society suggested by various government leaders have included:

(1) the idea of Singapore as home;[25] (2) to assist decentralization and self-governance in local government;[26] (3) to assist in the delivery of welfare, education, and other services, so that voluntary welfare associations can make greater contributions in tandem with the government, including in terms of funding.

The above reasons reveal the concept of civil society and political participation that the Singapore political leadership holds. This can be compared to the different and more liberal conceptions of civil society as being opposed to the state, representing a pluralist society with increasing democratic participation. The Singaporean conception of "civil society" would, in contrast, be expected to be relatively conservative socially and politically, largely middle class, and nationalistic.

From 1998, civil society in Singapore received increasing emphasis from the government with a major conference and the Singapore 21 process. At the conference, the keynote speech given by George Yeo, the then Minister for Information and the Arts, recognized that civil society would rise in parallel to the government, as its equal.[27] He saw this as inevitable, given technological and other changes, and recognized that civil society would be better than government in a number of areas:

> [S]tate-society relations in Singapore … [are] also going through a major transformation. In the old paradigm, the state was hard while society was soft. In the web world, the state and society exist in parallel. The organization of Singapore is becoming less hierarchical.[28]

> Many government committees have become civic committees, like those involved in keeping Singapore clean and green, discouraging smoking, promoting healthy lifestyle and the speaking of Mandarin. … Civil society is also flourishing in other sectors. The number of civic organizations based on religious beliefs have increased. Many are involved in running community hospitals, hospices, halfway houses and other welfare facilities.

Beyond this, the Minister also recognized some groups that were encouraging Singaporeans to be "more socially conscious", such as the Association of Women for Action and Research (AWARE), the Roundtable, and Sintercom, a website-based group that hosts discussion on policy and political events. Minister Yeo, however, also gave more cautious signals to the emergent civil society. He called on civil society groups to act within the national interest, or what the Minister called, "the Singapore idea": "Today, [these groups] operate within the bounds of the state and increasingly with a common Singaporean starting point. … As our common consciousness grows, the bounds of debate will be relaxed but, realistically, we will always need an outer perimeter to hold our society together". The Minister also cautioned that "old instincts" of top-down control are "sometimes die-hard", and that Singaporeans would have to strike a balance between bottom-up approaches and top-down concerns.[29]

The Singapore 21 process involved another young leader, Education Minister Teo Chee Hean, and ten Members of Parliament, appointed by Prime Minister Goh to consider the changes in attitudes and "heartware" that would be necessary for Singapore in the twenty-first century. This work commissioned five committees for specific subjects, including one to study the processes of decision-making and participation and their relationship to state power and efficiency. This was framed as the dilemma — "consultation and consensus versus decisiveness and quick action" — to recognize the tensions in policy.[30] The committee on this issue was co-chaired by a union leader Lim Swee Say (who is now Acting Minister for the Environment) and by Nominated (non-party) Member of Parliament (NMP), Simon S.C. Tay.

After considerable public participation and comment, the Singapore 21 report was published as, "Together, We Make the Difference". One outcome of the report, by the Ministry of Community Development, was a volunteer centre, to serve as a clearing house for ideas as well as a training centre for skills and know-how needed for the management of non-profit organizations. The Singapore 21 report was debated in Parliament and endorsed, albeit with some reservations.

Senior Minister Lee Kuan Yew perhaps exemplified these reservations in his remarks in the parliamentary debate on the Singapore 21 report.[31] He suggested that achieving even half of the recommendations of the Singapore 21 report, including its recommended principles that "Every Singaporean Matters" and for "Active Citizens", would take twenty years and "that [would be] a tremendous achievement".

On active citizens, in particular, Senior Minister Lee disagreed with the analysis of NMP Simon Tay.[32] NMP Tay had argued that "[o]ur desired society is not one in which government is strong and people are weak". He had urged that the rise of civil society (or "active citizens") be seen as an independent entity that, without being oppositional, would complement the state. He had concluded that, as civil society grew, then "if a government of the future should fail ... but if there is an active, able and responsible people sector, it need not be our (that is, Singapore's) end." The Senior Minister disagreed. He suggested that it was not likely that civil society would "throw up another leadership". This was because of Singapore's different culture and history.

In this exchange, we see both the differences and the limits in political discourse in present-day Singapore. Civil society in this context is not a simple release of energies, with an underlying trust that its activities will be within the bounds of law and order and other concerns, and largely beneficial.[33] Rather, the government policy seems to suggest mixed imperatives of encouragement, control, and (ultimately, in the mind of Senior Minister Lee) containment. This suggests a deliberate and deliberated project to manage Singaporean civil society.

Nevertheless, the years since 1997 have witnessed an increase in public advocacy in Singapore by civil society groups and individuals. This was demonstrable in a number of different areas of interest, including the environment and international issues of concern, and was reported widely by the media. Some examples include:

1. Reactions to reports of riots and rapes in Indonesia in June 1998 by the Singapore women's rights group, AWARE, which launched a public petition to the Indonesian Government, organized an exhibition, and issued public statements condemning the gross human rights violations, and calling for full investigations by the Indonesian authorities and the United Nations;

2. Environmental issues, such as the haze caused by Indonesian fires, were taken up by the Singapore Environment Council, the umbrella organization for green groups. On 4–5 June 1998, it held its first international dialogue involving regional and international non-governmental organizations (NGOs) and issued a statement calling for action by the Indonesian Government, and other actors. In mid-June 1998, it met with senior ASEAN officials to present the major recommendations of the statement. At the end of 1999, a delegation of NGOs visited Indonesia to meet government officials and Indonesian NGO counterparts.

3. The emergence or increasing activity of civil society groups that emphasize civic and political freedoms. These have included the Roundtable, which includes two Nominated Members of Parliament; the working committee on civil society (known as TWC) that served as a coalition or umbrella organization for different groups of diverse interests, including the arts and social welfare; and the Think Centre, that has held a number of political talks, and organized a rally to mark International Human Rights Day in 2001.

4. The creation of a "Speaker's Corner" that allows Singapore citizens to speak in public without prior permit, after a proposal by a civil society group.[34]

5. In late November 2000, a wide array of Singaporean civil society groups took part in the first ASEAN People's Assembly. This event, organized by the ASEAN Institutes of Strategic and International Studies, brought together some 300 representatives from NGOs and other civic groups to discuss regional issues in parallel to the ASEAN Summit. They included members from AWARE, the Roundtable, the Singapore Environment Council, Youth Environment Council, Sintercom, TWC, academic activists, and others.

These events are not monumentual, compared with the vast changes that have swept other countries in the region. They are, however, notable in view of the fact that the Singapore economy was spared the sort of crisis that triggered off political and social changes among its neighbours. They are also notable in an environment in which a wide array of laws continue to control the constitutional rights of speech, assembly, and association.[35]

The developments in Singapore's civil society are also noteworthy in the context of globalization in that a number of the issues, such as the events in Indonesia and the regional haze pollution, have had cross-border, or even global, ramifications. There are signs that Singapore's civil society is developing more connections to the regional and international community, as part of what some have called "globalization from below".[36] The corollary of this observation is that Singaporean civil society has not drawn strong links to the domestic socio-economic issues of globalization, such as the dominance of GLCs in the economy, the possibility of structural unemployment, and the widening income gap.

However, while civil society has grown in Singapore and forged some links with regional and international groups, the Singapore Government still polices its connections to political society. In 2000, a Political Donations Act was passed in Singapore that allows the authorities to declare a civil society group as a political organization and then to forbid it from receiving any donations from sources outside Singapore.

One particular incident in early 2001 may exemplify the limits that civil society groups face and the tentative nature of political change in Singapore. In organizing an event to mark International Human Rights Day, the Think Centre political discussion group invited a number of speakers and an audience to the Speakers' Corner. Subsequently, however, the group was investigated by the police for organizing an illegal demonstration. This was the first and only incident, so far, to be investigated. The event could possibly be construed as an illegal demonstration because, under the existing law, the permission to speak, which is given freely at the Speakers' Corner, does not abrogate the need for a licence for a demonstration. The definition of a demonstration, moreover, includes any organized assembly of five or more persons. The police also drew attention to the fact that the participants at the event clenched their fists and chanted slogans, indicating that it was a demonstration. The issue was debated in Parliament between the government and a Nominated Member of Parliament, with concerns that the case, and the overly broad laws, could have a chilling effect on free speech and the use of the Speakers' Corner.[37] In the event, the organizers of the event were issued a warning by the police but not prosecuted in the courts.

This incident suggests a number of different elements in the political landscape of Singapore. The first element is that, contrary to what some believe, citizens and civil society groups in Singapore, while still relatively conservative, are not moribund. A second element is that the attitude of the government in dealing with civil society groups is ambivalent and shifts between allowance — by creating the Speakers' Corner — and close inspection, in scrutinizing any possible "abuse" of its use. A third element that may be noted is that public and parliamentary discussion of the incident was considerable and quite unconstrained. In this context, the outcome — the issuance of an official warning but no prosecution — may be interpreted as showing the tentative nature of government acceptance and accommodation of political changes in Singapore.

More signposts, and perhaps more incidents, may be expected in the run-up to and the conduct of the next general election, which is due before the end of 2002, and widely expected in the second half of 2001.

The Context of Globalization

What do these recent economic, social and political changes in Singapore mean in the broader context of the region? Is Singapore an economic, social, and political anomaly in Southeast Asia? Or are there examples that can be shared and adapted in dealing with the aftermath of the crisis and the continuing challenge of development in the face of globalization? These are significant issues not just for Singapore but also for the region and how we think of globalization.

When globalization first became a buzzword, the emphasis was on its inevitability and, largely, on its benefits. The benefits were chiefly, but not solely, economic. Openness to the international market, and the harnessing of foreign investment and trade, in concert with new technologies, promised a new impetus for growth and development in both developing and developed countries. The promise was felt with special keenness in East Asia, particularly the newly industrialized economies (NIEs) and the ASEAN-4. This bloom of optimism has faded in the economic crisis that swept through the region. In the wake of the crisis, there are increasing questions about international economic structures as well as about national policies in response to the realities of international finance. Some countries that were already open to the international system have erected partial barriers, such as the currency and other controls in Malaysia. Others who were only beginning to open themselves may give pause to further liberalization. A greater awareness and caution about the process of liberalization and the institutional prerequisites for sequenced and successful liberalization is to be welcomed. In the aftermath of the crisis, and in the wake of the chaos and disagreement at the WTO ministerial meeting in Seattle, many more openly doubt the benefits of globalization.

With globalization, the nation-state has not disappeared but its ability to effectively govern on its own has diminished.[38] A global law has arisen in tandem with globalization. This intrudes into arenas that were traditionally considered to belong to a state's "domestic" jurisdiction. In the economic sphere, global law limits the range of actions that a state can take against private investors, and increases the rights that such non-state actors hold against the state. This is notwithstanding that such private actors are mere companies within the territory of that state. In international trade, the WTO regime binds states to observe certain rules and principles, and restricts their freedom to close their borders as they choose. The power of a state to control its domestic economy and markets as it chooses are thought to be increasingly constrained. So too are state policies to subsidize, to protect companies owned by the state or preferred nationals, to tax, and to provide social services as a safety net. Global law is also controversial in areas such as human rights and environmental protection. Both often challenge the internal system and policies of state.[39] Both fields are strongly associated with non-governmental organizations and what has come to be called "international civil society". For these reasons, many states, especially those from the developing world, have resisted these aspects of global law as intrusions on their sovereignty.[40]

In this context, many have made calls to change the international system in order to address the ill-effects of globalization.[41] These range from relatively modest but often sophisticated changes in the governance of various international institutions to bolder, more politically strident suggestions, such as an international tax that would be shared out to the developing countries.

There are strong reasons for revisiting the questions of global governance. Yet even if most agree that something must be done, there is no consensus on what that should be. What has received considerably less attention in this debate, however, is what each state can and should do for itself at the national level, in facing globalization.

States need not give up in the face of globalization. They are not faced with an "either/or choice" in response. There is no "golden straitjacket" for the state, as argued by Thomas Friedmann. In the economic sphere, despite the increased movement of people and companies, states can still raise taxes. This is provided they have demonstrable competitive advantages over competing states, for example, in physical or social infrastructure.[42] In the social sphere, a state has choices for the allocation of resources to provide social safety nets, education, and other public goods. These choices can vary in quality and philosophy that will make real and significant differences to the citizen, especially those nearest the bottom and those struggling to cope with globalization. In politics, states can still use traditional police powers over their citizens, or even control culture and social values in their societies. Even the Internet can be policed.[43] Such controls may draw occasional criticism but the international community will react only where there are gross and systemic violations of human rights and other norms.

Globalization is, as such, not predestined. It is a consequence of policies actively chosen and pursued by the state. Viewing globalization as a choice does not of course suggest that it is a choice without potential costs. Consequently, state policy towards globalization is neither one of complete control nor of unreserved openness. Like the common Asian saying, it is not a matter of opening the windows, but of putting up a screen against flies, or of having a fly swatter handy.

Singapore, in this context, provides an example of state policy in the face of globalization. The Republic has traditionally been porous to foreign trade, investment, and influence and is increasingly so today in the post-crisis period. A recent study to measure globalization has in fact ranked Singapore as number one in the world.[44] Indeed, sovereignty and power are constant concerns for a small state like Singapore. Some may fear such openness as a potential source of external interference that can adversely affect their economy, national stability, and cohesion.

What can such a small and globalized state do in the face of globalization? The choices made by Singapore are often overlooked or it is assumed that it has no choices at all. Too often, in the heyday of the "Asian" miracle, the formula for success was in danger of being over-simplified to mean more openness to everything and the diminution of governance in all areas. The danger in the aftermath of the Asian crisis, however, is that the lessons of pain will also become over-simplified. In reaction to the crisis, some may come to believe that openness to the international markets and globalization is bad, and therefore borders should be closed.

Singapore, however, has gone the other way. In the face of the crisis, the country has not only sought to weather the storm but indeed to, consciously and without external IMF compulsion, open more windows and doors to allow in foreign influence, investors, and competition. Its domestic economic policies from the late 1990s and into the new century must be understood in this context, with their increasing emphasis on liberalization, privatization, and markets. The role of the state as an active and dominant actor in the economy is more limited. The role of the state in regulating economic activity must be lighter, as well as controlled by good governance. However, the role of the state continues, and indeed can and should be stronger in providing incentives and infrastructure for new investments and new sectors, and in promoting efforts to groom local enterprises.

In politics, the regional crisis has been accompanied by dramatic social and political changes, as seen in the Philippines and Indonesia. Some view this as a demonstration of the worldwide trend towards democracy. Singapore has not, in contrast, witnessed street protests and demonstrations, or pushed existing leaders out of office. This, however, should not be mistaken for the perpetuation of the status quo. During the crisis years, and despite continued political control, smaller but perceptible changes can be discerned in Singapore's politics. There have been a number of signals that demonstrate the Singapore Government's greater acceptance and even encouragement of civil society and greater participation by citizens.

In social policies, the Budget of 2001 shows a range of assistance that a state can give to its citizens, provided that it has been fiscally prudent and successful in providing overall growth, without the more traditional and more costly methods of state welfare or high income-tax rates. The Singaporean policies in these spheres demonstrate that it has the makings of a novel approach for a new age of globalization. It shows that the state can and should make special efforts to target assistance to the less well-off and to empower them to participate in and benefit from the new economy. In Singapore, there is no safety net that is comparable to the elaborate systems seen in some European states. Instead of a safety net that can save but also ensnare, the approach here may be characterized as a "trampoline" to help citizens, when they fall, to bounce back up and go higher.

The changes and emphases that we can see in Singapore through the crisis years and into 2001 — in education, training, the creation of special programmes to target the less well-off and most vulnerable — are by no means perfect or accepted by all. They are, however, national policies that attempt to deal with the social and political elements that emerge alongside economic globalization. In this regard, they are an example of what a state can do — pending any change in the global system — to take its own initiatives to govern globalization.

Singapore and the Region: Driving or Suffering?

What do the developments of the crisis years mean for Singapore's relations with its neighbours and its role in ASEAN? Are Singapore's policies towards globalization bringing it closer to its neighbours or driving it further away? Is Singapore "driving" or "suffering" the region?[45]

With increasing economic progress and political stature, the PAP government in Singapore has been able to demonstrate considerable strength in relation not only to domestic politics and the people of Singapore but also in its management of relations with many of the neighbouring states and multinational companies. Some, such as Ambassador Tommy Koh, have indeed suggested that Singapore is "punching above its weight".[46] Others suggest that Singapore is becoming more global in outlook, with a "more central position on the world stage".[47] The argument is that while Singapore is small, size alone is no longer the indicator for assessing a state's relative importance. With economic strength and the increasing importance of multilateral institutions and processes, Singapore is believed by the proponents of this view to rank more highly than it did in the past and more highly than some larger states today.

On the other hand, others such as the late Michael Leifer provide a more realist reading of the current situation of Singapore in the context of the region. While admitting both the diplomatic and economic achievements of Singapore, Professor Leifer gave more emphasis to Singapore's vulnerability. He examined the tensions between Singapore and both Indonesia and Malaysia during the crisis and its aftermath, and concluded that the state had come "full circle" to the initial period of instability and vulnerability that characterized the circumstances surrounding Singapore's independence in 1965. Leifer said:

> Singapore's vulnerability is not only a function of its minuscule size but also of a confined location wedged between politically unpredictable neighbours, which have always been uncomfortable with the island-state's prevailing ethnic-Chinese identity and its accompanying economic role. … They are facts of geopolitical life that cannot be wished away.
> […]

> Matters have come full circle for Singapore but with a difference. An initial experience [upon independence] of an acute vulnerability was succeeded by economic and then diplomatic accomplishments with most likely adversaries transformed into working regional partners. Indeed, with the end of the Cold War, Singapore was able to ... drive the region in the direction of unprecedented multilateral security dialogue. That ... was succeeded by a dramatic reversal of economic fortunes with political turbulence. ... Singapore served as a soft target for political fall out. ...[I]ts security environment ... displays a disconcerting continuity.[48]

There are differences between the views of Koh and others, and those expressed by Leifer. However, these are not black and white disagreements but nuances that relate not so much to the basic facts as to the weightage given to different elements in Singapore's foreign policy. A survey of Singapore and the region in 2000 shows both elements of the state driving the region and suffering it. The same actions that allow and perhaps require Singapore to try to drive the region also tend to add to its "suffering" the region. Developments in the external economic policy as well as Singapore's security concerns demonstrates this duality.

External Economic Policy
In external economic policy, Singapore in 2000 aimed to reach out to and influence others in Asia to continue with policies of openness, especially in the sphere of trade. This is clearly seen in the bilateral trade agreements that Singapore has undertaken, or is studying. In 2000, Singapore concluded a bilateral free trade agreement with New Zealand. By the end of 2000, it had also begun negotiations with Japan, the USA, and Mexico.

Singapore's bilateral initiatives came in the wake of the failed WTO ministerial meeting in Seattle at the end 1999 and the stall in negotiations thereafter. They should also be viewed in the context of demonstrated limits to regional economic and trade agreements in ASEAN and the wider Asia-Pacific.[49] Singapore's initiatives do not constitute an abandonment of the global or regional level efforts, however. Rather, they are meant to be catalysts for global and regional liberalization. Singapore is not the only state in the world seeking to do this,[50] although it is by far the most active state in ASEAN on this issue.

By these bilateral initiatives, Singapore is thus seeking to drive not only the region but the global processes too, in tandem with other like-minded states. There is, of course, a national interest in this: Singaporean companies, consumers, and the economy do stand to gain from the free trade initiatives. This is not surprising, given the fact that trade is 300 per cent of Singapore's gross domestic product and is the economy's life-blood. The initiatives also connect to the domestic policies to liberalize in order to increase competition and efficiencies, surveyed earlier in this chapter. Singapore's example demonstrates the continued belief of its government in economic openness as opposed to isolation, and free trade over protected trade.

Singapore's bilateral initiatives, if concluded successfully, will also help strengthen Southeast Asia's links to its major trade partners in Northeast Asia and across the Pacific. The bilateral agreements should not produce closed trade arrangements; rather, they should be regarded as building blocks for the regional and global trade liberalization regimes. They must be WTO-consistent, or even go beyond WTO commitments in covering new areas.[51] The bilateral initiatives have not hurt anyone. There has been no reduction or delay in Singapore's commitments to ASEAN countries and to the ASEAN Free Trade Area (AFTA).

From this, one might expect at least a neutral response from other ASEAN members. Yet, there are signs that misunderstanding and perhaps envy are brewing over Singapore's free trade initiatives. Malaysian premier Mahathir Mohamad has voiced concern that goods transiting through Singapore could enter other ASEAN countries through the "back door", in the process circumventing AFTA provisions.[52] To this, there is a relatively short answer: trade agreements provide for rules of origin that stipulate what goods will qualify. For AFTA, only goods with 40 per cent or more of domestic inputs will benefit. As such, there is no "back door", as Dr Mahathir fears.

Beyond this, however, there are general reservations that are more difficult to address. A number of ASEAN states have become more reserved about globalization after the Asian crisis, as noted earlier. Malaysia has not only erected capital controls but delayed the opening of some sectors, most notably their automobile industry. This is despite the fact that, in general, the Malaysian economy is one of the most open in the world.[53] Other states that are more closed, like Vietnam, have remained cautious. ASEAN as a whole has decided against linking AFTA to the economic zone of Australia and New Zealand. It may, therefore, be disturbing for these states to see Singapore going ahead on its own, even if there is no agreed reason to prevent it from doing so. In this regard, the main basis for the reaction of some against Singapore's free trade initiatives may not be so much economic, but political.

Seeing Singapore ride out most of the crisis and coming out stronger has produced a certain envy in some quarters and renewed tensions between neighbours. Seeing it taking a "driving" role on trade issues, and in bilateral discussions with many of the major economies of the world, could have compounded that sentiment.

These sentiments show that even as Singapore seeks to "drive" the issue of free trade, it is "suffering" the region. Similar factors can be seen in Singapore's security concerns.

Security and Vulnerability

From late 1999, Singapore's vulnerability showed in the context of marked instability in the neighbouring states and tensions with both Malaysia and Indonesia. The viability of ASEAN as an institution for peaceful co-existence and closer co-operation also required attention.

Ties with Malaysia had deteriorated after 1996, following comments by Singapore's Senior Minister (and first Prime Minister) Lee Kuan Yew concerning Malaysia's preferential treatment of its Malay population. In 1997, further controversy arose over comments by Senior Minister Lee on high crime rates in the Malaysian state of Johor. By 1999, a slew of differences divided the two neighbours over problems such as the continued supply of water from Malaysia to Singapore; the redevelopment of land in Singapore belonging to the Malayan Railway; the re-siting of Singapore's customs checkpoint from the city to the northern point of Woodlands; the right of Malaysian citizens who have worked in Singapore to withdraw their money from Singapore's Central Provident Fund when they leave the country; and the accusation by Malaysian leaders that currency and share speculation in Singapore had undermined Malaysia's economy. Despite a number of meetings between the premiers of both countries, these issues were not resolved.

Against this background, Singapore's relations with Malaysia witnessed some improvements in 2000. In August, Senior Minister Lee visited Kuala Lumpur to meet with senior leaders. As the deterioration in bilateral ties had been triggered by his comments, the visit was seen as an effort in personal diplomacy. Senior Minister Lee expressed the hope that the differences he had with Malaysian leaders of his generation might be lessened with a succeeding generation. The visit was met with wide and positive media coverage in both countries. Exchanges followed between the two countries, such as between arts groups and the youth wings of the dominant PAP and UMNO political parties.

In January 2001, the Malaysian Deputy Prime Minister, Abdullah Badawi, made a high profile visit to Singapore, bringing several other ministers and state chief ministers with him. The visit to Singapore was, like the Senior Minister's visit to Malaysia, held in an amiable and friendly atmosphere. More ministerial and other visits will follow.

The possibility of a deterioration in sentiment cannot, however, be ruled out. In October 2000, a remark by the Senior Minister concerning medium-range missiles to be purchased by Singapore from the United States provided a spark. His off-the-cuff response to a question by a journalist that, "The missiles will face nowhere, but they are there to welcome whoever intends harm" was regarded as provocative by sections of the Malaysian media. Notably, however, Malaysian leaders did not respond negatively. In early 2001, both sides became involved in discussing how Malays, a minority in Singapore and the ruling majority in Malaysia, had fared under the different policies of the two states. This again raised tensions on both sides of the border.

In both cases, efforts to put ties on a more even keel can be discerned. It remains an open question, however, whether the two governments can make progress on the outstanding issues between them. Much will depend not only on Singapore but on the internal dynamics of Malaysia.

Ties with Indonesia also fluctuated in 1999-2000. From the 1970s and into the early 1990s, ties between Singapore and Indonesia under President Soeharto had been strong. Unease set in, however, from the mid-1990s, with concerns over succession to President Soeharto. From 1998, ties deteriorated sharply when Senior Minister Lee remarked that "the market" was uncomfortable with the then Science and Technology Minister, B.J. Habibie, becoming the Vice-President to Soeharto. Upon assuming office as Vice-President and then President, after Soeharto's resignation, Habibie continued to resent Singapore. He claimed that it was a country of "real racists" and referred to Singapore as a "little red dot" on the map.

Against this background, the new Indonesian President Abdurrahman Wahid promised a new start at better ties. President Wahid made Singapore the destination of his first overseas visit. Singapore Prime Minister Goh Chok Tong reciprocated, visiting Jakarta with offers of support and new schemes of financial assistance. Singapore also joined other ASEAN member states in supporting Indonesia's unity against separatist movements. Despite this, however, Indonesia's instability and troubles in different provinces continued to be a potential source of concern for Singapore.

Moreover, in November 2000, President Wahid surprised many by lashing out at the Singapore Government immediately after the ASEAN Informal Summit, held in Singapore. In remarks to Indonesians gathered at the Indonesian embassy in Singapore, President Wahid accused Singaporean leaders of being unsupportive of Indonesia and of his initiative to include East Timor and Papua New Guinea in ASEAN. He alleged that they looked down on Malays and suggested that Indonesia might join Malaysia to cut off Singapore's water supply. President Wahid came under criticism from within Indonesia for his remarks. The Singapore Government also issued a number of clarifications and corrections about his statements. The foreign ministers of the two countries met soon after at the sidelines of an ASEAN meeting. They appeared to play down the differences.

In early 2001, President Wahid came to Singapore to preside over the opening of a billion dollar natural gas pipeline between Indonesia and Singapore. This seemed to suggest a reassertion of rationality and shared long-term interests. Correspondingly, Senior Minister Lee Kuan Yew visited Jakarta as he had earlier accepted a role as an adviser to President Wahid. Nevertheless, a degree of unease has come into the bilateral relationship, that adds to Singapore's sense of vulnerability in relation to neighbouring states.

Given these perceptions of vulnerability, Singapore has been a strong advocate of a balance of power in the region, involving non-regional actors. The U.S. presence continues to be encouraged by Singaporean leaders as a cornerstone for regional security.[54] Similarly, the Five Power Defence Arrangement, involving Australia, New Zealand, and United Kingdom together with Malaysia and Singapore, continues to occupy an important place in Singapore's defence policy.

Beyond security, Singapore's approach is generally to favour inclusive processes in different circles of political engagement and to creatively link

ASEAN to wider groups. This can be seen in different fora. In the ASEAN Plus Three process, Singapore and others have linked the ten ASEAN members to China, Japan, and Korea. Yet even here, Singapore has emphasized that this process should not be a closed bloc that seeks to displace the wider Asia-Pacific forums, such as the Asia–Pacific Economic Co-operation (APEC) and the ASEAN Regional Forum (ARF). In the new East Asia–Latin American Forum that Singapore initiated with Chile, Australia and New Zealand have joined on the East Asian side. These efforts, as well as the bilateral trade and economic initiatives reviewed earlier, help Singapore to engage with non-ASEAN members and keep them interested, involved, and active in regional issues.

Co-operation with Other ASEAN Members
Despite these tensions with Indonesia and Malaysia, the Singapore Government continued to give attention and priority to ASEAN and its members. Ties with the other members on balance were positive, and those with Thailand and Brunei, especially, were strong.

The Singapore Government continued to be active in promoting ASEAN as a means of regional co-operation, focusing its efforts on addressing the division between older and newer ASEAN members and on economic initiatives. Foreign Minister S. Jayakumar was perhaps the most self-critical speaker at the 2000 ASEAN Ministerial Meeting. Singapore continued to work towards greater economic integration with its neighbours through AFTA, the ASEAN Investment Area (AIA), and e-ASEAN initiatives. Deeper economic integration will enhance ASEAN's attractiveness as a destination for global foreign direct investments (FDIs). Singaporean leaders and analysts believe that this is particularly crucial, given the rise of China and the diversion of foreign investment and interest to Northeast Asia.

However, the pace of ASEAN integration is not up to Singapore alone to "drive". It must depend on the consensus of members. Indeed, if Singapore were to seek to strongly "drive" integration on its own, it is likely that it would be resented. As such, Singapore has refrained from pressing other ASEAN members, and instead given more emphasis to assisting members in making the necessary adjustments for further and faster integration.

At the ASEAN Informal Summit, Prime Minister Goh announced initiatives to assist the newer ASEAN members in training and other measures to develop "e-ASEAN", linking the countries of the region through the Internet and other technologies. While modest, the efforts demonstrate an increased willingness of Singapore to assist and fund its neighbours as part of its multilateral diplomacy. These efforts go towards helping to address and close the "two-tier" divide between the founding countries and those that are better off, on the one hand, and Cambodia, Laos, Myanmar, and Vietnam, on the other.

Singapore's proposals in 2000 include attachments to skills development training institutes in the newer ASEAN states, as well as receiving students in Singapore. The programme for training institutes involves the training of trainers, consultants, and researchers in areas such as trade development, export promotion, and human resource development. In information technology (IT), a five-year package of IT "Train-the-Trainers" courses for each of these countries has been offered, with ten courses for 2001. Teacher and trainer development will be another focus to help develop teaching skills for economic and social development in Cambodia, Laos, Myanmar, and Vietnam: sixty vocational, polytechinc, and university lecturers from these countries will be attached to local Singaporean institutions annually. Additionally, the Singapore scholarships under the Singapore Co-operation Programme will be doubled from thirty to sixty per academic year. In a number of these efforts, Singapore will likely work with other, non-ASEAN countries, including Japan, Australia, and New Zealand.

Singapore has offered technical co-operation for some years, to both ASEAN members and other developing countries. Nevertheless, these latest efforts represent something of a change for the Republic because of the increase in scale and their links to policy goals. They can be read as a way of trying to help "drive" the integration of the ASEAN region, without "suffering" from resentment in the process. Help is less resented than exhortation and pressure. The corollary is also true. By giving a stronger policy direction to its assistance to fellow ASEAN members, Singapore lessens pressure from other ASEAN countries still recovering from the crisis to seek more generous assistance and "hand-outs". A concern expressed by some in Singapore as well as a number of regional commentators such as Leifer is that if Singapore gave monetary assistance, it would be like "pouring money down a black hole".

Conclusion: Governing an Island in the World

Singapore is more open to globalization and to regional forces than most other countries. This is a result not only of its geographical location, size, and ethnic composition. It is also a result of the deliberate choice of the state to pursue globalization, to reach out to the region and the wider world beyond ASEAN. This choice impacts on both economic progress and security.

In 2000, such economic openness paid off well. Strong external demand was the cause of Singapore's surge in growth. The world economy is estimated to have expanded by 4.7 per cent in 2000, the highest growth rate in twelve years. In particular, the U.S. economy was the key driver behind global demand. The bursting of the dot-com bubble did not stop the United States from registering a stellar growth of 5.0 per cent.

For 2001 and beyond, external economic prospects have become less rosy. The U.S. economy has decelerated quite sharply in the early months of 2001, with poorer corporate results and weak stock markets leading to slower consumption and investment. The consensus view in early 2001 is that the U.S. economy will grow by only 2 to 2.5 per cent. Compounding these concerns, the Japanese economy is expected to remain weak. The early shoots of recovery in 2000 have shown signs of withering, with low household expenditure caused by job worries and continuing deflation. In the rest of Asia, while the crisis has receded, banking systems remain weak, and there is still much restructuring to be done. Internal political problems complicate the potential recovery in several Asian countries.

Yet Singapore has thrived by being plugged into the global economic network and can be expected to continue to strengthen its economic linkages with the rest of the world. In 2000, the total trade of $470 billion was about three times Singapore's GDP. Thus, while Singapore remains committed to the launch of a new multilateral trade round in the WTO, and to regional efforts like APEC and AFTA, it is clearly in its vital interest to also pursue deeper trade liberalization initiatives with like-minded countries through bilateral agreements. Closer links with Europe and some of the countries in the former Eastern Europe will also likely be developed in the coming years. This will help to ensure that Singaporean exports are fairly well spread out among the major markets in the United States, the European Union, and Asia. The Singapore economy has undergone many changes and will experience another period of transformation, as surveyed in this chapter, to adjust to global conditions in search of sustained economic growth. In these respects, Singapore's place and policy in relation to the wider world is relatively settled.

Singapore's national policies complement globalization. The domestic scene is being transformed from the outside in and at a rapid pace, and economic changes have social and political connections. The domestic policies on economic issues, education and training, and social assistance surveyed in this chapter are responses to the challenges posed by globalization. They are, of course, not the only possible policies.

In 2000, these transformations wrought by globalization and the policies to deal with its ill-effects have been largely and peaceably accepted by the populace. In some measure, however, this was because of Singapore's rapid growth. The robust growth, together with the social and other measures taken by the government to help lower-income or unemployed Singaporeans, have tended to reduce the volume of a growing disquiet over social issues such as the inflow of foreign talent, and the widening income gap. However, if the economy turns sharply wrong in the near future, such disquiet may well grow and find a louder political voice of dissent than is presently heard. In such a scenario, the progress of civil society that has been noted in this chapter may be only the beginning of a much more robust political and civic development, provided that the civic groups (or opposition political parties) are able to mobilize themselves and public opinion on such issues.

Short of this, however, national policies in Singapore will continue to deal with the worst effects of globalization without straying from the objective of continuing to be open to the outside world economy and to "upgrade" Singapore and Singaporeans to take their place in it.

In this way, the PAP government in Singapore is not as dominant or omnipotent as is sometimes believed. Its first choice of globalization does restrict the succeeding policy choices open to it. To fiddle with an American adage, the Singapore Government cannot ignore all of the people all of the time. Yet, there are real and meaningful choices that can be made at the national level. The example of Singapore, as such, suggests that there is no "golden straitjacket"; globalization is a choice, and the national policies in education, social assistance, and other areas do make a difference.

Regional policy remains a much more difficult and open question. Peaceful co-existence and co-operation with its ASEAN neighbours will continue to challenge Singapore. In part, this is despite its economic success and place in the wider world, and another part, because of it. The globalized Singaporean economy cannot afford to be constrained by the region if, after the crisis, some in the region do not want to move more quickly towards economic integration and further openness. Yet the Singaporean polity cannot be too far out of step in the region lest it stirs the politics of envy and resentment. Indeed, as Singapore tries to drive the globalization agenda through its bilateral trade agreements, these may in fact increase the tensions between itself and some of its neighbours. If Singapore tries to "leapfrog" the region, it may well find itself pulled back to regional realities. Emphasizing the win-win nature of Singaporean initiatives will be a much more important and workable strategy.

Dialogue to exchange views and clear up misunderstandings can help somewhat. After all, Singapore has strong reasons of national interest to pursue these initiatives, and there are safeguards to ensure that harm is not done to others in the process. Efforts to increase assistance and co-operation towards ASEAN integration can also ameliorate the situation, but only to a degree. Singapore's vulnerability dictates that it cannot give too much lest it be seen as a soft touch, susceptible to pressure.

In these issues, there is a duality. Singapore cannot be "driving *or* suffering" the region but has to settle for both "driving *and* suffering" the region. That is to say, Singapore only finds worth and some security if it is ahead of the region in some areas, especially on the economic front, and trying in some ways to lead it. Yet this requires that its policies, priorities, and even the Singaporean ethos must be somewhat different from others in the region. These differences, along with historical disputes, tend to make relations with neighbours tense.

The end of the Cold War brought about Francis Fukuyama's predictions of the end of history and the victory of free market democracies. The Asian and ASEAN states seemed to defy that prediction with their long period of "miracle" growth and relatively authoritarian structures. The Asian crisis has, however, revisited such predictions of the inevitability of combining open markets and open societies. Some, including this author, do to a degree believe that open societies can provide the necessary mechanisms and processes for citizens and consumers to deal not just with their own governments but also with globalization.

In many respects, globalization in the Singaporean context has emphasized and indeed welcomed external influences in the spheres of trade, investment, and commerce. In contrast, influences on politics and society have often been subject to criticism and screened out as being "interference" in the state's domestic and internal affairs. Can these separations between economics and politics be maintained? Or will Singapore inevitably seek the path of convergence?

Globalization is a choice that a state makes and can mediate. That mediation, however, is not always guaranteed and is not made without cost. A regional location is not something that can be chosen. The choice of Singapore's policies for economic openness, increasing competition, and economic creativity will likely bring social and political changes. Some external factors can foster prosperity and militate towards greater accountability and participation for the Singaporean citizen. Others can bring recession and perhaps instability. As argued in this chapter, in seeking globalization and links to the wider world, Singapore must depart from the region in some respects, try to lead it in other respects, and will suffer from the region in yet others.

An island is small enough to be governed and dominated by a strong state and an entrenched party like the PAP. Yet an island is also open to the world and susceptible to the influence of larger countries and continents around it and to the flux of the international economy and polity: these are the dilemmas and tensions from which Singaporeans must construct a future.

NOTES

* This chapter is dedicated to the late Professor Michael Leifer of the London School of Economics and Political Science, a scholar of Singapore and the region, who passed away in March 2001, to the loss of all those who learnt from him, as students or friends.

1. The term is originally attributed to Schumpeter. See Joseph A. Schumpeter, *Capitalism, Socialism, and Democracy* (London: Allen and Unwin, 1976). In the context of the Asian crisis, those who have spoken about "creative destruction" include political leaders such as Singapore's Senior Minister Lee Kuan Yew and the ousted Malaysian Deputy Premier Anwar Ibrahim.

2. All sectors enjoyed higher growth in 2000. In particular, manufacturing, wholesale, and retail trade grew by a strong 15 per cent. Financial and business services rebounded from marginal growth in 1999, to 4.1 per cent and 6.6 per cent respectively. The contraction of the construction sector continued, but was less severe than that in 1999.

3. Thomas Friedman, *The Lexus and the Olive Tree* (Harpercollins, 2000), pp. 101–11, especially p. 105.

4. Vital U.S. interests in the Middle East and elsewhere, however, still do play a role in limiting U.S. criticism of non-democratic governments there.

5. For a study of the particulars of law-making in Singapore to illustrate the deep penetration of global influences into domestic laws and policies, see Simon S.C. Tay, "The Singapore Legal System and International Law: Influence or Interference", in *The Singapore Legal System*, edited by Kevin Tan, second edition (Singapore University Press, 1998), pp. 467–506.

6. Michael Leifer, *Singapore's Foreign Policy* (Routledge, 2000), especially chapter 5, "Driving and suffering the region", from p. 131.

7. The Prime Minister's National Day Rally Speech is a major occasion for the government to publicly review the year, much like the U.S. President's State of the Union message. For the full text of the Prime Minister's Speech in 2000, see "Prime Minister's National Day Rally Speech 2000" (Singapore: Ministry of Information and the Arts, 2000), or <http://www.gov.sg>.

8. Ibid., p. 19. The Prime Minister made specific reference to the work of Gary Hamel, *Leading the Revolution* (Harvard Business School Press, 2000).

9. *Asiaweek* 26, No. 11 (24 March 2000). Senior Minister Lee was quoted as saying: "We need to get our people to be more willing to undertake risk. It requires a completely different mindset". Like a major mental overhaul, to hear the former Prime Minister put it: "For us, the change means the abandonment of rules which have served us well for 30-plus years. [...] Societies must be flexible in re-inventing and refining their economic system. The strength of the American system is that it has always embraced change and creative destruction". See <http://cgi.cnn.com/ASIANOW/asiaweek/magazine/2000/0324/cover1.html>

10. "Contribution of Government-linked Companies to Gross Domestic Product", Occasional paper (Singapore: Department of Statistics, 2001).

11. It is conceivable that the large role of government in Singapore may be reduced, together with the domination of GLCs, only to be replaced by large private companies in an imperfect, oligopolistic market, perhaps with foreign owners. The Singaporean citizen and small entrepreneur may welcome such a scenario even less than the continued domination by the government and GLCs.

12. The Singapore Economic Development Board (EDB) in 2001 set up a $1 billion research and development fund and a $1 billion investment fund to attract life-sciences research and development and start-up activities, with specialized hubs and infrastructure. A pharmaceutical park will be developed at Tuas, and space for life sciences facilities will be set aside at the Buona Vista Science Hub. To support research and development, the amount committed by the government has more than doubled, from $2 billion allocated for the first five-year National Technology Plan to a $7 billion Science & Technology Plan from 2001 to 2005.

13. To raise the performance of local enterprises, the Productivity and Standards Board (PSB) will help firms to modernize their management, adopt IT, and increase efficiency. It will assist companies in restructuring and to move up the value chain, or to move into growth sectors. For those local enterprises that are promising, governments will seek to groom them into world-class companies. The existing Economic Development Assistance Scheme (EDAS) provides local firms with technical assistance and training, and helps them to adopt new technologies, among other initiatives.

14. Recounted by Prime Minister Goh in his National Day Rally Speech 2000.

15. Ibid.

16. Budget Statement 2001, made in Parliament by the Finance Minister, Dr Richard Hu, in March 2001.

17. This is a widely held perception, notwithstanding some evidence that more globalized economies have more equity than others. More globalized economies in Europe, such as the Netherlands, have considerably less inequality than, say, India and Brazil, which are far less globalized. This observation is drawn from the Foreign Policy-Kearney Globalization Index. See "Measuring Globalization", *Foreign Policy*, January–February 2001, pp. 56, 62–63.

18. Budget Statement 2001.

19. Prime Minister's National Day Rally Speech 2000.

20. Ibid, p. 24.

21. For 2001, the government will be giving utilities rebates totalling $350 to households living in 1 to 3-room HDB flats, $300 to households living in 4-room flats, and $250 to households living in 5-room flats. These will be given in ten equal monthly payments from July 2001 to April 2002. There will be two months in the year in which households have to make full payments, so that they will be encouraged to save on water and electricity. As such, this scheme will be renamed Utilities Save. Any unutilized amount of the Utilities Save given in any month will be rolled over to be used in the subsequent months. This Utilities Save scheme is more generous than the $100 and $200 utilities rebates given in 2000, and amounts to a total of $226 million. The government will extend and increase the rebates on HDB Service and Conservancy (S&C) charges and rentals granted over recent years to Singaporeans living in rented and owner-occupied HDB flats. The new package will be the most generous to date. Households living in 1-room flats will receive rental rebates of $12 per month, rebates for S&C charges of $8 per month, four months' net rent and five months' net S&C charges. Households living in 2-room flats will receive rental rebates of $8 per month, rebates for S&C charges of $7 per month, two months' net rent and four months' net S&C charges. Households which live in 3-room flats will be given rebates of $4 per month for S&C charges and four months' net S&C charges. As for households living in 4-room and 5-room flats, they will be entitled to three months and two months of net S&C charges respectively. The estimated cost of the entire package of rebates is $107 million. Low-income households which do not live in HDB flats can continue to receive help from the Citizens Consultative Committees' (CCCs) Assistance Scheme.

22. To help pensioners drawing low pensions cope with inflation, in 1974 the government introduced an *ex-gratia* allowance called the Singapore Allowance as an additional payment over and above the pensions that the government pays to pensioners residing in Singapore. The Singapore Allowance was last revised in August 1997, when the quantum was increased by $10, from $130 to $140 per month, and the gross pension ceiling raised from $900 to $950. The government has decided to increase the Singapore Allowance further by $10 to $150 per month, and raise the gross pension ceiling from the current $950 to $1,050 per month. The revision will give an additional $1.7 million a year to pensioners residing in Singapore, of which there are about 12,100. The ElderCare Fund was set up to help lower-income and lower-middle income households with the cost of nursing home-care, while the Medical Endowment Fund helps lower-income individuals with their medical bills so as to ensure that no one will be left without access to medical care because they cannot afford it. To further build up the ElderCare Fund and the Medical Endowment Fund, the government will contribute $250 million to the ElderCare Fund (bringing the total to $750 million) and $100 million to the Medical Endowment Fund (bringing the total to $800 million) in FY2001.

23. See Simon S.C. Tay, "Civil Society in 21st Century Singapore: Three Dimensions of Change", in *State-Society Relations in Singapore*, edited by Gillian Koh and Ooi Giok Ling (Singapore: Institute of Policy Studies and Oxford University Press, 2000), pp. 170–90.

24. See George Yeo, "Civil Society — Between the Family and the State", *Speeches* 15, No. 3 (Singapore: Ministry of Information and the Arts, 1991), pp. 78–86, especially pp. 79 and 86.

25. Ibid, p. 79: "The problem is how to make Singapore more than just a nice hotel to stay in, how to make it a home worth living and caring for."

26. Ibid, p. 82. On CDCs in particular, and on government-initiated institutions generally, see Ooi Giok Ling and Gillian Koh, *State-Society Synergies: New Stakes, New Partnerships in Singapore: Re-engineering Success*, edited by Arun Mahiznan and Lee Tsao Yuen (IPS and Oxford University Press, 1998), pp. 98, 101–3.

27. Speech at the Institute of Policy Studies (IPS) Conference on Civil Society, 6 May 1998. The full text of the speech is pending publication by the IPS. Excerpts of Minister Yeo's speech were released in "Worldwide Web: Strengthening the Singapore Idea", *Speeches 1998* (MITA, May–June 1998). In his 1991 speech, Minister Yeo preferred the term "civic society". In 1998, he used the term "civil society".

28. Ibid., pp. 50–55. "In discussing the role of civil society, we need first to look at the way the world is going for we do not exist in isolation. ... The world is going through a major transformation brought about by the revolution in information technology. The current Asian crisis, which is both economic and political, is part of it. Old structures are being undermined, while new structures have yet to crystallize. ... We are moving from a hierarchical world to a web world. ... The power of the state is weakening".

29. Ibid., pp. 56–57.

30. Although framed as dilemmas, Minister Teo publicly acknowledged that these issues could be resolved and were therefore not true dilemmas.

31. *Parliamentary Debates* (Singapore), Thursday 6 May 1999, col. 1646–55.

32. Ibid., Minister Yeo's speech, col. 1619–1629.

33. A wide array of laws exist in Singapore to license and manage the constitutional rights to speech, assembly, and association. See Tay, op. cit.

34. A simple permit can be obtained on the spot, in place of elaborate and time-consuming procedures. However, the normal laws of the land apply, including some that might constrain speech, such as the laws of defamation and sedition. The proposal was first aired by the Roundtable group, after the unlicensed public speeches by opposition politician, Dr Chee Soon Juan, led to his imprisonment for violating the Public Entertainments Act. The idea was then endorsed by Senior Minister Lee Kuan Yew at a public discussion at the World Economic Forum in Davos.

35. These laws include: (1) the Internal Security Act (Cap.143) that allows for detention without trial; (2) the Official Secrets Act (Cap.213); (3) the Sedition Act (Cap.290) that creates an offence if statements or actions tend to bring into "hatred or contempt or to excite disaffection against the Government"; (4) the Miscellaneous Offences (Public Order and Nuisance) Act (Cap.184) that provides that any assembly or procession in a public place may be prohibited or restricted if the authorities are satisfied that it might result in public disorder, property damage, or disruption to community life, and also provides that public processions, and demonstrations must be licensed; (5) the Penal Code (Cap.224) that creates an offence for unauthorized public demonstrations; (6) the Maintenance of Religious Harmony Act (Cap.167A), enacted in 1990, allows for orders to be made restraining an official or member of a religious group, or any other person, acting in such a way that might cause feelings of enmity between different religious groups; (7) defamation laws which have been the basis for government leaders (in their private capacity) bringing suits against opposition politicians for considerable sums in damages; (8) the Undesirable Publications Act (Cap.338) allows the prohibition of publications on the grounds that it is against "the public interest"; this can be interpreted quite broadly to relate to morality, security, or other exceptions; (9) the Newspaper and Printing Presses Act (Cap.206) that requires all newspapers to be licensed yearly and creates a controlling share for government to dispense; and (10) the Public Entertainments Act (Cap.257) that provides for the licensing of public performance (including political speech). The Public Entertainments Act was amended in 2000 to ease rules for public events, but not political speech. The new Act is entitled the "Public Entertainments and Meetings Act". See the *Straits Times*, "Govt to ease rules on public events", Thursday 14 November 2000, p. 1.

36. Richard Falk, "The Quest for humane governance in an era of globalization", in *The Ends of Globalization*, edited by D. Kalb et al. (Lanham, MD: Rowan and Littlefield, 2000).
37. See the *Straits Times*, "Is a clenched fist a protest?" 6 March 2001, p. H11.
38. For a recent overview of the issue, see Martin Wolf, "Will the Nation-State Survive Globalization?", *Foreign Affairs*, Jan/Feb 2001, from p. 178.
39. Global concerns for human rights, for example, led to the United Nations resolutions against South Africa for apartheid. In the area of the environment, to conserve biodiversity and control climate change, rainforests in one state have been proposed as a "global heritage" of all states.
40. The idea of an international civil society is wider, including NGOs but also networks of scholars and individuals, religious and other voluntary organizations, research institutes, and media. This "society" is not confined to any state, but relies upon the global telecommunications, media, and the Internet as well as the supporting symbols and values of such systems to organize themselves for common causes, across borders. Proponents of international civil society have urged a convergence of morals and laws, to accompany the economic convergence, towards a deeper integration between the continents. In this, global civil society is seen as a counter-balance to the negative effects of globalization. Often, in practice, civil society groups co-operate with governments to achieve their ends. But they can also oppose the state, as civil society groups did in the former Soviet bloc.
41. See, for example, Ethan Kapstein, *Winners and Losers in the Global Economy*, *International Organization* 54, no. 2 (2000): 359–84; Dani Rodrik, *Has Globalization Gone Too Far?* (Washington, D.C.: Institute for International Economics, 1997); and Richard Higgot, "Contested Globalization", *Review of International Studies* (forthcoming).
42. See Wolf, *Will the Nation-State Survive Globalization?*, pp. 185–89, for a discussion of the new environment for state taxation and economic policy.
43. Culture and social values are reinforced or re-created as part of nation-building. This can be seen in Indonesia's Pancasila ideology, and the promulgation of national values in Singapore in the early 1990s. Language, or moral instruction, is also to be protected or reinvigorated against foreign influence. In Vietnam, there are persistent crackdowns on English language signage for stores. Even in Singapore, where English serves as the common language of commerce, administration, and university education, the 1990s have witnessed a re-emphasis on Mandarin and other "mother tongues". These efforts are explicitly to provide for a cultural ballast, that is, to strengthen the sense of self and to shield the population against the negative effects of "Western" influence. Policing culture and social values is evident in attempts to censor the media and the Internet as channels of global influence. Often, access is limited to the select or commercial purposes. In Myanmar and Vietnam, Internet and even fax machines are to be licensed and controlled. The case of Singapore is somewhat more complicated as the city-state is part of the global network of telecommunications and media. Satellite dishes are available to businesses and diplomatic establishments, but proscribed for ordinary households. Homes are being wired up to provide for both cable television and broad-band computer access as "an intelligent island" but this is matched by a supervision of content, and the promotion of "decent" materials. There are selected and symbolic bans of materials such as *Playboy*.
44. *Foreign Policy*, January–February 2001, pp. 56–65. The AT Kearney/FP Globalization Index on a country-by-country basis seeks to quantify a large number of indicators for globalization. These go beyond the flow of investment and trade to include the level of personal contact by combining data on international travel, overseas telephone calls, and the penetration of the Internet.
45. Leifer, op. cit., p. 131 onwards.

46. Tommy Koh, "Size is not Destiny", in *Singapore: Re-engineering Success*, edited by Arun Mahiznan and Lee Tsao Yuan (Singapore: Institute of Policy Studies and Oxford University Press, 1998), pp. 172–87.
47. See Jean Louis Margolin, "Singapore: New Regional Influence, New World Outlook?", *Contemporary Southeast Asia* 20, no. 3 (1998): 319, at p. 327.
48. Leifer, op. cit.
49. With a stall in trade negotiations at the global level, regional efforts have returned to prominence. In Asia, however, there has been no broad push for free trade on a regional basis. The Asia-Pacific Economic Co-operation (APEC) forum has not given further momentum to free trade across the Pacific. The progress of the ASEAN Free Trade Agreement (AFTA) has been limited by reservations by Malaysia over its automobile industry. Discussions to link AFTA to Australia–New Zealand have also been blocked by objections by some ASEAN members, notably Malaysia. In contrast, initiatives in other regions are being pushed ahead. The United States has re-emphasized the objective of negotiating a Free Trade Agreement of the Americas, covering North, Central and South America. The European Union has proceeded with its plans for wider membership and closer economic ties with a number of former Eastern European nations.
50. The United States has concluded bilateral agreements with a number of smaller countries, including Israel and Jordan. Japan is exploring such arrangements with South Korea, Mexico, and Singapore. These represent a new direction for a country that, despite being the world's second largest economy, has traditionally focused on the WTO. Mexico has concluded over twenty bilateral agreements.
51. Given that its partners, like Japan, the United States, and Australia, are developed countries, the agreements are obligated to observe Article XXIV of the GATT, a higher standard than that placed upon developing country agreements like AFTA. Indeed, in some areas and some agreements, Singapore will likely go beyond WTO commitments. As Singapore is almost a free port, with few tariffs, the bilateral initiatives will potentially demonstrate approaches to dealing with new, non-trade issues that are or may be of interest in the broader WTO or regional context. In the case of its discussions with Japan, for example, the study has recommended a "new age" agreement that will potentially give a greater emphasis to non-tariff areas, such as business facilitation, mutual recognition of standards, and promote broader economic co-operation in many fields, including telecommunications, finance, and transportation. For this reason, the study has led to the bilateral treaty being tentatively entitled the Japan-Singapore Economic Partnership Agreement, rather than a free trade agreement.
52. Trade diversion is another possible concern stemming from bilateral agreements, but it is potentially harder to demonstrate. This is because traditional economic analysis of bilateral initiatives tends to misunderstand the nature of trade and globalization today. It underestimates the potential benefits of bilateral trade arrangements because it is based on the assumption of a static framework. Bilateral agreements can increase the volume of interactions between the two economies involved and facilitate a dynamic growth in benefits.
53. Malaysia was ranked No. 20 in the FP/Kearney study on globalization, cited above. It is the only Asian country other than Singapore in the top twenty.
54. Singapore is not a formal ally of the United States and no military bases are provided. Military co-operation has, however, increased in the 1990s, especially with the closure of the U.S. bases in the Philippines. In 1998, a Memorandum of Understanding was signed for U.S. Navy ships to use the Changi Naval Base, due for completion at the end of 2000. In 2000, the two countries signed an agreement to implement the administration of the U.S. Forces' access. Estimates are that by the late 1990s, more than 100 U.S. Navy vessels visit the island-state annually. By these modest but real measures, Singapore has demonstrated its support for a continued U.S. military presence in Asia, of which it has been one of the leading advocates.

ON BABIES, FOREIGN TALENT AND OLDER PEOPLE
The Great Balancing Act

Yap Mui Teng

Introduction

On 20 August 2000, Singaporeans must have been pleasantly surprised when Prime Minister Goh Chok Tong announced in his National Day Rally address that the government would be giving out "baby bonuses" worth up to $9,000 and $18,000 respectively for second and third children born on or after 1 April 2001. While this was not the first time that Singapore had used financial incentives for demographic purposes, it was the first time that the government had offered outright gifts to families for babies. Characteristically, the "baby bonus" was only one of several incentives served up by the government in its latest effort to revive the sagging Total Fertility Rate (TFR).[1] The latest package comprised a fixed government payment, as well as a matching government co-contribution towards a savings account for the first six years after birth for second and third children; paid maternity leave for third births, with the government covering the increased costs to employers; and measures to ease women's work and familial roles, such as increased childcare places and more family-friendly workplace practices in the civil service. Measures have also been announced to increase opportunities for young men and women to meet with a view to raising the marriage rate. The latter is important in a society such as Singapore's where out-of-wedlock births are viewed negatively, and the fall in the birth rate can be attributed at least in part to changing marriage patterns.

Implications of the "Baby Deficit"

The latest "baby incentives" came amidst the continuing decline in the TFR to almost unprecedented low levels of 1.494 and 1.475 children per woman in 1998 and 1999 respectively (see Figure 1). The only other time this low level was reached was in 1986 when the TFR fell to 1.433 children per woman. Among the three major ethnic groups, the TFR for Chinese and Indian women fell to 1.3 and 1.58 respectively in 1999, and it was only among Malay women that the TFR was above the level required for generational replacement level, at 2.42 children per woman (although this figure is still lower than in 1990).[2] Although there were extenuating circumstances on both occasions, these being

---

Yᴀᴘ Mᴜɪ Tᴇɴɢ is a Senior Research Fellow at the Institute of Policy Studies, Singapore.

economic recession and the unfavourable "Year of the Tiger" (in 1986 and 1998), they occurred under different population policy regimes.

As Figure 1 shows, Singapore experienced an extended post-World War II baby boom lasting until the mid-1960s. A national family planning and fertility control programme was launched in 1966 as part of a two-pronged strategy to control the rate of population growth and the attendant problems of high unemployment, poverty, and slum growth. A two-child family policy was adopted in 1972.[3] Fertility declined rapidly following the adoption of the anti-natalist policy as well as rapid social and economic development. From the mid-1970s, Singaporeans consistently produced children below the 2.1 average required for couples to replace themselves and for the population to maintain a constant size and a balanced age structure in the long run. While demographers, such as Saw Swee Hock, had called for a relaxation of the stringent anti-natalist measures following the achievement of replacement level fertility in 1975 and 1976, it was not until 1983 that the subject was given official attention. Following the publication of the results of the 1980 Census, Senior Minister (then Prime Minister) Lee Kuan Yew kicked off a chain of events with a National Day Rally speech in 1983 in which he warned of the consequences of the failure, particularly among educated women, to marry and to replace themselves. Dubbed the "great marriage debate", this was followed by the implementation of policy measures to redress the "lop-sided" pattern of procreation. Eventually, on 1 March 1987,

FIGURE 1
Live Births and Total Fertility Rate (TFR), 1957–99

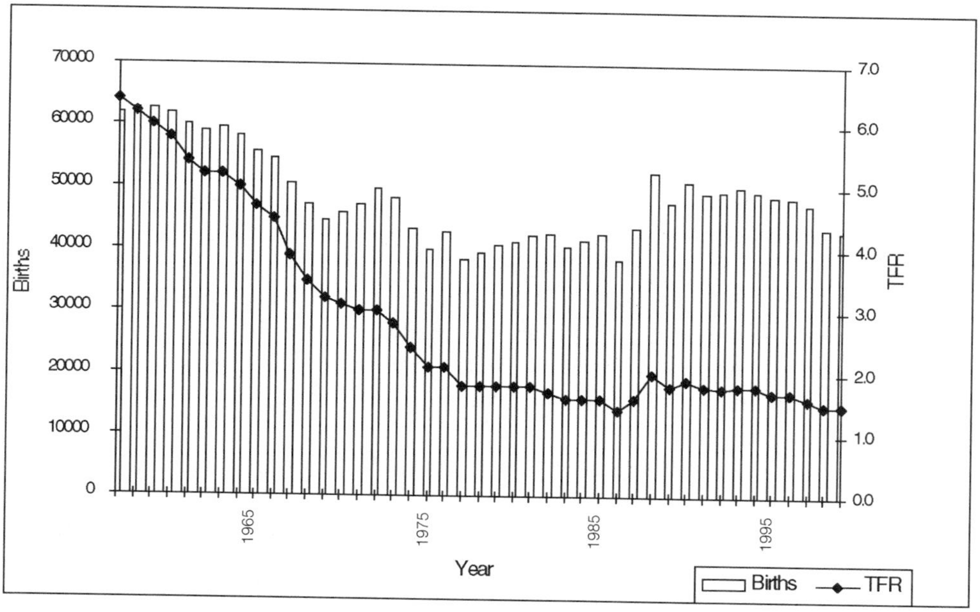

NOTE: TFR figures from 1980 are for the resident population only.

Prime Minister Goh, then First Deputy Prime Minister, announced the reversal of the "two-child family" policy and its replacement by the "three (children) or more if you can afford it" policy. The objective was to return fertility to replacement level by 1995 and then to keep fertility at this level indefinitely. The "three or more" policy was to make up for those who did not produce any children (either because they did not marry or because they did not want or could not have any children) or had only one child. Fertility above the replacement level would lead to an ever-growing population, with increasingly larger numbers of the young to be provided for, while persistent below-replacement fertility would result in an increasingly older population with a growing number and proportion of the elderly in the population that would require support. Under the latter condition, the size of the population, and the size of the work-force, would also decline once the population momentum created by the earlier high fertility had worked itself out.

In the event, the TFR resumed a downward trend after an initial rise to nearly two children per woman in the early years of the new policy regime (1988–90). It returned to the pre-1987 level of about 1.6 children per woman by the mid-1990s, and as mentioned earlier, the figure for 1999 was only 1.475 — 30 per cent below the level required for long-term replacement of the population. Not only were more Singaporeans remaining single, more of those who were married were either remaining childless (the proportion rose from 2.6 per cent in 1989 to 7.3 per cent in 1999) or had only one child (the proportion rising from 8.5 per cent to 15 per cent over the same period).[4] According to the Prime Minister, Singapore's resident population would decline from 3.2 million to 2.7 million in fifty years if fertility remained at 1.48 children per woman and there was no in-migration. The figure would fall further to 2.4 million if the TFR declined to 1.2 children per woman, as in Spain and Italy. The resident labour force would also fall in conjunction.[5]

The impact of fertility decline on the shape of the population age structure is shown in Figure 2. The changing shapes of the population age profile reflect Singapore's transition from a high-fertility population in the post-World War II "baby boom" period, with a large proportion in the youthful age groups, to an increasingly older one, with a growing proportion in the upper ages. According to official projections, the proportion of the population aged 65 and over would increase to 18.9 per cent in 2030, from 7.3 per cent in 1999.[6] In other words, in about thirty years, nearly one in five Singaporeans would be a retiree. The median age of the population would rise from 33.4 years to 41.2 years over this period.

On a positive note, the decline in fertility to date has resulted in a reduction of the number of young dependants to be provided for. Moreover, the maturing of the baby boom cohorts, together with the in-migration of foreign workers and permanent residents, had resulted in a growing population of work-force age, typically taken to be the 15–64 years age range. This "demographic bonus", however, could be expected to be eroded in the future as the large cohorts of

FIGURE 2
Age Profile of Population, 1957–2000

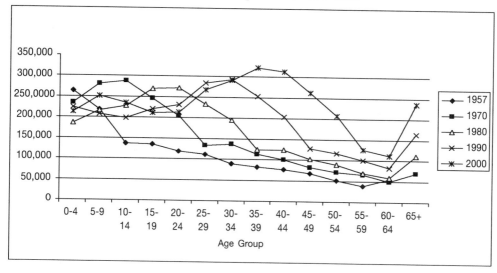

the baby boomers reach old age and are replaced by smaller cohorts born since the mid-1960s. The same set of official projections cited above show that the working age population would decline to 64 per cent of the total population in 2030, after rising to 72 per cent in 2010.[7] The composition of the work-force would also change as the large baby boom cohorts reach the older groups and are replaced by smaller cohorts of younger workers. The population of the old, aged 65 and over, has been projected to exceed the young, aged below 15 years, by 2025, and thus, while the "dependency burden" has declined on account of the number of young to be supported, the care burden could rise again on account of the growing number of the elderly. This could be the case even if the elderly of the future might be healthier, better educated, and better able to look after themselves. The vast majority of the oldest group would also likely be female (as women outlive men), who would likely not have adequate savings for their old age because of their disrupted or even non-existent work history.

Economic, Social, and Political Implications

There has been much discussion in local and international literature on the economic, social, and political impact of population ageing. The Organization for Economic Co-operation and Development (OECD), for example, addressed the issue of population ageing and economic prosperity in its publication, *Maintaining Prosperity in an Ageing Society*, thus:

> The goods and services produced by an economy mainly determine the material living standards of a society. The amount of goods and services produced depend mainly on the number of people working and their

productivity. If productivity continues at its post-1973 average growth rate of 1.5 per cent annually, the decline in the proportion employed (due to the ageing population) would mean that the growth in material living standards will be cut in half in the decades after 2010.[8]

Similarly, Prime Minister Goh, in a 1986 speech at the Nanyang Technological Institute (NTI), argued that:

> We have to pay close attention to the trend and pattern of births because of their consequences on our prosperity and security – in fact, on our survival as a nation.
> … (W)hy having fewer babies can result in a less prosperous nation… Economic growth comes from two sources – growth in the size of the work force and growth in its productivity. Productivity itself depends on the ability of the population. If the work force does not increase, then productivity must increase to generate economic growth.
> But there is a limit to productivity growth as the economy becomes more developed…
> Economic growth will slacken for another related reason. With fewer babies each year, the proportion of the younger people in the population will become smaller. Put in another way, our work force will become increasingly older…
> Will our work force be vigorous and dynamic? Will investors be attracted to a country which does not have enough young workers? Even now, you can see that many companies prefer to employ younger workers. Not only are they cheaper to employ, but they are also more nimble with their hands, and are more up-to-date in their skills and training.[9]

There is also the question of the sustainability of the pension and health-care financing systems in the United States and the established welfare states, such as Germany and Sweden.[10] While Singapore does not subscribe to the pay-as-you-go system where the current generation of workers pay for the retirement benefits of the present elderly, and relies instead on saving for one's old age in the form of the provident fund and on family support, an ageing population does have fiscal implications. As Prime Minister Goh put it:

> … How are you going to support yourselves when you are no longer working?
> You may say that your children can support you, but bear in mind, at the rate we are going, many Singaporeans will have only one or even not a single child in their lifetime.
> The population that is without a steady income will need medical care, housing and to move around *(sic)*. These services will have to be paid for, not by the Government, but by those who are working.
> Singapore has no natural wealth. The only way for the Government to raise the required revenue to take care of the older population is to levy more taxes on those who are working. And they will squeal.

> The tax burden can be extremely heavy if it has to support some 30 per
> cent of the population who are over 60 years old. How do we reconcile
> the interests of the young and the needs of the old? How do we solve
> the dilemma?"[11]

The potential conflict between the generations has indeed been the subject
of discussion, particularly in the United States and Europe.[12] In the United
States, in particular, much has been made of the potential influence of elder
groups using the power of their votes to arrogate resources to themselves,
possibly at the expense of the young, although this too has been disputed.[13]
In Singapore, Senior Minister Lee Kuan Yew has suggested that the one-man
one-vote system may have to be revised to give greater weight to those in the
productive ages, who would be voting on their children's behalf as well, to
counterbalance the weight of the elder vote.[14] While the issue of cohesion and
conflict between the generations was studied in the latest review of policies
with regard to the ageing population conducted by the Inter-Ministerial
Committee (IMC) on Ageing Population in 1999, the Committee proposed
that "[i]ntergenerational cohesion is best fostered in the context of the family"
and that "[i]ntergenerational transfers should also only take place within the
family. This will help diffuse tensions between the old and young and ensure
that social services remain financially sustainable".[15] As regards the changing
of the electoral system, the IMC did not support the proposal but nevertheless
ventured that "we should monitor the situation and raise this issue for public
discussion periodically".[16]

In his 1986 address to NTI students, Prime Minister Goh noted another
reason for increasing the birth rate, thus: "Put simply, there will not be enough
young men to defend the country".[17] The security implications of low fertility
are further elaborated by Rand researcher Brian Nichiporuk:

> First, shrinking youth cohorts mean that the military force (the low
> fertility countries) can put into the field will become progressively smaller
> in terms of personnel. This is probably not critically dangerous because
> the growing prominence of technology suggests that numbers may matter
> somewhat less on future battlefields. Second, increasing numbers of
> elderly citizens at the top of the age pyramid will demand increasing
> amounts of government funding for pensions, medical care, etc., which
> could "crowd out" significant amounts of defense investment. Fiscal
> challenges such as these will undoubtedly reduce the funds available for
> defense over the long run in the major European NATO nations and
> Japan.[18]

Redressing the Imbalance: The Demographic Levers

There are four demographic levers by which the issues of population size and
age structure balance could be redressed. These are births, deaths, in-migration
and out-migration. Singapore has, of course, chosen in-migration and
influencing the birth rate (more of which will be discussed below). Raising

mortality, or the number of deaths, either through neglect or denial of care is not an option in Singapore, as elsewhere. A less radical and less controversial option would be to encourage out-migration of the elderly. Out-migration could become an increasingly viable option, as witnessed by the granting of "silver hair" visas by Malaysia to senior citizens, aged 50 and older, meeting certain financial conditions who would like to live out their "golden years" in the country.[19] Out-migration could be an option for the asset-rich baby boomers looking for a lower cost of living and a less hectic pace of life. There could, however, be important economic implications for the country if large numbers of baby boomers moved their CPF savings and other assets overseas. In 1998, Central Provident Fund (CPF) members aged 50 and over held S$14,779,249,000 in balances, and total withdrawals by those aged 55 and above amounted to S$1,285,555,000.[20]

In-migration
Selective in-migration of foreigners, either on a permanent or temporary basis, bring with it the advantage of an immediate boost to the productive work-force both in terms of numbers and the age and quality of workers required. This would be obtained at minimal financial costs to the receiving country because, unlike newborns, investment in their health and education would have been borne by the migrants' countries of origin. There would be a further advantage in that the lag time between birth and labour force entry, typically about twenty years, given current requirements regarding skills and formal education, is cut. However, projections carried out by demographers elsewhere (in countries such as Germany and Canada) have suggested that the numbers required to rejuvenate the population would be so enormous as to be socially and politically unacceptable. The United Nations Population Division, in a paper entitled "Replacement Migration: Is it a Solution to Declining and Ageing Populations?" concluded its literature review on page 11, thus:

> In sum ... available research studies reach several conclusions. First, inflows of migrants will not be able to prevent population declines in the future, nor rejuvenate a national population, unless the migration streams reach comparatively high levels. Second, international migration can only act as a partial means to offset the effects of population ageing arising from below-replacement fertility. The inadequacy of migration to serve as a counter for population ageing, and in most cases for population decline, has been further consolidated by questions regarding the feasibility of formulating and adopting suitable migration policies. In many countries, additional large volumes of immigrants are likely to face serious social and political objections, even as a means of slowing population decline and population ageing. Therefore, regulating the level and composition of replacement migration streams to reach a desired population size or population age structure poses enormous challenges for Governments that may wish to do so.

In Singapore, the number of foreigners living and working in the country has grown significantly, particularly in the decade of the 1990s. According to the Census of Population 2000, Singapore citizens made up 74 per cent of the total population while permanent residents (PRs) and other visa holders made up the remaining 26 per cent. The proportion of the resident population (that is, citizens and PRs) who were born overseas increased from 15 per cent in 1990 to 18 per cent in 2000, after having declined in the previous three decades through attrition of the earlier immigrant cohorts. Singapore has adopted an open immigration policy (after having closed the country to immigrants immediately after independence in 1965) both to make up for the slowing growth of the indigenous work-force and to bridge the gap in skilled manpower required to meet the needs of the economy. Indeed, the educational attainment of the population has risen over the past decade, partly because of the inflow of well-educated permanent residents.[21]

The rationale for Singapore's immigration policy has been articulated by Prime Minister Goh, thus: "I see foreign talent, or global talent, not as a quick fix to make up for the shortage of local workers. This is a long-term strategy to enable Singapore to sustain its vitality, competitiveness, and prosperity. If we can absorb a steady inflow of global talent into Singapore, our ideas and outlook will stay fresh and vibrant, and we can be a competitive, global player".[22] However, Goh has himself articulated what must have been on the minds of many Singaporeans — that Singapore could not rely only on foreigners. In the Prime Minister's words: "... we will bring in foreigners and new immigrants. They will complement our needs, but they cannot replace us".[23] Apart from the need for national servicemen, which the Prime Minister referred to in his 1986 speech (see above), some political issues associated with a large immigrant population could be whether they would stay in times of trouble and the issue

TABLE 1
Highest Qualification Attained
(In percentage)

	Singapore Residents		Citizens		Permanent Residents	
	1990	2000	1990	2000	1990	2000
No Qualifications	31.3	19.6	31.5	20.9	27.2	7.5
Primary	27.0	23.1	26.8	23.6	30.9	17.6
Secondary	26.5	24.6	27.0	25.3	16.7	18.5
Upper Secondary	7.3	14.9	7.3	14.5	7.1	18.4
Polytechnic	3.5	6.2	3.4	6.3	3.8	5.2
University	4.5	11.7	4.0	9.5	14.2	32.7

Source: Department of Statistics, "Singapore Census of Population 2000 Advance Data Release No, 1: Changing Education Profile", at <*www.singstat.gov.sg/C2000/adr-edu.pdf*>, Table 1.

of divided loyalty (for which reason Singapore has been reluctant to allow dual citizenship). The above are quite apart from the question of conflict and competition for resources, particularly when times are difficult. As an example, Singaporeans are already beginning to worry about unemployment when the population is increased to 5.5 million, part of which would undoubtedly be made up of immigrants. Seventy-eight per cent of those polled by a Channel NewsAsia/Gallup poll felt that Singapore should restrict the number of foreign workers as the population expands.[24] How this will work out in view of the expected increase in structural unemployment remains to be seen.

As with other immigrant-receiving countries, the ethnic/racial composition of the in-takes can also be a sensitive issue. As this author has noted elsewhere, the ethnic balance featured as an issue in the public debates that followed the announcements of the new population and immigration policies in the 1980s.[25] The government had declared then its intention of maintaining the existing ethnic distribution as it believed this had contributed to Singapore's rapid economic development in the past. While there is no publicly available information on the composition of the migration streams, a hint of this is provided by the results of the 2000 Census of Population. While Malay Singaporeans have consistently (except for a short period in the 1970s) reported the highest fertility level, their share of the total resident population has remained fairly stable over the last decade, at about 14 per cent. On the other hand, the proportions of the Indians and "Others" have increased from 7.1 and 1.1 per cent to 7.9 and 1.4 per cent respectively. Indeed, the proportion of Singapore's resident population who were born on the Indian sub-continent and elsewhere (indicated in Table 2 by "Others") has increased disproportionately over the last decade, compared with the Malaysian-born, and there has even been a decline in the proportion born in Northeast Asia (China, Hong Kong, and Taiwan). Singaporeans have so far reacted with equanimity to the presence of large numbers of foreigners from diverse sources in their midst. This is perhaps because of the multiracial character of the society, quite unlike more homogeneous societies, such as Denmark for instance.

TABLE 2
Resident Population by Country of Birth
(In percentage)

	1970	1980	1990	2000
Singapore	74.4	82.5	84.8	81.7
Malaysia	9.0	6.6	7.2	9.4
China, Hong Kong, Taiwan	11.7	8.0	5.5	5.0
India, Pakistan, Bangladesh, Sri Lanka	2.5	1.6	1.3	1.9
Indonesia	1.3	0.9	0.8	1.0
Others	1.1	0.3	0.4	1.0

SOURCE: Department of Statistics, "Singapore Census of Population 2000 — A Quick Count", at *www.singstat.gov.sg/C2000/census.html*, Table 8, p. 8.

Pro-natalist Policies

Singapore's experience with the pro-natalist policy since 1987, as well as experiences elsewhere, has shown clearly the uphill task faced by states attempting to address the low fertility problem. Be that as it may, the best solution for population rejuvenation, at least from the demographic perspective, is to raise the fertility level of the domestic population.[26] For this reason, it is also necessary to understand the reasons underlying childbearing decisions in order to address them. While admitting that the Singapore situation is typical of developed countries, Prime Minister Goh, as characteristic of the People's Action Party (PAP) regime, valiantly declared that "we must at least try arrest the problem (because) not to try is to give up on Singapore".[27]

The reasons given by Singaporeans for not marrying or having more children typically revolve around pragmatic considerations such as the financial costs involved, problems of childcare and parenting, and the opportunity costs to their careers, particularly among women.[28] Elsewhere, it has also been found that "children's education" was the main parenting worry among married couples — "42.7% express this concern as they emphasise the importance of education for their children's future".[29] Singaporean parents are estimated to have spent $320 million annually on tuition for their children.[30]

The policy measures introduced to date are intended to reduce the obstacles to marriage and childbearing.[31] These are, however, short-term solutions, and indeed, both the Prime Minister and Senior Minister expected them to have a short-term impact. The attitude towards marriage and childbearing displayed by Singaporeans, as journalist Asad Latif correctly pointed out, reflect "… the self-expectations generated by the explosion of economic opportunities which have been accompanied … by the higher sanctions of failure in the marketplace. The stakes have risen for individuals seeking recognition in their own careers and fearful of how their children might fare in an increasingly competitive education system that will determine their status in the marketplace of the future".[32] A Channel NewsAsia/Gallup poll showed that younger Singaporeans are putting off marriage for careers — "[s]tarting a family takes second place to finding a good job"[33] — perhaps not surprising, given the amount of investment they and their parents put into their schooling. Similarly, a twenty-something bank executive interviewed by the *Asiaweek* magazine reported that "We have been conditioned to think that the only thing that matters is economic success".[34] In this, Singapore's young are not different from their contemporaries elsewhere in Asia, as *Asiaweek* noted: "… today's youth are free to chase their dreams. For the moment, those dreams largely mean material happiness and creature comforts, rather than children or community". The above point to what political scientist Ronald Inglehart has identified as a "materialistic" world-view, a concern with economic and physical security — as opposed to individual self-realization and quality of life, which he characterized as "postmaterialist"[35]. Combined with this is a traditional sex-role ideology,[36] whereby women continue to bear the main responsibility for the household even if they are employed, thus rendering child-rearing, especially a large number of children, a rather unattractive proposition.

Interestingly, renowned demographer Dirk van de Kaa has noted, based on findings from the fertility and family surveys conducted in Europe, that among the younger respondents, "postmaterialists almost invariably report a higher average number of children as ideal for a family in the country they live in than their materialist counterparts".[37] This suggested to him that "having children as such is appreciated quite positively by postmaterialist men and women (and that it) may constitute an important element in their perception of well-being and self-realization". Van de Kaa suggested further that as postmodernization continued, postmaterialists could well find it easier to combine child-rearing and other activities and thus have larger family sizes than their materialist counterparts. However, the author also accepted that current evidence supporting this thesis is as yet not strong, though the results for West Germany and Sweden pointed in this direction.

If van de Kaa is right, then the extremely materialistic world-view displayed by Singaporeans need to be re-examined. Changing it, and thereby the attitudes of Singaporeans towards marriage and childbearing, would however require time. Will this come about naturally as society matures, or will there be a role for the government? Perhaps the role of the government is to provide an open environment for postmaterialist values to grow.

Concluding Remarks

As the new millennium dawns, Singapore is on the second leg of its attempt to achieve a more balanced population growth and age structure. Following the very rapid fertility declines in the 1960s and 1970s, the population is now greying rapidly and the main source of population growth in the past decade has been in-migration rather than a natural increase of its indigenous population. These demographic developments have important economic, social, and political implications for the country and need to be redressed. The latest round of procreation incentives announced in 2000 is an effort in this direction, even though the success rate of such policies has not been encouraging. Nevertheless, Singapore has never been a country to shy away from a challenge, and this will be one of its major challenges. However, it should be understood that incentives are not a panacea for all ills, and longer-term solutions should look to the underlying causes, especially values. A society with greater diversity of views, other than materialism, need not be a bad thing as Singapore gets on its way in the New Economy.

NOTES

1. This is the average number of children a woman can expect to have by the end of her reproductive span if she gave birth at each age at the rate observed for the current year. The TFR has been criticized primarily because it is influenced by changes in marriage and birth timing. See, for example, John Bongaarts and Griffith Feeney, "On the Quantum and Tempo of Fertility", *Population and Development Review* 24, no. 2 (June 1998): 271–91.

2. *Straits Times*, 19 August 2000.

3. A two-child family would give an actual TFR of 2 only if every woman born is married. This was not the case in Singapore where the singlehood rates have been rising.

4. Goh Chok Tong, *National Day Rally Speech by Prime Minister Goh Chok Tong, 20 August 2000* (Singapore: Ministry of Information and the Arts, 2000) p. 33.

5. Ibid., p. 34.

6. Ministry of Community Development (MCD), *Report of the Inter-Ministerial Committee on the Ageing Population* (Singapore, 1999), Table 1-1, p. 29.

7. Author's computation based on MCD (1999), Table 1-1, p. 29.

8. OECD, *Maintaining Prosperity in an Ageing Society* (Brussels, 1998), p.10.

9. Goh Chok Tong, "The Second Long March" (Speech delivered at the Nanyang Technological Institute on 4 August 1986), reprinted as Annex D in Saw Swee-Hock, *Changes in the Fertility Policy of Singapore*, IPS Occasional Paper No. 2 (Times Academic Press for the Institute of Policy Studies, 1991), pp. 62–63. Not all economists agree with this view, however. For an alternative view, see, for example, James H. Schulz, "Population Ageing: Economic Growth and Generational Transfers (Labour, Productivity and Saving Issues)", in *Population Ageing: Challenges for Policies and Programmes in Developed and Developing Countries*, edited by Robert Cliquet and Mohammed Nizamuddin (New York: United Nations Population Fund, and Brussels: Population and Family Study Centre, 1999).

10. See, for example, Gary Burtless, "The Fiscal Challenges of an Aging Population", in *As the Workforce Ages: Costs, Benefits and Policy Challenges*, edited by Olivia S. Mitchell (New York: ILR Press); *and Financial Times*, 10 November 2000.

11. Goh (1986), pp. 62–63.

12. See, for example, "Equity Between Generations", Interview with Sam Preston by Alan AtKission, *In Context*, no. 21 (Spring 1989) (<*www.context.org/ICLIB/IC21/Preston.htm*>); Fernando Gil-Torres, "Productive Aging in the 21st Century: Social and Political Lessons from the United States" (Paper presented at the 6th Asia/Oceania Regional Congress on Gerontology, Seoul, 1999); and Alan Walker and Gerhard Naegele, eds., *The Politics of Old Age in Europe* (Buckingham: Open University Press, 1999).

13. See, for example, John B. Williamson and Diane Watts-Roy, "Framing the Generational Equity Debate", in *The Generational Equity Debate*, edited by John B. Williamson et al. (New York: Columbia University Press, 1999); *The Economist*, 11 January 1997, pp. 21–22. Schulz has described the "intergenerational conflict" prediction as "one of the worst abuses in the use of demographic numbers" (Schulz, op. cit., p. 135).

14. *Straits Times*, 8 May 1994.

15. Ministry of Community Development (1999), p. 21.

16. Ibid., p. 22.

17. Goh (1986), reprinted in Saw, op. cit., p. 63.

18. Brian Nichiporuk, "Summary", *The Security Dynamics of Demographic Factors*, MR-1088-WFHF/RF/DLPF/A, p xvi. (<*www.rand.org/publications/MR/MR1088*>).

19. *Straits Times Interactive*, 15 June 2000, and 7 November 2000. Dubbed the "Silver Hair" programme, individuals must have monthly incomes of RM7,000 (S$3,100) or fixed deposits of RM10,000 in a Malaysian bank or financial institution. The respective

amounts for couples are RM10,000 and RM150,000. They must also have medical insurance; those unable to obtain such insurance must provide proof. Those granted visas under this programme are not allowed to be in gainful employment but they may take part in voluntary organizations (<*Immi...Malaysia_Silver Hair Programme.htm*>).

20. Central Provident Fund Board, *Annual Report 1998*, n.d., p. 70).
21. Department of Statistics, *Singapore Census of Population 2000 Advance Data Release No. 1: Changing Education Profile*, at *www.singstat.gov.sg/C2000/adr-edu.pdf*.
22. Goh (2000), p. 12.
23. Ibid., p. 35.
24. Channel News Asia, 30 May 2000.
25. Yap Mui Teng, "Low Fertility and Policy Response in Singapore", in *Low Fertility and Policy Responses to Issues of Ageing and Welfare*, Research Paper 2000-1 (Korea Institute for Health and Social Affairs, and United Nations Population Fund [UNFPA], 2000), pp. 122–23.
26. See, for instance, Carl P. Schmertmann, "Immigrants' Ages and the Structure of Stationary Populations with Below-Replacement Fertility", *Demography* 29, no 4 (1992): 595–612.
27. Goh (2000), p. 37.
28. *Straits Times Interactive*, 11 September 2000.
29. Stella Quah, *Study on the Family* (Singapore: Ministry of Community Development, 1999), p. 27.
30. *Straits Times Interactive*, 28 November 2000.
31. Goh (2000), p. 35.
32. *Straits Times*, 15 November 2000, p. H15.
33. Channel NewsAsia, 27 September 2000.
34. "Being 25", *Asiaweek*, 24 November 2000, p. 36.
35. Cited in Dirk van de Kaa, "Postmodern Fertility Preferences: From Changing Value Orientation to New Behaviour", ANU Working Papers in Demography No. 74 (Australian National University, 1998). According to *Asiaweek*, "When it comes to ideals (such as freedom or fairness), young Asians are split. There are those who believe society can't be changed ... Yet other twenty-somethings rail against corruption, injustice and narrow-mindedness. Some do so for ideals".
36. See Quah (1999); and *Straits Times Interactive*, 13 November 2000.
37. Van de Kaa (1998).

THAILAND

THAILAND
A Moment of Transition

Abhinya Rathanamongkolmas

Never before in modern Thai political history has a civilian government sustained its full term in office. However, Chuan Leekpai has achieved this, albeit with a weakening of his credibility. In other words, he and his government struggled to complete the full term, in the face of serious criticism and outright challenges from various sectors.

At the beginning of 2000, the Chuan government survived no-confidence votes, especially on the motion of a false declaration of assets by his Deputy Prime Minister and Minister of Interior Affairs, and concurrently the General Secretary of his Democrat Party, Sanan Kachornprasart. When the case of Sanan was first submitted to the National Counter Corruption Commission (NCCC), and then forwarded to the Constitutional Court, Sanan was found guilty. The opposition Members of Parliament (MPs), mostly from the New Aspiration Party (NAP), tried to use this verdict to force Chuan to declare the dissolution of Parliament by their *en masse* resignation from the House in June.[1] Neither the politicians nor others could successfully pressure him into an early resignation, however. They had to wait until 9 November, only eight days before the official termination of government at full term, when Chuan finally declared the dissolution of Parliament. The elections were held on 6 January 2001. There were people who had come to believe that there was no alternative to the old style of politics, and that the sluggish election procedure operating under the umbrella of the Election Commission (EC) would delay the election results. There were others who expected that the elections would bring about a political transition towards democratization. If the elections had failed, it could have been seen as a setback for democracy not only in Thailand but also in Southeast Asia.[2]

The end of the Chuan government marked a constitutional transition from the old constitution to the new one promulgated in 1997. The new constitution alters the parliamentary composition, which used to comprise of 393 members. It now consists of 500 members — 400 elected individually via

ABHINYA RATHANAMONGKOLMAS is an Associate Professor in the Department of International Relations, Faculty of Political Science, Chulalongkorn University, Thailand.

constituencies, and another 100 selected from party lists based on the number of votes received by each party. Voters now have two votes each, one for a district representative and one for a party. The constitutional drafters expected different roles for the two kinds of MPs. Those elected from constituencies would be the legislators responsible for putting forward the demands of the people as inputs for the public policy formulation process, and to take accountability for policy implementation. Since they were from the constituencies, they would be more reponsive to the demands of the localities. Those MPs selected from the party lists would perform in the executive branch as the Cabinet because they would have specific potentialities and qualifications. The Cabinet would consist of 35 members, instead of 45 previously. Furthermore, MPs could not switch from one party to another within five years. This provision would help to strengthen the party system. However, the mandate brought some confusion to Thai politics prior to the end of the Chuan government. Numerous former MPs were "pulled" into various parties, especially the Thai Rak Thai Party of telecommunications tycoon, Dr Thaksin Shinawatra. Therefore, the January 2001 elections brought with it fierce competition between the Thai Rak Thai Party and Chuan's Democratic Party.

Independent Organizations: Mechanism for Political Reform
The year 2000 saw renewed efforts to improve the election process. On 4 March, the Election Commission organized the first elections for the Senate. The main objective of the Election Commission was to deter fraudulent candidates from entering the Senate. Thus, all means of electoral campaigning were closely monitored. The Election Commission took strong action in some provinces against candidates alleged to have cheated. Even in Bangkok, two further rounds of elections had to be arranged to get "clean" senators to replace those who were disqualified. The Senate elections saw an unprecedented voter level of 72 per cent. However, this enthusiasm declined rapidly in later by-election rounds. Owing to a ban on party affiliation for those running for office, the elected Senate comprised well-known former academics, technocrats, non-governmental organization (NGO) leaders, retired military officers, and others.

In the election for Governor of Bangkok Metropolitan Administration on 23 July, Samak Sundaravej, the outspoken rightist, achieved a landslide victory over Thai Rak Thai's Sudarat Keyurapan and other more liberal candidates. In this election, much information was collected by the EC concerning the campaigning behaviour of candidates and the amount spent during the election campaign.

The scope of the EC's power to suspend disqualified candidates, and the budget to be spent on further electoral rounds or by-elections, became the subject of a heated discussion in the run-up to the general election in early 2001. With mixed interpretations of the scope of its power, based on the EC draft regulation, confusion emerged over the expulsion of disqualified electoral candidates. In the end it took nearly five months to complete the Senate election process. The expulsion clause, known as the "red card" in the EC draft regulation, was also found to be in breach of the election law. The Constitutional Court at that time ruled that the EC did not hold such a mandate.

The struggle over political reform was obvious from the tug-of-war between the House of Representatives and the Senate over the Election Law Amendment Bill in October 2000. This was designed to empower the Election Commission to prevent disqualified electoral candidates from carrying out their campaigns, to abolish the election rights of candidates who cheated, and to declare as void party-list ballots that were cast for parties which violated the election law. This amendment should have been urgent business for the House but it has been prolonged for years. During the battle for the chair of the joint committee for amendment issues, the chairman (from the Senate) cast a decisive vote on disputed issues to iron out differences over electoral amendments. The four disputed issues were the requirement that the EC take legal action against disqualified candidates; the time-frame within which the EC can remove elected MPs and senators for cheating; the authorization of election officials to search houses without warrants; and the Senate's measure requiring constituent MPs and their parties to shoulder the by-election costs of MPs appointed to the Cabinet.[3] On 7 November, the Constitutional Court ruled out the implementation of the Election Law Amendment Bill. The Court also upheld the Senate's contentious requirement that the parties of Cabinet-bound constituency MPs should shoulder the costs of by-elections.[4]

The major factor in candidate disqualification was involvement in any form of vote-buying. However, for ministers, the application for disqualification goes further to cover any false declaration of assets and undeclared business shareholdings during their tenure in the Cabinet. This measure, in reality, is a two-edged sword. On one hand, it prevents money politics. On the other, it serves to defame or destroy political rivals via the functions of the National Counter Corruption Commission (NCCC) and the Anti-Money Laundering Commission.

Sanan Kachornprasart was the first politician in 2000 to be charged with false asset declarations. He opted to resign from all government posts following the Constitutional Court's verdict. Although Thaksin was cleared from alleged money-laundering charges, the NCCC investigated him for failing to adhere to constitutional rules governing shareholdings when he was Deputy Prime Minister for a short period. Whether he will be banned from politics for up to five years for concealing his stockholdings by transferring them to his maid, driver, and nanny, will be subject to NCCC investigation and the verdict of the Constitutional Court.[5] The investigation continued during the election campaign. There was an expectation that the verdict would have controversial impact for him as well as his party members, since Thai Rak Thai was gaining more popularity at the expense of the Democrats. Thaksin's political rivals, Chuan and Banyad Bantadtan, the Interior Minister, together with other Democrat ministers, have faced similar accusations (ministers from other parties have also been the subject of investigation).

On 26 December 2000, before the general election was held, the NCCC voted 8 to 1 to indict Thaksin on a false declaration of assets charge. Meanwhile, on the same day, they ruled that both Chuan and Banyad's failures to report on their stocks did not benefit them in any significant way. Eventually, the two leading Democrats were cleared.[6] Thaksin declined to accept this verdict and has been waiting for the final mandate from the Constitutional Court. However, this verdict of the NCCC did not deter him from becoming the twenty-third Prime Minister of Thailand. His Thai Rak Thai party crushed Chuan Leekpai and his Democrats on both constituency and party lists, taking just over half of all the seats in the House on election night[7] (however, disqualifications altered the final result so that Thai Rak Thai held 248 seats).

A complaint was submitted to the NCCC by the Bank of Thailand on 7 April, charging that Sirin Nimmanahaeminda, the younger brother of the then Minister of Finance, Tarrin, had been involved in financial irregularities between 1995 and 1997.[8] Sirin, the then Krung Thai Bank president, was tried under the State Enterprise Act of 1959 (given the bank's status as a state enterprise). The NCCC found him guilty of misconduct and negligence of duty, and forwarded the case against him to the office of the Attorney General. To some extent, this case has undermined Tarrin's political reputation.

The related work of the Constitutional Court, the National Counter Corruption Commission and the Anti-Money Laundering Commission offered a better environment for the Election Commission to bring about political reform. Coupled with legislation disallowing Cabinet members to sit in the legislature, these bodies have also successfully ousted violators of the constitution from the House and Senate. The decision of the Constitutional Court on the Electoral Amendment Bill will have immediate and long-term impacts. In the short term, political parties have to determine which candidates will be placed in constituencies and which will be placed on party lists (it cannot be both) in order to win the elections, as well as to decide who will become ministers. In the long run, Cabinet seat aspirants would be gradually eradicated. In the 2001 elections, voters would be given clearer choices of genuine legislators from the constituency elections and the potential Cabinet members from the party lists. The Senate elections of 2000 and the general election at the start of 2001 represent the new phase of political reform provided by the 1997 People's Constitution.

It was noteworthy that many people demonstrated their dedication to political reform and dared to challenge the influence of politicians and bureaucrats by filing information on vote-buying and other non-transparent actions to independent organizations. Sanan's case was brought to the NCCC for investigation by Veera Somkwamkid, president of the Group for Protection of the People's Freedom. The cases involving Cabinet members were submitted by Amara Amaratananont, the co-ordinator for the October People's Network. The business newspaper *Prachachart* disclosed Thaksin's reportedly dubious transfer of shareholdings.

Political Reform by the People

Non-governmental organizations played a significant role in political reform through an institutional mechanism, but direct social action by the people was also important at times. In 2000, Thailand witnessed attempts to practise the popular participation of civil society according to the new constitution, as well as attempts to maintain the status quo of the existing system. Economic and social problems were used to catalyse and to stimulate an increasing and strengthening social movement to manifest social conflict between central government and civil society. Therefore, the rationale behind social conflicts in Thailand during the year 2000 was mostly based on the consequences of national socio-economic developmental strategies. These were reactions against government policies that disrupted localities and resources, and changed their economic patterns of self-sufficiency, as well as causing adverse environmental impacts.

Some of those conflicts, for example, the Pak Moon Dam case, escalated to bloodshed between the state and its supporters on one hand, and protestors on the other. By mid-2000, the villagers from Kong Chiam district and its vicinity in U-Bon Ratchathani province, accompanied by the leading rural NGO, the Assembly of the Poor, and supported by other NGOs, set up demonstration camps near Government House. They requested the government to continue taking action in the process of compensation for the cost of their lands and livelihood, which they had lost to the Pak Moon Dam site construction. During the former Chavalit government, the Cabinet had decided on resolutions, on 26 April 1996 and 17 April 1997 respectively, to compensate the villagers on the basis of proven landownership rights. Some compensation had already been paid before the resignation of the Chavalit government. However, the Chuan Cabinet made a decision on 30 June 1998 that reversed the previous resolutions. The government argued that the villagers' demands were illegal, since they could not claim landownership rights as the construction site was partly in the national forest area. Villagers who had lived in such an area were deemed to be encroachers. Moreover, the government accused some compensation recipients of cheating the system (this included the politician in the former government who was responsible for this policy).

Villagers, both in the encamped demonstrations in Bangkok, and in their villages at the dam site, put pressure on the central government and the Electricity Generating Authority of Thailand, which produces electricity from hydraulic power from the dam. Violence resulted between state forces and the villagers.[9] At the end of the Chuan government, this conflict was still not resolved. The case reflects the increasing power of the local people, which could symbolize to some extent unity against state power when it comes to protecting property and rights.

Since the new constitution offered participation by the people in state decisions and affairs that will impact on their way of life, the number of social movements escalated throughout 2000. On 29 July and 21 October respectively, the local people from Songkhla province, including academics and students from Songkhla Nakarindara University, joined by NGOs, notably the Federation of Students of Thailand and the Committee for Democracy Campaigning, to protest against the public hearings on the Thai-Malaysian gas pipeline project. The reasons behind these protests were threefold: the fear of environmental mismanagement owing to the route of the gas pipeline from the source in the Joint Development Area (JDA) to the gas separation plant at Jana district; the alleged misconduct of the public hearings; and the hazardous impact of an industrial estate. Later on, the Ministry of Science and Technology confirmed that a study on the environmental impact of this project had been discounted.[10] The first hearing failed to achieve a compromise as each side stood firm on its stance. The second hearing was marred by chaos and some violence. A few days later, the Chuan Cabinet decided to continue the public hearings on the project.[11] The police also decided to arrest leaders of the protest movement and other persons involved.

Besides performing the role of a unified pressure group on the allocation of natural resources and environmental issues, the NGOs also tried to enforce accountability for government expenditure and other issues. On 7 November, during the last Cabinet meeting of the year, 1,000 members of Assembly of the Poor protestors blocked the entrance to Government House in an attempt to stop the Cabinet from "squandering" 20 billion baht before its term expired. Meanwhile, Deputy Prime Minister Banyat Bantadtan considered this action a violation of the law.[12] In the swift operation to clear the blockade, police and protest leaders suffered minor injuries.

Not all social movements deal with environmental and poverty problems, and not every social movement employs protest as a means to achieve an end. When the Chuan government took office in the middle of the year without an effective opposition in Parliament to provide a check on his administrative and legislative power, an alliance called the Democratic Group for People (*Po x Po* in Thai) was formed and led by Dr Seksarn Prasertkul, a highly respected intellectual. This NGO occasionally proposed socio-political and economic alternatives to Thai society. In its first attempt, the members proposed that Parliament be dissolved as the government should accept responsibility for Sanan's case.[13] On another occasion, Dr Seksarn urged economic liberation from the International Monetary Fund (IMF) and other capitalist institutions, to restore the national economy.[14] This urge was similar to that of Meechai Ruechupand, the previous Chairman of the National Assembly, in his satirical article "Letter to the Boss".[15]

Economic Recovery: Illusion or Illusive?

Throughout the year, the economy remained the main concern of the Thais. Finance Minister Tarrin Nimmanahaeminda was the target of criticism from many corners. Even the former economic tsar, Boonchoo Rojanasathira, who is a fellow Democrat Party member, subjected Tarrin to harsh criticism. Tarrin was blamed for an ineffective policy to assist economic recovery. However, the Democrat members who held positions in the Cabinet supported Tarrin and assured him that he had not failed in tackling the economic crisis. They maintained their confidence in him as minister.

In fact, the economy was not as bad as many perceived it to be. According to the report distributed by the Ministry of Finance on 9 October 2000, there was a recovery in the national economy as a whole.[16] Together with the statement of the General Secretary of the National Economic and Social Development Board (NESDB), and leading businessmen, they confirmed that there had been some effective measures to stimulate the economy, as seen in the expansion of exports, increasing domestic investment, and the allocation of 910,000 million baht for government expenditures for the 2001 fiscal year.[17] Although the macroeconomy looked better, academics and business people were sceptical about the financial and productive sectors.

Ammar Siamwalla, a prominent economist, analysed the cause of Thai economic stagnation in his article entitled "AMC: An idea whose time has gone". He argued that the economic crisis stemmed from the adoption of the modern banking system in an unstructured Thai economy, which relied upon unrealistic public companies, and unsystematic businesses. Therefore, the implementation of the bank-based, high debt model of banking, with the hope of reducing non-performing loans, could not work. He suggested the adoption of the market-based prudential model instead.[18] Business people were also hampered in their efforts by the government's financial measures which needed to be adjusted. In another approach, Banthoon Lamsam, the president of Thai Farmer Bank (TFB), for example, urged the government to intervene in the financial institutions as well as to stimulate the production sector.[19] His opinion was similar to that of the president of the Federation of Thai Industries, Thawee Butrsunthon.[20] Meanwhile, others in the commercial sector proposed a temporary retreat or delinkage from the world capitalist economy, which they believed to be the only measure to help Thailand out of its crippled situation.

Tarrin resolutely held on to his policy. Prior to the dissolution of Parliament, he had initiated a range of economic measures aimed at cutting business costs, helping farmers, and raising household income. Programmes under these measures would be financed with unused funds from existing loans from international institutions, with no new borrowing that would cause taxation rate increases. The Cabinet approved these programmes, and the issue of new bonds for the Finance Institutions Development Funds on 31 October 2000.[21] However, the economy remained generally lethargic, which helped to undermine the Democrat Party in the 2001 general election.

Whether or not the economic recovery was illusive, the reality is that between 1997 and 2000, poverty levels rose from 11.4 per cent to 16.0 per cent, and Thailand already had one of the worst income distribution ratios in the world.[22] According to an NESDB statement, economic growth during the third quarter of 2000 was below market expectations. The major factors for this economic deceleration were weaker domestic demand and rising fuel prices. These factors pulled the anticipated growth rate of 3.6 per cent down to 2.6 per cent for year-on-year growth. However, a growing export sector was the main driving force for the 4.7 per cent overall economic growth for the first nine months of the year. Statistics from the Bank of Thailand's data portrayed the 18 per cent increase in export growth year-on-year against a growth in imports of 18.8 per cent. Inflation was estimated to remain low at 1.7 per cent for 2000.[23] Meanwhile, the IMF had observed the risk to economic recovery for 2001 and suggested that Thai authorities maintain an accommodative stance on interest rates, and to push ahead with the restructuring of corporate debt.[24]

The economic situation offered a good chance for most political parties to sell ideas of raising household income, especially in the agricultural sector. Thai Rak Thai, for example, had promised farmers a three-year debt moratorium, loans to each of Thailand's 80,000 villages to stimulate employment, and a tax cut — all apparently without running up a budget deficit.[25] For the whole year, the government had supported small and medium enterprises (SMEs), but the credit crunch in the financial system brought difficulty to small entrepreneurs. Many financial institutions have experienced a refusal to repay loans from countless defaulting borrowers, and the legal system is too ineffective to enforce loan payment. A policy of encouraging domestic investment in SMEs thus presents a "chicken and egg" situation. Moreover, foreign investment appears to lack confidence in Thailand, viewing it in the same light as Indonesia or the Philippines, where economic uncertainty is beset by political instability.[26]

Foreign Relations: Regionalism as an Essential Mechanism

In general, the Thai voting public are not interested in foreign relations, nor do they regard themselves as being affected by foreign policy decisions. The current economic crisis has made the public more aware of the role of international financial institutions in their daily lives. Unpleasant activities from Myanmar's dissidents in Thailand are other events that may stir their interest in foreign affairs from time to time. However, foreign relations are still perceived by the majority of Thais as an élite task that is far beyond the understanding of laymen. Foreign policy was not an issue in the 2001 general election.

The Chuan government was fortunate to have Dr Surin Pitsuwan and M.R. Sukhumbhand Paribatra as, respectively, the minister and the deputy minister of foreign affairs. Prior to entering the political arena, both had accumulated respect as outstanding academics in the field of international relations. They both have extensive networks with regional and international élites and institutions. With the application of theory to practice, both of them have given Thai diplomacy a high reputation. As a Muslim, Surin was able to pursue a close link with Islamic countries. Both Surin and Sukhumbhand have successfully implemented a proactive approach to ASEAN and to co-operation with the international community. Thailand played a leading role in establishing the agendas for both conventional and human security in the Southeast Asian region through the ASEAN Regional Forum (ARF) and the ASEAN Ministerial Meeting (AMM), as well as other venues. Thailand joined the International Force for East Timor (INTERFET), assuming the deputy command under Australia, in order to keep the regional peace and security, and in respect of the non-intervention principle. Thailand continues to stand by the enlargement of ASEAN membership, especially the controversial acceptance of Myanmar as a member, and will continue its efforts to urge political change in Myanmar. Moreover, Thailand contributed its effort to co-ordinate the ASEAN-Europe Ministerial Meeting (ASEM) held in Vientiene in late November 2000. This meeting had been postponed for more than two years because of the European Union's displeasure with Myanmar's dictatorial military regime, which engages in massive forced labour and generally has a dismal human rights record. In order to prevent the spillover of domestic conflict from neighbouring countries (especially from Myanmar with which Thailand shares its longest border), Surin had proposed a "flexible engagement" policy several years earlier. This was designed to allow for greater discussion of transnational issues in ASEAN. This policy was, however, not welcomed by the majority of ASEAN members, but did find favour with the Philippines.

Myanmar's political unrest and economic hardship caused the flow of both Burmans and ethnic minorities, as refugees, displaced persons and illegal immigrants into Thailand. The need for cheap labour in some industries and services, such as fisheries and restaurants, was another supporting factor that led to human trafficking from Myanmar. Thai diplomats were caught in the dilemma of deciding between good state-to-state relations and maintaining humanitarian support. On 24 January 2000, nine members of a Myanmar rebel group called God's Army seized Ratchaburi Hospital in Suan Pung district,[27] taking hostage hundreds of patients, medical personnel, and visiting relatives. All the rebels were later killed in a Thai rescue mission.[28] Again, by 31 December 2000, while Thai villagers at Wai Noi Nai village in Suan Pung district were celebrating New Year's Eve, an unidentified group of gunmen (claiming to be God's Army also), robbed a grocery store and killed six Thais, including two children.[29] These two incidents exhibited the desperate need of God's Army to survive, by seizing a hospital to seek medical care and supplies, and a store to steal food. These cases ignited furious reactions from Thais, not only against the God's Army but also towards innocent displaced persons. Later, on 16 January 2001, the symbolic leaders of this group, who are twin teenagers, with fourteen other group members sought political asylum in Thailand.

Although people-to-people relations were frustrating, and the "flexible engagement" policy could not be employed as a mechanism for preventive security, in the final analysis Thailand still places importance on regional co-operation as an essential factor in responding to diplomatic relations with Southeast Asia,[30] including Myanmar.

Conclusion

The general election on 6 January 2001 set an unprecedented political mandate for both Thaksin Shinawatra of Thai Rak Thai Party and Thai politics. For Thaksin, it gave him both the legitimacy to administer the country, and relatively strong bargaining power to form the coalition government. His two-year-old Thai Rak Thai Party appeared to have gained more than half of the seats in the House of Representatives on election night. For Thai politics, this is the first time in history that one party has won so convincingly. After the second round of voting following the disqualification of some candidates, Thai Rak Thai (TRT) took 248 seats, which overwhelmed its nearest rival, the Democrats with 128 seats. TRT has formed a coalition with two smaller parties: Chart Thai (41 seats) and NAP (36 seats). A third minor party in the house is the Chart Patana (39 seats). The popular mandate was also strong with approximately 70 per cent of voters turning out. This was also the first time that a party's policies were enthusiastically employed and promoted in what can only be described as a political marketing campaign. Thai Rak Thai aroused the political awareness of voters by presenting and advertising campaign policies, which convinced them that the party was a viable alternative to the Democrats. Promises of a three-year debt moratorium, an endowment fund for village loans, and a new programme for medical care were attractive to poverty-stricken Thais.

Equally, the Democrats lost the elections because of their increasing unpopularity. This included a slow economic recovery, implementation of unpopular reforms, a declining stock market, a surge in oil prices, and lower returns from agricultural exports. Furthermore, many "godfathers", or political fixers, in Thai politics lost their seats. Their losses in this election are partly due to the change in the way the ballot was counted, from individual stations to a regional centre for each constituency. This nullified the effects of vote-buying because even if a vote was purchased, the buyer could not know whether or not the vote sellers had voted for them. Various small parties did not survive either. The present composition in Parliament sees the Thai Rak Thai and Democrat parties as the two leading parties, while the New Aspiration Party, Chart Thai and Chart Patana have become much smaller in size. Thus, the elections have altered Thailand's previously fractured political scene. If this general election is able to bring in a government with a greater moral commitment and, crucially, administrative capabilities, then this transitional moment will have been worth the wait.

The year 2000 saw Thailand confirming its political transformation. It was a transitional period from old-style politics to further democratization. This process has been kept moving by independent organizations and a growing awareness in civil society. Interactions and interplay among and between political institutions have played essential roles in pressing for accountable government policies, and their implementation and administration, especially those related to corruption scandals. The continuation of effective accountability is expected since there have been attempts to establish more independent bodies, according to the new constitution. Some are in the process of emerging, such as the new National Broadcasting Commission and the new National Telecommunications Commission, which will wield powers in deregulating national telecommunications. A new Human Rights Commission will guarantee basic human rights. Reformist senators and intellectuals have supported the establishment of these organizations. These changes in governance and society will constitute a genuine reform movement.

Conservative forces seeking to maintain the old-style system still remain, however, with some support within the country. Nevertheless, there is an expectation that the strengthening of political participation will facilitate this socio-political transformation. With the compromise and conciliation brought by democratic rule, Thailand will most likely see better governance and eventually nationwide political stabilization.

NOTES

1. <http:www.parliament.go.th>
2. See, for example, "A Moment of Truth for Democracy", *Far Eastern Economic Review*, 9 November 2000, p. 15.
3. "Senate, MPs begin reform tug-of-war", *Nation*, 14 October 2000, pp. A1, A6.
4. "Constitutional Court: Ruling clears the way for election", *Bangkok Post*, 1 November 2000, p. 1.
5. "Broken Dreams", *Time Magazine*, 6 November 2000, p. 28.
6. "I will be prime minister: Thaksin", *Nation*, 27 December 2000, p. 1.
7. "National Election", *Sunday Nation*, 7 January 2001, p. 2.
8. "Sirin guilty over loan irregularities", *Nation*, 8 November 2000, pp. A1, A6.
9. "Violent clashes spark rallying cry", *Nation*, 18 July 2000, pp. A1, A6.
10. "News Report", *Matichon*, 11 November 2000, pp. 1, 24.
11. "More hearing on pipeline set", *Nation*, 25 October 2000, pp. A1, A2.
12. "Riot police break up Assembly rally", *Nation*, 8 November 2000, p. A6.
13. "Report on the first conference of PO x PO", *Matichon*, 28 August 2000, pp. 2, 6.
14. "Seksarn Prasertkul urged Thais to resolve crisis, liberation from 'World Capitalist'", *Matichon*, 15 October 2000, pp. 2, 6.
15. <http:www.meechaithailand.com>.
16. "Ministry of Finance shows figures to counter 'Committee of the Senate' to confirm an economic recovery", *Matichon*, 11 October 2000, p. 2.
17. "Perspectives on economic situation from public and private sectors", *Thai Rath*, 23 October 2000, p. 8.
18. "AMC: An idea whose time has gone", *Nation*, 3 October 2000, p. A4.
19. "Banker urges intervention in key sectors", *Nation*, 25 October 2000, p. B14.
20. *Thai Rath*, 23 October 2000, p. 8.
21. "Tarrin fine-tunes recovery", *Bangkok Post*, 1 November 2000, Business Section, p. 1.
22. *Far Eastern Economic Review*, 9 November 2000, p.19.
23. "Statistics reveal little change", *Bangkok Post*, 30 December 2000, Business Section, p.1; "Economy a mixed picture", *Nation*, 30 December 2000, p. A7; and "Third-quarter slow down deals blow to GDP outlook", *Nation*, 19 December 2000, Business and Finance Section, p. B1.
24. "IMF warns weak market may hit recovery", *Bangkok Post*, 22 December 2000, Business Section, p. 1.
25. *Time Magazine*, 6 November 2000, p. 27.

26. *Far Eastern Economic Review*, 9 November 2000, pp. 15, 19.
27. Suan Pung district, Ratchauri Province, is the site of the Myanmar refugee camps.
28. "God's Army seized Ratchaburi Hospital", *Matichon*, 31 December 2000, 10 Top News of the Year, p. 2.
29. "Burmese rebels slay 6 Thais in raid on shop", *Nation*, 1 January 2001, p. 1.
30. HE M.R. Sukhumbhand Paribatra, Opening Statement, Address to an International Conference on "Democratization and Conflict Management/Prevention in Southeast Asia in the 21st Century?", organized by UNPA/UNDP and ISIS, Thailand, at Riverside Mariot Hotel, Bangkok, Thailand, 16–19 January 2001.

THAILAND'S RELATIONS WITH THE NEW ASEAN MEMBERS
Solving Problems and Creating Images

Chayachoke Chulasiriwongs

The second Chuan Leekpai government was defeated in the 2001 general election owing to its unpopularity by the end of its term. The government, which was first elected in late 1997, was at first hailed as a saviour as there was a strong expectation that with its "economic dream team" Thailand's economy would be revitalized following the economic crisis. In the three years since it came to power, the government has been found by the majority of the population to be incapable of reversing the critical plight of the country.

Although the outgoing government has proven to be unpopular, including Prime Minister Chuan Leekpai, who has been the object of considerable adverse media attention, this does not mean that the overall performance of the outgoing coalition government, led by Chuan's Democrat Party, was a total failure. For instance, while the government claimed an economic recovery of around 3–4 per cent in the year 2000, some business sectors actually fared better than others, depending on the extent of remedial measures introduced by the government.

Nevertheless, people in general still felt the "pinch" and considered the full commitment that the Chuan government had given to the International Monetary Fund (IMF) as a mere sell-out of the country to foreigners. This has given rise to an inward-looking neo-nationalist upsurge among the Thai people, who have embraced the notion of "localism".[1] This implies some endogenous concepts re-introduced by the Thai King, such as self-sufficiency and self-reliance, less reliance on consumerism and industrialization, and nostalgia for the traditional rural community.

How does this political and economic situation relate to Thai foreign relations in the year 2000? As it turned out, during 2000 Thailand was occupied with problems concerning Myanmar and Laos, while the state of its relationships with other neighbours was comparatively normal. Yet, one wonders why Thailand fares better when it deals with countries further away, and also when it handles regional and global issues.

CHAYACHOKE CHULASIRIWONGS is with the Faculty of Political Science, Chulalongkorn University, Bangkok, Thailand.

Friendly and Unfriendly Neighbours

Thailand's external relationship with its neighbours was prominent throughout 2000. This relationship requires some discussion as it touches not only on security issues but also on the economic well-being and social matters affecting Thailand and its people.

Perhaps one can better appreciate these relations if one understands the meaning of the term "neighbour" in Thai, which is *peun-ban*. This term does not merely mean "a person", but "a friend" who lives next door or near one's residence. Yet within the three years of the Chuan administration, it had, to the people's chagrin, successfully caused much resentment among some of Thailand's neighbours. Therefore, it makes one wonder if the term *peun-ban* can still be applied.

A Long-Standing Conflict with Myanmar

Thailand's sour relations with its neighbour to the west, namely, Myanmar (or Burma), began in the 1960s under the Ne Win regime when Myanmar suspected that the Thai Government, through its humanitarian policy, was giving support to the Burmese minorities fleeing into Thailand. As the minority issue was at the core of Myanmar's security, this became a serious concern throughout the past thirty years. In recent times, the relationship between the two countries reached its lowest ebb after the siege of the Myanmar Embassy in Bangkok on 1 October 1999 by a group of student dissidents known as the Vigorous Burmese Student Warriors (VBSW). Conflict resolution methods which the Thai Government used complicated the relations between the two countries. Critical comments made by Major General Sanan Kajornprasart, the then Interior Minister, on the general conditions in Myanmar, gave rise to the siege, and the authorities allowed the culprits to go free without any punishment. These events clearly angered the Yangon government.

During the first month of the new millennium, the Thai Government encountered more problems, but it also helped to loosen up the tense relationship between Thailand and Myanmar. Almost four months had gone by after the Embassy incident when another seige occurred. This time, at least two of the released students, and their friends from the VBSW, together with another four dissidents calling themselves God's Army of the Karens, made a daring attempt to capture the Ratchaburi Centre Hospital in the early morning of 24 January. The Thai hospital is situated about 70 kilometres from the Thai–Myanmar border. After a twenty-two-hour ordeal, the ten terrorists were all killed, and the eight hundred hostages then freed. However, according to some reports, there may have been some accomplices who later fled to the God's Army Kamaplaw camp in Myanmar's Karen stronghold.

Although the Yangon government was appeased by the Thai authorities' handling of the Ratchaburi crisis, the relationship between the two countries was far from normalized. Throughout most of the year, Thai–Myanmar relations were riddled with incidents. Not only were there skirmishes along the

2,400-kilometre common border, but there were also conflicts and misunderstandings over Myanmar's ethnic minorities, the issue of drugs and methamphetamine production and trade, illegal immigrants and labourers, and various issues on human rights. Although these problems may have actually originated from conditions within Myanmar, Thailand's mishandling of the issues, and its resulting inconsistent policy, did not help the situation.

Clearly, the seizures of the Myanmar Embassy in Bangkok and the Ratchaburi Centre Hospital were in part a result of inefficient intelligence and lack of proper administration on the part of both the Thai Government and its civil service.[2] The incidents were the culmination of the long history of a murky Thai policy towards the armed Myanmar minorities residing on both sides of the porous border. The "buffer state" or "buffer communities policy", which should really be called a practice, has been applied since pre-modern times. Protectorate or dependent states in Ayuthaya and the early Bangkok periods, and the "Khmer Seri" and "Lao Issara" on the eastern border during the Cold War, had kept Thailand free from direct confrontation with its major foes and communist neighbours. This practice, especially during military rule, allowed the Thai armed forces to determine and direct what they believed to be the best way to pacify the border areas. This foreign policy approach during the period of military rule in Thailand, however, has left a legacy which the Yangon junta finds difficult to forget. This is especially so after renewed fighting occurred between the minorities and the Myanmar forces along the border throughout 2000,[3] and some of these attacks were seemingly even launched by some Myanmar minority groups from inside Thailand.[4]

For the past three years, the elected government under Chuan Leekpai had tried its best to lead the country's foreign policy. However, the civilian government was not able to control policy-making without the security forces along the border lending a willing hand. Therefore, whatever occurred along the border should have been under the control of the central government in Bangkok. Apparently, this did not happen. This raises the doubt whether Thai policy towards Myanmar changed much during the year 2000, and whether its policy engendered trust from its western neighbour.

A more serious threat to Thailand's stability, in terms of security, economic and social matters, is the problem of illegal migrants and drugs coming from the western border. Thai leaders at all levels have always maintained that these problems are rooted in Myanmar. Therefore, if the Myanmar Government cannot redress its internal problems and does not give a willing hand to Thailand to stop the human exodus and the export of drugs, then the Thai Government will never be able to eradicate these problems. This assertion may be true to a certain extent. However, Thailand should also realize that it has to take a major share of the blame because of, *inter alia*, the short-sighted government policy, corrupt politicians and civil servants, and domestic demand for narcotics.

The problem relating to illegal immigrants is a dilemma for Thailand. It also touches on national security issues and foreign relations at all levels.

The summation of these problems can be found in an editorial note in the *Nation* newspaper, which states:[5]

> Acting Foreign Minister Sukhumbhand Paribatra ... has already said that Thailand needs to review its policy towards immigration, as well as ties with Burma. In fact, Thailand should have done this review a long time ago. But because of domestic political and internal constraints, some of the policies were not implemented. As Thailand continues to adopt a proactive policy with human rights and democracy as its diplomatic pillars, it is still being held hostage by its bilateral relations — especially by countries which do not respect fundamental rights of human beings. As a principle, Thailand must provide humanitarian assistance to the Karen refugees as it has done in the past five decades.

During the past few years, as a result of the Yangon junta's practice of political persecution and forced labour, as well as the economic plight in Myanmar, hundreds of thousands of Myanmar people (consisting of various ethnic groups) have illegally entered Thailand. These people can be roughly categorized into three groups. There are those who are put in the refugee camps scattered along the Thai–Myanmar border; students whom the United Nations' High Commission for Refugees (UNHCR) has granted the status of "person-of-concern" (POC); and those who, after entering Thailand, are employed as labourers.

For the first group, the Thai policy is to provide humanitarian assistance and when the political condition in Myanmar has improved, they will supposedly be repatriated. Recently, the policy of humanitarian assistance has become very confusing and problematic for Thailand to the extent that its international image has been tarnished and its internal security adversely affected. This is due to the work of corrupt Thai officials, the escape of refugees from camps to seek employment (a cheap and manipulable labour force for national industry), and the accusation made by the Myanmar Government that Thailand will make use of these refugees to secretly undermine their homeland.[6] As a result, the Thai Government has sought assistance from both Yangon and the UNHCR.

In relation to Myanmar, the repatriation of these refugees has been very difficult to enforce. One reason for this difficulty is that the relationship between the two countries is not on equal terms. Apart from the existing problems and occasional exchanges of verbal accusations, the mistrust and the perception which each country has about the other has definitely played a major role. While Myanmar is suspicious of Thailand's accommodation of Myanmar's ethnic minorities, the Thai Government is tired of this never-ending problem because the Myanmar junta, as always, adheres firmly to its own method of conflict resolution. In any case, the then Thai Foreign Minister, Surin Pitsuwan, at the preparatory meeting for the ASEAN Informal Summit in Singapore at the end of November, secured from his Myanmar counterpart, Win Aung, a "formal acceptance" that Myanmar would take back its refugees. Both ministers also agreed on the need to ensure that these refugees return in safety.[7]

Before the middle of 1998, Thailand was not a member of the United Nations Convention on Refugees. It also had no formal link with the UNHCR in handling the country's refugee problems. There were historical reasons for not wanting to formally allow international organizations, or even non-governmental organizations (NGO), to help Thailand to deal with these problems. This was because Thailand had experienced a large and uncontrollable number of Indochinese refugees flocking into the refugee camps some two decades ago, and wanted a free hand to deal with the problem as it saw fit. The number of refugees at that time increased to more than one million people, causing much hardship for the Thai Government.

In the case of Myanmar, the Thai authorities did not want a rerun of the risks associated with the massive migration of impoverished people. This would impose human security problems on Thailand, as well as invite criticism from foreign agencies on Thailand's handling of the refugees.[8] Even informally, the Thai Government, following an exchange of memoranda with the UNHCR in June and July 1998, only allowed this international organization a limited role in overseeing refugees in the eleven camps along the border, and a repatriation camp for Myanmar students (POC) at Maneeloy in the Ratchaburi province, near the Thai-Myanmar border. As for the rehabilitation programme in the eleven refugee camps, the Thai Government also allowed many NGO agencies to participate, such as the Burmese Border Consortium (comprising fourteen agencies), the Catholic Office for Emergency Relief and Refugees, Medicins Sans Frontiers-France, and others.

In terms of the repatriation of refugees, the Thai Government found it expedient for the UNHCR to facilitate this process. As a neutral international body, this agency was able to convince the Yangon junta to take back its people. This was a significantly enlarged role for the UNHCR, which had previously only given assistance to the refugee camps. Therefore, throughout 2000, Thai leaders tended to call on the UNHCR to increase its role in order to solve the refugee problems. By allowing the UNHCR to act, Thai policy became more open to solving the problem of Myanmar refugees. However, the policy did not make much news during the year until Sadako Ogata, the UNHCR High Commissioner, visited the Tham Hin camp in the Suen Peung district, Ratchaburi, where some 8,200 Karens live. The conditions of the campsite, visited on 18 October 2000, reportedly shocked High Commissioner Ogata. Ogata later mentioned that "if you are a refugee, you should be protected properly — minimum standards should be maintained, whether they [the refugees] go back tomorrow or next year."[9]

It seems that the Thai policy on Myanmar was again mismanaged in this instance. However, from the Thai official perspective, even while stressing Thailand's humanitarian policy, there is no intention of allowing refugees to stay in the country permanently. Furthermore, if the UNHCR wants to help Thailand to improve the conditions in the camp, it should provide funds for this because the Thai Government has the primary responsibility of providing for its own impoverished citizens. There are as many Thai villagers living in equally poor conditions, many living nearby, and if the refugees were to receive special treatment from the Thai Government this might cause jealousy and antagonism.

With a yearly budget of about 10 million baht, Thailand now has to take care of more than 100,000 refugees living in the eleven camps. Additionally, it has to care for hundreds of newly arrived refugees and the increasing number of new babies born within the camps (at the Tham Hin Camp alone, the birthrate is about 20 new babies a month). In such cases, overcrowded and unhealthy conditions can be expected.

However, if Thailand takes full responsibility for its refugee problems, leaving the UNHCR in a powerless position, while UNHCR officials are allowed to visit the camps on a regular basis, then, for humanitarian reasons, the Thai Government should see to it that its officials stop mistreating the Myanmar refugees. This mistreatment has included economic exploitation, rape, and murder. Preventing this is important in terms of Thailand's adherence to democratic rule, and respect from the international community. Above all, the refugees should not be treated as criminals being held in camps, but as victims of injustice and exploitation in their homeland.

With regard to the exiled Myanmar students (POC), the Thai Government has long understood that under an obligation with the UNHCR, the agency would provide assistance in the form of welfare and education until these students find a third country for their resettlement. However, the issue has become a dilemma because while Thailand would like the 2,000 students (or the POC) at the Maneeloy Holding Centre in Ratchaburi to be resettled by early 2001 and the Centre closed down, this must not be done by forced repatriation.[10] Furthermore, the dilemma appears in two other forms, the first being that the resettlement process is extremely slow. After the hostage incident at the Myanmar Embassy in October 1999, only about 130 students were resettled by late January 2000. By the end of 2000, only 455 students were granted permission to resettle, while another 555 were awaiting repatriation interviews. The other problem, which has caused much anxiety for the Thai Government, is that some of the POC do not want to be resettled. They simply want to stay in Thailand and await the chance to return to Myanmar when the political situation has improved. Apart from this future uncertainty, the Thai authorities have found out that some students from the Maneeloy Centre had taken part in the seizure of the Embassy and the Ratchaburi hospital incident. This latter problem had some negative effects on Thai–Myanmar relations. However, as always, the leaders in Yangon have charged that it was the intention of the Thai Government to exploit these people at the expense of Myanmar's security.

As a matter of fact, the Thai security watchdog has been rather haphazard in its tasks. Most of the time, security control is lax, as long as there is no serious incident. There have been reports that some POC at Maneeloy can venture quite freely in and out of the centre. Normally, permission is required before one is allowed out, but the security officials have not been vigilant in ensuring that the POC follow the proper procedures. Therefore, many POC may be either in Bangkok, or anywhere else in the country. Furthermore, the POC members at Maneeloy may be only a fraction of all the Myanmar students seeking asylum in Thailand; the UNHCR believe that more of them are probably in Bangkok.[11] Hence, it is not surprising that some of these students took part in the seizure of the Embassy and the hospital, while others have plotted some mischief against the Myanmar Government.

As a measure for controlling these POC, to ensure that they would not create any security risk for either Thailand or Myanmar, the head of the Thai National Security Council, Kachadpai Burusapatana, has repeatedly warned that all exiled students living outside Maneeloy must register with the UNHCR. He has further stated that they must return to the camp or face charges of illegal entry.

Another important factor, which has created security risks for Thailand, and damaged Thai–Myanmar relations, is the never ending problem of illegal labourers. According to some estimates, more than one million illegal Myanmar citizens are residing and seeking employment all over Thailand. The Thai Government does not classify these people as refugees because most of them, though affected by both economic and political hardships, prefer to take a risk and leave their country to seek a better livelihood. Therefore, in labelling these people "illegal labourers", the government believes they should be pushed out of Thailand. This happened at the end of 1999, when forced repatriation was used. However, the policy failed completely because not only did many of these people sneak back into Thailand, but a large number of their compatriots, who had not been in Thailand before, undertook the same venture.

There are many reasons why illegal Myanmar migrants seek shelter in Thailand in increasing numbers, despite reports of ill-treatment towards Myanmar citizens residing in Thailand. Firstly, it is clear that a major cause stems from the repressive nature of the Yangon government and the economic hardships in Myanmar. Therefore, it is quite natural for these people to seek alternatives where possible.

Thailand has become a land of opportunity for many Mons, Karens, Shans, Burmans, Bangladeshis, and Indians living in the border areas. The country has to allow entry to thousands of refugees and illegal migrants of various ethnic minorities from Myanmar, including Arakanese, Chin, and Kachin, for short-term settlement. Secondly, at a time when the current economic crisis in Thailand has thrown tens of thousands of Thai nationals out of work, Thai businessmen and women, and entrepreneurs prefer to employ the abundant illegal labourers from Myanmar. The advantages of hiring these people are many: they can be paid below the minimum wage; no welfare or medical benefits are provided; and they can endure the heavy and strenuous workload better than the Thais. Thirdly, the Thai foreign labour policy of "no illegal labourers" and forced repatriation will never work as long as the Thai private sector is concerned with its own interests and collaborates with various corrupt officials who, while taking bribes, turn a blind eye to the situation.[12] Finally, the Thai Government has been very indecisive and has not tackled the problem seriously. Only when crises occur, such as the seizure of the Myanmar Embassy and the Ratchaburi Center Hospital, or the jail-break in Samut Sakorn at the end of November, will the government pay due attention to the policy.

In the international arena, Thailand has decided to display a more strict policy with regard to forced labour in Myanmar. In March 2000, after a year of mild warnings to the Myanmar Government to solve its human rights abuses, the International Labour Organization (ILO) decided to take action on Myanmar in order to make it "comply with its rules" on labour treatment. In mid-June, it became quite clear that the international body would invoke a special article in the ILO rules allowing action to be taken against Myanmar by the end of 2000. It was to no one's surprise when the governing body of ILO on 17 November maintained that there had not been sufficient progress in the dissolution of forced labour in Myanmar. It therefore invoked Article 33 (Convention 29) of its Constitution to call on member states to enforce sanctions against Myanmar, with effect from the end of November 2000.[13]

Although the consequences of forced labour in Myanmar have a profound effect on the country and its society, Thailand generally avoids any overt criticism of the regime in Yangon. As it happens, however, whenever Thai authorities make comments relating to Myanmar's handling of its nationals, Myanmar will make a quick response on the exploitation and benefits Thailand has gained from the plight of Myanmar labourers. Nevertheless, in the international arena, Thailand has always been consistent in its decision to abstain from voting on sanctions of any kind against Myanmar. However, this time it acted differently in that, apart from abstaining from voting on the sanction measures, it also refused to join other ASEAN countries in attempting to protect Myanmar from those sanctions. The decision, of course, caused some disappointment for Yangon's military regime.

The most significant issue, which occasionally causes tension in Thai–Myanmar relations, is the question of drugs, especially the production of methamphetamines in Myanmar which are then smuggled into Thailand. The issue here entails a number of problems in both domestic and international affairs. In terms of domestic problems, Thailand now has at least two million methamphetamine addicts and the number is increasing. The country suffers in terms of the huge amount of money spent by addicts on these drugs, in addition to the increasing crime rate and the related social consequences. In international matters, relations between Thailand and Myanmar have been strained as a consequence of the cross-border trafficking of illicit drugs.[14]

The reasons why methamphetamine abuse is so widespread in Thailand is not difficult to comprehend. Apart from the external reasons explained above, the Thai Government is also to be blamed as it has not given much attention to its drug policy. The government was preoccupied with trying to solve the national economic crisis and to salvage itself from the dissolution of Parliament at the end of the year. The outgoing Democrat-led government clearly made little effort to eradicate the production of illicit drugs, despite the occasional rhetoric from Thai leaders calling attention, from both the Myanmar Government and the international community, to solving the crisis in Myanmar. The government also made a direct appeal to the Yangon government for co-operation with Thailand. Moreover, the lenient punishment for drug offences does not constitute a real deterrent, combined with the crumbling of social values in Thai society, especially when the use and sale of drugs among workers, the youth, and people from many walks of life can be found just about anywhere.

Above all, the inability of the country to eradicate crime affecting human security is probably caused by corrupt officials and politicians who have a stake in illicit drugs. As reported in the *Bangkok Post*, a leader of the Shan State Army, Sao Hser Harn, said that the "Burmese ethnic groups are not the sole producers of methamphetamine sold in Thailand. Domestic producers, among them influential figures and politicians, are playing a major role".[15] Instead of tackling the cause of the drug problem within the country, the Thai Government has looked instead at external factors. However, there has been little positive response from Myanmar when Thailand calls for international co-operation. In addition, criticizing the Yangon military leaders has only received a response that Thailand is interfering in Myanmar's internal affairs. Indeed, a frequent response from Myanmar has been that it is not producing any precursor chemicals, and therefore if the illegal entry of these chemicals into Myanmar can be halted, the illicit drug production along the common border can be eliminated. In defending Myanmar's drug policy at the conference marking the end of the ASEAN Post-Ministerial Conference in Bangkok, Win Aung said that Western governments should lay the blame on ethnic groups such as the Wa National Army and the Shan State Army with bases in Thai territory. These groups, often ignored, were also trafficking in drugs.[16]

Thailand cannot really deny the accusations from Myanmar, when the Third Army, which supervises drug suppression in the North, categorically admitted that the Shan State army did collaborate with the United Wa State Army and that both groups were directly involved in the illicit drugs trade.[17] What then can Thailand do to persuade its neighbour to the west to co-operate? It seems that the options are limited, as M.R. Sukhumbhand, the then Deputy Minister for Foreign Affairs, frankly admitted. Thailand has little leverage with the Yangon government and can only use the "sweet words" of diplomacy in its contacts with its neighbours, and "in the case of Myanmar we don't have any stick to use".[18]

This comment by the Thai Deputy Minister for Foreign Affairs seems to be true because since late 1988, when Myanmar became more open to foreign trade, Thailand had depended heavily on the import of timber and sea resources under concession rights. After many years of dealings, mainly on the part of unscrupulous Thai entrepreneurs, and the seizure of the Myanmar Embassy in

Bangkok in October 1999, Yangon ordered that all concessions be halted indefinitely. The order clearly had negative effects on the Thai logging and fishing industries; the effect on the latter was particularly severe as the fishing and allied industries were losing at least 150 million baht a day.

At the present time, except for the logging industry which has resumed its activities, the Thai fishing fleet is still barred from Myanmar waters, although concessions have been granted to boats registered in India, Cambodia, Malaysia, and Singapore.[19] In the struggle for survival, the Thai trawlers have either registered their vessels in neighbouring countries, or ventured into the fishing grounds of other neighboring countries, namely Indonesia, Malaysia, and India, where many have been caught and imprisoned. For these problems, the industry has blamed the Thai Government for being slow in negotiating with the neighbouring countries, especially Myanmar. However, prior to the January 2001 elections, a number of political parties such as the Chart Thai, and the Thai Rak Thai, apart from the Democrats, had made an overture towards the Yangon leaders in order to revive cordial relations in the future.

Troubled Neighbour — Laos

In an interview given to the *Bangkok Post* in early July 2000,[20] the then Thai Foreign Minister, Surin Pitsuwan, repeatedly stated that disturbances in the neighbouring countries were internal matters. Furthermore, he stated that as a consequence of the economic downturn as well as ethnic problems, Thailand could not develop investment and economic co-operation. However, he believed that the problems were manageable and that many of these countries would eventually emerge from the economic crisis. The interview came at a time when Thai–Lao relations had reached another low ebb, although not as low as when open conflicts erupted between Thai and Lao troops in the village of Romklao, Pitsanuloke province, in January 1988. At that time, opposing forces had confronted each other, leading to fatalities on both sides. However, after the cessation of the conflicts, some regional committees were established to resolve the many conflicting issues. Since that time, there has been greater technical and economic co-operation between the two neighbours.

For over twelve years, the relationship between the two neighbouring countries had been normalized. Then, on 3 July, following a spate of bombings in Vientiane, and in Pakse in Southern Laos during the first half of 2000, a group of sixty men launched a major attack on the market and state offices at Wang Tao village in Laos, opposite the Thai village of Chong Mek, in Ubon Ratchathani province. Although the Thai Foreign Minister denied any involvement on the part of the Thai Government, blaming it instead on Thai individuals, the Vientiane government accused Thailand of having direct interest in some of the bombings and the Wang Tao incident. In the latter case, the Lao Government radio had come out quite strongly against Thailand, to the extent of pointing out that "the surrounding circumstances" showed "Thailand's dark conspiracy" to swallow Laos step by step and make it a colony.[21]

In policy matters, while emphasizing that Thailand would never allow its soil to be used as a staging area for attacks on Laos, the Thai Government's action towards the crisis seemed dubious to the Lao authorities. There were some good reasons why the Lao Government doubted the sincerity of the Thais. Firstly, one has to look at other related issues, which might have some relevance. Currently, Laos has not only economic problems, but it is also vexed with security problems with regard to the highland Hmongs of the North, and the Central plain. Moreover, there is the anti-government group under the name "Lao Neutral, Justice and Democratic Party" with its stronghold straddling the Lao–Thai–Cambodian borders.

The bombings in Laos, believed by some commentators to be the work of the Hmongs, may have been aimed at embarrassing the central government which was planning its 25th anniversary celebrations. Thailand was blamed for the accommodation of "rebellious elements" at Thamkrabok Temple in Saraburi, and in some camps in the northeastern border. At various bilateral meetings, Lao officials had raised this issue and asked that the Thai authorities keep these people under control. Secondly, the raiders of Wang Tao, supposedly based at Chong Mek in Thailand, had finally fled across the border after their unsuccessful attack. The twenty-eight rebels, eleven of whom held Thai identification cards, were of Lao origin. They were also suspected of being part of a plot to raise funds among Lao migrants in the United States, Canada, and Europe with the aim of ending communist rule in Laos. Although it seemed that Thailand had no part in the scheme, the apparent tardiness and indecisive handling of the case by the Chuan government caused Vientiane to continue to nurture the suspicion. For instance, Thailand has turned down the demand for the immediate extradition of the twenty-eight rebels, pointing out that they would first have to be tried under Thai law before being considered for extradition. Legally, this is allowed because some of these people did not have any formal identification, and therefore would be put on trial for illegal entry, in addition to the possession of weapons. Furthermore, the bilateral extradition treaty signed in 1999 had not yet been ratified by either government, and therefore the extradition could only be considered under Thailand's 1929 Extradition Act. Even then, the Act does not allow for the extradition of Thai citizens to face charges without specific provisions in a bilateral agreement.

The argument put forth also shows that Thailand was standing firm on the issue of sovereignty. However, legal and diplomatic wrangling like this would not serve Thailand well if it wants to maintain a good relationship with Laos. The Thai Government was quite right in its argument not to extradite these people. However, it requires action and not just words to prove and show to Vientiane that, as Chuan said, "Thailand does not want anyone to use its soil as a base to create problems for another country".[22]

By the end of the year, the Wang Tao-Chong Mek incident seemed to taper off while relations between Laos and Thailand looked generally calm, except for a minor incident on the Mekong River in early September when Lao troops took over three small islands on which both countries laid claim. On the positive side, Thai and Lao delegates had cordial meetings to solve various problems, including the demarcation of their common border and the occupation of the islands mentioned above. In late October, the Thai Deputy Foreign Minister M.R. Sukhumbhand Paribatra went to Vientiane for a *kathin* merit-making ceremony at the end of the Buddhist lent, as a sign of goodwill.

Working Harder for a Friendly Neighbour — Cambodia
Thailand made little progress in improving friendly relations with the neighbouring countries in 2000. The then Deputy Foreign Minister stated in early July 2000 that Thai foreign policy was practical in that:

> Thailand must remain sensitive towards its neighbours and must be responsive to their requests and provide assistance whenever necessary, something which the country has done in the past through the Thai Aid Programme. Thailand can be a good regional partner and a good global citizen, even though, for the time being, it is unable to be a good neighbour owing to vast differences with Burma and Laos.[23]

In summary, the Deputy Foreign Minister stressed that it was in Thailand's best interests to "turn dilemma into opportunities". However, the outcome of the relationship with its neighbours cannot be considered "an opportunity" for Thailand, as long as there is still a "dilemma".

In the case of Cambodia, the relationship between the two countries is still marred by some bilateral issues. For example, the Thai Government was in a dilemma when Cambodia demanded the extradition of Sok Yoeun, who had allegedly attempted to assassinate the Cambodian Prime Minister, Hun Sen, at the end of 1998. It was subsequently found at the end of 1999 that Sok Yoeun had come into Thailand through the UNHCR refugee programme. His presence in Thailand was revealed through a Channel 5 television programme. The matter became more complicated for a while for the Democrat-led government during the censure debate in Parliament in early January 2000. It backfired on the New Aspiration Party leader (General Chavalit Yongchaiyudh) when it was later revealed that he had actually met with Sok Yoeun some time earlier. However, the situation became even worse when the Thai Government had to find a way to keep Sok Yoeun in custody in Thailand, while at the same time postpone the extradition request. The outcome was that Sok Yoeun was charged with illegal entry and was put in jail for six months, after which time the two governments would work out extradition proceedings based on the 1929 Extradition Act.

In general, Thai–Cambodian relations have been sound since the visit to Phnom Penh by Prime Minister Chuan Leekpai in mid-June 2000. High on the agenda for the visit was the co-signing of the Memorandum of Understanding relating to the 798-kilometre Thai–Cambodian boundary, based on the 1904 France-Siamese Convention and the 1907 Treaty and Protocol. This is the latest in a number of attempts by Thailand and Cambodia to resolve their contested boundary. However, the border problem cannot be resolved easily because in early February, another incident flared up which amounted to a Cambodian incursion of Thai territory around the border crossing at Klong Luek in Sra Kaew province. Klong Luek is opposite the township of Poipet in Cambodia. Here, some Chinese investors and Cambodian developers, trying to establish a casino site on the bank of the canal, had encroached onto a part of the boundary. Although a minor incident, the Cambodian provincial authorities did not respond to a complaint from the Sra Kaew governor. Therefore, the matter was brought up at a meeting in Phnom Penh in mid-June 2000. Although Cambodia admitted the mistake, both governments had to refer the dispute to their legal experts, a proceeding which can take some time before a solution is found. In addition to these problems, the number of casinos in Poipet has now increased to seven and, according to the Thai authorities, ten more are being planned. These will probably be constructed on land claimed by both Cambodia and Thailand.

Besides the border disputes, other important issues were also included in the agenda. These included: co-operation for the suppression of narcotics and other illegal trade along the border; the setting up of joint bodies on trade and investment; the increase in Thai investment in Cambodia; the use of Ubon Ratchathani province as the centre for a tripartite economic plan (which would include Thailand, Cambodia, and Laos); the prevention of cross-border vehicle smuggling from Thailand; more Thai aid programmes for the development of basic infrastructure in Cambodia; and joint fishery ventures. It seems that Thailand is in a position to make co-operation with Cambodia a reality, following years of mistrust and confrontation between the two countries. Hence, in late August, the Thai Council of Economic Ministers approved the drafting of a ten-year master plan for economic co-operation with Cambodia, especially in the areas of trade, investment, infrastructure, agriculture, education, and tourism. The assignment was given to the National Economic and Social Development Board, with the joint effort of the Ministries of Commerce and Foreign Affairs, to draft the framework document and a comprehensive plan of action through consultations with the Cambodian Council for Development.[24] However, the success of any bilateral co-operation also depends no less on the agreeable attitude of the Cambodian Government.

Vietnam

The general perception of the Thais towards their neighbours, especially during the Cold War, was that Vietnam, as well as Myanmar, were their long-term adversaries. However, for Vietnam, the year 2000 saw a completely new chapter in relations with the Thais. Instead of dwelling on the previously existing security issues, a Thai business delegation, headed by M.R. Sukhumbhand, visited the Vietnamese capital early in the year with a trade target of US$1–2 billion. In the previous three years, trade volume had reached an annual average of about US$735 million, with Thailand ranked eleventh in Vietnamese foreign trade. During the recent tour, talks ranged from fisheries, food processing, construction, cement, and chemicals, to office automation.[25] This was followed by a successful talk in March on an agreement to waive visa requirements for thirty-day visits by nationals from both countries, the first of its kind ever agreed to by Vietnam for any ASEAN member. In early May, the bilateral relationship received another boost when Vietnamese Prime Minister Pham Van Kai made a three-day visit to Bangkok. By this time, Thailand had already referred to Vietnam as its regional partner desiring co-operation in rice exports, rather than a rival in trade. Furthermore, Thailand also urged more co-operation in the development of the Mekong subregion, or the East-West Economic Corridor cutting across the poor regions of Thailand's Mukdahan, Laos' Suvannakhet, and Vietnam's Da Nang.

In drawing Vietnam into this threshold, Thailand's dream of reviving regional tourism was becoming a reality. The name "Suwannabhumi", or "Golden Land", covers Cambodia, Laos, Vietnam, Myanmar, and Thailand, and the next step would be to draw southern China into the scheme.[26] Of course, the idea has yet to be fully realized because there are several stumbling blocks — namely, the development of infrastructure in the region, entry formalities, and tourist restrictions in certain border areas. However, perhaps the most serious obstacle is in the name itself, as some members, such as Laos, do not favour the term "Suwannabhumi". The Thai authorities are now trying hard to resolve this issue.

Looking for Greener Pastures

Although during much of 2000 Thailand was occupied with mostly negative issues related to its neighbouring countries, there were times when Thailand tried to create a better image in activities only indirectly related to its neighbours.

The Thai Foreign Minister, Surin Pitsuwan, as Chair of ASEAN until late July 2000, had clearly given his best effort in trying to alter the perception of the organization as being an ineffective, or "sunset", organization. A most controversial realization from the meeting, proposed by Minister Surin, was the so-called "Troika", a mechanism for resolving intra-ASEAN crises. Although it was formally accepted by all members, some, such as Myanmar, openly stated that whatever the Troika did, it should act on the consensus of the member states.[27] Basically, it was a reflection of Surin's original two-year-old "flexible engagement" proposal. In this proposal, the ASEAN members were to be more responsive to regional crises and to talk candidly to one another on matters of mutual interest. However, the Thai Minister admitted that whether the ASEAN Troika would work or not depended on the chairman's creativity, or his powers of persuasion. Nevertheless, credit should be given to Surin for his tireless effort and his proposal of an "un-ASEAN" way to boost ASEAN's credibility and to make it a more relevant regional organization capable of handling crises in its own region. Nevertheless, the actual success lay in the manner in which it was proposed. The informal gathering before the actual meeting was held was the key to this success. Another such informal gathering was proposed by Myanmar for 2001 in either Bagan or Mandalay to discuss the issue of drugs and security.[28]

A second highlight was the proposal by Thailand at the 33rd ASEAN Ministerial Meeting for an ASEAN Trade Fair where member countries could bring their products to the international community and promote more economic intra- and extra-ASEAN collaboration. Thailand also called on the international community to assist in the integration of Myanmar, Cambodia, Laos, and Vietnam by supporting the development of their infrastructure and human resources. Indirectly, this was also a call for much needed effort in the development of the Mekong subregion, which China, the country controlling the source of the river, had to be included. The proposal was in fact timely as the Economic and Social Commission for the Asia–Pacific (ESCAP) region had, at the beginning of the year, proposed that 2000 to 2009 be the "Decade of Mekong Development".

Another noteworthy event was Thailand's effort in bringing North Korea into the ASEAN Regional Forum (ARF) held in Bangkok, on 27 July. The substance of the meeting was not directly related to Thailand's security or its well-being. However, it was significant that Thailand was able to bring in North Korea, represented by its Foreign Minister Pak Nam-sun, to meet counterparts from South Korea and the United States, the major players in the Korean peninsula's stability. At the ARF meeting, Thailand also proposed a high-level meeting of nations to address the illicit drugs problem, especially with the co-operation of the United Nations Drug Control Programme. This, of course, was another relentless effort by the Thai Government in dealing with its neighbouring country to the west.

The Last Tango of Bangkok

The Thai Government under the Democrats, which saw its final days at the end of 2000, had been quite busy throughout the year. In domestic politics, with the dissolution of Parliament in early November and the general election set for 6 January 2001, outgoing Prime Minister, Chuan Leekpai, had to manoeuvre politically to get an upper hand over other parties, including his coalition partners. The government tried to prove itself capable of managing Thailand's foreign policy, which had been plagued throughout the year by problems with its immediate neighbours, while at the same time prove itself capable of being an effective actor.

Problems with two of its immediate neighbours, namely, Myanmar and Laos, had taxed Thailand's resources. Apart from some goodwill visits by different government leaders, co-operation on trade and tourism, and technical aid programmes, which amounted to approximately 67 million baht to Laos, and 11 million baht to Myanmar, the overall picture of their relations was not in good standing at the end of 2000. The Thai military, in believing that it has the capability to settle certain accounts with the neighbouring countries, did show its prowess by hosting a meeting of Southeast Asian army chiefs at the end of November 2000 in an army unit in Prachuab Khiri-khan province. It was disappointing to the Thai army that Myanmar and Laos did not participate in the event. Worse still, Myanmar's army chief, General Maung Aye, sent an invitation that his government would be happy to host a future meeting.[29]

Thailand's relations with Cambodia, Vietnam, and even Malaysia can be considered "normal" when compared to the vexing problems with Myanmar and Laos. It seemed that relations with countries further away from Thailand often bore good results. While Thai troops stationed in East Timor received cordial thanks from Xanana Gusmaõ when he visited Bangkok in February 2000, and again during the ASEAN meeting in July, Thailand was also able to maintain very good relations with Indonesia throughout the year. This was shown by the fact that President Abdurrahman Wahid came to Thammasat University in early May to receive an honorary law doctorate, and the Thai fishing fleet was boosted by a fisheries agreement which allowed Thai boats and businessmen to fish and invest in Indonesia.[30] Through relations with Muslim countries such as Indonesia, Malaysia, and Brunei, which are all ASEAN members, and through Thailand's membership of the BIMST-EC (Bangladesh–India–Myanmar–Sri Lanka–Thailand Economic Co-operation), the government had been pursuing cordial co-operation with South Asian countries and the Indian Ocean rim economic organization, IOR-ARC. With Surin's visit to Oman in the middle of the year when the association was having a meeting, Thai membership was almost complete. Being a Muslim helped Surin to travel widely in the Middle East. Starting in March when he delivered a speech at the King Faisal University in Jeddah, Saudi Arabia — a task which was much needed after the murder of four Saudi diplomats in 1990 and 1991 — the Minister visited Libya and then Iran in May and July. In line with the "Look West" policy, the Thai Government had also been sending trade missions to Africa and urged more of its investors to explore Africa. With a total population of 725 million and as many as 53 countries, representing about one-third of the votes in the United Nations, Africa was important to Thailand's foreign trade policy.[31]

In East Asia, especially with China, the relationship was extremely cordial. Chinese Vice-President Hu Jintao's Bangkok visit in late July led to a bilateral agreement that China would lend support to Thailand in the suppression of illicit drugs. From this event, it can be seen that the Thai Government would like to gain advantage from the connection as Beijing has maintained strong relations with Yangon. At the same time, China also favour a good relationship with Thailand. As the figure on trade and investment shows, the volume of bilateral trade in 1999 amounted to about US$4.2 billion, while Thai investments in China reached US$4.8 billion.[32] In making the relationship more binding, Queen Sirikit and Princess Sirindhorn made an official visit to China in late

October 2000. In other areas of the world in which Thailand had no previous interest, missions were sent to strengthen economic ties. This included visits by the then Deputy Foreign Minister, M.R. Sukhumbhand, to countries in Latin America.

In relation to Thailand's involvement with international organizations, not to mention the significant relations with ASEAN, ASEM and the WTO, of which Thailand would take over the leadership in 2002, two events are noteworthy. Firstly, the UNCTAD X (United Nations Conference on Trade and Development) meeting in Bangkok on 12–19 February 2000 was a major achievement for Thailand in the international arena. Although it spent more than 100 million baht, and was spurned by many developed countries which sent smaller contingents and minor officials as heads of delegations, the Thai Government was praised for its efforts in bringing many developing countries together. Thailand's gains from the meeting included an agreement to set up an international institute for training in trade and development at Chulalongkorn University, to which the country would contribute about 10 million baht towards a fund. Furthermore, to the great excitement of the Thai Government and especially the Prime Minister, the Group of Eight (G-8), for the first time ever, invited Chuan Leekpai and three other leaders of developing countries to its annual summit in Okinawa. The occasion was considered a landmark event that would set the tone and direction for international co-operation in the new century. However, the reason that the Thai leader was invited was that he was the presiding chairman of ASEAN and the president of UNCTAD at the time. At the summit on 20 July 2000, the Thai Prime Minister urged conciliation from leaders of the major economies on issues such as a more accessible market for developing countries, a "real" reform of the international financial and trade institutions, the promotion of technology transfer, and the development of human resources.[33]

Conclusion

Overall, Thai foreign policy in 2000 displayed a certain degree of ineffectiveness in its dealings with some neighbouring countries. While the Thai Government had numerous problems with Myanmar and Laos, relations with other neighbours could have been more effective, although a number of co-operative arrangements were initiated. In dealing with issues related to ASEAN and other nation states outside Southeast Asia, including international organizations, the image of the Chuan administration fared better. The final assessment of Thai foreign relations is that the decisions of the government in many instances had puzzled Thais at large. If government action had been made clear to the public, the question of transparency would not have been raised. The new government in 2001 will have to deal with the outcomes of the ineffectiveness of the previous government. In this matter, various contending parties have expressed their desire and willingness to forge more effective links with the neighbouring countries, with whom good relations are sorely needed.

NOTES

1. For a full discussion, see Kevin Hewison, "Resisting globalization: A study of localism in Thailand", *Pacific Review* 13, no. 2 (2000): 279–96.
2. "NSC given lead role in intelligence", *Bangkok Post*, 27 January 2000, p. 2.
3. "The border is heated: Myanmar demands for a return of 3304 base", *Matichon*, 24 November 2000, p. 28.
4. "Burma slams Thais over rocket attack", *Bangkok Post*, 15 May 2000, p. 1.
5. "Editorial", *Nation*, 25 January 2000, p. A4.
6. "Junta raps Thailand for helping refugees," *Bangkok Post*, 21 May 2000, p. 2.
7. "Junta feels let down on ILO vote", *Bangkok Post*, 25 November 2000, p. 4.
8. Interview with a high-ranking official from the National Security Council, June 2000; and Ministry of Foreign Affairs, "The roles of the UNHCR and problems of refugees along the Thai–Myanmar border", 1997.
9. "Overflowing camp can't be expanded", *Bangkok Post*, 19 October 2000, p. 4.
10. "Maneeloy camp to be shut down after repatriation," *Bangkok Post*, 28 November 2000, p. 5.
11. "UNHCR urged to tighten screening", *Nation*, 28 January 2000, p. A2.
12. "Smuggling of illegals is on the rise again," *Bangkok Post*, 21 August 2000, p. 2.
13. "Editorial", *Bangkok Post*, 18 November 2000, p. 12.
14. "Envoys set to talk with Wa Army", *Bangkok Post*, 3 July 2000.
15. "Suppression officers are being 'misled'", *Bangkok Post*, 26 April 2000, p. 2.
16. "Junta blames neighbours", *Bangkok Post*, 25 February 2000, p. 2; and "Reports on drug trade 'biased'", *Nation*, 30 July 2000.
17. "Brass confirms Wa working with Shan", *Bangkok Post*, 7 August 2000; and "Drug threat mounts as Wa army takes control", *Bangkok Post*, 4 September 2000, p. 1.
18. "Sweet words only", *Bangkok Post*, 27 September 2000, p. 7.
19. "Fishing in troubled waters", *Bangkok Post*, 5 June, 2000, p. 10.
20. "The good neighbour", *Bangkok Post* (Perspective), 9 July 2000, p. 6.
21. "Laos accuses Thailand of colonial plot", *Bangkok Post*, 19 July 2000, p. 1.
22. "Chuan urges Vientiane to name names", *Bangkok Post*, 14 June 2000, p. 4.
23. "Regional Perspective", *Nation*, 3 July 2000, p. A4.
24. "Thai-Cambodian cooperation plan gets go-ahead", *Nation*, 29 August 2000, p. A6.
25. "Delegation hopes to wind back trend to falling trade", *Bangkok Post*, 19 February 2000, p. 3.
26. "New frontiers opening", *Bangkok Post*, 23 November 2000, p. 11.
27. "The Thais almost failed in its Troika proposal", *Matichon*, 26 July 2000, p. 19.
28. "Editorial on ASEAN Troika", and, "Troika set up to keep watch over region", *Nation*, 26 July 2000, pp. A4–A5.
29. "Regional top brass to meet", *Bangkok Post*, 3 November 2000, p. 4.
30. "Wahid calls on region to follow Thai lead", *Bangkok Post*, 11 May 2000, p. 4; and "Thailand and Indonesia agreed to cooperate in fishing", *Exporters Review*, May 2000, p. 23.
31. "Thai firms eye South Africa investments", *Nation*, 2 August 2000, p. B4.
32. "Enhance trading ties for mutual benefits says Hu", *Bangkok Post*, 21 July 2000, p. 4.
33. "Chuan calls on G8 states to open up their markets", *Bangkok Post*, 21 July 2000, p. 4.

VIETNAM

VIETNAM
Light at the End of the Economic Tunnel?

Russell Hiang-Khng Heng

Vietnam's economy spiralled downwards in the last three years, disappointing an international community that, in the earlier half of the 1990s, had expected the country to be the next "tiger" economy. While the 1997 regional financial crisis did contribute to the economic slowdown, the self-generated ineptitude of the Vietnamese state was a significant cause as well. A slate of social and political problems also points to bad governance. Against this background of lacklustre economic results, some emerging positive indicators may give the impression that the year 2000 marked the beginning of Vietnam's passage out of the economic doldrums. Evidence of initial recovery in some regional economies bolsters this optimism about Vietnam. However, since an earlier confidence in the growth imperative of Vietnam's economy proved misplaced, economic forecasting will have to be more circumspect, the second time round. During America's Vietnam War, a catchphrase summed up the United States' hopefulness that it was getting on top of the struggle with Hanoi's guerrilla forces: seeing the light at the end of the tunnel. That light was illusory. There may be an analogy in this for Vietnam's economic woes. Is its economy really on the mend or is the light at the end of the tunnel a mirage?

The sustainability of economic progress is intimately related to the issue of governance. If official mishandling of economic reforms had hobbled economic growth three years ago, is it realistic to expect that governance has improved sufficiently to know how to nurture the dynamics of recovery. Two factors are central to any discussion of governance in Vietnam — the role of ideology and the cohesiveness of its leadership. This chapter will look at these factors but first, it is important to take a measure of the economic malaise.

Economic Upturn?

After a few years of media reports highlighting Vietnam's stalled economy, positive publicity is making a comeback. In September, Vietnam's General Statistics Office raised the gross domestic product (GDP) growth estimate to 6.7 per cent, a clear lead over the World Bank's and International Monetary

RUSSELL HIANG-KHNG HENG is a Senior Fellow at the Institute of Southeast Asian Studies, Singapore.

Fund's earlier projections of 5 and 4.5 per cent, respectively. By November, exports had chalked up a 25 per cent increase over the previous year's total. In August, various media reports pointed to stagnant property rentals beginning to climb again, both in Hanoi and Ho Chi Minh City.[1] Again in 2000, the country could well have overtaken Columbia as the world's second largest producer of coffee.[2] Vietnam also ranks second in the world as a cashew nut exporting country.[3] With all these accolades being won in agricultural production, it is not surprising that by the end of 2000, agriculture accounted for a large 25 per cent (exceeding the set target of 19–20 per cent) of Vietnam's GDP structure.[4]

However, these statistics need qualifying. Although it has been revised upwards, the GDP growth rate is still below the pre-1997 average of 8.2 per cent. According to the Ministry of Planning and Investment's (MPI) estimate, the year's GDP per capita, estimated to be 80 per cent higher than the 1990 figure, still falls short of the official target of a 100 per cent increase.[5] While the Asian Development Bank is also prepared to raise its projection of GDP growth for 2000, it has warned that government growth projections of at least 7 per cent in the next few years would only materialize if there was steady progress in implementing reforms.[6] The impressive export earning was largely due to a leap in crude oil sales and not any significant increase in productivity. That streak of luck was offset by the drastic drop in international prices for rice and coffee, both of which are Vietnam's major export items. Since the rural sector still employs some 70 per cent of the country's population, the poor market for these agricultural products has affected the livelihood of a large sector of the population. Furthermore, if agriculture has exceeded its targetted share of GDP it may mean that other sectors have not been pulling their weight, relatively speaking.

Vietnam's economic shortcomings come into sharper relief if developments are viewed over a time-frame of several years. The August figures released by the MPI warned that the total foreign direct investment (FDI) capital during the past five years has been estimated at US$36 billion, compared with a planned US$42 billion. Furthermore, all sectors except agriculture had an average growth rate below objective, lending credence to the observation that non-agricultural sectors were not delivering optimal results.[7]

TABLE 1
Economic Performance, 1996–2000

Annual Growth Rate %:	Actual	Targetted
GDP	7	9–10
Industrial sector	13	14–15
Service sector	7	12–13
Agricultural sector	5.5	4.5–5

Judged by its own targets, this is an under-performing economy. Moreover, a welter of worsening social problems — drug addiction, decline of already poor social services, youth unemployment, and so on — has contributed to an overall picture of bad governance. However, the situation does not threaten an economic collapse or inevitable regime demise. To be fair, these statistics are not that dismal. They indicate growth, even if somewhat short of the official plan. Some may argue that, of themselves, these figures are quite respectable. Public disgruntlement is discernible but the aggregate mood is far from being volatile. The absence of crisis-level social economic, and political pressures may be attributed to the dynamic agricultural sector, which produces more than enough to feed the country. For many Vietnamese who remember the chronic shortages and negative growth of the pre-reform socialist economy, the current situation does not approach that same level of desperation. Given that degree of public sufferance, any regime has considerable leeway for muddling through.

A few high-profile events in 2000 also played a big part in bringing back a buoyant mood to Vietnam. They include the implementation of an Enterprise Law that took effect on 1 January, the U.S.-Vietnam Bilateral Trade Agreement (BTA) on 13 July, the opening of a stock exchange in Ho Chi Minh City on 20 July, and the visit of U.S. President Bill Clinton on 16–21 November.

The Enterprise Law seeks to remove bureaucratic hurdles that have stood in the way of domestic investment. Although the Vietnamese state has pledged to mobilize domestic capital for its economic reforms programme, ideological uncertainties over the desirability of an indigenous private sector have deterred the development of home-grown entrepreneurs. The drastic decline in foreign investment in recent years has forced the leadership to be more encouraging of the private sector, as a result of which the Enterprise Law makes it much easier for small and medium enterprises to set up shop.[8] By December, 12,000 new enterprises had been registered under this new law, which is an exponential increase over the 600 in the entire period 1995–98.[9]

The BTA means that Vietnam-made goods would get access to the U.S. market under the same low tariffs accorded to nations which have normalized trading relations with the United States. This increases Vietnam's attraction to foreign investors. Adding to the impact of the BTA was the opening of the Ho Chi Minh City stock exchange that very same month. Having a bourse means that Vietnam has taken one more tottering step towards running a proper market economy where there will be a market place for investing capital. The greater importance of both these events is their political significance against a background of ideological discord at the top that had allegedly held them up. The BTA was supposed to have been signed in September 1999 but the Vietnamese changed their minds at the last minute, after agreeing to terms that had taken three years of careful negotiation to finalize. Plans for a stock market had begun in the early 1990s in the euphoria of FDI rushing into Vietnam. The market was supposed to open at the end of 1999 but the launching date was delayed so many times that until the actual opening day, nobody was sure if it would actually happen. The realization of these projects implies that the political obstacles standing in their way have been breached. Politically, that means wisdom has prevailed in Vietnam or, at the very least, that those obstructive forces to economic liberalization have been moderated. If these events have any impact on foreign investors, it will be to persuade them that after years of policy entanglement, Vietnam may have finally found a way to move forward.

Foreign Relations

Like its economic indicators, foreign relations also provided Vietnam with a few triumphal events. Negotiations with China to resolve longstanding border demarcation problems — both land and maritime — finally bore fruits. In the wake of a land border treaty on 30 December 1999, Beijing and Hanoi signed an agreement to settle their disputes over the Gulf of Tonkin on 27 December 2000. However, the rival claims over the Spratley and Paracel islands remain unchanged. Realistically, these diplomatic results, while effective in reducing tension up to a point, are not expected to remove deeply entrenched ethnic and historical mistrust.

Related to this is Vietnam's sensitive relationship with its two Indochinese neighbours, Laos and Cambodia. A section of the Laotian political élite is rumoured to be shifting from its traditional alliance with Vietnam and seeking more solidarity with China. Hanoi–Phnom Penh ties are formally warm since both governments have longstanding revolutionary connections, but the centuries-old mistrust and antipathy at the grass-roots level remain high. China too has its own close relations with Cambodia's political élite. Under the circumstances, Sino-Vietnamese rivalry will continue to be a key factor in Indochinese geopolitics.

In July 2000, Vietnam also assumed for the first time, the chairmanship of the ASEAN Standing Committee. While this contributes to Vietnam's image as an active ASEAN member, the Association's loose and flexible agenda will make no great demands on any diplomatic skills or leadership. In the nature of this job, nothing outstanding or disastrous is expected from Hanoi's chairmanship.

The most significant event in Vietnamese foreign policy in 2000 was the visit of U.S. President, Bill Clinton. Clinton's arrival in Vietnam signalled another step forward by the country's leadership after years of vacillating over how close it wants to get to the United States, a nation the regime still perceives as a major strategic threat to its ideological underpinnings. The media reported Clinton being warmly received by crowds of enthusiastic Vietnamese, way beyond what the Hanoi leadership expected and would like to see. Whatever the hiccups, Vietnam's controlled media portrayed the visit positively. In an intangible way, these images are hopeful signs of dogmatic politics having turned a corner and a new commitment to reforms following from here.

However, these early encouraging signs, both in domestic reforms and foreign relations, are more expectant than substantial. They should not be dismissed but, at the same time, they should also be tempered with a clearer understanding of two major factors that will shape governance in the immediate future: ideology and leadership.

Ideology as a Power Device

Ideology was one cause of the Vietnamese economic downturn even before the Asian financial crisis. The regional crisis merely aggravated a situation where foreign investors were already getting tired of the policy incoherence and bureaucratic high-handedness that mired their investments in endless red tape. More specifically, in the first half of 1996, an intense power struggle in the Politburo turned into a fight over what should be the permissible size of the country's private sector. Some leaders wanted to limit the expanding private sector on ideological grounds, arguing that a private sector predominant over the state sector was not in the interest of a socialist polity where the Vietnam Communist Party (VCP) must have sole leadership. This was the year of the Eighth Party Congress. Underlying this ideological contention was actually a scramble by different interest groups within the party for the maximal number of key positions within the party establishment. Finally, the Congress affirmed the need to retain the state sector as the dominant component of the economy but was imprecise about how to define this dominance, for example, by size of contribution to GDP, the size of capital invested, the physical number of state enterprises, or the number of jobs it provides. This lack of precision provided the necessary room for compromise, but it also left the option open for further disputes. The result was an uncertain ideological climate where officials managing the economy played safe by shying away from making bold decisions in favour of market reforms. This played a part in delaying foreign investment projects and sapping the patience of investors. Thus, ideological dispute is not just a debate in the abstract over Marxist-Leninist doctrines that many Vietnamese, including senior cadres, no longer take seriously. Nobody is advocating turning away from the market economy and returning to the old state-planned collectivized system. However, ideology can still addle economic policy-making in a critical way. Backing out of the BTA with the United States at the last moment in September 1999 was an example of resident fears among the political élite over the speed and scope of contact with the capitalist world.

It is hard to reconcile the capitalist-based consumerism so evident in Vietnamese society today with this alleged concern for ideological fidelity at the top. This incompatibility between a growing market reality and the bluster of propaganda is easier to understand if ideology is seen for what it is: not as intrinsic beliefs but as a political tool that individuals or groups may use to secure their personal interests within the establishment. The content of ideology is no longer as important as the structure of its organized dissemination. Members of an intellectual and managerial élite who form this ideological sector persist because they are drawn into a nexus of power and privilege. Keeping ideology high on the agenda guarantees them positions in the power centre, a role in policy-making, institutional resources, a network of obliging subordinates, and other trappings of power and influence.

Ideologues do not naturally abhor the market economy for they and their family members may also be benefiting from the financially-enriching opportunities it brings. However, they would be wary of the growing importance of competitors in the leadership whose power and influence are derived from the dynamism of economic growth and linkages with the capitalist world. This was a major element that fuelled the power struggle over the permissible size of the private sector leading up to Eighth Congress. As of now, this dark-cloud situation has a possible silver lining. Having experienced the outcomes of reforms being grounded, all factions in the leadership are likely to want to appropriate the market liberalization agenda as their own because it is the popular mood of the moment. However, the spectre of ideology has not been totally removed. In its latest report on Vietnam issued in November, the World Bank sees the need to warn that "the climate for the private sector has been grudging rather than supportive", even though there has been a marked improvement over the years.[10] While licensing barriers have been removed, for private firms, the access to credit is still paltry compared to what state-owned enterprizes can get.

Politics and Leadership

Many Vietnamese accept leadership discord as a fact of life in their politics. As the ruling VCP prepares to hold its Ninth Congress in the first half of 2001, the wrangling within the party élite intensifies. As with previous congresses, a personnel reshuffle will not be confined to positions in the top party organs. A complex formula that seeks to balance various interest groups will re-arrange senior appointments throughout the whole party–government apparatus from central to provincial levels. Some scholars have called this power dynamic sectoral politics.[11] A coalition of the military and security agencies is said to comprise a major sectoral interest. Two other groups identified are those whose power base is in the party (for example, the various party commissions that oversee all aspects of governance) as opposed to those whose power base is in the government (for example, the Prime Minister's Office and the ministries).

The key figures of this competitive power play are leaders who had held or are holding top positions in those sectors. They include a triumvirate of party elders — Do Muoi, Le Duc Anh and Vo Van Kiet — who have retired to become influential behind-the-scene advisors. Anh and the incumbent party General Secretary, Le Kha Phieu, both military men, are said to represent the military-security sector. Kiet who was Prime Minister, and his immediate successor, the current Prime Minister Phan Van Khai, have the government bureaucracy as their power base. Do Muoi, the previous party chief, derives his influence from party organs. This is a very simplified rendition of a far more complex network of criss-crossing allegiances that are defined also by geographical identification (North and South), personal and familial ties, as well as ideologue versus reformist manoeuvrings. The intra-élite contestation does not shake out into two distinct competing sides neatly opposed on all issues. The alignments are multi-sided and dynamic, changing over time and according to issues, thus leading to a situation that has to be constantly managed to reach a working compromise. This makes for an unsettled pattern of leadership. It also slows down policy-making and obstructs implementation because decisions have to be filtered through such an intricate mesh of different affiliations.

Governance becomes a system built around powerful individuals entrenched in various sectors. Each person put into a key position by a mentor will gather supporters to form what the Vietnamese call an *e kip* (an approximate English term is "coterie"). As key appointments are traded according to a shifting balance of power, individual *e kip* gets dismantled and reassembled. Adding to the confusion of this mutable system, prerogatives are frequently not well defined, and lines of authority can be compromised by personal patronage. With such entrenched systemic requirements in personnel selection, it is unrealistic to expect that the Ninth Congress will break new grounds to find the most qualified person for any given position.

In this pre-Party Congress year, the most talked-about issue has been whether or not party General Secretary Le Kha Phieu and Prime Minister Phan Van Khai will continue in their jobs. At the end of 2000, the prevailing wisdom on the political grapevine held that Phieu, in his first term, is likely to remain because he has steadily consolidated his position. On the other hand, Khai is expected to go. In Hanoi, rumours have been circulating since May about Prime Minister Phan Van Khai's desire to resign.[12] While Hanoi's Foreign Ministry has officially refuted this, Khai's political fortunes have been the target of speculation since the mysterious detention of his private assistant, Thai Nguyen, in November 1999.[13] Khai took over from Kiet as Prime Minister in 1997 and foreign observers regard the two men as leaders who are most friendly towards market liberalization in a leadership where ideology can still be used to obstruct reforms.

However, this is no more than second guessing the Byzantine politics of Hanoi which, in recent years, had surprised seasoned observers with its unpredictability, such as when Nguyen Ha Phan was suddenly evicted from the Politburo in the months leading up to the Eighth Party Congress. Indeed, the 1996 Eighth Congress was an example of how personnel selection can be an intractable problem, so much so that no final agreement on the make-up of the Politburo was reached. The much-expected change in the General Secretary appointment had to wait a year and a half to be concluded at the Fourth Plenum (Eighth Congress) in December 1997.

In the public perception, leadership appointments are often meshed with the country's endemic corruption problem. As the problem of impropriety in high places can no longer be hidden, media publicity is garnered to highlight state efforts at bringing senior cadres to trial. However, corruption continues as part of the Vietnamese reality and this fuels the public feeling that the corrective measures are not matched by political will and have not reached high enough into the system, thus losing credibility. To date, the most senior official to be publicly reprimanded is Deputy Prime Minister Ngo Xuan Loc in November 1999. But after the Party Central Committee requested his removal from that high office, a prime ministerial appointment in April 2000 made Loc a State Commissioner in the key areas of industry, construction, communications, and transportation.[14] Another cursory bid to fight corruption is the use of obsolescent revolutionary tactics — for example, launching a "criticism and self criticism" campaign. In a press interview, Politburo Standing Board member Pham The Duyet said that the eighteen-member Politburo underwent individual criticism sessions for twelve days and collective criticism for another seven to eight days.[15] His cautiously-framed conclusion was: "No serious problem was found but some issues had to be raised. These were not related to the official but to the family members." Such cursory statements do not lessen the public belief that corruption prevails at the top, and may, in fact, aggravate the cynicism that the country's leaders are unwilling or unable to solve the problem.

In 2000, a major point of curiosity about the Ninth Congress in 2001 was not whether any new configuration of power will reduce these embedded leadership problems but which individuals will get the better of them to survive. In this context, whether or not General Secretary Phieu lasts another term in his position is a particularly engaging question. Since the Sixth Congress of 1986, the top party position has changed hands frequently, deviating from the established pattern when the late Le Duan held the post for twenty-six years until his death in 1986. Le Duan's successor, Nguyen Van Linh, lasted one term. Linh's successor, Do Muoi, lasted slightly more than one term. Will Phieu remain as General Secretary indefinitely, thus reverting back to the practice of Le Duan? This unfolding pattern of top leadership will provide an indication of how much the mechanisms of power within the VCP are being remade by the changing times. Meanwhile, the mutability of élite politics does not give cause to believe that the leadership is united enough to provide good governance.

The Repackaging of Bad Governance

The VCP regime survives this reputation of corruption, red tape, ideological politicking, and lack of unity at the top, by using what may be termed the "repackaging" of bad governance. This is easier to understand if we see "governance" as a process made up of several segments, which include identifying a problem, thinking out the solutions, and implementing them to achieve the target, or the best possible results, in the shortest possible time. Repackaging this poor quality product to make it look better involves highlighting those segments of governance which the regime can be seen to be doing something. Even if these measures fail to achieve their targets, some credit can be taken for the mere act of intending to carry out reforms.

For a start, the Vietnamese Government has become quite good at identifying problems. Increasingly, it is also capable of drawing on a range of technocratic solutions that are sound in principle and widely used in comparable situations around the world. For instance, in response to the challenge of red tape, the leadership speaks of reducing the size of the bureaucracy and introducing "one stop service" in bureaucratic procedures. Vietnam's leadership has also allowed United Nations' agencies, foreign donors of aid, and foreign business communities into its own official initiatives to troubleshoot policies. External auditing of this sort enforces a certain discipline to see that things get done, are seen to be done or, at the very least, are kept on the agenda of reforms.

The Vietnamese leadership has also been promoting watchdog roles for domestic institutions. It has allowed the National Assembly unprecedented leeway to criticize government policies. Over the years, Assembly members have been boisterous in highlighting issues, such as corruption, red tape, ineffectual policies, and almost anything and everything that relates to government incompetence. National Assembly sessions telecast on television has enabled citizens to see Cabinet ministers grilled by elected representatives and made to apologize for their failings. In addition to elected representatives, the media is also given a role to highlight what is officially called "negativism" (*tieu cuc*) — a catch-all term for all bad things, including bad governance.

Be that as it may, the irregularities of the system continue to mount and overwhelm the party-state machinery. In response to the deluge of public complaints about an unresponsive bureaucracy, in 2000, the government set up five high-level multi-departmental teams, led by ministerial-ranking officials. They were then sent out to supervise the performance of provincial people's committees in enforcing the law and implementing policies.[16] All these actions add up to an impression that the government is aware of what is wrong with the system, prepared to admit to difficulties and shortcomings, and is crafting policies to address them. Such an impression helps the government to avert criticisms of being totally inept or irresponsible.

In the economic doldrums of the last three years, there were examples of such responsiveness to problems. Rules and regulations that hampered foreign and domestic investments have been made more transparent and/or liberalized. To slice through red tape, the power to license FDI has been devolved to provincial governments. By June, 84 licences incompatible with the Enterprise Law were abolished.[17] Huge infrastructure projects have been launched using overseas development assistance (ODA) or foreign loans to inject money into the economy and make up for the slack caused by the exodus of foreign capital. A prominent example is the new north-south highway to be built along the old Ho Chi Minh trail in the jungles.[18] In a nutshell, the Vietnamese state has generated a flurry of activities that have their share of critics, but are also not without a supporting logic. These projects are likely to run into their share of problems, given the administrative record of the country, but at the stage of commencement, they can be marketed as sound policy options to foreign and domestic constituencies.

Governance in Vietnam can claim some success stories. The most prominent record in this regard must be its good macroeconomic management that has kept its currency and prices stable. The Vietnamese currency slid from 11,000 to 14,000 dong to the U.S. dollar in the past three years. This performance is not bad when measured against the decline of other regional currencies. Foreign lenders have also given the Hanoi authorities credit for bringing down inflation from 67 per cent in 1991 to 3.8 per cent in 1997, and 0.1 per cent in 1999.[19] All these help to create a stable macro climate for economic development. Whatever its many failings, this government has maintained a semblance of order which influences people to tolerate instances of bad governance more.

Another feather in the cap for Vietnam's leadership is the country's agricultural output, but the credit for that should go more to the Vietnamese farmer for his initiative and hard work than to the role of the state. The currently high-performing agricultural sector became possible when the state pared down its intervening role, beginning in the 1980s. The outstanding growth of coffee production rode on the back of large-scale illegal migration to the Central Highlands. These migrants cleared the land and learned to cultivate coffee by relying on their own resources and support network.[20] The state's greatest contribution may be that it has refrained from stopping them. Put another way, official inefficiency becomes tolerable when that very inefficiency provides loopholes for citizens to do what they want to do. This describes an overall psychology that makes it possible for the Vietnamese state to get away with poor governance.

Starting from a very low level of development, it is easy for a country to register impressive early gains when implementing reforms policy. For example, Deputy Prime Minister Nguyen Tan Dzung was able to announce that Vietnam is ranked among the top ten countries in terms of telecommunications development rate. A statistic that supports this claim is Vietnam's twenty-fold increase in telephone subscriptions in the 1990s. However, this impressive growth rate only amounts to 4 subscriptions per 100 people.[21] Developmental figures from Vietnam generally look promising because of this factor. It contributes to an image of an achieving result-oriented government.

Conclusion
Vietnam's reform agenda is embedded in a process of repackaging substandard governance to appear better than what it is to both foreign and domestic constituencies. In the future, the Vietnamese state will continue to deliver a stream of high-profile projects bolstered by sound technocratic arguments. However, their competent implementation remains uncertain because there is no quick answer to some entrenched political problems of the Vietnamese

system. These are the related issues of ideology and leadership and how they are incapable of producing a managerial infrastructure staffed with the appropriate personnel for good governance. This political culture will be around for a while and not expected to change quickly even as the economic pressures continue to force the momentum of market reforms.

Finally, to say that the Vietnamese state repackages bad governance implies a level of deceit among its political leaders. That would be too harsh a reading of the reality. It is more accurate to say that the VCP regime is able to recognize the problems the country faces and wants to solve them but the required means are not to be found within present political dynamics. Given such a situation, the next best thing to do is to cobble together what seems like the best option of the moment and not expect too much. One scholar has called this "immobilism", which results in a "middle course of muddling through".[22] Both Vietnamese state and society see this reality for what it is. Bad governance gets repackaged in this process but not really as a carefully thought-out ploy to pull the wool over people's eyes.

If such is the Vietnamese reality, it is sensible not to believe too readily that the country has seen the light at the end of the economic tunnel.

NOTES

1. Nguyen Hanh, "Rosier Times Reported by Apartment Ventures", *Vietnam Investment Review*, 31 July–6 August 2000; Internet version on *http://www.vir-vietnam.com/index.htm*; Bich Ngoc, "Hanoi housing market might be hotting up", *Vietnam Investment Review*, 7–13 August 2000, Internet version; and Thien Nhan, "Hi-rise market bounces back", *Saigon Times Daily*, 17 August 2000, p. 1.
2. Paul Solman, "Commodities and Agriculture: Vietnam to take Second Place in Growers League", *Financial Times*, 13 June 2000, p. 48.
3. "Vietnam's Cashew Nut Exports Increase 22.3% in Jan–July Period", *Vietnam News Agency*, 2 August 2000.
4. Thai Thanh, "Vietnam Fails to Realize Decade Targets", *Saigon Times Daily*, 8 August 2000, p. 1.
5. Ibid.
6. *Reuters*, "ADB sees Vietnam 2000 GDP Growth at 6.1 per cent", 30 November 2000.
7. Thai Thanh, op. cit.
8. In the author's visits to Vietnam in February and September 2000, conversations were held with five Vietnamese businessmen individually. Their ready consensus was that the act of registering a private business has really become much easier. Two were from Hanoi and the others from Ho Chi Minh City. One of the three southern businessmen said that registration takes only two weeks with the local authorities whereas, previously, it needed at least three months. The improvement may be less evident away from these two major economic centres. The interviewees also added that this did not mean that all the bureaucratic problems associated with setting up business have been solved with the Enterprise Law.
9. The 12,000 figure is from the daily *Vietnam News*, and cited in "Vietnam Boosts Non-State Economy", *Xinhua News Agency*, 14 December 2000. The 600 figure is from "Transforming the Rural Economy", in *Vietnam 2010: Entering the 21st Century — Vietnam Development Report 2001* (World Bank, 2000), chp. 3; available at <*http://www.worldbank.org.vn*> p. 14.

10. "Creating a Supportive Climate for Enterprise", ibid., chp. 2, p. 7.

11. The sectoral politics approach was initiated by Carlyle Thayer, in "The Regularization of Politics: Continuity and Change in the Party's Central Committee, 1951–86", in *Postwar Vietnam: Dilemmas in Socialist Development*, edited by David Marr and Christine White (Ithaca: Cornell Southeast Asian Programme, 1988). For an updated expansion of the topic, see Thaveeporn Vasavakul, "Sectoral Politics and Strategies for State and Party Building from the VII to the VIII Congress of the Vietnamese Communist Party (1991–96)", in *Doi Moi Ten Years after the 1986 Party Congress*, edited by Adam Fforde (Canberra: Political and Social Change Monograph 24, Research School of Pacific and Asian Studies, Australian National University, 1997).

12. "Vietnam says PM Resignation Report 'Groundless' ", Reuters, 17 August 2000.

13. Huw Watkin, "Corruption Crackdown being used to Settle Scores, say Critics", *South China Morning Post*, 1 December 1999.

14. "Vietnam: Former Deputy Premier gets Industry, Construction Job", *Saigon Giai Phong*, 27 April 2000; in *BBC Monitoring Asia Pacific — Political*, 8 April 2000.

15. Pham The Duyet, "Van de Hom nay - Chong tham nhung khong tru bat cu ai, bat cu cap nao" [Today's Issue — Anti-corruption efforts make no exception for any body or any rank], *Saigon Giai Phong*, 26 August 2000; <http://www.sggp.org.vn>

16. See the series of media reports in the folder entitled "Hoat Dong cua Doan Cong tac Chinh phu" [Activities of the Government Working Teams] on the website of the newspaper *Lao Dong*, <http://www.laodong.com.vn>

17. "Five thousand enterprises licensed in five months", *Vietnam News Agency*, 10 June 2000.

18. Critics have pointed out that this US$380 million project uses up too much resources and it would be financially more sound to upgrade the existing Highway One. Environmentalists among them charged that the new highway would slice through stretches of national parks, which should not be permitted. See Huw Watkin, "Green row over highway", *South China Morning Post*, 30 May 2000.

19. "Virtually Static Prices End Five Months of Deflation in Vietnam", Agence France Presse, 22 August 2000.

20. Stan B-H Tan, "Coffee Frontiers in the Central Highlands of Vietnam: Networks of Connectivity", *Asia Pacific Viewpoint* 41, no. 1 (April 2000): 51–67.

21. *Vietnam News Agency*, 16 August 2000, "Post and Telecommunications Sector on Integration and Development Route".

22. Brantly Womack, "Vietnam in 1996 — Reform Immobilism", *Asian Survey* 37, no. 1 (January 1997): 79–87.

STATE-SOCIETY RELATIONS IN VIETNAM
Strong or Weak State?

David Koh

It is easy to assume that because Vietnam is a communist country, the state and the Vietnamese Communist Party (VCP) dominate the society. This assessment was most likely true during the Vietnam War, when the northern Vietnamese regime effectively mobilized people and resources. With more in-depth research on Vietnamese state–society relations from the 1980s, this assessment has come under greater scrutiny. Some scholars now view the Vietnamese state as being weak, as opposed to the long-accepted idea that it is strong. The current mode of thinking about state–society relations in Vietnam is thus divided into the dichotomy of a "strong" or "weak" state.

That is the state of affairs regarding the literature on state–society relations in Vietnam today. The view that the Vietnamese party-state dominates, leaving very little space for society, has prevailed for some time. While this view is stark, it rightly points out that with a pervasive administrative machinery, the Vietnamese party-state permeates every level of society and controls and directs it. In this view, not only is there structural dominance of society by the party-state, but the party-state also makes policies and then directs local authorities to implement those policies, which the society meekly accepts. There is also a parallel view that the political system in Vietnam is "bureaucratic socialism" because bureaucrats dominate the socialist party-state which in turn dominate the society. According to this view too, the party-state machinery is authoritarian and unresponsive to the people. These two views see the Vietnamese party-state as "strong" in controlling and influencing Vietnamese society.[2]

What was missing from the picture was a systematic questioning of the assumption that dominance equals effectiveness. Valid questions include whether the policies decided by the Vietnamese state would be implemented to the letter, or whether what really happened was what was intended by the party-state. Furthermore, if the *doi moi* (renewal, or reform) reforms of the late 1980s were responses to society's pressures for change, of what currency is the view that the Vietnamese party-state dominates society? Indeed, research since the mid-1980s has managed to examine these questions in the light of

DAVID KOH is a Fellow at the Institute of Southeast Asian Studies, Singapore.

a new situation for state-society relations in Vietnam after the war. Some of the insights gained have been fascinating and have contributed to a revision of the top-down, authoritarian view.

In particular, there has been an alternate view that the Vietnamese party-state is accommodating to society, in the sense of being responsive, or catering to society's demands, or accepting practices and activities that contradict the centre's directives or even the very core of official ideology. Ultimately, proponents of this view argue, there is much space in which society can manoeuvre and rework the state's boundaries to society's benefit, even though this effort is often disorganized. In this sense, the state that the VCP has been building should be considered fairly weak in some aspects of its relations with society.[3]

Which of these two schools of thought is more in tune with what is really happening? There is a need for a synthesis, based on the author's understanding that the Vietnamese party-state is strong in some ways, but weak in others. In this view, both schools of interpretation are not wrong but in their analysis they have tend not to recognize fully the paradoxical features of the Vietnamese party-state. That is, those who stand on the strong state interpretation tend to underestimate the ability of the political system to cater to local issues and people's needs, even if such accommodation may be unintentional or simply due to the incompetence of state officials. Accommodation also occurs when the party-state faces contradictory interests and then has to respond in ways that satisfy the practical interests of the situation. Even today, the best illustration is the willingness of the party-state to sanction society's experiments with private contract farming in the early 1980s in Do Son prefecture of Hai Phong City. Private contract farming, which raised farm output significantly, was not appropriate to official ideology, but the results opened up possibilities for the alleviation of food hardship. This encouraged the party-state to put behind the ideological policy of collective farming which lagged far behind private farming in terms of output.

On the other hand, scholars who think that the Vietnamese party-state is accommodating tend to argue so without fully recognizing the capability of the state machinery, especially when it is well-focused, or when the VCP's position may be threatened. Examples of strong state action include many restrictions on civil freedom that citizens of many other countries take for granted, the clamping down on the slightest dissidence, the pervasive party-state administrative machinery which penetrates society, and many more. The VCP eliminates all sorts of overt political opposition, especially those who are not within their ambit of legal control. It has even embedded its "overlord" position in the constitution and through its domination of the state.

This chapter argues that the dichotomy between "strong" and "weak" in efforts to accurately label the Vietnamese party-state is a false one, and it is time for a synthesis of views. It deliberates on the nature of state-society relations through an analysis of the relationship between the party-state, local officials, and society at the urban basic level. It notes how the failure to control local level officials by the central authority in Vietnam often led to state ineffectiveness, even though the state is apparently strong.

The way the Vietnamese party-state's administrative machinery works, especially at the level of the ward — an urban grass-roots level of state administration — displays the "strong" and yet "weak" paradox in the state-society relations of Vietnam. Basic level officials make a vast difference to how one would normally view state-society relations in Vietnam. Therefore, this chapter will analyse the ward level of state administration and demonstrate how the wards are organized and operated. It will then argue that inefficiencies at the ward level reduce the effectiveness of the party-state and make for a more accommodating state than the appearance and structure of its operation would suggest. Yet, if necessary, the ward machinery can become an effective tool to achieve the aims of the party-state.

Party-State Administrative Structure and the Ward Level

The Socialist Republic of Vietnam has three levels of local authority: a) province and central cities; b) provincial cities and districts (urban *quan* or rural *huyen*); and c) wards (urban) and communes (rural).[4] The ward and commune are, respectively, the urban and rural units at the bottom level.

Each of these local units of state authority has a people's council and a people's committee, with the former acting as the constitutional forum for local affairs. The committee is the executive of the people's council but it plays the more substantial role as the local branch of national government. Both the council and the committee relate to other government agencies vertically and horizontally. Thus, they are accountable to councils and committees at levels above it, right up to the National Assembly and the government. While the people's council theoretically oversees local affairs, the people's committee is the more powerful body. The people's committee comprises departments that report directly to officers of the respective departments of higher committees. There are, therefore, three chains of command (council, committee, departments) and each chain is quite long.

The law governing local authorities is thus supposed to dictate clear, effective control over the local authorities by the upper levels as well as by the chief executive of each level. The reality, however, is one of confusion as multiple agencies can have responsibility over the same set of affairs. This situation usually means that no one has responsibility at all, and the Vietnamese proverb "nobody cries when everybody's father dies" (*Cha chung khong ai khoc*) aptly describes it. At the ward level, the people's committee supposedly oversees and co-ordinates the work of departmental specialists who are from professional agencies, such as ministries. In actual fact, however, the ministries do not give up control over these specialists, and this adds to the confusion in authority. Moreover, higher level authorities often interfere in the affairs and authority of the lower levels, but may yet not have the power to compel them to do things according to what they want. Neither the government (which determines the laws) nor the VCP (which determines policies) has managed to resolve this issue of multiple and contradicting centres of power, which is the most important paradox of state authority in Vietnam today.

While the two local authority organs briefly described above belong to the state, the third and most important part of any local authority is the VCP machinery. In the ward, it is the ward branch of the VCP. The ward party branch, legally speaking, is separate from the state structure, but in practice, because the Communist Party has layers of administration that parallel the state all the way down to the ward (and directs the state apparatus), distinguishing the party from the state is very difficult. In fact, VCP officials' remuneration is determined by the state and follows the rates of state employees. Ultimately, of course, VCP members occupy the most important state positions, as would be evident by further analysis below.

The Communist Party in the Ward

The Communist Party at the ward level comprises two tiers. The upper tier is the ward party branch (WPB, *dang uy*) and the lower tier is the party cell (*chi bo*). The WPB holds a congress every two and a half years and elects a fifteen-member executive committee. The WPB executive committee elects a ward party standing committee (WPSC) and the party inspectorate.

The WPSC normally has six members: (1) secretary (top ward party official who usually chairs the ward people's council); (2) deputy party secretary (who usually chairs the ward people's committee); (3) head of the party inspectorate (or party inspector); (4) a member from the permanent committee of the WPB (a subcommittee of the WPSC); (5) a member who is usually the chief of police in the ward; and (6) another member who is usually the leader of the ward branch of a mass organization. The WPSC meets once a week.

If any checks and balances are to occur within the ward party organization, then the party inspectorate is the body to do it. The inspectorate usually has five members: an inspector, a deputy inspector, and three other members. The party inspector must be elected into the WPSC, because he is supposed to check on the top executives of the WPB and should be included in the inner circle in order to know what goes on. The checking role of the inspector may be impeded by collusion with party leaders or by deference. Meanwhile, party and ward-level meetings (except ordinary meetings of the people's council or ceremonial meetings of each organization) are not open to the public or even to the higher levels of party or state authority, unless invited. This makes supervision of the WPSC by the upper levels difficult.

The permanent committee (*Ban Thuong Truc*) is the subcommittee of the WPSC that oversees day-to-day affairs. This "subcommittee" usually has only one or two members (depending on the willingness of the WPSC members to serve), one of whom is the party inspector. If the inspector is the only member of the permanent committee, then the WPSC would in fact have only five instead of six members, because the same person would occupy both seat (3) and seat (4).

On a daily basis, the core leadership of the WPB comprises the ward party secretary and the permanent committee. Together with the chairman of the ward's people's committee (who is also usually the deputy party secretary, and a member of the WPSC) these three or four persons hold the reins of party-state power and authority within the ward. The VCP supervises state activities within the ward on a daily basis through the presence of the party secretary and the WPB permanent committee members in the ward office. Other WPSC members hold lesser but still important positions in state and mass organizations. The common pattern of interlocking leadership at the ward level is seen in Table 1.

TABLE 1
Common Distribution Pattern of Ward Leadership Posts among
a Group of Local Party Leaders in the WPB and WPSC[5]

WPB executive committee and WPSC (numbered) posts	State post	Mass organizations
(1) Secretary	Chair, Council	
(2) Deputy Secretary	Chair, Committe	
(3) Party inspector (permanent committee)		
(4) Senior member	Vice-chair, Council	Chair of one mass organization
(5) Senior member	Vice-chair, Committee	
(6) Senior member	Chief of police	
Other WPB executive committee members		Chairs and vice-chairs, mass organizations

The distribution pattern for the top two posts is not necessarily fixed. It is not uncommon for the WPB secretary to be the chairperson of the people's committee. In that case, someone else would occupy the chair of the people's council, most likely the deputy party secretary, or the chairperson of one of the branches of a mass organization such as the Vietnam Fatherland Front (VFF), or the Women's Association.

The Ward People's Committee
The ward people's committee ranks as the second main component of the ward machinery. It is the executive of the ward people's council and is elected from the council. It attends to the day-to-day governing of the ward, including routine state administration, and also the management of community relations. In official dictum, it "organizes and directs the implementation of the

Constitution, laws, directives of upper level state organs as well as the resolutions of the people's council of the same level."[6] Its size depends on the size of the ward population. Wards with more than 7,000 people have seven members on the people's committee, and wards with less than 7,000 people would have only five.[7] Besides the chairperson, there are one or two vice-chairpersons (two for the seven-member committee), a secretary, and the rest are ordinary members. Each committee member, including the chairperson, takes sole charge of one specialized area of ward responsibilities. A standing committee comprising the chair, the vice-chair, and the secretary makes decisions for both the people's council and people's committee (which meet once in three, and once every month respectively) when they are not in session. The standing committee of the people's committee is thus the core of the state's executive leadership in the ward on a day-to-day basis.

The Ward People's Council

The people's council represents local residents, but it also represents the state at the local level; it is at the same time both a people's organ of representation and a state organ of execution.[8] An important distinction, however, is that the council does not represent local residents to the state, but instead represent residents to settle local matters among themselves according to the laws and policies laid down by the party-state. In its state executive role, it is differentiated from the people's committee by its function in rubber-stamping state policies for implementation by the people's committee. The people's council election process emphasizes equitable representation from different social and economic sectors, and the selection of candidates is controlled by the VCP through the VFF. All election candidates, including independents, must be approved by the VFF, as required by the election laws.

Under the most recent 1994 Law on Organization of People's Councils and People's Committees, the ward people's council should have twenty-five members who must be living in the locality. They are elected for five-year terms and meet once in six months to discuss local affairs, approve reports and plans, review work-in-progress, and examine the work of the VFF. In between council sessions, the people's committee makes decisions on behalf of the council, in consultation with the council chairman. The council can hold extraordinary meetings but only at the request of the people's committee or one-third of council members. Members of the council volunteer or are voted into the subcommittees handling the political, economic, cultural, and secretarial work of the council. A council member cannot concurrently serve on the subcommittees of the council and on the people's committee at the same level. A similar rule applies to the head of any council subcommittee, who cannot be the head of specialized agencies of the people's committee, such as the police.[9] These two rules are to prevent conflicts of interest, but they do not affect the composition of the top leadership of the ward state machinery.

People's council members are not state employees but are volunteers, and so they are not paid by the state. Every month they receive a small compensation of 20 per cent of the lowest salary benchmark (US$15) for state workers, and receive fringe benefits such as health insurance, funeral allowance, and expenses for council work.[10] Leading council members who are also members of the people's committee and of the WPSC receive, in addition, party and executive remuneration for their roles in the party and in the committee.

Other Officials of the Ward Administration
A ward has two groups of expert officials who are employees of government ministries or the ward administration, but who are not members of the people's committee or people's council. Officials of the first group are stationed at the ward by central government ministries and departments to assist the ward in special areas of work. Police officers are a prime example. Others include officials handling taxation, children's welfare, land, housing, and market inspection. They are directed by the people's committee, but are also accountable to their ministries and departments. Officials of the second group, who are hired directly by the ward, comprise the accountant, the clerk, the security guard, and the tea lady (almost invariably a woman).

Scope of Responsibilities of the Ward
Another indication of how the ward has been a tool of the party-state in controlling society is the scope of ward responsibilities, although this scope has been reduced greatly since *doi moi* reforms of the late 1980s. From 1981, when the party-state established the ward, until the late 1980s, the party-state had given the local ward administration every conceivable type of administrative, economic, political, and social responsibilities, as if the ward was a tiny state in itself. The responsibilities are too numerous to be listed here.[11] Briefly, prior to *doi moi*, the state took care of every person's needs, from cradle to grave, and it interfered strongly in every aspect of people's daily lives. Consequently, on behalf of the state, the wards took care of registration of all births, deaths, weddings, divorces, employment, schooling, military service, housing, residence, travel, and many more. It also certified the residential status of all residents or acted as a guarantor when they wanted to deal with other agencies of the state outside the ward. It even operated food supply shops, distributed ration coupons, sold noodles and other cooked foods, besides taking charge of public sanitary and health duties. Apart from all these tedious everyday responsibilities, the wards also carried out propaganda and mobilization for the party-state.

The present responsibilities of the ward administration are just a tenth of what they used to be, but the wards still hold considerable sway over administrative procedures which people must perform to fulfill their obligations to the state.

Sub-Ward Party and State Organizations

Indicative of the depth of party and state penetration into the daily affairs of the people is that the WPB and the ward state machinery are not the lowest grass-roots organization of the VCP and state representation, respectively. Under the WPB and the ward administration are two organizations that are more informal in nature and operation but nevertheless can be influential on people. They are the party cells under the WPB, and the resident clusters and resident groups under the people's committee and people's council. These sub-ward organizations help to ensure, as far as possible, that people do comply with party-state policies. They can, however, also become escape hatches for those who wish to evade compliance.

The Party Cell and the Resident Cluster

The party cell and resident cluster are discussed together because they are usually mutually associated in the ward party-state machinery. The party cell relates to the resident cluster like the WPB relates to the ward state machinery. Each party cell comprises at least three members, up to a maximum of about thirty-five members. Usually one or more party cells are attached to a resident cluster, depending on the number of party members. Annually, the party cell elects a standing committee comprising a secretary, a deputy secretary, and one to three other members. To retain their positions, party cell secretaries must be elected as a delegate of the party cell to the next ward party branch congress, otherwise, they should resign for not retaining the confidence of members. Among the three ordinary members, one is in charge of inspection and answers directly to the ward's party inspector. This position is appointed by consensus among cell members at the cell's annual congress. If the party cells are too big, the ward party branch may create smaller organizations, called party groups (*to dang*), which have no formal leadership.

The VCP has two types of party cells. The first is called basic level party cell (*chi bo co so*) or street party cell (*chi bo duong pho*), also known informally as "retiree members' cell" (*chi bo huu tri*) because most members are retirees. The other type is the working members' cell (*chi bo duong chuc*). This type comprises party members working in government organizations or state enterprises in the locality. Working people can choose to participate in either or both of these cells, but most choose to participate only at the place of work and excuse themselves from participation in street party cells, thus contributing to a high average age of members in the latter. The average age of VCP members, however, is also high.[12]

What does the party cell do? According to one source:

> The party cell usually discusses and passes resolutions on issues such as building a civilized way of life, building a cultured family, securing neighbourhoods, building a new way of life in their area. They resolve contradictions among the people, help in the conduct of activities of the Vietnam Fatherland Front and other mass organizations; they conduct

charity work, look after the aged and the young, and espouse the political line, the policies, and main resolutions of the city, district, and ward authorities.[13]

The resident cluster (*cum dan cu*) is an informal neighbourhood organization situated between the ward and the resident group (*to dan pho*) and first established in 1984.[14] It is a collection of several resident groups. The resident cluster has sometimes been misunderstood as a level of administrative authority,[15] but it is not. Each cluster is led by a member of the ward's people's council, representatives of sub-branches of political and social mass organizations, and a party cell. Therefore, each cluster is a sub-ward forum through which the leading people's council member organizes low-level mass activities and conducts propaganda and mobilization.

The party cell is supposed to obtain suggestions from the resident cluster to overcome difficulties in policy implementation within the ward and to oversee (but not to command or direct) the cluster's implementation of policies decided by the ward. The resident cluster and the party cell have no power to mete out punishments to residents, or to make decisions on their own. They must report to the ward whatever suggestions or unlawful activities they discover, and let the ward take action. Thus, the WPB holds a monthly meeting with all the party cells of the ward and a regular Saturday meeting with each party cell to delegate tasks. The WPB usually consults the resident cluster on important or sensitive local matters where residents' views are sought. Where party matters are concerned, party cell officials provide references and reports on members living within the locality or active within the cell, for purposes such as evaluation, admissions, and disciplinary matters.

In spite of what it is supposed to do, the party cell has little political authority in the ward state machinery where implementation of state policies is concerned. This is because the heads of resident groups may deal directly with the ward people's committee, in effect bypassing the party cell (and the resident cluster). The party cells have no direct power over the leaders of the resident group within their territory for matters not pertaining to the party. Similarly, the resident cluster, led by the party cell, can only channel feedback to the WPB and has no say in how resident groups below them should conduct their affairs. Exceptions occur when relations between a party cell secretary and the resident group head within its area are close. In those situations, the party cell can play a leadership role.

Furthermore, at the level of party cells, resident clusters and resident groups, informality is the order of things. Discussions in recent years on the role of the resident clusters, and especially the role of the street party cell in the wards' work, demonstrate this point. The VCP wants to rejuvenate the party cells, because the majority of ward party cell members are old and are hampering the leadership of the party at the grass-roots and the co-ordination of state administration at the resident cluster level (which the party cells are supposed to lead). The reason is that street party cell members (being mostly retirees) are happy to contribute to party/community work but dislike social conflict. Thus, they do not like to moralize and discipline fellow members and neighbours on daily matters such as proper rubbish disposal, or use of public space such as the sidewalk, as they are supposed to do. Hence, the effect of having predominantly elderly members in the street party cells is to reduce the ability of the state to maximize its reach and effectiveness in punishing minor offences against social order.

The Resident Group (*to dan pho*)

Resident groups are the smallest formal grouping consisting of contiguous rows of houses and their occupants, with each group comprising 25 to 30 households. Residents have to deal with the resident group head for matters such as collection of monies on behalf of the ward, and references for such matters as registration of birth, marriage, and residence, mobilization of work on behalf of the state, and many others.

The government uses the resident groups to promote community spirit and ideology as well as to perform administrative duties. The leaders of resident groups are elected from the locality, and their relationship with fellow residents extends not only to government matters but also includes mutual help in daily needs. As such, resident groups have an informal and personal dimension. On the other hand, resident groups are responsible for the community's self-regulation and mobilization tasks, such as maintaining public health and order. Resident group leaders' mobilization role is different from that of the party cell in that they do the legwork for the ward and the resident cluster.

Like the party cells, the resident groups also emphasize informality. They hold an annual election of group heads (*to truong*) and assistant group heads (*to pho*). There is no official control of nominations for these two posts. Like party members in the ward party cell, most if not all resident group leaders are middle-aged or older. They do not have to be party members or have high socio-economic standing. Popular candidates are amiable, behave well, and possess a good family background — that is, they are from wholesome family units, and must not have committed offences or crimes against the law or the VCP. The author's house-mother in 1995–97 intimated that group heads and their assistants should set examples in their daily lives in order to gain the respect and thus the votes of the people. Referring to an assistant group head in her group, she said that he was unlikely to be re-elected because residents were unhappy with his family's illegal extension of their home which encroached upon public space.

The heads of the resident groups usually dislike their job. One Vietnamese observer described the status of the group head as having "powers light like straws but responsibilities heavy like stones" (*quyen rom va da*). What is meant here is that group heads do not have the power to perform their many duties properly, and are often blamed by the authorities for negative outcomes in their areas, such as the lack of compliance to the laws.[16] The author's house-mother, a group head, spoke of the lack of people willing to take over her position even though she, being over 60 years old, would like to retire after being on the job for more than twenty years. Moreover, group heads often find themselves in the uncomfortable dilemma of having to report on neighbours when the ward requires it. The group head and assistant group head could be blamed for punishments a family receives for minor offences against the law or state policies, and thus may attract personal revenge. On the other hand, for residents, group heads are important sources of information for the neighbourhood. When residents apply to register their marriage with the ward, ward officials require them to first ask their group heads to certify their marital status. People also approach group heads for information about many other things. Group heads may also be sources of information about the neighbourhood for the higher officials, although they might also protect neighbours from prying officials. The author's house-mother said that during her twenty years on the job, she was able to avoid telling on her neighbours when asked to do so by ward officials. She advised ward officials instead to have a policeman come to the resident group regularly to patrol and to ask discreet questions of residents. Generally, group heads see their relationships with their neighbours and their obligations to the ward as equally important, and they may not wish to report on every infringement they see in the group. In this sense, the group heads can shield people from the state.

Nevertheless, group heads can mobilize people personally, and in this sense, the state is not "faceless" but comes in the form of the eagle-eyed, amiable elderly neighbour, who, even without being the group head, already has some authority over younger neighbours. This is not to say that the old have the ears of the young all the time, but few people are likely to reject reasonable opinions and requests of senior members of the neighbourhood. A good example is a school-teacher talking about purchasing government bonds. She said she had never taken the initiative to buy any despite the intense campaign urging people to do so. If the group head, however, manages to "catch" her at home (she works full-time) when mobilizing people to buy bonds, then she would buy some, to oblige the group head.[17]

Lack of State Effectiveness: Causes at the Basic Level

The above section has briefly shown the degree of penetration of the party-state into the structure and content of the daily lives of the Vietnamese people. Paradoxically, this penetration has not brought about a commensurate domination of society by the party-state. This is because the ward, like other levels of local authority in Vietnam, suffers from a number of deficiencies that mediate state effectiveness. Consequently, it often becomes a tool of accommodation in state-society relations. People freely use this weapon to rework the party-state's boundaries to their benefit. Three broad reasons relating to the basic level account for the present mediation that takes place at the ward level.

Remuneration Paid to Officials

At the ward level, the most obvious reason for the state's ineffectiveness is insufficient pay for ward officials. This is part of the countrywide problem of low pay for bureaucrats, whose fixed salaries typically pay for only 25 per cent of the average household's expenditures.[18] Putting it in more vivid terms, a state salary is only sufficient to pay for an employee's daily breakfasts in Hanoi.[19] The details of remuneration at the ward level demonstrate the seriousness of the problem.

In 1997, the chairman of the ward people's committee received 390,000 dong in salary, while other state posts were paid less. Cadres involved in special duties or projects of the ward received extra payments for the work done. When cadres attended ceremonies or events of state organs on behalf of the ward, they also received from the host "envelopes" containing money for lunch and transport, the amount usually ranging from 20,000 to 50,000 dong. On the party side, the highest paid ward official was the secretary, who received 450,000 dong per month. State regulations determine that the difference in pay between the highest and lowest paid officials of the state cannot be more than ten times.

In 1999 and 2000, bureaucrats' salaries were adjusted twice, raising the salary base by 33 per cent, to 210,000 dong per month. However, evidently, these were very meagre increases, especially compared with the salaries of other occupations and the living standard. The pay of leading ward officials was comparable with other low-paying jobs (see Table 2).

TABLE 2
Approximate Salary Levels of a Sample of Officials of a Ward
and Other Low-Salary Earners in Non-Ward Employment[20]

Job	Approximate Official Salary per Month (dong, 1997)
Trishaw drivers	300,000 to 500,000
Roaming vendors	300,000 and above (10,000 to 20,000 per day)
Road sweepers	700,000 to 1,000,000
*State cadres**	200,000 starting salary (Head of a section got about 450,000.)
Ward policemen	300,000 onwards. (Policemen in service for about ten years received close to 1 million dong per month.)
Chairman of people's committee	390,000 (after twenty years of service)
Ward doctor	300,000 (about five to ten years of service)
Resident group head	50,000
Assistant resident group head	30,000
Ward party secretary	450,000 (more than twenty years of service)
Party cell secretary	30,000
Retirees	200,000 (retired senior ranks from the armed services, such as a senior colonel [*dai ta*] may get as much as 1,000,000)

NOTE:
* Jobs in italics are in direct party-state employment. Road sweepers are employed by state companies and thus indirectly under state employment).

Concerning living standards, the official statistics show that the average annual expenditure per capita in the urban areas of Vietnam in 1993 was close to two million dong. Food expenditure for the same year was about 1.11 million dong. For the whole household, the mean of annual total household expenditure in the urban areas was about 9.77 million dong, which works out to 814,166 dong per month.[21] These expenditure levels, identified in 1993, already exceeded salary levels of 1997. Any ward people's committee chairman would be living in heavy debt if his or her family relied only on 390,000 dong. A ward committee chairman that this author interviewed on many occasions in 1997 stressed that without his wife's roadside tea stall business, his family would not be able to make ends meet. The author subsequently discovered that he was paying for his children to have extra schooling, had recently bought a new motor-cycle, and possessed a number of fairly new electrical appliances, including a colour television set and a hi-fi set. Certainly, this ward chairman had other types of income. Tea-stall income alone would not be able to cover the shortfall between his salary and the family's real expenditures.

The situation therefore breeds a part of the informal economy revolving around official corruption on a collective and systemic basis. Ward officials fill the income-expenditure gap by providing mediation services for its residents, especially manoeuvring around cumbersome state regulations. These mediation services are of course done quietly. In contrast, the wider society loudly moans about pervasive state controls and the requirements of administrative procedures, but welcomes mediation by ward officials (or, in fact, officials from other and usually higher levels of authority, thus making the problem a systemic and collective one). Within the party-state machinery, groups of officials usually collaborate to mediate party-state policies so as to obtain informal income collectively, making the venture much more viable than if only one person was involved. Along the same vein, as a collective, the ward can obtain extra income, which is shared among ward officials (or goes into the ward's budget), by closing one eye to socio-economic activities that would not have been allowed or would have to be patrolled closely. Such activities include social vices under the cover of legitimate businesses (for instance, prostitution in restaurants or karaoke bars) and allowing illegal markets to flourish in order to collect rents from illegal stall operators. Currently, one of the best ways of earning more money for ward officials is to allow the illegal construction and renovation of houses, or to build on vacant land.

Lack of Control and Supervision

The lax supervision and control by the Vietnamese state over the basic level local administration system, and officials' behaviour are probably the most important contributors to a "leakage of authority" of the Vietnamese administration system.[22] In general, bureaucrats' misdemeanours, such as abuses of power and authority to secure economic benefits illegally, are widespread.

In 1988, one source noted that, among law offenders every year, an average of about 16 per cent of offenders were party members, cadres,[23] or civil servants. In Hanoi in 1996, among 631 offenders who illegally bought and sold 115.6 hectares of state land, 98 offenders (15.5 per cent) were state cadres. Ten per cent of these state cadres were chairmen of communes and wards.[24] In a 1997 newspaper survey, 55 per cent of the 4,000 respondents nation-wide listed corruption as the second most urgent social problem. Bureaucrats and cadres received 22 per cent of votes as the third top category of people whom respondents felt needed to be educated about a "civilized way of life", which included virtues such as the rule of law, discipline, being responsible and rational, and doing the right thing in solving social problems.[25]

Besides inadequate checks, the central authority may be providing disincentives to local officials and authorities to obey orders, thus causing them to lose out if they do the right thing. For instance, in 1979, in the attempt to speed up the circulation of goods to reduce shortages and inflation, the central authority ordered all highway and road checkpoints set up during the war to be closed, because they impeded legitimate goods transport. However, the central authority did not take into consideration that many local administration units imposed levies on goods transiting these checkpoints in order to gather revenue to make up for the shortfall in state budget allocations. In other words, those checkpoints were a local adaptation strategy. Closure orders were re-issued in 1986 and 1990 apparently because many localities continued to operate the checkpoints.[26] Another example was seen in the early 1980s. Attempting to control the use of video-cassette recorders in Hanoi, the party-state required all owners to register them. Many military, police, local authority, and party officials, however, used the machines to screen videos for a fee, which helped them to maintain a decent standard of living in the face of hyper-inflation. The ban was impossible to enforce without officials first setting the example. Murray Hiebert found more than 20,000 violators in 1989.[27]

Moral/Cultural Environment
Another cause of mediation space at the basic level is that ward officials also operate in the moral or cultural environment, not just in the legal or administrative environment. Contact with residents on a daily basis is a significant influence on the formal as well as informal behaviour of ward officials. Officials share a common local identity as members of the same neighbourhood and they are expected to help local residents when the latter face difficulties. These cultural dynamics place local officials in an "ambiguous political niche" with conflicting roles. First, they are expected to intervene for family and clan members. Referring to this imperative, Vietnamese use the old saying: "One of us becomes a mandarin and the whole clan gets favours" (*Mot nguoi lam quan, ca ho duoc nho*).

Furthermore, officials are often inclined, for the sake of feelings and good working and neighbourly relationships, to compromise with residents rather than press for full compliance to state laws. This cultural trait is encapsulated in a number of Vietnamese folk sayings, one of which is "Nine is accepted as Ten" (*chin bo lam muoi*).[28] This idea comes quite close to what William Duiker pointed out as governance that emphasizes moral virtues ("the Tao" in Chinese, or "the way") rather than laws.[29] One of these virtues, as Malarney has shown, is that local leaders should be forgiving of minor misdeeds of fellow community members.[30]

Furthmore, ward officials are sometimes moved by the difficult circumstances of the people and they become compassionate (the Vietnamese words are *thong cam*) and selective in applying laws and enforcing policies. A vivid example is the case of a woman living in one ward. She went to her ward office to register her daughter's birth. The child, however, had already reached school-going age. The mother had chosen not to register the child at birth because her "marriage" was unregistered and thus against the law. Instead of imposing a fine on her straightaway for not registering the child, the vice-chair of the ward women's association advised her to get her marriage and her child's birth "witnessed" retrospectively with the help of her resident group head. Once she had done that, this female official would help her register the child's birth retrospectively as well. By a stroke of compassion, state laws on the marriage, on the rights of women, and its population planning policy were evaded.[31]

The recent socio-economic context of this moral/cultural dynamic arose from the time of the mid-1980s when hyper-inflation lowered real incomes at an alarming rate. People with fixed incomes — which was almost everyone because most people were employed in the state sector, as the private sector was very small — found themselves unable to make ends meet, and therefore had to look for ways to participate in the informal economy. These activities were often against state laws but many local authorities overlooked the offences, because their political and moral intelligence told them to. These illegal activities included roadside vending and housing construction and renovation to expand on the poor standard of housing. Furthermore, they occurred on very large scales. Numerous offences were forgiven or overlooked by ward officers without the approval or knowledge of higher authorities. Undeniably, of course, the moral reason can become a cover for corruption, but it is fair to say that quite a number of officials genuinely acted from their hearts than from their heads.

Conclusion

With the brief analysis of how the ward level party-state machinery works and what its strengths and weaknesses are, it can be seen that there is a paradox of state-society relations in Vietnam. On the one hand, the party-state dominates the structure of administration, puts only the people it trusts into positions of power and authority at the ward level, and has policies which allow the wards to control residents. On the other hand, such power and authority are not automatically translated into policy effectiveness.

Furthermore, it is worth reiterating the point that the strength of the Vietnamese party-state is relative to the arena of state-society relations and the time of the action under investigation. An uneven picture can emerge across different arenas and time periods. Even within an arena that one would consider the party-state to be strong because of its penetration into society, such as the wards' administration of society, a paradox of concurrent strength and weakness exist. This is despite the best of times for party-state control, which was just after the war ended in 1975. Certainly, there can be no easy generalizations about how one views state-society relations in Vietnam.

Notes

1. This article was adapted (but substantially revised) from a chapter of the author's doctoral dissertation submitted to the Australian National University in April 2000. He did the fieldwork for the dissertation from 1996 to 1997.

2. For representative works, see Joel Migdal, *Strong Societies and Weak States: State-Society Relations and State Capabilities in the Third World* (Princeton, NJ: Princeton University Press, 1988); Carlyle Thayer, *Political Development in Vietnam, 1975–1985*, (1994) (*ftp://coombs.anu.edu.au/coombspapers/otherachives/asian-studies-achives/vietnam-archives/politics/vietnam-polit-devel-75-85.txt*); Gareth Porter, *Vietnam: The Politics of Bureaucratic Socialism* (Ithaca: Cornell University Press, 1993); and William S. Turley, "Party, State, and People: Political Structure and Economic Prospects", in *Reinventing Vietnamese Socialism: Doi Moi in Comparative Perspective*, edited by William S. Turley and Mark Selden (Boulder, Colorado: Westview Press, 1993).

3. Benedict Kerkvliet, "Village-State Relations in Vietnam: The Effect of Everyday Politics on Collectivization", *Journal of Asian Studies* 54, no. 2 (1995); Nigel Thrift and Dean Forbes, *The Price of War: Urbanization in Vietnam 1954–85* (London: Allen and Unwin, 1986); and Adam Fforde, "The Political Economy of 'Reform' in Vietnam — Some Reflections", in *The Challenge of Reform in Indochina*, edited by Borje Ljunggren (MA.: Harvard Institute for International Development, Harvard University, 1993).

4. In October 1997, Vietnam had 8,823 communes, 520 towns, and 949 wards. Nguyen Huu Duc, "Ve co cau bo may chinh quyen dia phuong hien nay" [On the present structure of local authorities], in *Cai cach hanh chinh dia phuong — Ly luan va thuc tien* [Local administration reform — theory and practice], edited by To Tu Ha, Nguyen Huu Tri and Nguyen Huu Duc (Hanoi: Chinh tri Quoc gia, 1998), pp. 96–97.

5. Gathered from various interviews with ward party leaders in 1997 and 1998.

6. Socialist Republic of Vietnam (SRV), *Luat to chuc Hoi dong nhan dan va Uy ban nhan dan* [Law on Organisation of People's Councils and People's Committees], 21 June 1994, Article 41.

7. SRV, *Luat to chuc Hoi dong nhan dan va Uy ban nhan dan* [Law on Organisation of People's Councils and People's Committees], 21 June 1994, Article 47.

8. Truong Hanh chinh Quoc gia [National College of Administration], *Ve cai cach bo may Nha nuoc* [On reforming the State machinery] (Hanoi: NXB Su That, 1991), p. 70.

9. SRV, *Quy che hoat dong cua Hoi dong nhan dan cac cap* [Regulations on activities of all levels of people's councils] (Hanoi: NXB Chinh tri Quoc gia, 1996), Article 29.

10. "Chu tich UBND thanh pho ra nhung quy dinh cu the nham bao dam thuc hien nhiem vu, quyen han cua HDND cac cap" [Chairman of City People's Committee promulgates specific regulations to ensure people's councils of all levels fulfill their obligations according to their powers], *Ha Noi Moi* [New Hanoi], 19 May

1988), pp. 1, 4; and to SRV *Quy che hoat dong cua Hoi dong nhan dan cac cap* [Regulations on activities of all levels of people's councils] (Hanoi: NXB Chinh tri Quoc gia, 1996), Article 48.

11. See David Koh, "Wards of Hanoi and State-Society Relations in the Socialist Republic of Vietnam" (Ph.D. thesis, Department of Political and Social Change, Research School of Pacific and Asian Studies, The Australian National University, 2000), Table 2-4.

12. The average age of communist party members in 1999 was 64. See Voice of Vietnam, "Former party official Pham Van Dong discusses party problems," via Reuters, 16 May 1999.

13. Van Chieu, "Nen to chuc chi bo theo to dan pho" [Should organize party cells parallel to resident groups], *Ha Noi Moi* , 7 May 1997, p. 2.

14. Nguyen Duc Tha, "Phuong Le Dai Hanh: quan chung tham gia quan ly xa hoi" [Le Dai Hanh ward: The masses participate in management of society], *Ha Noi Moi*, 20 February 1985, p. 2.

15. Nguyen Van Canh and Earle Cooper, *Vietnam under Communism, 1975–1982* (Stanford: Hoover Institution Press and Stanford University, 1985), pp. 89–92.

16. Dong Phuong, "To truong dan pho — mot trach nhiem khong nho" [The head of the resident group — not an unimportant position], *Ha Noi Moi*, 26 February 1997, p. 2.

17. I also asked the interviewee how she determined how many bonds to buy. She said that she would buy roughly the same amount as her neighbours. If she were the first person asked, she would ask the group head what an appropriate amount would be. Conversation with a school-teacher, 16 April 1999.

18. David G. Marr and Christine Pelzer White, "Introduction", in *Postwar Vietnam: Dilemmas in Socialist Development*, edited by Marr and White (Ithaca, NY: Southeast Asia Program, Cornell University, 1988), pp. 4-5; Vo Nhan Tri, *Vietnam's Economic Policy since 1975* (Singapore: Institute of Southeast Asian Studies, 1990), pp. 160–68; and DCSVN (Dang Cong San Viet Nam, or the VCP], *Chien luoc on dinh va phat trien kinh te — xa hoi nam 2000* [Strategy to stabilize and develop the economy and society until year 2000] (Hanoi: NXB Su That, 1991), p. 3.

19. Vietnam Economic News, "Full Breakfast But Empty Lunch," via Reuters 22 June 1999.

20. SRV State Planning Committee and General Statistical Office, *Vietnam Living Standards Survey 1992–1993* (Hanoi, September 1994), p. 20, Table 6.1.1, p. 179.

21. For trishaw drivers, see Minh Quang and Pham Hieu, "Chuyen trang: Xich lo Ha Noi" [Special Report: The trishaw in Hanoi], *Lao Dong* [Labour] 15 April 1997, p. 6. For road sweepers, see Thu Thuy, "Xichlo thanh pho Ho Chi Minh sau mot nam cam duong" [The Trishaw in Ho Chi Minh City after One Year of Road Ban], *Lao Dong*, 21 December 1996, p. 6. The figures for the others were gathered through interviews and conversations with ward officials and many contacts who were state cadres.

22. The term, first used by Anthony Downs in *Inside Bureaucracy* (Boston: Little Brown, 1967), refers to lower level officials preferring to satisfy their own goals when implementing upper level policies and having different purposes from those of their superiors. See Cameron Ross, *Local Government in the Soviet Union* (London and Sydney: Croom Helm, 1987), p. 183.

23. The term "cadres" (*can bo*) refers to officials who are in the permanent employment of the party-state and who occupy senior or leading positions in state organizations, while ordinary, non-leading state employees are referred to as "staff" (*vien chuc* or *nhan vien*). See Le Dinh Khien, "Xac dinh the nao la can bo quan ly hanh chinh nha nuoc" [How to define a state administrative cadre], *Dan chu va Phap luat* 6 (1996): 8–9; and Vu Duc Khien, "Nang cao hieu biet va y thuc ton trong phap luat cua can bo, dang vien" [Raise the understanding and consciousness among cadres

and party members in respecting the law], *Tap Chi Cong San* [Communist Journal], 1 (1998): 44–47.

24. Duong Duc Quang, "Tan man ve bao chi chong tieu cuc" (Rambling thoughts about newspapers against negativism), *Ha Noi Moi Tet Dinh Suu,* 7 February 1997, p. 18.

25. "Chuan muc nep song Viet Nam: Dang & se ..." [The Good Life Benchmarks: Present and Future], *Dai Doan Ket Cuoi Tuan, Xuan Dinh Suu* edition (1997), p. 12.

26. Tan Teng Lang, *Economic Debates in Vietnam: Issues and Problems in Reconstruction and Development (1975–1984),* Research Notes and Discussions Paper No. 55 (Singapore: Institute of Southeast Asian Studies, 1985), pp. 26-27; and Melanie Beresford, "The political economy of dismantling the 'bureaucratic centralism and subsidy system' in Vietnam", in *Southeast Asia in the 1990s: Authoritarianism, Democracy and Capitalism,* edited by Kevin Hewison, et al. (St Leonards, NSW: Allen & Unwin, 1993), p. 230.

27. Cited in Carlyle A. Thayer, *Political Developments in Vietnam: From the Sixth to Seventh National Party Congress* (Canberra: Department of Political and Social Change, Research School of Pacific Studies, Australian National University, 1992), p. 10.

28. Last heard spoken by the character of the retired village teacher, Mr Quy, in the Vietnamese film "Thuong nho dong que" [Nostalgia for the countryside]. The film is based on two short stories by Nguyen Huy Thiep, one with the same title as the film, and the other is "Nhung bay hoc nong thon" [Lessons from the countryside]. The film director is Dang Nhat Minh. The saying is featured only in the film, and it reminds the audience of the purpose of nine-pin bowling. In bowling, normally only when all ten pins are struck down is the result considered a "strike" and given full points; however, recognizing that most people are less than perfect in skills and luck, and to allow people to enjoy the sport even more, nine-pin tap competitions are also organized in which nine pins struck down is considered a "strike", that is, "accepted as ten." For other sources of this deeply-ingrained Vietnamese cultural trait, see the novel by Le Luu, *Thoi Xa Vang* [Time of the distant past] (Hanoi: NXB Hoi Nha Van, fourth edition, 1998); and Vu Dung, Vu Thuy Anh, and Vu Quang Hao, *Tu dien thanh ngu va tuc ngu* [Dictionary of Proverbs and Idioms], third edition (Hanoi: NXB van Hoa, 1997), p. 171.

29. William J. Duiker, *Vietnam: Nation in Revolution* (Boulder, Colorado: Westview Press, 1983), p. 71.

30. Shaun Kingsley Malarney, "Culture, Virtue, and Political Transformation in Contemporary Northern Vietnam," *Journal of Asian Studies* 6 (November 1997): 899–920.

31. Field notes, 11 June 1997 and 12 June 1997.